W. H. AUDEN
The Life of a Poet

W. H. AUDEN

The Life of a Poet

◇

Charles Osborne

For Barrie Reid
who introduced me to the poems
and
for Ken Thomson
who helped me cope with the poet

First published in the United Kingdom in 1980
by Eyre Methuen Limited, 11 New Fetter Lane,
London EC4 4EE

This book was designed and produced by
The Rainbird Publishing Group Limited,
36 Park Street, London W1Y 4DE
House editor: Beverley Moody
Picture researcher: Vanessa Whinney
Designer: Martin Bristow
Indexer: Vicki Robinson

Filmset, printed and bound by
W & J Mackay Limited, Chatham, Kent

ISBN 0 413 39670 3
Printed in England

Contents

Illustrations
Acknowledgments

JACKET FRONT *W. H. Auden* (Ink) © David Hockney 1968. Courtesy Petersburg Press
JACKET BACK Photograph by Cecil Beaton courtesy of Sotheby's Belgravia

Edwin Allen 266 *below*
John Auden/Weidenfeld and Nicolson Archives 75 *above*
P. G. Auden 65 *above left and right*, 66, 67, 68 *above*, 69, 72, 73
BBC Copyright/Weidenfeld and Nicolson Archives 175 *below*
Photographs by Cecil Beaton courtesy of Sotheby's Belgravia 162 *above right*, 176 *above left and right*, 257
The Britten Estate 174 *above*, 258 *below right*
Rosamira Bulley 70 (Weidenfeld and Nicolson Archives), 71
Camera Press 258 *below left*, 267 *above* (photo Peter Mitchell), 270 *below* (photo Billett Potter)
Sir William Coldstream 168 *above left*, *above right* (photo Sotheby's/Weidenfeld and Nicolson Archives)
Colorific! 176 *below* (photo Carl Mydans, © 1939 Time Inc), 259 *below* (photo Jerry Cooke, © 1946 Time Inc), 261 *above left* (photo Jerry Cooke, © 1947 Time Inc), 268 *below*, 269 *above* (photos H. Redl, Time-Life)
Robert Craft/Weidenfeld and Nicolson Archives 263 *above*
Ray Daffurn *frontispiece*
Louise Dahl-Wolfe 175 *above*, 258 *above right*
Daily Herald Picture Library 172
Daily Telegraph Colour Library 80 *above right* (photo Stephen Spender), 268 *above left and right* (photos Horst Munzig)
University of Durham 78
Mary Evans Picture Library 68 *below*
Faber & Faber 80 *above left*, 161, 164 *below left* (photo Angus McBean), 170 (Weidenfeld and Nicolson Archives), 173, 258 *above left*, 265 *above* (photo Mark Gerson)
Fox Photos 266 *above*
Mark Gerson 262 *below right*, 272 *below left*

GPO 166 (Weidenfeld and Nicolson Archives), 165 *above right*, 167 (Courtesy of National Film Archive, Stills Library)
Guy Gravett 265 *below*
Gresham's School 75 *below*
William Heinemann Ltd 74
John Hillelson Ltd 264 (photo Howard Sochurek)
King's College, Cambridge 79
Lincoln Kirstein 260 *above right*
John Lehmann 164 *below right*
David Luke 270 *above left*
The late Frank Lyell 259 *above right*
The Mander and Mitchenson Theatre Collection 169, 171 *above left and below*
Robert Medley 165 *above right*, 171 *right*
Metropolitan Opera Archives 263 *below* (photo Sedge LeBland)
National Portrait Gallery 162 *above left*, *below*, 163, 168 *below left* (photos Howard Coster)
© Copyright 1979 New York Review – Opera Mundi 267 *below right*
The New York Times 269 *below*
Ursula Niebuhr/Weidenfeld and Nicolson Archives 262 *below left*, 264 *above*
Observer 267 *below left*, 271 *above* (photos Jane Bown)
Oxford City Library Local History Collection 76, 77, 80 *below*
Billett Potter 270 *above right*
Radio Times Hulton Picture Library 165 *below*, 261 *above right*
Stephen Spender/Weidenfeld and Nicolson Archives 262 *above*
James Stern 174 *below*, 259 *above left* (photo the late Frank Lyell), 260 *above left* (Weidenfeld and Nicolson Archives), 260 *below*
Ken Thomson 271 *below*
Topix 272 *above*
Edward Upward 164 *above*, 168 *below right*
Yorkshire Architectural and York Archaeological Society 65 *below*
Photo by Bill Yoscary 261 *below*

Preface

Many of Auden's friends and mine have been generous with their help while I was at work on this book. I list a number of them below, but I am deeply indebted to four friends who have been especially helpful: Stephen Spender who shared his memories of Auden with me and allowed me access to his letters; my old mentor John Lehmann who talked to me about Auden and the thirties; Ian Hamilton who read my typescript and made a number of very helpful criticisms and suggestions from all of which I have benefited; and Edward Mendelson, Auden's Literary Executor, who also read my typescript, corrected some errors and suggested one or two useful leads, despite the fact that this is not an 'authorized biography'.

I am grateful also to the following: John Johnston Appleton; P. G. Auden; Jonathan Barker (Poetry Librarian of the Arts Council of Great Britain); C. D. Baxter (Librarian of Gresham School); Goran Bengtson (of the Swedish Broadcasting Corporation); Baron de Breffny; William Caskey; Nevill Coghill; Robert Craft; Brian Finney; John Fuller; Roy Fuller; Roland Gant (of the Heinemann Group of Publishers); Lawrence Gowing; Robert Halsband; Alan Hancox; Peter Heyworth; Christopher Isherwood; J. W. Lambert; Donald Mitchell; Charles Monteith; John Nevinson; Sir Peter Pears; Dilys Powell; the late John Pudney; John D. Root; Nikos Stangos; George Svenson; Alison Wade; Eric Walter White; Basil Wright; Michael Yates.

A number of libraries and institutions in England, America and Austria have been helpful, among them the London Library; the New York Public Library; the Bryn Mawr College Library; the Newberry Library, Chicago; the BBC; the Australian Broadcasting Commission; the United States Information Service; Granada TV Network Ltd. My thanks are also due to Norman Sims in England and to Scott Lackey in the United States for assistance with research, and to Al Ordover, widower of Rhoda Jaffe, for providing me with copies of Auden's letters to her.

My research expenses were alleviated by a generous grant from the Phoenix Trust.

C.O.

Chapter One

1907–1925

I must admit that I was most precocious
(Precocious children rarely grow up good).
My aunts and uncles thought me quite atrocious
For using words more adult than I should;
My first remark at school did all it could
To shake a matron's monumental poise:
'I like to see the various types of boys.'[1]

As a young man, Wystan Hugh Auden was described by his contemporaries as Nordic, and in later years he liked to refer to himself as a creature of the north. 'Auden' is probably an Anglo-Scandinavian corruption, 'Healfdene' or 'half Dane', though it could also be the old English 'Aelfwyne', 'elf-friend'. In any case, the family is said to have come originally from Iceland. The name 'Wystan' is English enough. Thomas de Marleberge's *Chronica Abbatiae de Evesham* tells the story of Wystan, son of Wimund, and grandson of Wiglaf, King of Mercia, whose uncle Bertulph conspired against him. On the eve of Pentecost in the year 849, while giving Wystan the kiss of peace, Bertulph drew a sword from beneath his cloak, struck Wystan on the head, and killed him. Wystan's body was conveyed to Repton Abbey in Derbyshire for burial. However, 'for thirty days a column of light, extending from the spot where he was slain to the heavens above, was seen by all those who dwelt there, and every year, on the day of his martyrdom, the hairs of his head, severed by the sword, sprang up like grass.' Ever since then the place, which is a mile and a half from the Shropshire village of Craven Arms, has been called Winstanstow. Not very far away is the village of Wistanswick, or 'Wistan's dwelling'.[2] W. H. Auden's account of the ninth-century Wystan's martyrdom is quite terse: 'Of my own saint, St Wystan, all that appears to be known is that he objected to the uncanonical marriage of his widowed mother to his godfather, whereupon they bumped him off. A rather Hamlet-like story.'[3] In 1966 Auden told an enquirer, 'I was christened

---

[1] From 'Letter to Lord Byron'.

[2] This information comes from *Shropshire*, an archaeological and historical guide, published in 1912. Its author is John Ernest Auden, M.A., F.R.Hist.S., who contributed to *Memorials of Old Shropshire*, 1906, edited by Thomas Auden, M.A., F.S.A., Vicar of Condover, Salop, and Rural Dean; Prebendary of Lichfield. Another contributor was Henrietta M. Auden, F.R.Hist.S. The family contained more than its fair share of clergymen and archaeologists.

[3] W. H. Auden: *A Certain World* (New York, 1970).

Wystan because my father was born in Repton to which church St Wystan's bones were removed after his martyrdom, later they were transferred to Tewkesbury.'[1]

Wystan Auden's father, George Augustus Auden, was born in Repton, Derbyshire, on 27 August 1872, and educated at Repton (as was, thirty years or so later, Wystan's friend Christopher Isherwood). George Auden read Natural Science at Christ's College, Cambridge, as a preparation for studying medicine, and became an intern at St Bartholomew's Hospital, London. Here he met Constance Rosalie Bicknell, who was three years younger than he. The daughter of Rev. R. H. Bicknell, Vicar of Wroxham, Norfolk, and the youngest of eight children, she had graduated from London University, where she specialized in French, and had taken up nursing at St Bartholomew's with the intention of eventually joining a Protestant medical mission in Africa. She and George Auden became engaged in 1898, and married the following year. They moved to York, where he set up as a general practitioner of medicine. Bernard, the first of their three sons, was born in 1900. John followed in 1903, and the youngest, Wystan Hugh, was born at 54, Bootham, York on 21 February 1907. In the following year Dr Auden gave up his quite lucrative practice in York when he was appointed School Medical Officer for the city of Birmingham, and Professor of Public Health at the University there. The family moved to Birmingham.

The Audens were a family of the professional middle class, but perhaps only just. When young George Auden had become engaged to Constance Bicknell, one of her sisters who was married to a clergyman said to her, 'If you marry this man, nobody will call on you, you know.' Wystan Auden in his adult years occasionally regretted not knowing more about his family and his forebears. His certain knowledge went back only as far as his four grandparents: an Auden, a Hopkins, a Bicknell and a Birch. He would have liked, he said, to know more about 'the Reverend Dr. Birch who for a time was tutor to the young Prince of Wales, the future Edward VII . . . and about the Miss Bicknell who, to the dismay of her parents, married Constable.'[2] Both his grandfathers were Church of England clergymen, and both died of heart attacks in early middle-age. One of them, his maternal grandfather, was apparently an unpleasant character, for his sons danced round the table for joy when they heard he was dead. Of Wystan's twelve uncles and aunts, six on each side of the family, two were mentally retarded: an uncle on the Auden side and a Bicknell aunt. Uncle Lewis was looked after by his housekeeper, and Aunt Daisy by Anglican nuns. In the opinion of the adult Wystan, his father's family were inclined to be phlegmatic, earnest, rather

<hr>

[1] Quoted in Alan Hancox Catalogue 114 (Cheltenham, 1969).
[2] W. H. Auden: 'As It Seemed to Us', a review of biographies in *The New Yorker*, 3 April 1965.

slow, somewhat miserly, and they usually enjoyed excellent health, while his mother's were quick of mind, short-tempered, generous, and subject to bouts of ill-health, hysteria and neurosis. Auden's view of himself was that, with the exception that he enjoyed good health, he took after his mother's side of the family.

Wystan's early childhood at home, before he was sent off to boarding school, was a happy and confident one. Treated with love and gentleness by their parents, the three boys were made to feel safe and secure. Wystan in later life referred to his parents as lovable and admirable human beings, though with their fair share of individual weaknesses or idiosyncrasies. His father he recalled as a man of solidity and common sense, and his mother as having the more imaginative temperament of the two. Dr George Auden was a voracious reader and also a published writer and translator of archaeological and psychological articles. Wystan's love of the printed word and of literature clearly derived from his father. Yet he felt closer to his mother, not only because of their temperamental affinity, for he also certainly inherited his father's common sense, but probably because, for five important years of his childhood, from the age of seven to that of twelve (1914–1919), his father was away from home, serving with the R.A.M.C. (Royal Army Medical Corps), in Egypt, Gallipoli and France. Wystan's relationship with his father, after the war, remained amicable, but George Auden's absence during those psychologically important years, combined with the fact that Constance Auden was the stronger personality of the two parents, led to Wystan's drawing closer to his mother. She was capable, at times, of behaving rather oddly. When Wystan was six years old, she taught him the words and music of the love duet from Wagner's *Tristan and Isolde*, which mother and son sang together on several occasions, Wystan taking the role of Isolde.

Childhood pleasures included visits to his maternal grandmother's house, the mid-Victorian smells and furnishings of which both delighted and comforted Wystan.

The Auden household was run fairly strictly, as one would expect of Victorian parents. In York, the servants included a cook and two maids who slept in the attic, and a coachman who lived out. Dr Auden insisted on their attendance at church on Sundays, and at prayers at home every morning before breakfast. Wystan's elder brothers remembered this in adult life, though he did not, for the move to Birmingham was made well before his second birthday. Wystan's earliest memories were of the unlovely industrial landscape of the midlands, of Birmingham and its outskirts, and of the mines. 'Clearer than Scafell Pike, my heart has stamped on/The view from Birmingham to Wolverhampton', he wrote in his thirtieth year in his long poem, 'Letter to Lord Byron', one stanza of which reads:

11

Long, long ago, when I was only four,
Going towards my grandmother, the line
Passed through a coal-field. From the corridor
I watched it pass with envy, thought 'How fine!
Oh how I wish that situation mine.'
Tramlines and slagheaps, pieces of machinery,
That was, and still is, my ideal scenery.

There is quite a lot of autobiography in 'Letter to Lord Byron'. Auden describes himself physically, the hazel eyes, the fair 'tow-like' hair, the adult height of five feet eleven, and the brown mole on the right cheek. He says his father's forebears were all Midland Yeomen, his mother's ancestors, from Somerset, had Norman blood, and 'My grandfathers on either side agree / In being clergymen and C. of E.' (In adult life Auden came to bear a strong facial resemblance to his mother.) He recalls his father's excellent library, the accomplishments of their old cook, Ada, and claims that his earliest recollection is of his father lancing a sore on their terrier's foot, on a white stone doorstep. He confesses to 'stuffing shag into the coffee pot/Which nearly killed my mother, but did not'. Dr Auden had a strong interest in the Icelandic sagas, which the young Wystan used to read until 'With northern myths my little brain was laden'. But his favourite story, he says, was Hans Christian Andersen's *The Snow Queen* (or, in another translation, *The Ice Maiden*).

In later life, Auden attempted to remember and to list the contents of his nursery library, dividing the books into three categories:

FICTION

Beatrix Potter	'All her books'
Hans Andersen:	*The Snow Queen*
Morris and Magnusson:	*Icelandic Stories*
Lewis Carroll:	*Alice in Wonderland*
	Through the Looking Glass
George Macdonald:	*The Princess and the Goblin*
Jules Verne:	*The Child of the Cavern*
	Journey to the Centre of the Earth
Rider Haggard:	*King Solomon's Mines*
	She
Dean Farrar:	*Eric, or Little by Little*
R. M. Ballyntyne:	*The Cruise of the Cachelot*
Sir Arthur Conan Doyle:	'The Sherlock Holmes stories'

POETRY

Hoffman:	*Struwwelpeter*
Hilaire Belloc:	*Cautionary Tales*

Harry Graham:	*Ruthless Rhymes for Heartless Homes*
NON-FICTION	
T. Sopwith	*A Visit to Alston Moor*
?	*Underground life*
?	*Machinery for Metalliferous Mines*
His Majesty's	
Stationary Office:	*Lead and Zinc Ores of Northumberland and Alston Moor*
?	*The Edinburgh School of Surgery*
?	*Dangers to Health* ('a Victorian treatise, illustrated, on plumbing, good and bad')

His favourite poem in Struwwelpeter was 'The Story of Little Suck-a-Thumb', although it failed to frighten him as he was not a thumb-sucker but a nail-biter. The fiction and the poetry in Auden's nursery are titles one would expect to find, but the non-fiction reveals a more idiosyncratic taste. Limestone landscapes were the young Wystan's ruling passion, the landscapes and the machinery of their mines. According to his brother John, Wystan came to love Alston Moor, Cumberland, above all other places, and 'Letter to Lord Byron' tells us that 'from my sixth until my sixteenth year/I thought myself a mining engineer'. Between the ages of six and twelve, one of Wystan's private, solitary games was to imagine to himself, in great detail, a secret world whose basic elements were '(a) a limestone landscape mainly derived from the Pennine Moors in the North of England, and (b) an industry – lead-mining.'[1] His parents and adult relatives were urged to procure for him the necessary geology textbooks, maps, catalogues and photographs, and were even persuaded to take him down real mines, 'tasks which they performed with unfailing patience and generosity'.[2] The landscape and the mines made up a world with rules and laws formulated by Wystan, imposing certain restrictions upon himself: 'I was free to select this and reject that, on condition that both were real objects in the primary world, to choose, for example, between two kinds of water turbine, which could be found in a textbook on mining machinery or a manufacturer's catalogue.' It was a world from which people, both real and imagined, were excluded, and it was a world whose technology Wystan treated with the respect due to a religious system. 'A word like *pyrites*, for example,' he said in a lecture forty years later, 'was for me not simply an indicative sign; it was the Proper Name of a Sacred Being, so that, when I heard an aunt pronounce it *pirrits*, I was shocked. Her pronunciation was more than wrong, it was ugly. Ignorance was impiety.' Throughout his life, Auden retained his

---

[1] *A Certain World.*

[2] W. H. Auden: *The English Auden* (London, 1977).

preference for the landscape of the north. The sunny blue skies of the south held no attraction for him: the winds and rains of autumn were his favourite weather.

In addition to the books bought for his nursery use, the young Wystan also read widely in his father's library, the nature and scope of which, he was to claim later, afterwards dictated his own adult taste. His father's shelves contained few novels, but a heterogeneous collection of books on many subjects, with the consequence that Wystan's adult reading was, according to him, 'wide and casual rather than scholarly, and in the main non-literary'.[1] As a child he already showed a passion for words – the longer they were the better – and he used to appal his aunts 'by talking like a professor of geology'. The images from his childhood which remained with him included, in addition to the books and pre-breakfast prayers, a rain-gauge on the lawn, a family dog, bicycle expeditions to collect fossils or to rub church brasses, piano lessons, family reading sessions in the evenings. The Audens were High Anglicans, or Anglo-Catholics, and so on Sundays there were services with music, candles and incense. At the age of six, Wystan was a boat-boy, carrying the bowl of incense from which the censers were replenished. On one occasion, his attention wandering, he was star-tled in the middle of a service to be hissed at by an older boy in need of an incense-refill, 'Come here you little bastard.' At Christmas time there was 'a crèche rigged up in the dining room, lit by an electric-torch battery, round which we sang hymns.' His mother, apparently, was often ill. His brother John, four years older than Wystan and so already at school in 1913, remem-bers their summer holiday of that year, spent at Rhayader in Wales, where the brothers became interested in the tannery, a ginger beer factory, and the three dams of the Birmingham waterworks. The two elder boys had bicycles of their own: Wystan rode pillion with his father. In 1914, at Easter, they climbed Cader Idris from Arthog and descended to Dolgellau. The seven-year-old Wystan had to be carried part of the way.

Years later, Auden told an interviewer: 'I remember at the age of seven seeing my pa and ma in drag, and bursting into tears. She had on his clothes and a false moustache, and he was wearing hers. They were going to a masquerade, I think, and I suppose they thought it would amuse me. I was terrified. It was one of the last times I saw him as a child.'[2]

There were visits to uncles, aunts and cousins, though Wystan did not really get on with most of them, regarding them as either hysterical or stupid, while they no doubt considered him an insolent, spoiled brat. The only relative he did get on with was Uncle Henry, his father's younger brother and a bachelor, who was some kind of authority on sulphuric acid.

[1] *The English Auden.*
[2] *Observer* Colour Magazine, 7 November 1971.

In August 1914, war broke out. In September 1915, the eight-year-old Wystan Auden left home to go to school for the first time. His prep, or junior, school was St Edmund's at Hindhead in Surrey, and he was to remain there until 1920. St Edmunds had been founded in Norfolk by Rev. John Morgan-Brown, and had been moved to Hindhead in 1901. At the time of Wystan's arrival, the founder's son, Cyril Morgan-Brown, was headmaster. The school was a typical late-Victorian country house, surrounded by extensive, hilly grounds. Wystan's elder brothers, Bernard and John, also went to St Edmund's, and John was still there when young Wystan arrived. The bespectacled John's solemn and birdlike appearance had earned him the nickname of 'Dodo', so his younger brother Wystan, when he appeared on the scene, became known as 'Dodo minor'. The name hardly suited him, however, for his school contemporaries remember him as a chubby, white-faced child with a short-sighted stare, thick, straw-coloured hair and, despite his podginess, a general air of anaemia. He was already a firmly self-possessed child, announcing to a startled matron upon his arrival at school that he liked to study the various types of boys. His precociousness and poise stood him in better stead with the boys than with the teaching staff, and the sexual knowledge he airily disseminated to his fellow pupils, having illicitly discovered it in his father's anatomical manuals, led many of them to regard him with awe.

There are several mentions of Wystan Auden in the *St Edmund's School Chronicle*. The first is in December 1916, when he had been there more than a year, and had contributed to an exhibition of objects of interest found by boys during the holidays: 'in the first class all the exhibits were distinctly above average. Auden (1) [i.e. John Auden] showed a very good collection of shells. . . . His brother's notes on the prehistoric remains in that part of Wales where their holidays were spent were also very neat and good.' In a later competition, Wystan exhibited a collection of insects, beetles, bees and flies. In 1917, he won the Novices' swimming race, managing to do one length in eight seconds. However, in the last term the Examiners of the Royal Life Saving Society thought him only 'Very fair, rather slow'.

Musically he showed greater accomplishment while at St Edmund's. He made good progress on the piano and, in a variety concert staged by the two top forms, the Fourth and Upper Fourth, in October 1919, he played the accompaniment for three other boys in a country dance 'which would have been excellent if the accompanist, Auden, had not taken the bit between his teeth and bolted.' Apparently he improved in his next accompaniment which he played 'with much skill', and he also recited. In June 1920, he won a prize for his proficiency as a pianist, and it was noted that his work was excellent not only in the learning of new music 'but also in the more humdrum but essential matter of care and accuracy in scale playing'. He was commended, too, for leading the choir, augmented by adults, in a rendering of Liza Lehmann's *Fairy Cantata* in the school chapel. At some time later, Mrs Auden presented a splendid crucifix to the chapel.

Wystan appears to have collected prizes at St Edmund's without much conscious effort: in the spring term of 1920 he won the Form Prize as well as first prize for mathematics. In his last term, he helped to form the St Edmund's School Literary Society with a fellow pupil, Harold Llewellyn Smith, and with the support and encouragement of Miss Winnie, one of the headmaster's daughters. Wystan was President, Llewellyn Smith Honorary Secretary, and there were seven members. Miss Rosa, the headmaster's other daughter, who also taught at the school, later remembered that 'It was a stately affair; members addressed each other with formality as "Mr" and on the last meeting of the term they partook of ginger wine and biscuits.'

In addition to his musical and literary activities, Wystan, somewhat improbably, played at soldiering. When an officer invalided from the army joined the staff and, as Miss Rosa recalled, 'organized the school into a military force which seemed to have considerably more officers and NCOs than privates', there was a climactic Field Day in the Devil's Punchbowl at Hindhead, when Corporal Auden (junior), representing an entire machine-gun corps, was observed rushing about and waving a police rattle wildly over his head, surrounded by boys wielding toy wooden rifles. 'Corpl. Auden (senior) then turned up and asked for advice. Corpl. Auden (junior) replied that the machine-gun was going to retire, and could he hold out a bit longer until he had reached the top and cover his retreat.' But although he later claimed not to have been very interested in poetry as a child, Wystan's interests at school were, in the main, literary and pacific rather than sporting and belligerent. One of his school fellows,[1] who remembers another Auden nickname – 'Wittie' (which sounds like the kind of family baby-talk for 'Wystan' which one of his elder brothers might have introduced into school use) – says he was 'a great reciter of verse who did not mind being teased. He had a wide repertory, not only the Alice in Wonderland, Just So Stories, Hilaire Belloc and the ballads we knew, but also American ballads. He must have had some training or encouragement in recitation.' His favourite poems of this time included Christina Rossetti's 'Uphill' and R. H. Braham's 'As I lay a-thynkynge'.

One of Wittie's party pieces was a ballad about Jim of California, a heroic miner who

> . . . stood
> With his back against the wall.
> 'Run for your life, Jake,

---

[1] Mr John Nevinson, in a letter to the author.

Run for your wife's sake,'
Said Jim of California.

At the line, 'This beastly old lamp makes my eyes to run', the reciter would solemnly break off in order to explain that here the narrator was in tears. Another item in his repertoire was 'The Village Blacksmith' which provoked from his listeners a parody: 'There stands Little Wittie, with small and grubby hands/And the muscles in his little sticks aren't strong as iron bands.' A piece of scatological verse which Wystan used to declaim, to the delight of his brothers, and which still seemed funny to him fifty years later, was

> While shepherds watched their flocks by night,
> All shitting on the ground,
> An angel of the Lord came down
> And handed paper round.

In his first years at St Edmund's Wystan's closest friend was Harold Llewellyn Smith. More than once they stayed at each other's home during school holidays. Llewellyn Smith still remembered, nearly sixty years later, the cultured atmosphere of the Auden home, the stimulating conversation, the much-used piano, and the way in which Mrs Auden clearly 'spoilt' her youngest son. He also remembered Wystan as being not only clever but very well aware of his cleverness, though not too aggressively. He was a sensitive child who tried to take pains not to appear so, and he was grateful to his headmaster's daughters, first Miss Rosa and later Miss Winnie, for taking a special interest in him and guiding him through the school jungle. The headmaster himself was seen by the boys as somewhat of a terror, and treated with wary respect. Wystan for a time cherished a grudge against him for having made him Head of the School a term later than he expected that honour to come his way; but in general he had no cause to be unhappy at St Edmund's, nor was he. He delighted in displaying his general knowledge, which was considerably wider than the average ten year old's, and, one day, when two classes which usually shared a room for preparation work were separated for some reason, Wystan referred to the event as 'The Great Schism' and delivered to his classmates an impromptu lecture on religion in the fourteenth century. He also had, for a child, an unusually well developed sense of justice, giving it as his judgment on one occasion, when some of the boys were ganging up on a fellow-pupil who had been caught cheating, that 'cheating to avoid punishment, though wrong, was less wrong than cheating to obtain a prize and that, in any case, both of them were less wrong than lynch-law'.[1]

[1] Harold Llewellyn Smith in *W. H. Auden: A Tribute* (London, 1974).

The School Literary Society not only presented papers at its meetings, it also read plays; Wystan was Peter Quince in a reading of *A Midsummer Night's Dream*, and one is faintly surprised that he had not appropriated a larger role. But he was to blossom, as an actor, at his public school. Meanwhile, as the war continued in Europe, the more imaginative of those boys still at school in England wondered if they would eventually find themselves going straight from school to the trenches. Lists of 'old boys' who had fallen were read out in chapel each week. Wystan's father was, for most of the war, behind the firing line, though he was exposed to real danger during the Gallipoli campaign. Wystan's eldest brother Bernard was called up, but he was still in training camp at the end of the war. Assistant masters at school came and went, 'becoming more peculiar each year'. To Wystan, with his rich interior life of mines and northern landscapes, occasionally interrupted by the demands of school, the war had little or no reality. To the extent that it affected him at all, it brought some variety into his routine of school terms alternating with holidays, for when his father enlisted, the lease of the family house in Solihull was about to expire. Instead of renewing it his mother relinquished the house, taking furnished rooms for herself and the three boys during the school holidays, each time in a different part of the country. Wystan found it exciting to spend his holidays discovering new and exciting places, and indulging, with the family, in very gentle 'war work' which consisted, in the main, of collecting sphagnum moss, 'when there was any', and knitting mufflers for the troops in the evening, while mother read aloud. These wartime holidays took Wystan to Dyffryn, Rhayader, Monmouth, Bradwell in Derbyshire, Clitheroe, Cleeve Hill, Totland Bay on the Isle of Wight, and occasionally to the house, surrounded by poplars, in Horninglow near Burton-on-Trent, where his paternal grandmother lived. In the summer of 1917, the ten-year-old Wystan visited the Isle of Wight with his mother and two brothers and the diary kept by the boys noted:

M.W and J went out shopping at Totland and then walked over by the fields to Freshwater Church (All Saints) to find out the services. Came back home in time for dinner. After dinner we walked onto Headon Hill and after we had seen the Tumulus we walked down into what looked like an old disused fort but when we got in there an Orderly turned us out saying that it was an Isolation Camp.* There were two large muzzle-loader guns there. Then we walked down into Alum Bay but it was High Tide so we could not go and see the different coloured rocks. Then we came home. We had by that time almost discovered the short cuts etc. It was a lovely evening and the sunset was beautiful. We saw some Larks and Robins and several other birds. The rooms are very nice. For the sitting-room see drawing on the first page, Mother's room is a nice large one other [sic] the sitting room. J & W's room is a nice one also with 2 beds in it.[1]

The brothers are referred to by the initial letters of their names, including, elsewhere, B (Bernard). M. is mother who is clearly responsible for the asterisk after 'Isolation Camp' referring to the footnote at the bottom of the page: '*M. heard it was cerebro-spinal meningitis – so felt anxious!'

Wystan and John studied menhirs and stone circles, gold and lead mines, caverns, churches and pre-Norman crosses. On country walks, when their mother retired behind a wall to perform a natural function, she would demand that the boys look the other way. Once, Wystan shouted a question over the wall: what would happen if they did look? The maternal voice dodged the question, ordering him not to be rude and cheeky. On holidays, they also compared churches and their rituals. To such staunch Anglo-Catholics, the Welsh churches were a sad disappointment compared with St Albans in Holborn, London, which they attended while paying visits to the boys' aunts who had a large apartment in Brooke Street, E.C.1.

School-boys traditionally complain of both the quality and the quantity of the food dished up to them, but Wystan found it in general quite palatable, although he hated the boiled cod on Fridays. He remembered, however, once taking a second slice of bread and margarine, which was permitted, only to hear a master remark 'Auden, I see, wants the Huns to win.' He was fortunate with his teachers, in the main, even in the headmaster who taught him Latin and Greek and who, if he was in a bad temper, would instantly beat any boy making an error in syntax. He could be brutal, Auden later recalled, but he was a born teacher. Clearly, young Wystan was a well adjusted, reasonably happy prisoner at St Edmund's, miserable only when he caught Spanish flu in the autumn of 1918: he was still recovering, in the school sanatorium, when peace was declared on 11 November 1918.

Many of the boys at St Edmund's had lost close relatives in the war. When C. Bradshaw-Isherwood appeared in class one morning wearing a black armband, Wystan realized this meant that his father had been killed in action. C. Bradshaw-Isherwood, who was later to drop the hyphen and become known as Christopher Isherwood, had become his closest school-friend. Christopher, two and a half years older than Wystan, was already at St Edmund's when Wystan arrived in 1915, but the two boys only got to know each other in 1918. This was Christopher's last year before going on to his public school, Repton, by which time Wystan had caught up with him in the Fourth form. Auden used to say in later life that his first glimpse of Isherwood was when he walked into a classroom and saw his future friend

[1] The diary is in the possession of Dr John Auden.

and collaborator carefully copying down the work of the boy at the desk next to him. In his autobiographical novel, *Lions and Shadows*, published twenty years later in 1938, Isherwood wrote of his life between the ages of seventeen and twenty-four, but also included a paragraph describing his friend at St Edmund's. The characters in Isherwood's book are thinly disguised under fictitious names – Wystan Hugh Auden becomes 'Hugh Weston':

> I remember him chiefly for his naughtiness, his insolence, his smirking tantalizing air of knowing disreputable and exciting secrets. With his hinted forbidden knowledge and shock of mispronounced scientific words, portentously uttered, he enjoyed among us, his semi-savage credulous schoolfellows, the status of a kind of witch-doctor. I see him drawing an indecent picture on the upper fourth form blackboard, his stumpy fingers, with their blunt bitten nails, covered in ink: I see him boxing, with his ferocious frown, against a boy twice his size; I see him frowning as he sings opposite me in the choir, surpliced, in an enormous Eton collar, above which his great red flaps of ears stand out, on either side of his narrow scowling pudding-white face. In our dormitory religious arguments, which were frequent, I hear him heatedly exclaiming against churches in which the cross was merely painted on the wall behind the altar: they ought, he said, to be burnt down and their vicars put into prison.[1]

Wystan and Christopher enjoyed the eccentricities of some of the teaching staff at St Edmund's. They derived particular pleasure from Captain Reginald Oscar Gartside-Bagnall who was given to distributing beer and biscuits to his more favoured pupils, while he read them scenes from his melodrama, *The Waves*, which apparently owed a great deal to Sir Henry Irving's *cheval de bataille*, *The Bells*. Wystan, years later, was still able to impersonate the playwright's reading of the climactic scene in which the villain sees the ghost of the boy he has murdered: 'The waves . . . the waves . . . can't you hear them calling? Get down, *carrse* you, get down! Ha, ha – I'm not afraid! Who says I'm afraid? Don't stare at me, *carrse* you, with those great eyes of yours. . . . I never feared you living, and I'm demned if I fear you now you're – *dead*! Ha, ha! Ha, ha! Ha ha ha ha ha ha ha!' Wystan was no less adept at impersonating the school chaplain giving his annual sermon on St Edmund's day. He also incorporated part of the sermon, which he knew by heart, into 'Address for a Prize-Day' in his book, *The Orators*, which he wrote at the age of twenty-four:

> Commemoration. Commemoration. What does it mean? What does it mean? Not what does it mean to them, there, then. What does it mean to

[1] Christopher Isherwood: *Lions and Shadows* (London, 1938).

us, here, now? It's a facer, isn't it boys? But we've all got to answer it. What were the dead like? What sort of people are we living with now? Why are we here? What are we going to do? Let's try putting it in another way.

In Wystan's performance, this sounded like 'Whur ders it *mean*? Nert – whur did it mean to *them, then, theah*? Bert – whur ders it mean to *ers, heah, nerw*?'

Wystan and Christopher, who were later to become literary collaborators, nearly began that collaboration at school, for one day in 1918, when they and Harold Llewellyn Smith were supposed to be participating in a cricket match, they spent most of the time surreptitiously planning an ambitious historical Gothic novel, to be set in Marple Hall, the ancestral seat of the Bradshaw-Isherwoods. The project, unhappily, did not survive the cricket match.

Isherwood departed from St Edmund's in the autumn of 1918 to go on to his public school at Repton, leaving Wystan to get through his final two years on his own. As he grew up, Wystan worked ever more assiduously. Much of his school routine he did not even regard as 'work' which, as he later formulated it, 'is action forced on us by the will of another'. If you enjoy doing it, it isn't work. To him, most lessons were play, and work meant something like playing football. He cheerfully put up with those aspects of school life he did not enjoy, fulminating only against the compulsory cold bath every morning which authority prescribed in the belief that cold water subdued the carnal passions. (As an adult, he asserted that he belonged to the first generation to resolve that, after school, they would never take a cold bath in their lives again.)

When the time came for him to leave St Edmund's, he did so with mixed feelings. He was a sophisticated child, but a child, nevertheless, and his view of the teachers he was leaving behind had both the clarity and one-sidedness of a child's view of the world around him: 'hairy monsters with terrifying voices and eccentric habits, completely irrational in their bouts of rage and good-humour, and, it seemed, with absolute power of life and death'[1] was how he expressed it in later life when he still, in part, believed it. But he also realized that, from his parents and his family and also from his first exposure to school life, he had learnt certain attitudes or prejudices which he was unlikely to shake off:

. . . that knowledge is something to seek for its own sake; an interest in medicine and disease, and theology; a conviction (though I am unaware of ever having held any supernatural beliefs) that life is ruled by mysterious forces; a dislike of strangers and cheery gangs; and a contempt for business men and all who work for profits rather than a salary.

[1] *The English Auden.*

He was thirty-two when he listed those attitudes. But, at thirteen, all he knew was that his five years 'as a member of a primitive tribe ruled by benevolent or malignant demons' were drawing to a close, and that he was now to embark, at public school, upon another five years as what he would in due course describe as 'a citizen of a totalitarian state'. In the autumn of 1920, he arrived at Gresham's school in Holt, a small market town in north Suffolk, about ten miles inland from Cromer, in flat, featureless country. Wystan just missed getting a scholarship to Gresham's, so found himself at first placed in a form too low, in which the work was so easy for him that he simply coasted along. In his second term, he wrote to Miss Rosa, his old friend and mentor at St Edmunds: 'The buildings are excellent and also the teaching. We all have studies. Your first few terms you share with about three others, then less; finally you get a single study.' He also gave news of his brother John who was in the Science Sixth Form at Marlborough and had just joined the English Literature Society. The next year, Wystan won the top scholarship at Gresham's, and began to enjoy life there even more than in his first terms. His mother wrote to Miss Rosa: 'He has also been acting and took the part of Miss Ashford in *The Private Secretary* [an adaptation by the American actor-playwright William Gillette of Moser's *Der Bibliothekar*]. This was in the house play and his acting was such that he has been chosen for a part in the school play which comes off in July.'

Founded in 1555, Gresham's appears to have been an excellent school of a kind which, in the first years of the century, was comparatively rare in its liberalism and modernity of outlook. It taught very little Latin and no Greek, but concentrated on science and history. It did not inculcate into its pupils snobbish attitudes regarding social class, and it frowned on corporal punishment and bullying. It clearly appealed to parents of the liberal intelligentsia. Although the school buildings were late Victorian and of no architectural distinction, their situation was a fine one: Wystan would remember with delight watching a snowstorm come up from the sea over the marshes at Salthouse, or walking by Hempstead Mill in a June Dawn. The library was magnificent, and the academic standard excellent. The cooking, if undistinguished, was quite adequate, the maids no more slatternly than elsewhere, and the attitude to sport and athletics was sensibly unfanatical. What more could a short-sighted, mentally precocious, bookish and solitary child require? This particular specimen took pleasure in it all, especially the expeditions of a sociological society which studied very little sociology but enjoyed itself with charabanc outings to nearby factories.

The morals of Gresham's pupils were kept in impeccable condition, at least in theory, by an honour system. Within a few days of his arrival, each new boy was interviewed separately both by his housemaster and by the headmaster, and made to promise three things: not to swear, not to smoke, and not to say or do anything indecent. A boy who broke any of these promises was expected to report himself to his housemaster; and if any boy was aware of anyone else falling by the wayside, it was his duty to attempt to persuade the culprit to report himself, or, in the last resort, to report him himself. Auden, after he had left school, looked back on this system with distaste as being Fascist. In an essay on Gresham's which he contributed at the age of twenty-seven to an anthology edited by Graham Greene, he wrote: 'It meant that the whole of our moral life was based on fear, on fear of the community, not to mention the temptation it offered to the natural informer, and fear is not a healthy basis. It makes one furtive and dishonest and unadventurous. . . . There is far too much talk about ideals at all schools. Ideals are the conclusions drawn from a man of experience, not the data: they are essentially for the mature.'[1]

However, Wystan did not suffer unduly from the system while he was at Gresham's: he simply ignored it and went his own way, throwing himself wholeheartedly into those activities which appealed to him, and keeping his distance from others. He took an active part in the Arts and Archaeological Society, gave a lecture on Psychology to a literary society, and another on Comparative Folklore, and in 1923, with a fellow pupil, Mervyn Roberts, organized and promoted a recital of modern music, including works by Delius, Bax, Ireland, Elgar, and the now almost forgotten Scottish composer John McEwan.

In the summer of 1922, the fifteen-year-old Wystan was cast in a leading role in the annual Shakespeare production in the open air theatre in the school woods. The play was *The Taming of the Shrew*, and Wystan played Katharina opposite the Petrucchio of Sebastian Shaw who was seventeen, already an experienced actor, and later to become well known in British films and on the stage. Shaw remembers his Katharina as 'a small, slightly puffy little boy with pink and white cheeks and almost colourless hair . . . red wrists projecting from frilly sleeves and never knowing what to do with his hands. His voice, however, was clear, and his diction excellent.' The review in the school magazine, *The Gresham*, conjures up a convincing picture of the amiable amateur Auden fighting a losing battle against the ambitious professional Shaw:

Another delightful setting in the theatre, a cast of exceptionally high standard, a splendid Petrucchio. Auden struggled nobly against overwhelming odds to give Katharina her rightful dominant position in the play, but was completely swamped by Petrucchio's all-pervading personality the moment he appeared. To do justice to the character Katharina is an extremely trying task for a mere male, and Auden was far from

[1] *The Old School* (London, 1934).

assisted by a poor wig and clothes that can only be described as shocking. Under so many adverse circumstances, however, it reflected the greatest credit on him that he contrived to infuse considerable dignity into his passionate outbursts and, moreover, by his spirited performance showed that determination can overcome almost insurmountable difficulties.

Comparing his early years, for the purpose of a book review, with those of Leonard Woolf and Evelyn Waugh, the adult Auden noted: '1920, period of ecclesiastical *Schwärmerei*. 1922, discovers that he has lost his faith.' Auden's 'hiatus of unbelief' was to last a good eighteen years, and whether he ever came back to the intense belief in Christianity of his childhood years may well be doubted. The religious infatuation of the pubescent leads inevitably to crisis as he progresses through adolescence, discovering the delights of the world and the flesh, but the young Auden's progress was made comparatively easy for him by his temperament and his intelligence, and also by three helpful and sympathetic adults whom he encountered at the right time. One of these was the master who taught Classics and English, a man with a magnificent bass speaking voice who inculcated a lively respect for the classics into his pupils: 'From listening to him read the Bible or Shakespeare I learnt more about poetry and the humanities than from any course of University lectures.'[1] Another was Walter Greatorex, the Music master, known to his pupils as 'The Ox'. An elderly man who concealed great kindness and tact under a haughtily indifferent manner, this fine musician communicated his love and knowledge of music to the young Wystan, who sang under him in the choir and heard him play most of the Bach preludes and fugues. Auden later wrote that it was to Greatorex that he owed not only such knowledge of music as he possessed but also his first friendship with a grown-up person.

As a musician he was in the first rank. I do not think it was only partiality that made me feel when later I heard Schweitzer play Bach on the organ that he played no better.

As a person he was what the ideal schoolmaster should be, ready to be a friend and not a beak, to give the adolescent all the comfort and stimulus of a personal relation, without at the same time making any demands for himself in return, a temptation which must assail all those who are capable of attracting and influencing their juniors. He was in the best sense of the word indifferent, and if the whole of the rest of my school days had been hateful, which they weren't, his existence alone would make me recall them with pleasure.[2]

It was in 1922, Wystan's fifteenth year, that his attention was turned away

[1] *The Old School.*
[2] *The Old School.*

from religion as a major interest, and towards poetry. He had already begun to read Freud, who has turned many a youngster's mind away from imagined God to real man, but he was now given a sudden and seemingly arbitrary push into the arms of poetry. 'I began writing poetry myself because one Sunday afternoon in March 1922, a friend suggested that I should,' said W. H. Auden during his inaugural lecture as Professor of Poetry at the University of Oxford in 1956. The friend was Robert Medley, who was later to make his name as a painter. Auden claimed that, until that afternoon, the thought of writing poetry had never entered his head: he often wondered what his life would have been had Medley not made that suggestion. He had read some poetry as a child, though not much: the English Hymnal, the Psalms, *Stuwwelpeter* and the mnemonic rhymes in Kennedy's *Shorter Latin Primer* were all he could recall in adult life.

Robert Medley, fourteen months older than Wystan, had arrived at Gresham's in the autumn of 1919. He remembers the exceptionally bright new boy, Auden, being put into the lower third on arrival only to be given an open scholarship the following year and moved up two forms, thereafter 'float[ing] up the senior school without effort', never bothering to make a show of his knowledge in class and therefore being thought by many to be lazy. Medley was absent from Gresham's in 1921 for most of the year, recovering from a bicycle accident; he and Auden did not meet until March 1922, and Medley remembers that it was by Wystan's contrivance that they met, in the bus which was taking the Sociological Society to visit a boot factory in Norwich.

Auden had been confirmed in 1920 at the age of thirteen. Although he dates his loss of religious faith from 1922, he appears in March of that year still to have been an excessively devout fifteen-year-old, for it was in this month, very early in their friendship, that, during the course of a walk towards the woods a mile or two from the school, Medley made an attack upon the church and was astonished to find that he had upset and angered his friend. In embarrassment, and in order to avoid what he feared might become a serious breach, Medley found an opportunity to go off at a tangent and ask Wystan if he wrote poetry, confessing in turn that he himself did. 'I was a little surprised that he had not tried,' Medley recalled in later years, 'and suggested he might do so.' Within weeks, Wystan was showing sheaves of poems, scrawled in his small, illegible hand, to Robert Medley and one or two other friends at school, and asking for their opinions. The poems rhymed conventionally and derived mainly from Edward Thomas and Thomas Hardy. Especially Hardy-esque was 'The Traction Engine':

> Its days are over now; no farmyard airs
> Will quiver hot above its chimney-stack; the fairs

It dragged from green to green are not what they have been
    In previous years.

Here now it lies, unsheltered, undesired,
Its engine rusted fast, its boiler mossed, unfired,
Companioned by a boot-heel and an old cart-wheel,
    In thistles attired,

Unfeeling, uncaring; imaginings
Mar not the future; no past sick memory clings,
Yet it seems well to deserve the love we reserve
    For animate things.

Another poem described the countryside where his family had a summer cottage, near Keswick in Cumberland, 'Where one can walk for miles and miles/And meet with neither gate nor stiles.'

These first *juvenilia* were perhaps not startlingly original, but they were surely unusual in the competence of their technique and the confidence of the poet's voice, and they were seized upon with admiration by Wystan's school-friends. At the end of 1922, Robert Medley left Gresham's to study art in London, first at the Academy School and later at the Slade, but he and Wystan corresponded, and Wystan continued to send batches of poems for Medley's approval. On 16 December his first published poem, 'Dawn', appeared anonymously in the school magazine, *The Gresham*.

Far into the vast the mists grow dim,
    A deep and holy silence broods around,
Fire burns beyond the vaporous rim,
    And crystal-like the dew bestrews the ground.

The last laggard star has fled the glowing sky,
    Comes a quiet stirring and a gentle light,
A vast pulsating music, throbbing harmony,
    Behold the sun delivered from the gloom of night!

In 1923, staying with the Medleys while in London to take an exam, Wystan gave Medley's sister an impromptu piano lesson before breakfast one morning, playing John Ireland's piano prelude, 'The Holy Boy', and explaining to her how it should be played. On this and other visits to London Wystan went to the theatre frequently with Medley; to Basil Dean's productions of Karel Čapek's expressionist drama, *R.U.R.*, and *The Insect Play* (by Čapek and his brother). They also went to Rutland Boughton's opera, *The Immortal Hour*, which was enjoying a long run at the Regent Theatre, and spent a lot of time browsing in Harold Monro's Poetry Bookshop.

The loss of religious faith which Auden later claimed to have suffered in 1922 was not at the time the dramatic event which it can be for fifteen-year-olds: it appears rather to have been an eventual awareness of loss of faith, possibly even no more than a lessening of interest in religion as other interests revealed themselves to him. Poetry was one such interest, and by the time he arrived at Oxford he was to know it as his vocation. At school, along with puberty had come that other obsessive interest of the teenager, sex. At Gresham's there was probably less homosexual experimenting among the boys than at many other schools, for the 'honour system' did its best to repress such perfectly healthy, normal activity. At this stage of their development, boys can be extraordinarily romantic creatures; the more sensitive natures among them tend to separate sex and love into different compartments, indulging in sexual activity with this school-friend but elevating that one into the unattainable image of the distant beloved, the not-to-be-besmirched-by-carnal-passion. Wystan appears to have developed a crush of this latter kind upon Robert Medley who, busily wrestling with his own adolescent problems, remained totally unaware of the devotion he inspired in Wystan and of its sexual basis.

Medley was an expert swimmer and diver. One day in 1922, when Wystan saw him at the swimming pool, diving off the top board with another boy on his back, he asked to be given a 'piggy-back' into the pool, too. 'After some difficulty in getting him to grip firmly with his legs,' Medley recalled a good fifty years later, 'and not to strangle me with his arms, all was declared ready, and off we went to disaster. Wystan emerged from the water with a badly bleeding nose. Feeling responsible, I was very upset, but it was the first time I had encountered his innate physical clumsiness. Also I suppose it was as near as we, or most of us, ever got to an embrace at Gresham's.' The following year, Medley stayed with the Audens during the holidays, and one night he and Wystan read over a number of Wystan's poems. The following morning Dr Auden discovered amongst them a poem describing Medley at the swimming pool, in which he thought he discerned an erotic content. Somewhat disturbed, he spoke to the two boys about it, explaining that he was sympathetic to close romantic friendships among young males, indeed that he himself as a youth had experienced such a feeling, but that it was highly undesirable that things should go 'that far'. Had things gone 'that far' between Wystan and his friend? The boys, no doubt highly embarrassed, were able truthfully to assure Dr Auden that their friendship was purely platonic. However, it very easily might not have been.

Despite the almost complete lack of help and guidance in sexual matters offered by the school authorities, by the time Wystan left school he had become aware of his own sexual nature which was predominantly homosexual. By his sixteenth birthday, he had realized that he was going to carry his sexual preferences into adult life. As a mature adult, Auden was inclined to think his homosexuality was caused by the absence of his father between 1914 and 1918. 'A child needs a mother up until the time he's seven. After that, he needs a father and mine was gone.'[1] He paid tribute to the one person who, he claimed, had helped him through his difficult years of adolescence. Referring to the fact that many people could look back and remember some adult who had taken an interest in them as children, an interest in which there was usually an element of homosexual feeling, whether sublimated or overt, he wrote that

> the corresponding figure in my life I had to meet clandestinely – my housemaster having forbidden me to see him, and not without reason, for he was a practising homosexual and had, I think, been to prison. Why he should have taken a shine to me I cannot imagine, since I was a very plain boy. He made advances, which I rejected, not on moral grounds but because I thought him unattractive. Instead of dropping me, however, he continued to give me books and write me long letters full of encouraging and constructive criticism of my juvenile verses. I owe him a great deal.[2]

Auden's housemaster may have disapproved of this figure, but it was Walter Greatorex, the senior Music master at Gresham's who, in fact, introduced him to Auden. The man was Michael Davidson, a twenty-six-year-old junior sub-editor on the *Eastern Daily Press* in Norwich. One day in 1923, Greatorex said to his friend, 'There's a boy you'd like to meet. Writes very good verse, I think. His name's Auden.' They met, and Davidson was immediately bewitched by Wystan, but mentally and spiritually, rather than physically. He was overwhelmed by the sixteen-year-old boy's intellectual maturity, his honesty and abhorrence of any kind of sham or falseness, and also touched by his adolescent vulnerability. He recognized genius in the young Auden, genius which needed guidance, sympathy and understanding. 'I saw,' Michael Davidson wrote nearly forty years later in his autobiography,[3] 'that I had found my boy Keats or Chatterton, on whom I would lavish all I could muster of literary maternalism. I was in love; but I think I deliberately chose to be in love.'

Their relationship was conducted, for the most part, by post, with letters, poems and books flowing almost daily between Norwich and Holt. Wystan sent his poems to Davidson who returned them with long letters of criticism, or discussion of poets whom they had discovered, such as Edward Thomas, Robert Frost and Walter de la Mare. Davidson bought the latest books of

---

[1] *Observer* Colour Magazine, 7 November 1971.

[2] W. H. Auden *Forewords and Afterwords* (London, 1973).

[3] *The World, the Flesh and Myself* (London, 1962).

verse and of literary criticism and presented them to Wystan, who kept many of them to the end of his life. 'It must have been a strange, and rather touching, correspondence,' Davidson remembered:

> Mine were love letters as well as literary ones; though I did my best to filter the love out of them, so afraid was I of offending his detestation of the sentimental. His were calm, mature, rigidly unemotional. I tremble still today when I think what nonsense I must often have written; for my outlook on poetry was a romantic, traditionalist one, and sadly uninstructed. Although I was supposed to be the counsellor, the critic, of ten years' seniority, I learned much more from Auden than I could teach him. . . . He knew, of course – better than I, having the entire psychological pentateuch at his finger-tips – the nature of my feelings for him. I think he rather enjoyed them – he could study me, so to speak, clinically; he once told me, as if stating an interesting scientific fact, that I was the first adult homosexual he had met. But his understanding of my devotion was never more than tacit; and once, when I was fool enough to post him some wretched verses I'd written to him, he never referred to their existence. He was kind enough to ignore their poetic dreadfulness and stern enough to keep silent on the sentiment they conveyed (he knew of course that sentiment far better than my feeble and misguided effusion could tell it).

Although, at the instigation of Robert Medley and with the encouragement of Michael Davidson, he was now writing poetry, Wystan had by no means decided to make poetry his profession. At this time he was reading widely in Freud and Jung, and told Davidson he hoped to become a psychologist. For poetry to take its place in the modern world it was going to have to become scientific. The poet, henceforth, would also be the scientist. The young Auden found his truth in science and the scientific approach, and his conversation now, and later at university, was loaded with the specialist terminologies of science and psychology.

When Wystan's housemaster expressed his disapproval of Wystan's friendship with Michael Davidson, the relationship continued clandestinely, even after Davidson received a letter from Mrs Auden formally requesting him to see no more of her son. Wystan was not one to be browbeaten by authority, parental or scholastic. He went, occasionally, to stay with Davidson in Norwich, sleeping in the only bedroom while his host 'chastely slept downstairs'. Occasionally they met in King's Lynn, or they would take long walks together, over fen and through wood, exchanging ideas, hesitantly on Davidson's side, with authoritative fluency on Wystan's. In his autobiography Michael Davidson wrote:

> I angered him by springing a surprise which I hoped (with the fevered excitement of a lover bearing gifts) would give him pleasure. I had

discovered that some firm of publishers was putting out an annual volume called 'Public School Verse'; and choosing what I thought the best from my stock [of poems by Auden], I submitted a poem without saying anything to him. Of course it was accepted; and I had the additional joy, when the book appeared, of reviewing it in the *Eastern Daily Press* and devoting the whole review to Auden. But he was furious and I, in consequence, chagrined. Yet I think his anger was justified: his work by then was far too mature to be ranked with that of schoolboys.

A nice story, but not supported by the facts. Whoever may have submitted a poem or poems, Wystan certainly knew about it in advance, for he wrote to his parents from school, in the autumn of 1923: 'I also have a little surprise for you. I have had some things accepted for the 1924 volume of *Public School Verse*; so shall make my first appearance in print so to speak next year.'

If 'some things' were submitted, only one was accepted. The poem, 'Woods in Rain', duly appeared in *Public School Verse*,[1] though the poet's name was misprinted as 'Arden', perhaps through an absent-minded compositor's association of forests and Arden. Furthermore, Michael Davidson, far from devoting the whole of his anonymous review to Auden, merely quoted a few lines of 'Woods in Rain' which he referred to as 'a charming poem reminiscent, perhaps, of John Clare'.[2] If this is not as much as Michael Davidson claimed, at least he was responsible for the first critical reference in print to Auden.

Among Wystan's school friends was John Pudney, two years his junior, who was to become well known as poet, novelist, and journalist. (One of his short lyric poems, 'For Johnny', written for a film about the RAF in World War II, *The Way to the Stars*, reached audiences far wider than those of most twentieth-century poets.) Pudney remembered Wystan Auden at school as 'a Nordic, sagacious, heavy-footed boy', and was bowled over by his defiance of convention and by his independence of mind. Wystan, who was in another house at school, initiated a friendship with Pudney simply by walking across to his house and engaging him in conversation about poets and poetry, psychology, sexual hygiene, homosexuality, and politics. Not surprisingly, young Pudney found it an 'explosive experience' to be forcefully liberated from Swinburne and the other Victorians he admired, and to be introduced to D. H. Lawrence, Freud and Jung. The two boys went on 'long didactic walks', Wystan deliberately choosing paths that were out of bounds, stopping at a local farmhouse for massive teas of eggs and strawberries and cream. The friendship had its romantic excitements, too, for

[1] Edited by Martin Gilkes, Richard Hughes, and P. H. B. Lyon, *Public School Verse, Volume IV, 1923–24* was published by William Heinemann Ltd in September 1924. (See p. 74.)

[2] *Eastern Daily Press* (Norwich, 26 September 1924).

Wystan was given to climbing up a drainpipe into the younger boy's study in the early hours of the morning, to leave messages or to correct the school-work which Pudney had left out on his desk.

Clearly, Wystan helped and guided young John Pudney through his years at Gresham's. Equally clearly, Pudney helped Wystan by reacting suitably to his poems when Wystan read them to him or gave them to him in hand-written copies which were 'neat, emphatic, just a little difficult to read'. Some of the poems which Auden wrote at school were kept by his mother and later given to a friend, E. R. Dodds, for safe-keeping in case Auden might destroy them. They were lucky to have survived, for Wystan at school was fiercely self-critical, and one summer morning in 1924 he announced to Pudney that, bad though Pudney's poems were, his, Auden's, were even worse, for they were more pretentious. The two boys were walking through the school woods. 'It was a Wagnerian scene,' Pudney remembered, 'with East Anglian winds sounding gusty chords of doom.'

> The climax was dreadful. As we approached the larger of the school ponds, I was commanded to stand back while the poet, tossing back his pale straight hair, drew his manuscripts from his pockets and went on alone, to commit literary suicide by casting them into the depths. I leant against the fretted bark of a great wet tree, shivering and facing away from the calamity. I felt ashamed that my own juvenilia, carefully copied out in an exercise book, remained undestroyed but dishonoured, hidden in my tuck-box beneath the defenestrated volumes of Swinburne which I had secretly retrieved.[1]

Wystan laughingly announced to his shivering disciple that he had now got poetry out of his system and intended to devote his life to science. But later that same day the ex-poet appeared at Pudney's study window in the damp twilight, beckoning him again to the woods. Another boy from Wystan's house, Neil Pearson, joined them, and as the three boys made their way to the pond in the woods the fearsome thought crossed Pudney's mind that perhaps they were now to witness the actual suicide of Wystan Auden, and that science, as well as poetry, would have to fend for itself. But no, what they were to witness, or rather what they were to assist by keeping watch, was the poet's attempt to retrieve his poems. Wystan informed them that he regretted his hysterical action earlier in the day; when they reached the pond he waded in, after posting Pearson and Pudney on the only two paths along which intruders or school staff might approach. The two boys could hear sloshing sounds, and their nostrils were assailed by the abominable stench of the stagnant water. Pudney called out to ask if Wystan was all

[1] John Pudney: *Home and Away* (London, 1960).

right, and received a snappish answer. Eventually the poet reappeared, wet and smelly, but clasping all the pages of his manuscript poems which, saved by scum, had scarcely penetrated the surface of the water. To suspect that they had been carefully placed earlier that day so as to facilitate their later retrieval would be unkind.

Walter de la Mare's anthology of poetry, *Come Hither*, had just been published, and Wystan devoured its contents greedily. He was later to remark that, more than any book he had read before or since, it taught him what poetry was.

In his last year at school, he served on the library committee and, perhaps less predictably, chose to go to the annual Officers' Training Corps summer camp, at which boys from a number of public schools were given a week's training under professional army officers. He revelled in the absurdities of this, and enjoyed noting the way some of Gresham's 'pure and virtuous' behaved when thrown into contact with boys from less inhibited schools. In his final term at Gresham's, the summer of 1925, Wystan made his last appearance in the annual school play. It was *The Tempest*. He was determined to play Caliban, for he had firm views about the role's interpretation. Caliban's inheritance of the island on the departure of his master Prospero whom he loathed and feared was seen by Auden as an opportunity to make a protest against Gresham's honour system. He succeeded in getting the role, but whether he also succeeded in making his protest clear through his performance is by no means certain. The producer of the play was Wystan's housemaster whom he had cordially hated ever since the housemaster caught him writing a poem during prep, and sneered, 'You shouldn't waste your sweetness on the desert air like this, Auden.' Ten years later, Auden still could not think of this man without wishing him evil.

When Wystan left Gresham's in the spring of 1925, he had won a scholarship in natural science at Oxford, and knew he would be entering the university in the autumn. Looking back on the school ten years later, when he himself was a young schoolmaster, Auden remembered his time there as having been, for the most part, enjoyable. He had found solitude when he wanted it, and companionship when he wanted it. All the staff were conscientious and some of them were efficient; and, if the boys were not given any real sense of the problems of the world or of how to attack them, then that was probably too much to ask of any English public school, for the system was dedicated to the mass production of gentlemen. He remembered some masters – and one prefect, Michael Fordham – with affection, and could look back tolerantly on other masters who either shouted in class ('a horrible habit') or came up behind one on bicycle rides and pinched one's bottom. Aided by some and hindered by others, Wystan had done a pretty good job of educating himself.

Chapter Two

1925–1928

On Sunday walks
Past the shut gates of works
The conquerors come
And are handsome.[1]

Wystan's summer holiday in 1925 was a trip to the continent with his father, as a reward for having done so well at school. They went to Austria, visiting Salzburg during the festival and also the spa resort of Kitzbühel in the Tyrol. At Kitzbühel, he met an Austrian woman, Hedwig Petzold, with whom he kept up a tenuous kind of friendship in later years. In the autumn, Wystan went up to Oxford and settled into his rooms in 'The House', as his college, Christ Church, is familiarly known. Oxford in the twenties has been much written about by a number of his contemporaries, among them C. Day Lewis, Louis MacNeice, Richard Crossman, Tom Driberg, Stephen Spender, Harold Acton and A. L. Rowse. They have described the glittering social and academic life enjoyed by the well-to-do students: the drinking parties, the hearty sportsmen, the elegant aesthetes, the raids upon the rooms of the latter by the former, the extraordinary degree of undergraduate freedom, these elements have become clichés of Oxford between the wars. (Tom Driberg recalls that, during his first interview with one of his tutors, a young man put his head round the door to say to the tutor, 'I thought I'd just let you know that I shan't be coming to any tutorials or lectures this term, because I've managed to get four days' hunting a week.'[2])

Into this world of hearties and aesthetes, the mature, serious minded, eighteen-year-old Wystan Auden, who was neither hearty nor aesthetic, was thrust in the autumn of 1925. Sir John Betjeman, his senior by some months, remembers being introduced to the 'tall milky-skinned and coltish' youth in corduroys, who was unimpressed by Betjeman's grand friends such as Harold Acton, Bryan Guinness and Christopher Sykes, uninterested in the fashionable Sitwells, and 'really admired the boring Anglo-Saxon poets like Beowulf'. Although Auden consistently refused Betjeman's invitations to lunch with various peers and baronets whom the young socially minded future Poet Laureate was cultivating, the two of them became friends. Their tastes in poetry may have differed widely, but they

[1] From 'On Sunday Walks'.
[2] Tom Driberg: *Ruling Passions* (London, 1977).

shared certain admirations, enjoyed discovering unknown poets amongst the Victorians and Edwardians, and reading out their discoveries to each other. Politically, they differed even more than poetically. The elegant Betjeman combined his enjoyment of the good things of life with a great reverence for those who possessed them – the landowning classes with their great houses and parks – while the shambling Auden was aware of, and concerned about, slum conditions in Birmingham and the mining villages. However, they came together in their eccentric obsessions, from country churches to Bradshaw's railway timetables. They discovered and read together the works of the Rev. Dr E. E. Bradford who wrote bad verse which Betjeman has described as 'innocent and touching about the love of "lads" '.

Auden's beautifully proportioned, oak-panelled rooms were in the north-west corner of Peckwater Quadrangle (known as Peck), on the third floor. In addition to his sitting-room and bedroom, there was a small cupboard-like space into which a piano had been squeezed and whose walls had been covered by a previous occupant with a startling mural of scarlet and black cubist design, described in due course by Christopher Isherwood as apparently representing 'a series of railway accidents and copulations between traction engines and pyramids'. It was in these rooms that Auden would hold court with the small group of acolytes who began to assemble around him, reading aloud his own poems and those of other poets whose work impressed him. In middle age, Auden tended not so much to converse as to lecture, and even at the age of eighteen his discussions of the poetry of, say, Emily Dickinson or Wilfred Owen were, more often than not, monologues. They were, however, monologues which his listeners found quite fascinating, occasionally as much for the oddly impressive, somewhat portentous manner of his delivery as for his actual words. Betjeman was impressed by Auden's oracular quality, and thought him 'a born schoolmaster and lecturer'. He was equally impressed by Auden's refusal to adopt the fashionable undergraduate pose of looking down on one's parents as boring philistines: this young man spoke with affection and respect of his parents, and of Birmingham and the country around it with interest and, almost, nostalgia. Clearly, he fitted into no Oxford pigeon-hole.

There was a strong element of the poseur, the role-player, in the mature Auden. He would adopt an attitude or an intellectual position, sometimes in order to test his own ideas, at other times to goad a response out of someone else. His intellectual ebullience was such that he could present with equal force and conviction the opposing sides of an argument, and he frequently did so. As a young man, he was already indulging this ability, assuming the roles of prefect, philosopher or headmaster, as the mood took him. This chameleon-like attribute extended, apparently, to his personal appearance, for descriptions of him as a student are more than ordinarily contradictory:

'a fresh, unwrinkled, pink face' (Rex Warner); 'loosely put together, flat-footed, with big chubby hands and well-bitten nails, fumbling with a cigarette, and a big mobile face good at expressing contrived emotions' (Gabriel Carritt); 'he had almost albino hair and weakly pigmented eyes set closely together, so that they gave the impression of watchfully squinting' (Stephen Spender); 'he had physical beauty too: he was tow-haired, chubby-cheeked, innocent looking' (Tom Driberg); 'moving with his phenomenally long, ungainly stride, and talking incessantly, his words tumbling over one another in the hurry to get out, a lock of tow-coloured hair falling over the brow of his rather puffy but wonderfully animated white face' (C. Day Lewis); 'frightfully unappetizing as this apparition was' (A. L. Rowse).

Schoolboys of Auden's generation tended not to care about their physical appearance, unlike the clothes-conscious children of the sixties and seventies. But students of his generation, in their late teens, were concerned to be fashionable: for men, it was the period of the Oxford 'bags', singularly graceless garments to the eyes of today, but at that time the ultimate degree of elegance. Wystan Auden expressed his contempt for fashion sometimes by wearing what his contemporaries thought to be extremely outlandish costumes, and sometimes simply by dressing dowdily in whatever was nearest to hand. His clothes were described by friends as 'the idiosyncratic, ill-fitting, smelly clothes he shambled about in' (Rowse); 'an extraordinary black, lay-reader's type of frock-coat which came half-way down to his knees and had been rescued by him from one of his mother's jumble sales' (C. Day Lewis); he was 'conventionally dressed and tidy, but wore his clothes as if they did not fit' (Gabriel Carritt); 'this tough youth in corduroys' (John Betjeman); 'absurdly dressed in a brown double-breasted suit' (Stephen Spender).

Along with his eccentricities of appearance and dress went eccentricities of behaviour, though these were sometimes disguised as impeccable social concern. Gabriel Carritt and Wystan, travelling in Cumberland, had occasion to use the lavatory at the railway station in Oxenholme. As the towel in the lavatory was filthy, Carritt dried his hands on a handkerchief. Wystan immediately accused him of harbouring feelings of disgust for his fellow men, and ostentatiously dried his face and hands in the dirty towel as an expression of his solidarity with the working classes. But if such behaviour sounds priggish it was apparently leavened with self-deprecatory wit: he was always able to laugh at his own absurdities, and was prone to amiable self-parody which, his friends claimed, was extremely funny. At one moment he would be woefully complaining about his flat feet, and at the next asserting that a paragraph in a student magazine attacking him was certain proof that its author was in love with him.

When invited to the homes of his friends he would usually make an effort to behave with conventional politeness, though he still appeared wildly eccentric to most strangers. Rex Warner's parents thought Auden had charming manners: that he was given to raiding their pantry in the middle of the night, or that he took down the curtains in his bedroom and used them as blankets, was tactfully ignored. When he stayed with the Carritts, he removed their stair-carpet, still in search of nocturnal warmth, and placed it on his bed. He always got on well with Mrs Carritt, even though at breakfast on the first morning he tasted his tea and then said flatly, 'Mrs Carritt, this tea is like tepid piss.' He also hated the porridge Mrs Carritt served, and once vomited up his breakfast all over the geraniums in the front garden of the local post office, apologizing by going inside and announcing to the postmistress, 'I'm sorry, madam, but it's the Carritts' porridge.'

In general, although he professed firm likes and dislikes, he was not interested in food other than as necessary fuel for the body, wolfing it down quickly in order to get back to his cigarettes. In later life, at a dinner party at which he was guest of honour and thus seated first, he managed to finish the food on his plate before the last of the other guests had sat down.

In public, the young Auden's innate shyness could take one of two courses. Either he would sit self-effacingly and quietly, hardly uttering a word, or else he would flamboyantly draw to himself the attention of strangers by making intentionally shocking remarks as loudly as possible. Once, on the occasion of his birthday, he insisted on buying champagne ('the best bubbly') for all the farm workers in the bar of a country pub. If there was a piano in the pub he was drinking in, he would most likely play hymn tunes or accompany himself in German *Lieder*. Brahms' 'O Tod, wie bitter bist du', one of the *Vier ernste Gesänge*, was perhaps the gloomiest of his party pieces.

The walk along the side of the canal by the gasworks and the municipal rubbish dump which, according to Stephen Spender, Auden thought the most beautiful walk in Oxford, was certainly one which he took frequently with friends. He was fond of taking extremely long walks, especially after a doctor had advised him not to do so because of his flat feet; but, despite his professed and, in its way, real love of the bleak Pennine country of his childhood, he was usually not greatly aware of his physical surroundings except when he reminded himself to be aware of them. So he would walk with his friends and disciples as happily through the back streets of Oxford as in Wytham woods or through the downs outside Wantage. As one of his Oxford friends noted, he was not really interested in nature unless nature was at work reclaiming old mines or derelict machinery. It was the evidence of man in nature that intrigued him. Rex Warner, the future novelist, often accompanied him on walks in the vicinity of the Oxford gasworks, and even on expeditions up foul-smelling tunnels in a canoe. Wystan was quite fond of canals and waterways, it seemed, as long as they were overgrown or neglected, but he was completely unmoved by rare or beautiful flora or fauna. On walking expeditions, his friends often had difficulty keeping up with him, for his angular, flat-footed stride was very fast, his arms and head jerking about as he strode. His reading in psychology had convinced him that most illness had a psychological rather than a physical basis, was self-induced, and so could best be cured by being ignored. Hence, presumably, the thirty-mile walks in defiance of his foot condition.

The talks, the lectures to his friends, went on not only during these long walks, but also in the privacy of his rooms, where friends were encouraged to visit him singly. All his life, Auden tended, as many people do, to keep his friends apart and in separate categories, so that it was possible for two quite close friends of his not to know each other at all, or only very casually. He liked, even in his Oxford days, to adopt an avuncular attitude in one guise or another, and was much given to issuing advice which verged on instructions on how to live the good life. The advice to would-be poets was always frank, and never misleadingly kind. When Gabriel Carritt (who in adult life became a Marxist and proletarianized his first name to Bill) showed Auden his poems, he was told, 'Gabriel, you're good at rugger.'

Those who knew him at Oxford agree on the range and volubility of Auden's conversation, or rather his monologues, for, like many of those renowned for their conversational powers, he was disinclined to converse, preferring to harangue. Like Wilde, he was a performer, though his manner was decidedly more Johnsonian than Wildean. Frequently, the ideas which he propounded with such dogmatic emphasis were simply those which he himself was tentatively exploring, trying out. Often, the role he assumed was that of the poet technically experimenting with words. He did and said everything with an air of superb confidence which impressed even those who disagreed with his ideas or were not mentally well enough equipped to understand them.

Auden wrote a great number of poems at Oxford, and enjoyed reading them to his friends. He would recite from the depths of his armchair, in a flat, clinical voice, careful not to allow meaning or interpretation to obtrude, but occasionally highlighting individual words by an odd emphasis, and always marking the rhythm, or at any rate the line endings, very clearly. Much of his Oxford poetry, which he destroyed then or later, was in the manner of T. S. Eliot, whose long poem, *The Waste Land*, had appeared in 1922, exciting and impressing its readers by the poet's unconventional technique and the bleak pessimism of his philosophic doubt. Another influence which continued to be strong was that of Gerard Manley Hopkins, the Victorian religious poet whose intricate experiments with rhythm intrigued the young Auden as much as the spiritual content of his poetry.

The conviction that he could, through positive thinking, control illness and perhaps even events, was strong in Auden as a student, and was justified on at least one occasion: he was walking on the downs with a friend, and discovered that he had lost three pound notes which he had put loosely into a trouser pocket and must have dropped when pulling out a handkerchief. 'Never mind, we'll pick them up on the way back,' he said; and some hours later, as the two students retraced their steps, they came across the three banknotes fluttering along in the breeze. Auden, still talking, picked them up, stuffed them casually into his pocket, and walked on.

Sex at school tends to be furtive, and at university gregarious. Oxford in the twenties certainly exemplified this tendency, as a good many memoirs of the period reveal. Auden, however, was not part of the prevailing gregariousness. To him, sex was a private matter. He had no inhibitions about discussing it, graphically and clinically, with anyone, but he would never have been seen at a party, as Evelyn Waugh and another young man were, rolling on a sofa 'with (as one of them said later) their "tongues licking each other's tonsils"'.[1] Auden's sexual nature had by now confirmed itself as predominantly homosexual, and as a young man his sexual appetite was voracious. He tended to have affairs with his friends, almost as an extension or consolidation of their friendship: sex was certainly not the most important ingredient in these relationships, which usually continued and developed long after the sexual aspect had disappeared. At the same time, however, he enjoyed the casual pick-up, the chance encounter and the one-night stand, though he would rarely go out of his way to seek them. They seemed just to happen to him, and he would pick up young men in Oxford pubs or on the London train, later describing his experiences in salacious detail to his friends.

One of the friends to whom Auden was in the habit of reading his new poems was A. L. Rowse, four years his senior and a Fellow of All Souls. Occasionally these readings would take place after lunch at All Souls, in the big quad on summer afternoons. Once, after lunch, Auden suggested instead that they go back to his rooms in Christ Church. When they arrived, he shut both inner and outer doors, closed the shutters, drew the blinds, switched on the green-shaded desk lamp and donned the green eye-shade. Thus far, the ritual was proceeding along its normal course. But what Auden proceeded to read to a highly embarrassed and nervous Rowse was not poetry but a long letter from someone in an oil company in Mexico describing in explicit detail his sexual encounters with Mexican youths. If this was intended to have an aphrodisiac effect, it dismally failed, for the young

[1] Tom Driberg: *Ruling Passions.*

Rowse was conventionally guarded on the subject of his own sexual idio-syncrasies, and escaped from the room as soon as he decently could, if not sooner.

Another friend and, briefly, lover at Oxford was a handsome fellow student, Richard Crossman, later to distinguish himself in politics. Cross-man frequently accompanied Auden on visits to the Carritts, and a summer holiday that Auden and Crossman spent with the Carritt family on the Pembrokeshire coast is celebrated, though with a masterly obliqueness and obscurity, in a passage written five years later in 'Journal of an Airman', a section of Auden's second published volume, *The Orators*:

> There was a family called Do:
> There were Do-a, Do-ee, and other Do-s
> And Uncle Dick and Uncle Wiz[1] had come to stay with them
> (Nobody slept that night).
> Now Do-a loved to bathe before breakfast
> With Uncle Dick, but Uncle Wiz . . .
>
> Well?
>
> As a matter of fact the farm was in Pembrokeshire.
> The week the Labour Cabinet resigned
> Dick had returned from Germany in love.
> I hate cold water and am very fond of potatoes . . .
> You're wondering about these scratches?
>
> Well, I thought perhaps . . .
>
> Merely the gorse between Stumble Head and Llwndda.
> Gabriel was entertaining a young couple, so . . .

Having begun his Oxford life as a scholarship student in Natural Science, Auden briefly flirted with Politics, Philosophy and Economics before finally deciding to switch to English. Interviewed by his future English tutor, Nevill Coghill, he was asked what he intended to do when he left the university. 'I am going to be a poet,' he replied. Uncertain what to make of this, Coghill said, hesitantly, 'Well, in that case you should find it very useful to have read English.' There was a pause, and then Auden spoke again. 'You don't understand: I'm going to be a great poet.' It was certainly not long before he became a great rival to the authority of his tutor, for Coghill many years later recalled that, frequently, when he criticized the ideas of his other students, they would exclaim 'Well, Wystan says it's all right.' And it was Auden who

[1] Auden's Oxford nickname.

led his tutor towards a proper understanding and appreciation of T. S. Eliot:

> One morning Mr Wystan Auden, then an undergraduate at Christ Church, blew in to Exeter College for his tutorial hour with me, saying: 'I have torn up all my poems.'
>
> 'Indeed! Why?'
>
> 'Because they were no good. Based on Wordsworth. No good now-adays.'
>
> 'Oh . . . ?'
>
> 'You ought to read Eliot. I've been reading Eliot. I now see the way I want to write. I've written two new poems this week. Listen!'
>
> He recited them.
>
> I was brought up to demand a logical as well as a sensual meaning in poetry, so his recitation was completely incomprehensible to me, though I was struck by some of the images that had a sudden but seemingly irrelevant force. I can still remember one of a man by a gate looking into a field, though its 'meaning', in a context unintelligible to me, escaped. I complained of this, and Auden explained with clarity and pity that to 'understand' a poem was not a logical process, but a receiving, as a unity, a pattern of co-ordinated images that had sprung from a free association of sub-conscious ideas, private to himself. He again recommended the works of Mr Eliot.
>
> All this was towards 1926–7. I had of course already made some tenta-tive soundings in Mr Eliot's poetry and decided it was too deep for me, or else one of us was off the track of poetry. Perhaps he was a fad or fashion; if only my more advanced pupils would stop talking about him, there was a chance he might blow over . . . Or must I swot him up? It was that morning's tutorial hour that convinced me I must. 'Auden,' I thought, 'is in the imperative.'[1]

The imperative Auden had himself only recently been introduced to Eliot's great poem, *The Waste Land*, by Tom Driberg, with whom he read it as they stood side by side in Driberg's rooms in Peckwater Quad. Nevill Coghill was to find Auden not only imperative in mood but also, on occa-sion, capable of affecting an irritatingly impudent style of behaviour. One day, Coghill arrived late for a tutorial to find Auden already there, sitting at his tutor's desk and reading his letters with an air of great concentration. Looking up, Auden said, 'Ah, you're here. Good. What have you done with the second page of this letter?'

While not losing contact with one or two of his old school chums, among them Robert Medley, who had come to stay at Christ Church for a weekend

[1] From Nevill Coghill's contribution to *T. S. Eliot: a Symposium* (ed. Richard March and Tambimuttu. London, 1948).

as soon as Auden felt settled enough to invite guests, he met at Oxford a handful of people who were to remain his friends for life. One of these was William (later Sir William) Coldstream, who was then seventeen and about to become an art student at the Slade. Others were Stephen Spender, who of all his friends was to remain closest to him, Cecil Day Lewis and Louis MacNeice. But before any of these appeared on the scene, Auden renewed acquaintance with someone he had not seen since his prep school days: Christopher Isherwood. In December 1925, at the end of Auden's first term at Oxford, a mutual acquaintance who was having tea with Isherwood took Auden along with him. The scene is described by Isherwood in *Lions and Shadows*:

> I found him very little changed. True, he had grown enormously; but his small pale yellow eyes were still screwed painfully together in the same short-sighted scowl and his stumpy immature fingers were still nailbitten and stained – nicotine was now mixed with the ink. He was expensively but untidily dressed in a chocolate-brown suit which needed pressing, complete with one of the new fashionable double-breasted waistcoats. His coarse woollen socks were tumbled all anyhow, around his babyishly shapeless naked ankles. One of the laces was broken in his elegant brown shoes. While I and his introducer talked he sat silent, aggressively smoking a large pipe with a severe childish frown. Clumsy and severe, he hooked a blunt dirty finger round the tops of several of the books in my shelves, overbalancing them on to his lap and then, when his casual curiosity was satisfied, dropping them face downwards open on the floor – serenely unconscious of my outraged glances.

However, when the third person had gone, Auden relaxed somewhat, and before long the two friends were exchanging school reminiscences and gossip, reviving old jokes and falling about in helpless laughter as they recalled their former teachers and their eccentricities. Isherwood was surprised when, just before he left, Auden mentioned that he now wrote poetry, for he thought of Auden as a scientific type, and expected that any verse he might produce would be pretty poor stuff. Condescendingly, he suggested that Auden should send him some of his verses, and the poet responded not very graciously with 'All right, if you really want me to.' Isherwood was surprised when a large envelope containing a number of poems arrived in the post a few days later, for the poems were, in his opinion, 'Neither startlingly good nor startlingly bad; they were something much odder – efficient, imitative and extremely competent.' He was relieved to find that Auden's handwriting was still as bad as he had remembered it to be, or worse, and claimed many years later that there were still whole lines in the poetry which he had never been able to decipher.

41

In May of the following year, 1926, Wystan Auden indulged in his first overtly political act, albeit a somewhat quixotic one. The occasion was the General Strike. Nearly half of Great Britain's six million trade-unionists had gone on strike in support of the coal miners. Volunteers, mainly from the upper classes, helped to maintain essential transport and other services, and a large number of students played their part in this. A smaller number, however, mainly Socialists and Communists, supported the Trade Union Council and the strikers. Among them was Wystan who drove a car for the TUC. One day he had driven a prominent trade-unionist to his house in Mecklenburgh Square. A female cousin of Auden's, married to a stock-broker, lived a few doors away, so Auden paid an impromptu call and was invited to stay to lunch. The three of them were just sitting down at table when his cousin's husband asked Auden if he had come up to London to be a Special Constable. When Auden replied 'No, I'm driving a car for the TUC,' he was immediately ordered to leave the house. 'Mayn't I have my lunch first?' he enquired plaintively but practically. The strike was called off after nine days, which was fortunate not only for the nation but for Auden, for he was, and remained, an unimpressive and erratic driver.

Having found each other again, Auden and Isherwood began to meet and to correspond frequently. Isherwood had just come down from Cambridge, where his closest friend had been Edward Upward, who was to become a novelist. Isherwood and Upward, in rebellion against the academic conventionalities of Cambridge, had invented a village called Mortmere and peopled it with a number of fantastic characters, continually assuring each other that they would collaborate in writing a magnificent novel about their secret world. Isherwood told Auden about Edward Upward and about Mortmere, and Auden became interested in Upward and began to correspond with him. He and Upward met for the first time over dinner with Isherwood in a Soho restaurant in the early summer of 1926. By this time, Auden had sent a number of his poems to Upward who was impressed with their technical competence and the promise they revealed. At their first meeting, the talk turned to religion. Upward, who was later to embrace Communism, was then briefly toying with spiritual solutions to the world's ills, and suggested that it might be a good idea to invent an entirely new religion. He was astonished at the vehemence of Auden's antagonism to this, and at Auden's complete objection to any kind of religion. Auden, at the time, was certainly not conscious of any feelings of nostalgia for the comfortable faith he had rejected in his rational teens.

His habit of bullying and needling his friends asserted itself on the occasion of this first meeting with Upward. Christopher Isherwood, much addicted to gossip, as indeed was Auden, had obviously revealed to Auden one of Upward's idiosyncrasies; he never let his flesh come in contact with a lavatory seat. Upward's reason, apparently, was that he found the rough texture of the wood too uncomfortable. Auden, however, was not aware of this, and made a point of attacking, 'forcefully and loudly enough for other diners around us to become interested',[1] the sort of person who refused to sit on a public lavatory seat for fear of catching a venereal disease! Despite this kind of misdirected aggressiveness on Auden's part, he and Upward became firm friends.

For part of the summer vacation that year, Auden joined Isherwood who was staying at the seaside, at Yarmouth on the Isle of Wight. He arrived one day in July. 'I see him striding towards me, along Yarmouth Pier,' wrote Isherwood,[2] 'a tall figure with loose violent impatient movements, dressed in dirty grey flannels and a black evening bow-tie. On his straw-coloured head was planted a very broad-brimmed black felt hat.'

Isherwood disliked that hat from the moment he saw it: in fact, he took against all of Auden's hats, which he claimed were simply part of the poet's disguises. There was an opera hat, worn during the period when Auden felt that poets should dress like company directors; a workman's cap which he bought during his Berlin period a couple of years later, and which finished up in the fire after he had been sick into it in a cinema; a panama with a black ribbon, representing what Isherwood thought of as his friend's 'conception of himself as a lunatic clergyman'; and, of course, a schoolmaster's mortar-board, which Auden never had the courage to wear in Isherwood's presence. (The hat trick did not last. In later life, Auden gave up wearing any form of headgear, and disapproved of his friends wearing anything on their heads!)

The broad-brimmed black felt hat was enough to be going on with, for it was the cause of much astonishment and amusement in the village where Isherwood was staying. Auden was not displeased by this, and announced smugly, 'Laughter is the first sign of sexual attraction.' He embarrassed Isherwood by talking loudly and oddly on the local bus in a resonant Oxford accent: 'Of course, intellect's the only thing that matters at all . . . Apart from nature, geometry's all there *is* . . . Geometry belongs to man. Man's got to assert himself against Nature, all the *time* . . . Of course, I've absolutely no use for colour. Only form. The only really exciting things are volumes and *shapes* . . . Poetry's got to be made up of images and form. I hate sunsets and flowers. And I loathe the *sea*. The sea is formless . . .'

Isherwood found that Auden's literary tastes had changed considerably since their first meeting the previous December, as a consequence of his having read *The Waste Land*. Eliot had replaced Hardy and Edward Thomas as a major influence on Auden's poems, which were now liberally strewn

---

[1] Edward Upward: in *Adam* (Nos 379–384, 1973–74).

[2] In *Lions and Shadows*.

with quotations from scientific and psycho-analytical jargon, his equivalent of Eliot's classical allusions and fragments of German, French and Italian. Words like 'eutectic', 'sigmoid', 'Arch-Monad', 'ligature', and 'gastropod' now tended to occur. The effect he was seeking, Auden claimed, was a clinical one. The poet must be clinical, austere, removed from the everyday passions of the common herd. 'Austere' was a word Isherwood would become very tired of during the course of his friend's visit, yet he was touched to find that Auden admired him and looked up to him as a kind of literary elder brother. Like many highly prolific writers who over-produce in order to stave off the demon sloth, Auden was essentially and engagingly lazy, and he tended to accept without question Isherwood's suggestions for improvements to individual lines or words in his poems. Isherwood claims, perhaps not entirely seriously, that much of the obscurity of diction in Auden's early work is due to the poet's habit of saving up lines that Isherwood had liked in otherwise unsatisfactory poems, 'until a poem had been evolved which was a little anthology of my favourite lines, strung together without even an attempt to make connected sense'.

When they were not testing out their ideas on each other, the two friends went bathing in the sea, or drinking at the village pub, or sang hymns to Auden's accompaniment on the upright piano in their lodgings. Auden, throughout his life, loved to play the piano, and would sit at any keyboard he encountered in public or private and bang out hymn tunes, as often as not with his hat on (in his younger days) and a cigarette or pipe in his mouth. To Isherwood, he explained his incessant smoking as 'insufficient weaning – I must have something to suck'. He also drank innumerable cups of tea each day 'as if,' said Isherwood, 'his large, white apparently bloodless body needed continual reinforcements of warmth.' Throughout this summer holiday he liked to have a fire in the sitting-room whenever possible, and he invariably slept with two thick blankets, an eiderdown, both his and Isherwood's overcoats and all the rugs in his bedroom piled onto his bed.

Isherwood found his visitor stimulating, exasperating, and also disturbing. Stimulating was the literary talk; exasperating were the nicotine stains and dirty thumb marks in precious books, not to speak of the hole burnt in his only overcoat by a cigar; disturbing were Auden's shameless descriptions of his sexual adventures, and his amateur psychoanalysis of his host. He felt sorry for himself and lonely when the time came for Auden to go. They had enjoyed each other's company, and both realized that their friendship would develop, that there was no need for them to work on it. They complemented each other admirably, Auden with his superb analytical intellect, Isherwood with his intuitive intelligence.

But Isherwood was a prose writer, a novelist. The names that were to be linked with Auden's in the early thirties as belonging to a new poetic group were those of his Oxford contemporaries, Stephen Spender, Louis Mac-Neice and C. Day Lewis. The first of these whom Auden met was Cecil Day Lewis, when Day Lewis was in his last year at Oxford. Auden impressed Day Lewis with his vitality as much as his intellectual power, and though the older man (by three years) recognized his dogmatism, intellectual bossiness and tendency to try to run his friends' lives for them, he found Auden intensely stimulating, as did most people who met him at this stage of his life. Day Lewis was determined not to become completely swamped by Auden's personality, and decided to take him in small doses. But the two saw a great deal of each other at Oxford, not only in Day Lewis's last year as a student but also the following year when he was teaching in Oxford. That a certain degree of mutual jealousy or at least rivalry existed between them is suggested by Day Lewis in his account of an episode that occurred during a week's holiday they took together at Appletreewick in Yorkshire, in the summer of 1927:

> Walking the moors there one day, we approached one of those dark walls which wind over their contours like strips of liquorice. A hundred yards from the wall, as if on a common impulse, we both began to walk faster: at fifty or sixty yards, we broke into a trot, and we were sprinting all out over the last thirty yards or so. Arriving simultaneously at the wall, we gave each other an amused but also sheepish look.[1]

It was during this holiday that Auden and Day Lewis wrote down the names of all the living English poets they could think of, and divided them into three lists: those whom, in their opinion, they themselves already excelled; those whom they would one day excel; and an extremely short list of those whom they thought they had little hope of ever excelling.

Day Lewis may have successfully resisted having his poetic personality shaped by Auden, but he was unable to resist musical tuition. Auden decided to improve his friend's musical taste by teaching him the *Vier ernste Gesänge* (Four Serious Songs) of Brahms, four very sombre songs whose words are from the German translation by Martin Luther of Ecclesiastes and I Corinthians. Supported by what he described as Auden's 'loud, confident but wonderfully inaccurate' piano accompaniment, Day Lewis finally mastered the songs, which, to the consternation of his fiancée and her friends and relatives, he and his accompanist performed at a party on the eve of Day Lewis's wedding. Emboldened by what he regarded as his pupil's success on this occasion, Auden next persuaded the promising young composer Lennox Berkeley to allow Day Lewis to perform three new songs of his at the Oxford Musical Union. Day Lewis's lyric baritone sailed through Berkeley's setting of a sixteenth-century French poem easily enough, but came to grief

[1] C. Day Lewis: *The Buried Day* (London, 1960).

45

in the two 'rather unmelodious settings' of poems by Auden, limping through the first and actually breaking down in the second and having to begin again. His performance was 'received by the audience with a sustained outburst of silence'.

Auden took another trip abroad with his father for three weeks in July and August 1927. They visited Zagreb, Dubrovnik and Split, and Auden later enthused to Spender over the beauty of Yugoslavian youth.

In the twenties and early thirties, annual volumes of poetry by Oxford undergraduates were published. *Oxford Poetry 1926*, which came out in November of that year, was edited by Charles Plumb and W. H. Auden, and includes three poems by Auden, whose admonitory voice can clearly be discerned in this passage from the Editors' preface:

> In this selection we have endeavoured to pacify, if not to content, both the progressive and the reactionary. And to the latter, who will doubtless be in the majority, we would suggest that poetry which does not at least attempt to face the circumstances of its time may supply charming holiday reading, but vital interest, anything strictly *poetic*, it certainly will not. If it is a natural preference to inhabit a room with casements opening upon Fairyland, one at least of them should open upon the Waste Land.

Reviewing the volume, the student magazine *Oxford Outlook* regretted that 'the Eliot school predominates to such an extent'. But the Eliot school was to predominate even more strongly in *Oxford Poetry 1927*, for the editors this time were W. H. Auden and C. Day Lewis. Auden included only one poem by himself, and he and Day Lewis wrote alternate paragraphs of the preface, which reads very portentously, but which Day Lewis later claimed was written as a burlesque of solemnity. The editors were broadminded enough to include 'Souvenir des Vacances', a parody of T. S. Eliot's most obscure manner, by Christopher Isherwood, though not under his name, for he was not, nor had he ever been, an Oxford student.

It was at this time that Auden and Isherwood began going to bed together. To say that they became lovers would hardly convey the nature of their relationship at all accurately or sensitively. Sex was, for them, a logical extension of the close friendship between two men, a possibility latent in any close friendship whatever the gender or genders involved, but usually allowed to remain latent when the two friends are predominantly heterosexual males. In the case of Auden and Isherwood, it would probably be appropriate to refer to them at this period of their lives as loving friends: though they continued to have sex together, on occasions, for the following ten years or more, neither found the other all that exciting, physically; and temperamentally they were too alike, despite the differences in their types of intellect. Each would no doubt have preferred a non-intellectual lover of a completely different type. (It is customary, when making that kind of statement, to add a phrase like 'as, apparently, do many homosexuals'; however, the same is broadly true of male and female heterosexuals, at least in their day-dreams.) Christopher Isherwood described the exact nature of his personal relationship with Auden many years later, in his autobiographical volume, *Christopher and His Kind*, in which he refers to himself in the third person:

> They couldn't think of themselves as lovers, yet sex had given friendship an extra dimension. They were conscious of this and it embarrassed them slightly – that is to say, the sophisticated adult friends were embarrassed by the schoolboy sex partners. This may be the reason why they made fun, in private and in print, of each other's physical appearance . . . The adults were trying to dismiss the schoolboys' sex-making as unimportant. It was of profound importance. It made the relationship unique for both of them.

Early in December 1927, Isherwood made an overnight visit to Auden at Oxford. University life, he could see, suited his friend, who proudly but hurriedly showed him over his small suite of rooms, drawing attention to the piano on which he now played Bach (whom he had momentarily decided was 'the *only* composer') as well as hymn tunes; the model which he himself had made from a Meccano set on the mantelpiece; the Picasso etching of two young acrobats ('frightfully *emo*tive') which hung above the writing-table; Gertrude Stein's curious novel, *The Making of Americans* ('my God, she's good!'). Hardly given time to notice these, Isherwood was then made to listen simultaneously to Auden's reading of a poem by Christian Morgenstern (although Isherwood at this time knew no German) and a gramophone record of Sophie Tucker singing 'After you've gone'. Then it was time to go to dinner, and Auden entertained Isherwood in great style at the George, Oxford's most expensive restaurant (since closed) on the corner of George Street and Cornmarket. Dinner was accompanied by champagne ('the only *possible* drink, except whisky of course') and by Auden's ebullient lecture on the subject of entertainment. The cinema (which had still to discover its speaking voice) was dead, for there had been nothing of the slightest interest since D. W. Griffith's sentimental melodrama *Way Down East*, seven years earlier. Modern drama since Chekov was quite impossible, and the theatre lived on only in music hall, though in time perhaps something might be done with puppets. The ballet ought to be forbidden by Act of Parliament. The only possible forms of entertainment in the evenings were the dog races, the dirt track or boxing. Auden's own preference was for the dog races because they were so marvellously English. 'English', Isherwood discovered, was his friend's latest term of approbation: 'All this coninentalism won't *do*, it simply doesn't suit us. And we do it so *frightfully* badly.'

After dinner, there being no dog or dirt track races or boxing to be found in Oxford, Auden decided to take his guest to a meeting of the college Essay Club, muttering darkly 'You may as well see what Oxford's really *like*.' The meeting was held in a large crowded room, and Auden brusquely introduced his friend to about two dozen undergraduates and several dons. The students in particular eyed Isherwood with frank curiosity: it was only much later that he discovered Auden had been loudly proclaiming him throughout Oxford as the author of 'the *only* novel' since the war. (This was *Seascape With Figures*, which Auden had read in manuscript during their Isle of Wight holiday. Isherwood's first novel, it was to be published the following year under the title of *All the Conspirators*.) Isherwood was, for the most part, bored by the jejune proceedings of the Essay Club, though momentarily amused when a student's remark that it would have been better to hold the meeting the following week caused Auden to leap to his feet and shout 'I take that as a personal insult to my guest!' Both the remark and the protest it gave rise to were duly entered in the club's minutes.

Though Auden first met Louis MacNeice at Oxford, it was not until the thirties that they saw much of each other. MacNeice, in his memoirs, described Auden in his rooms in Peck, 'dressed like an untidy bank clerk and reading in a self-imposed blackout all sorts of technical unaesthetic matter or flapping his hands while he denounced the wearing of bright colours or the cultivation of flowers'.[1]

The most extensive and most memorable accounts of Auden at Oxford are those provided by Stephen Spender in *World Within World* and elsewhere. Spender had been at Oxford for several months before he met Auden, for, although his brother and some of his friends knew the poet, they did not think Spender worthy of the honour of being presented to him. Eventually, Spender and Auden met at a luncheon party given by one Archie Campbell. During the greater part of the meal Auden ignored Spender, after an initial 'clinically appraising' glance, but, over coffee, suddenly asked him 'Who do you think are the best poets writing today?' Spender, with the nervousness of one fully two years Auden's junior and thus even more awed by him than his exact contemporaries were, managed to produce the name of a poet, whereupon Auden exclaimed 'If there's anyone who needs kicking in the pants, it's that little ass.' However, as Auden was leaving, he invited Spender to visit him in his rooms, much to Spender's surprise.

Spender duly called on Auden, and, like so many before him, made the acquaintance of the darkened study with its atmosphere of the psychiatrist's consulting-room; the outer door closed (in Oxford parlance, 'the oak

[1] Louis MacNeice: *The Strings Are False* (London, 1965).

sported') as a sign to casual visitors that the doctor had a patient with him and was not to be disturbed; the terse and clinical manner of young Dr Auden himself as he conducted the examination. On this first visit, Spender was asked a number of questions about his life, his opinions and his ambitions. He admitted to liking the poetry of Edmund Blunden, which was allowed, but the second name he produced was dismissed by Auden as 'Up the wrong pole'. The third had written 'ravishing lines, but has the mind of a ninny'. He was told whom to admire: T. S. Eliot, of course, and Wilfred Owen, Gerard Manley Hopkins, Edward Thomas and A. E. Housman.

He told me that the subject of a poem was only the peg on which to hang the poetry. A poet was a kind of chemist who mixed his poems out of words, whilst remaining detached from his own feelings. Feelings and emotional experiences were only the occasion which precipitated into his mind the idea of a poem. When this had been suggested he arranged words into patterns with a mind whose aim was not to express a feeling, but to concentrate on the best arrangement that could be derived from the occasion.

Auden derided most contemporary poets and admired few beyond those I have mentioned. He thought that the literary scene in general offered an empty stage. 'Evidently they are waiting for Someone,' he said with the air of anticipating that he would soon take the centre of it. However, he did not think of himself as the only writer of the future. He had the strongest sense of looking for colleagues and disciples, not just in poetry but in all the arts. He looked at a still life on the wall and said: 'He will be The Painter.' This was by Robert Medley. His friend Isherwood was to be The Novelist. Chalmers [Edward Upward] was another member of the Gang. Cecil Day Lewis was a colleague. A group of emergent artists existed in his mind, like a cabinet in the mind of a party leader.

At our first meeting he asked me how often I wrote poetry. Without reflecting, I replied that I wrote about four poems a day. He was astonished and exclaimed: 'What energy!' I asked him how often he wrote a poem. He replied: 'I write about one in three weeks.' After this I started writing only one poem in three weeks.

I took to showing Auden my poems. I would arrive with my pockets stuffed with manuscripts and watch him reading them. Occasionally he would grunt. Beyond this his comment was restrained to selecting one line for praise. I showed him a long poem, after reading which he said:
    '"In a new land shooting is necessary,"
is a beautiful line,' and immediately the line entered as it were his own poetic landscape of deserted mines, spies, shootings – terse syllables

enclosed within a music like the wind in a deserted shaft.

After I had known him six weeks he must have approved of as many of my lines. Therefore it was rather surprising to discover that he considered me a member of 'the Gang'. Once I told him I wondered whether I ought to write prose, and he answered: 'You must write nothing but poetry, we do not want to lose you for poetry.' This remark produced in me a choking moment of hope mingled with despair, in which I cried: 'But do you really think I am any good?' 'Of course,' he replied frigidly. 'But why?' 'Because you are so infinitely capable of being humiliated. Art is born of humiliation,' he added in his icy voice – and left me wondering when *he* could feel humiliated.[1]

As Spender was leaving Auden's rooms on that first occasion, he noticed the copy of Gertrude Stein's *The Making of Americans* which Auden had so enthusiastically recommended to Christopher Isherwood only some months earlier. 'Is this any good?' he asked. 'Tripe,' Auden answered, 'I'll sell it to you for fifteen shillings,' and apparently expected Spender, on that recommendation, to buy it.[2] There is, in youth, a quick turnover of tastes and opinions.

There is also, in youth, impatience, self-absorption and a perhaps not consciously formulated feeling that human relationships are a luxury of middle-age. Auden possessed these attributes to a greater degree than most, which must have made him, a cold fish, appear a positively refrigerated one to someone of Stephen Spender's warmth and sensibility. Warmth and sensibility are desirable, indeed enviable qualities, but they can degenerate into the direst sentimentality if they are not leavened with both intelligence and humour. Spender, then as now, had a good measure of both, as well as a rare honesty with himself and others, which has occasionally got him into trouble with others. He observed his new friend at Oxford with clarity and affection, and wrote of him twenty years later with that just balance of gentleness and malice which can only be achieved by a true friend:

> For his Oxford contemporaries the most impressive thing about Auden undoubtedly was that, at such an early age, he was so confident and conscious a master of his situation. Not only did he hold very definite views about literature, but he also had a philosophy of life which, if juvenile, at least explained to him his own actions and those of his friends. He saw himself – as I then envisaged him – with certain poten-

[1] Stephen Spender: *World Within World* (London, 1951).

[2] This brief piece of dialogue is not to be found in the published *World Within World* but in an earlier draft of an excerpt which appeared in *Partisan Review* (November 1948), in which Auden's remark about art and humiliation is given as: 'All literature springs from humiliation.'

tialities and talents, certain desires, certain attitudes of mind, living within a community governed by certain rules and traditions, and consisting also of people with different potentialities, desires and attitudes. His aims were to fulfil his potentialities, obtain satisfaction for his desires, and maintain his attitudes, without prejudice and without accepting any authority outside his own judgment. At the same time he avoided coming into unnecessary conflict with the interests and views of those around him. As a youth he was outrageous, but he was not a rebel. His clinical view of living, whereby he regarded life as an operation performed by a surgically minded individual upon the carefully analysed and examined body and soul of the society round him, was amoral. He rejected, quietly and without fuss, the moral views of both his preceptors and his fellow undergraduates. The only generally accepted virtue which he himself accepted was courage: because courage was required by anyone wishing to achieve his own independent development. The extreme edge of his youthful philosophy was that he accepted suicide as the 'right of choice' of an individual who, having failed in what he set out to do, wished to end his game with life.

. . . At this time Auden had fantastic fads. He was extremely particular about food, grumbled outrageously if everything was not arranged as he wished, sometimes carried a cane and even wore a monocle. Generally he organized the people around him where he stayed to suit his whims, but he kept his hosts in a good humour. He was not witty. His humour was of a buffoonish kind and consisted partly of self-mockery. 'I have a face of putty,' he said, 'I should have been a clown.' Or, 'I have a body designed for vice.' He smoked, ate, and drank cups of tea all in great quantities.[1]

One day, in commenting on a prose narrative Spender had shown him, Auden said that it was really pure poetry. The following day the two of them went on a picnic together, and Auden said he had now changed his mind: Stephen should not write poetry but autobiographical prose narrative. Lying on top of a hill in open country with a wide view of the undulating landscape, they opened their luncheon baskets and began to discuss poetry. Or rather, as usual, Auden defined poetry and the poet: 'In a revolution, the poet lies on his belly on the top of a roof and shoots across the lines at his best friend who is on a rooftop of the other side. Of course, at heart, secretly, the poet's sympathies are always with the enemy, because he so hates the idea of there being sides and propaganda that he inevitably must hate most the side of which he hears and sees most, namely his own . . . When he is in love, the poet always prays that his loved one will die. He thinks more of the poem that he will write than of the beloved . . . The tragic, at its best, is

[1] *World Within World.*

always funny. "Enter Lear with Cordelia dead in his arms. Lear: Howl, howl, howl, howl!" Or that scene in *War and Peace* where Pierre rushes into the burning building to save a baby and the baby turns and bites him.' Later, he told Spender that he must drop the 'Mad Shelley stunt. The Poet is far more like Mr Everyman than like Shelley and Keats. He cuts his hair short, wears spats, a bowler hat, and a pin-stripe suit, and goes to the job in the bank by the suburban train.' Needless to say, this picture of the young T. S. Eliot was not one which Auden himself ever attempted to emulate.

Auden, who by this time had enticed the virgin Stephen into his bed, came to London in the summer vacation to stay with Stephen at the Spenders' house in Hampstead, and the two young men got to know each other even better away from the atmosphere of the university, though it was only later that their friendship deepened, partly because at this time Spender tended both to keep his friend on a pedestal as a poet and critic to be admired without reservation, and also to regard him as an amusing performer to be applauded when on form and forgiven when not. One day in his famous Oxford rooms Auden allowed Spender to meet Isherwood. He had shown Spender's prose narrative to Isherwood with the comment, 'He's mad: I think it's very good indeed.' Isherwood was impressed and asked to meet its author. On the occasion of their meeting, Spender arrived early at Auden's rooms ('blushing, sniggering loudly, contriving to trip over the edge of the carpet – an immensely tall, shambling boy of nineteen, with a great scarlet poppy-face, wild frizzy hair, and eyes the violent colour of bluebells', according to Isherwood.)[1] He had interrupted a session in which his mentor's poems were being examined critically by his mentor's mentor. 'I really don't see the image of a "frozen gull flipped down the weir": it sounds like cold storage,' Isherwood told Auden, who, blushing, struck out the lines with a thick pencil. (He later reinstated them, however.) When his session with Auden was over, Isherwood turned to Spender and made him a 'quite formal little speech' saying he thought Spender's manuscript one of the most striking things he had read by a young writer for a long time. Shortly after this Spender met Isherwood in London and they soon became close friends.

It was in his last term at Oxford that Auden met Basil Wright through whom he was later, briefly, to find employment with the GPO Film Unit. Basil Wright had been to school with Cecil Day Lewis, and had then gone on to Cambridge University. When Wright paid a visit to his old friend at Wadham College, Oxford, Day Lewis, whose second book of verse, *Country Comets*, was about to be published, arranged a luncheon party to celebrate its publication and also to enable his friends to meet each other. Basil Wright remembers the impact of Auden's personality that day as 'colossal': he was

[1] In *Lions and Shadows*, in which Spender appears as Stephen Savage.

hypnotized as much by the style as by the content of Auden's conversation, and accepted him at his own valuation as the coming poet of the age.

Despite the awe with which he was regarded by his Oxford contemporaries, despite, or more probably because of, the hours he spent in his darkened room solving the problems of his friends and fellow students, and ministering to their spiritual ills, Wystan Auden went down from Oxford in July 1928 with a rather poor third-class degree. This seemed not to bother him in the slightest, for a great poet needed no degree, he needed only great poems. Auden went down from Oxford with, perhaps not great poems, but a manuscript of poems sufficient in number for a first book, and a second manuscript, a short play in prose and verse, 'Paid on Both Sides', which was nearly finished, and which he completed before the end of the year. He called 'Paid on Both Sides' a charade, for his view was that the country house charade was one of the most significant dramatic forms of the day, the others being the music hall and the Christmas pantomime. Having been invited to a friend's country house in August, he hoped to have the play performed there, but, as he wrote to Isherwood, 'They refuse to do the play, as they say the village won't stand for it.' 'They' were surely right, for 'Paid on Both Sides' is an essentially private work much more likely to have been appreciated and partly understood by Auden's fellow students at Oxford than by the guests at a house-party in the country, however intellectual. Its world, as Christopher Isherwood was to observe some years later,[1] is a blend of the Old Norse sagas with the Officers' Training Corps of a public school:

> I once remarked to Auden that the atmosphere of *Gisli the Outlaw* [one of the northern sagas] very much reminded me of our schooldays. He was pleased with the idea: and, soon after this, he produced his first play: *Paid on Both Sides*, in which the two worlds are so inextricably confused that it is impossible to say whether the characters are really epic heroes or only members of a school O.T.C.

It is possible to view 'Paid on Both Sides', as it is possible to view most works of art, successful or unsuccessful, as an image of the essential human condition. But the terse, elliptical telegraphese of the play's prose dialogue and the curiously hieratic quality of its verse, equally taut and cerebral, full of private references decipherable only by a handful of the young author's friends, militate against its complete success in performance. Nevertheless, despite being only partially susceptible to intellectual understanding, it is undoubtedly entertaining to read.

Auden's university days were now over, and his entrance onto the stage of the outside world was about to be made. Many years later, he committed

[1] In 'Some Notes on Auden's Early Poetry' (*New Verse*, November 1939).

to print some of his impressions of his time at Oxford, embedded in a review of memoirs by Evelyn Waugh and Leonard Woolf, allowing his middle-aged self to comment on the young Auden:

. . . the Oxford of the twenties was frivolous indeed . . . Looking back now, I find it incredible how secure life seemed. Too young for the war to have made any impression upon us, we imagined that the world was essentially the same as it had been in 1913, and we were far too insular and preoccupied with ourselves to know or care what was going on across the Channel. Revolution in Russia, inflation in Germany and Austria, Fascism in Italy, whatever fears or hopes they may have aroused in our elders, went unnoticed by us. Before 1930, I never opened a newspaper.

. . . The lunch parties were still going on. The George Restaurant was still crowded. Panache and elegance were still much admired. Making friends was still of much greater importance than the academic studies we were ostensibly there to pursue. 'It was a male community,' says Mr Waugh. 'Undergraduettes lived in purdah.' This was still the rule, but I knew of exceptions to it. There were three or four girls in my day who had somehow managed to get out and, like token Jews in a Wasp community, were accepted by us. Not every lunch party was stag, but at a mixed one the female faces were always the same.

. . . If at Oxford and for many years afterward I drank little, this was a matter of chance (none of my friends drank heavily) and of money (I could not afford to drink much or often) . . . I preferred then, as I do now, to see my friends one at a time; I never entered the doors of the Union; the only club I belonged to was a Christ Church Essay Club; and though I was just as academically idle as Mr Waugh, I spent a good deal of time by myself reading . . . I had no intention of studying English literature academically, but I wanted to read it, and the English School would give me official licence to do so. At that time, Christ Church was far too snooty to have an English tutor, so I was farmed out to Mr Nevill Coghill, at Exeter, who became a lifelong friend. He was not a guru of the Moore kind; I never took a deep breath before knocking on his door. On the contrary, he put me so at my ease that I felt I could say anything to him, however silly, whether about literature or my personal life, without fear of being laughed at or rebuked.

. . . Beneath the fun I was always conscious of a dull, persistent, gnawing anxiety. To begin with, I felt guilty at being so idle . . . I knew very well what sort of degree I was going to get and what a bitter disappointment this was going to be to my parents. More important than guilt, however, was ambition . . . I had been quite certain since the age of fifteen of what I wanted to do. At nineteen, I was self-critical enough to know that the poems I was writing were still merely derivative, that I had not yet found my own voice, and I felt certain that in Oxford I should never find it, that as long as I remained there, I should remain a child.

. . . no college scholarship was sufficient to live on without a parental contribution . . . I received £250 [per annum] and almost managed [to keep out of debt], but only by staying at home during the vacations; I went down owing some fifty pounds to Blackwell's for books.

. . . I know too little about fiction to be able to give any accurate picture of undergraduate taste and fashions in that medium during my time. Henry James, if I recall rightly, had gone into the shadows, awaiting his triumphant re-entry in the nineteen-forties. Meredith the novelist was no longer read; on the other hand, Meredith the poet, author of *Modern Love*, who seems to have gone unnoticed twenty-five years before, was greatly admired. As for the poets of the past, the most striking change in our ranking of them had resulted from the rediscovery of the metaphysical poets of the seventeenth century. The modern stars were, of course, Eliot, the early-later Yeats, Wilfred Owen, and I would add the names of two who, though they had lived in the nineteenth century, had only recently been published – Emily Dickinson and Gerard Manley Hopkins. I don't think any of my friends shared my enthusiasm for Thomas Hardy, Robert Frost, and Edward Thomas, whom I had discovered at school.

The world as we now know it, created by the automobile, the airplane, the phonograph, radio, television, and social conscience, was only just beginning to take shape – a world without earth privies, oil lamps, gas jets, horses, domestic pianos, maids, governesses, and silence, and it would seem, soon to be without open space.[1]

---

[1] From 'As It Seemed To Us': a review of *A Little Learning*, by Evelyn Waugh, and *Beginning Again*, by Leonard Woolf. Contributed to *The New Yorker*, 3 April 1965, and reprinted in *Forewords and Afterwords* (Selected by Edward Mendelson. London, 1973).

Chapter Three

1928–1932

Seekers after happiness, all who follow
The convolutions of your simple wish,
It is later than you think; nearer that day
Far other than that distant afternoon
Amid rustle of frocks and stamping feet
They gave the prizes to the ruined boys.
You cannot be away, then, no
Not though you pack to leave within an hour,
Escaping humming down arterial roads:
The date was yours; the prey to fugues,
Irregular breathing and alternate ascendancies
After some haunted migratory years
To disintegrate on an instant in the explosion of mania
Or lapse for ever into a classic fatigue.[1]

'But why do you take everything I say so seriously?', Auden once said to Stephen Spender when they were both at Oxford. And it is true that not only Spender but most of Auden's friends and acolytes took his pronouncements much more seriously than he himself did. Auden realized that he frequently play-acted even when consciously he was quite serious, well before his audience became aware of the fact; and this was bound up with his understanding that the arts are, to a very large extent, sheer play. To accept this is in no sense to denigrate or undervalue the arts, for play is an essential aspect of life. Today, however, when the arts are seriously undervalued by being considered as vehicles for the transmission of ideas sociological, philosophical, political and educational, it may be difficult for the indoctrinated young to comprehend this. But it is an important tenet of Auden's faith, and is present in all his poetry from his student days, through his time of interest in politics to his later, quasi-Christian period after World War II, even though later on he had, intermittently, a positively Goethe-like appreciation of his own importance, and would have been quite likely to say to Stephen, 'Why do you not take everything I say seriously?'

In his sixties, Auden could at least still laugh at his twenty-year-old self. 'When I was twenty,' he remembered, 'I wrote a line which, had I intended it to be a caption for a Thurber cartoon, I should today be very proud of; alas,

[1] From 'Consider'.

I did not, so that I now blush when I recall it: "And Isobel who with her leaping breasts pursued me through a summer."' Unless a derisory remark from the stern Isherwood had led to its being expunged, this line might well have been part of the book of poems which Auden submitted to the publishers Faber & Faber in June 1927. T. S. Eliot, who then read poetry for the firm of which he later became a director, took a good three months to reply, and then returned the poems to Auden with a letter of qualified rejection: 'I am very slow to make up my mind. I do not feel that any of the enclosed is quite right, but I should be interested to follow your work.' Auden tried not to feel too dejected over this: 'On the whole, coming from Eliot's reserve I think it is really quite complimentary,' he wrote to Isherwood. The typescript of poems was shown to the new firm of Victor Gollancz Ltd and no doubt to other publishers, but no one was enthusiastic enough to want to publish Auden. No one, that is, except Stephen Spender, who possessed, at his family home in Frognal, Hampstead, a small Adana printing set of the kind used by chemists for printing labels, which he had bought for £7. On it, during the long summer vacation of 1928, after Auden had gone down from Oxford, Spender printed a little volume of his friend's poems (six of them being poems also embedded in the charade 'Paid on Both Sides') in an edition of about thirty or forty copies. At least, he began to print the volume himself, but the printing set, and Spender's patience, broke down, and he took the remaining poems to the Holywell Press in Oxford who finished the volume and had it bound. So W. H. Auden's first published volume was produced as a labour of love by a friend, and the copies were given away by the poet to other friends and relations.

One of the most accomplished, certainly one of the most 'Audenesque' of the poems, is one written in January 1928 which survived to be given the title of 'The Secret Agent' in the 1945 *Collected Poetry of W. H. Auden*:

Control of the passes was, he saw, the key
To this new district, but who would get it?
He, the trained spy, had walked into the trap
For a bogus guide, seduced by the old tricks.

At Greenhearth was a fine site for a dam
And easy power, had they pushed the rail
Some stations nearer. They ignored his wires:
The bridges were unbuilt and trouble coming.

The street music seemed gracious now to one
For weeks up in the desert. Woken by water
Running away in the dark, he often had

Reproached the night for a companion
Dreamed of already. They would shoot, of course,
Parting easily two that were never joined.

That same summer, Auden became very ill. Putting into practice his theories about the psychosomatic nature of most illness, he refused to consult a doctor, and instead went off on a long bicycle ride. The result was that he nearly killed himself, and had to take to his bed for several weeks. He recuperated at the resort of Spa in Belgium during August. On his recovery, he decided to take advantage of his father's offer of a year abroad after he had finished at university, and chose to spend that year in Berlin. He was led to this choice by his lack of interest in the Mediterranean countries and by a mild dislike of French culture, inculcated in him by the previous generation's excessive adulation of it. Perhaps, also, he was aware that in Berlin there were about a hundred and fifty cafés recognized by the authorities as meeting places for homosexuals. He knew no German and was ignorant of German literature, so thought he could make good use of a year spent in Germany. Also, as he was to remember only later, he had associated Germany with the idea of forbidden pleasures ever since his prep school days during the war, when his request for another slice of bread led to his being accused of wanting the Huns to win. Paris and Rome were places too familiar, territory too well covered by other writers: Berlin was a more adventurous choice, as well as a slightly eccentric one. English men of letters did not flock there, as they did to France, Italy or Greece. Very well, Auden would go. It was a decision he was never to regret.

On his arrival, in October 1928, Auden lodged with a family in a middle-class suburb of Berlin. However, this proved not entirely satisfactory, for one of the objects of his stay in Berlin was to learn German, while the family he was with spoke a little English and wanted to improve it. Realizing he would do better in an environment where English was not understood, he moved, in December, to Furbingerstrasse in the working-class district of Hallesches Tor, and there he remained until the following June, when he went to the Harz Mountains for a month before returning to England.

Berlin, in the last days of the Weimar Republic before the advent of the Nazis, was an exhilarating place. It was a time when social and artistic life had a great variety of excitements to offer; when there was, for instance, as much experimental music to be heard in the concert halls and opera houses as there was experimental sex to be had in the streets leading off the Kurfürstendamm. Something in the much lauded Berlin air seemed to be conducive to both a mental alertness and a moral laxity. Music, theatre, cinema and the visual arts all flourished. The collaboration of Bertolt Brecht and Kurt Weill had produced *Die Dreigroschenoper* (The Threepenny Opera) which opened at the Theater am Schiffbauerdamm, with Weill's wife Lotte Lenya as Jenny, some weeks before Auden's arrival in Berlin and which he saw soon afterwards. The political cabaret was still very active and influential, though, as later events were to prove, not quite influential enough. Auden revelled in his newly found freedom – from immediate responsibility, from study, from his friends and his family. If he did not immediately fling himself into the middle of Berlin's sea of delight, this was because he remained, by nature, an observer rather than a participant. But he observed closely from the shore, and he paddled with increasing confidence as the weeks passed.

Quite soon after his arrival in Berlin, Auden got into conversation in a café with an Englishman called John Layard, a thirty-seven-year-old anthropologist, who had once been a patient and pupil of the American psychologist, Homer Lane. Layard, who impressed Auden for quite some time before being dismissed, albeit affectionately, as 'loony Layard',[1] belived that disease of the body was disguised disease of the soul and that all illness, therefore, was spiritual in origin. Layard's mentor, Homer Lane (1876–1925), had been a labourer who became in turn a teacher, a superintendent of reform schools and, in London, an unconventional consulting psychologist. There is nothing about psychosomatic disease in Lane's only published work, *Talks to Parents and Teachers*, which was assembled posthumously from his manuscripts and lecture notes, though, according to Layard, it had been one of the basic tenets of his teaching. Layard found in Auden a ready listener to such talk, for Auden's reading of Freud and Georg Groddeck had already led him some distance along these paths with, as already noted, almost fatal results in the case of his own illness. Lane-Layard mixed a little of Freud with a lot of spiritual hot air: the problem, when dealing with a patient, was to discover which of the conflicting elements within him was God, and which the Devil; God appears unreasonable because we have stifled and imprisoned him within us, while the Devil, in conscious control, is reasonable and sane; one of the greatest evils of civilization is the idea of pity which is never a healer but always a destroyer; diseases are warnings from God, and to attempt to cure disease is to serve the Devil. All of this seemed heady stuff to Auden, presumably because to him as a poet ideas did not have to be prosaically testable, they had merely to stimulate poetry. He soon became an enthusiastic convert to Lane's ideas as propounded by Layard. When he returned to England briefly in December to spend Christmas with his family, he took the opportunity to spread the gospel to Christopher Isherwood. Isherwood, who had been simultaneously trying to finish writing a novel and to sit his final chemistry exams, complained of not feeling well, but was instantly reproved

[1] In the first of Six Odes in *The Orators* (1932).

by Auden: 'You've got to drop all that. When people are ill, they're wicked. You must stop it. You must be pure in heart.'

'What nonsense,' Isherwood replied. 'How can I stop it? There's nothing the matter with my heart. It's my tonsils.'

'Your tonsils? That's very interesting. I suppose you know what that means?'

'Certainly. It means I've caught a chill.'

'It means you've been telling lies!'

Refusal to make use of one's creative powers could lead to cancer. Stubbornness found physical expression as stiffness of the joints, the deaf and the blind were attempting to shut out the physical world, and Stephen Spender was so tall because he aspired to heaven. When Isherwood asked how these misfortunes were to be avoided, Auden assured him it was quite simple: one had merely to be pure in heart. Before long, Isherwood too was waving this phrase about as a panacea. John Layard was revered as the one man who was pure in heart, who was therefore without guilt or fear, and consequently unable to contract disease, and who was profoundly, fundamentally happy. When Auden told Isherwood that in Berlin were to be found not only this paragon of virtue but also a large number of bars where one could pick up boys easily and cheaply, without the guilt or fear attendant upon such activities in England, Isherwood decided to pay Auden a visit in Berlin the following spring.

After Christmas, Auden returned to Berlin. His German was already serviceable, though by no means impeccable, and he managed to write in that language a sequence of sonnets which, despite its grammatical howlers, a 'German critic of great sensibility' to whom Isherwood showed the poems recognized as the work of a poet of the first rank. Auden had completed and partly rewritten his charade, 'Paid on Both Sides', incorporating into it the ideas of Homer Lane and John Layard, and he also found their influence infiltrating into the poems he wrote during the remainder of his stay in Germany. Homer Lane's concept of love as a creative force also began to find its way into his writing and thinking:

> The loving act is hopeful behaviour, the hateful act is fearful behaviour. And he who serves his fellow men by effort of will is making love a virtue; it is unnatural to mankind. According to his conception of authority man will either progress towards perfection, obeying the master-wish, or regress to the primitive. The only true authority is love, and the only true discipline is founded upon hope. The authority that is based upon force will transform love into hatred and hope into fear.
>
> If a man's love be not extended to all mankind and all communities, he cannot be completely happy; for love is dynamic and universal. Any

distrust or fear of another community than his own, will infect his own community with hatred, and destroy its harmony. For hatred makes a community sick, as it makes each human sick. Every man must choose for himself. No man can be compelled to love, for love is itself the highest form of compulsion.[1]

In March, Isherwood arrived in Berlin for a visit of ten days, and Auden took him to his favourite pick-up bar, 'The Cosy Corner', in Zossenerstrasse. Auden had not formed any but the most casual relationships with the boys he had met in this and other bars, but Isherwood, more romantic in temperament, met and fell in love almost immediately with a handsome, blond, Czechoslovakian youth, Berthold Szczesny, known to his friends as 'Bubi'. Like many of the boys who frequented such bars, Bubi was there for the money. Some of the boys were basically heterosexual, others liked to pretend that they were and that they went to bed with men merely to subsidize their heterosexual activities. Bubi was probably one of the former, for Auden discovered that much of the money he got from Isherwood was in turn spent by Bubi on female prostitutes. Bubi had no English, and Isherwood at this time no German, and certainly no Czech, so the two of them communicated mainly in bed. They spent several hours together every day throughout Isherwood's stay, but the relationship was not a serenely happy one, for Isherwood was absurdly jealous of the naturally promiscuous Bubi, much to Auden's ironic amusement.

Isherwood was, of course, introduced by Auden to John Layard, but was too preoccupied with Bubi and 'The Cosy Corner' to pay much attention to Auden's guru. In any case, the profoundly happy Layard was not at his most impressive, as he was in a state of deep depression for which there appear to have been two equally unlikely causes: his unreciprocated passion for Auden, and his conviction that Homer Lane, who had died while Layard had been undergoing psychoanalysis with him, had done so purely to spite him and had also caused another of his patients, a beautiful Italian called Elta, to turn against Layard. To Auden and Isherwood, and to Margaret Gardiner, a friend of Layard's, who was visiting him from England, Layard announced that he intended to shoot himself. Margaret Gardiner was much distressed, and consulted Auden who merely said, 'If he wants to kill himself, you should let him. You've no right to interfere.' A few days later, while Margaret Gardiner was searching for the beautiful Elta in Paris, to try to persuade her to write to Layard, she received a telegram from Auden: 'John shot himself but is alive. Writing.'

Layard had shot himself in the mouth, but had made a mess of the operation. Finding himself still alive, he had put on a hat to conceal the

---

[1] Homer Lane: *Talks to Parents and Teachers* (1930).

wound, pocketed the gun, and staggered to the lift, and thither, with the aid of the doorman of his apartment house, to a taxi which he took to Auden's address, collapsing outside the door. When Auden came out to see what the noise was all about, Layard held out the pistol and begged him to shoot. 'I would if I dared,' said Auden, 'but I don't want to be hanged.' Instead, he sent for an ambulance and had Layard conveyed to hospital where a bullet was extracted from the top of his head. Miraculously, Layard made a complete recovery and lived on for another forty years, but it is perhaps not unreasonable to assume that his influence on Auden began, from this time, to wane.

Auden had acquired a regular boy-friend, Otto Küsel, a cheerful, good-natured youth whom he took with him to the Harz Mountains in June, where they stayed in a romantic village called Rotehütte, surrounded by forests. Isherwood travelled out to join them, and Bubi was supposed also to make his way there from Berlin. When Isherwood arrived, he found that Auden had completely transformed his room at the village inn into the kind of room he always inhabited, with books and manuscripts strewn about in apparent confusion. He was already a popular character in the village, and his impromptu recitals on the piano in the refreshment-room of the railway station had become a feature of local life. The villagers even accepted with equanimity his wrestling naked with Otto in a meadow.

Isherwood became anxious when Bubi failed to arrive from Berlin. It was eventually discovered that, wanted by the police, he had fled to Amsterdam and was about to depart for South America. The police arrived at Rotehütte in search of Bubi, and, in questioning Auden, Isherwood and Otto, they discovered that Otto's papers were not in order. It turned out that he had escaped from a reformatory. Not surprisingly, the police, when they left, took Otto with them, much to Auden's annoyance. Isherwood now wanted to get to Amsterdam as quickly as possible to see Bubi before he sailed: Auden, his idyllic mountain holiday ruined, agreed to accompany him. The innkeeper at Rotehütte was tolerant of their sexual preferences, despite having had the police on his premises. 'I expect,' he said to Auden, 'a lot of things happen in Berlin that we wouldn't understand.'

In Amsterdam, Bubi was found, tearful farewells were said, a farewell gift of money offered and accepted, and Bubi sailed off to South America as a deck-hand. Relieved to be alone together after their recent excitements, Auden and Isherwood spent the next day together in Amsterdam, talking and laughing happily as they cruised through the canals and the harbour in a tourist launch. Bubi and Otto were forgotten. Disembarking after their tour of the harbour, the passengers were asked to sign a guest-book. After his name, Auden wrote two lines from the Russian poet Ilya Ehrenburg's poem about the Revolution:

Read about us and marvel!
You did not live in our time – be sorry!

Isherwood returned to England, while Auden made his way back to Berlin. In addition to having a regular boy-friend in Germany, Auden also appears to have had an affair at about this time with a young woman in Berlin who may have been a nurse. He was informally engaged to her, and apparently was quite seriously contemplating marriage, until talked out of such heterosexual foolishness by the chauvinistically homosexual Isherwood.

In 1929 Auden was visited in Berlin by his brother John, now a geologist and mountaineer and on leave from an assignment in India. John spoke of K2, the second highest mountain in the world, which inspired the eventual title of a play, *The Ascent of F.6*, which Auden and Isherwood were to write several years later. Meanwhile, Auden had begun to write a play which was to go through a couple of drastic revisions before achieving its final form. Its working title was *The Reformatory*. When he returned to England in July, Auden finished it in collaboration with Isherwood, its title then being *The Enemies of a Bishop* or *Die When I Say When: A Morality in Four Acts*, and they dedicated it to their two Berlin boy-friends, Otto Küsel and Berthold Szczesny. Edward Mendelson says of it:[1]

> The title is unfortunately the play's high point. Its various sketchy plots – a governor of a reformatory becomes infatuated with a boy in drag who escapes from his reformatory and later becomes the target of a white-slave ring; the governor's brother (the central character, accompanied by a Spectre who keeps reciting Auden's poems at inconvenient moments), who is manager of a lead mine, seduces his under-manager's wife and is then ruined by the mine's failure – are resolved by the appearance of Bishop Law, who, the authors seemed to think, was modelled on Homer Lane.

Isherwood said of this hotch-potch, which he and Auden made no attempt to publish or to stage: 'The play was no more than a charade, very loosely put together and full of private jokes. We revised the best parts of it and used them again, five years later, in *The Dog Beneath the Skin*.[2] It was inspired by a play they had seen in Berlin, *Revolt in a Reformatory* by Peter Martin Lampel, a rather poor documentary piece which had amused them.

[1] Preface to *The English Auden*.
[2] In an article in *New Verse* (November 1937). But Isherwood's memory was at fault. It was *The Chase*, a play he and Auden worked on in 1934, which in due course became *The Dog Beneath the Skin*. A lost play, *The Fronny*, which Auden wrote in 1929–1930, its title deriving from the nickname of a Berlin friend, Francis Turville-Petre, is probably the play Auden and Isherwood plundered for *The Chase/The Dog Beneath the Skin*.

In July 1929, after nine months of living in Berlin, Auden returned to England. He had written to several friends asking if they could find him a teaching job, and for a time he acted as Latin coach to one of the sons of the writer, Naomi Mitchison. Through John Layard's friend Margaret Gardiner he was engaged to tutor a friend's son (Peter Benenson, who in adult life was to found Amnesty International). Before starting his job, Auden went to stay with Margaret Gardiner in Gaminglay, a village near Cambridge, where she taught at the local school. Miss Gardiner lent him her car during the day while she was at work, and he took himself for drives around the countryside. One afternoon, on his return, Auden announced to her, 'I've brought you a present,' and produced a soft, warm, dead chicken from behind the driving seat. 'I ran over it by mistake and I didn't want to waste it.'

'What did the farmer say?'

Auden grinned. 'I didn't wait to ask him.'

After visits to his parents, and to Yorkshire to stay with Robert Medley, Auden moved into the Benensons' house in London and took up his post as tutor to their son. He became friendly with the family and their circle, especially Mrs Benenson's sister, Manya Harari, who was young, rich, intelligent and beautiful, and a close friend of Margaret Gardiner. It was at Manya Harari's house, one evening, that Auden, to their mutual amusement, tried on all her clothes. He would not have made a very fetching woman, and there is no other known instance of his getting into drag.

Margaret Gardiner, years later, remembered Auden at this time coming to stay for a few days at her mews flat in Knightsbridge:

Mrs Wilson, my charming and gentle daily woman, was uncharacteristically indignant. Not for any personal or moral objection that she had to his staying with me but because of his extreme untidiness and the way he scattered ash over everything. She herself was so very neat and clean. But Wystan, always polite and friendly towards domestic helpers and aware of them as people, never, I think, discovered her hostility or could have guessed its cause.

In those days he loved gossip, he loved talking about his own and his friends' affairs. Never maliciously but with a kind of benevolent curiosity. He wanted to arrange things for his friends, to see to it that they met suitable people and parted from unsuitable ones. He was indignant on their behalf if he thought that their partners were ill-treating them and pleased if he heard that all was running smoothly. There was a conspiratorial element in his friendships, a zestful love of intrigue. I remember him telling me that he felt the time had come for one of his young boy friends to be initiated into the knowledge of woman. 'To help

LEFT Auden's mother, Constance Rosalie Bicknell. The daughter of a clergyman, she was accused by her family of marrying beneath herself.
RIGHT Dr George Augustus Auden, a practising GP in York at the time of his son Wystan's birth in 1907.
BELOW Bootham, York: number 54, where Auden was born, is the fifth house from the left of the photograph.

LEFT Wystan at the age of about fifteen months, with his cousins and his elder brother John, staying at Perkins Farm, Monmouth, in 1908.
RIGHT Feeding the chickens at Perkins Farm.
BELOW Wystan and John with their parents in 1909.

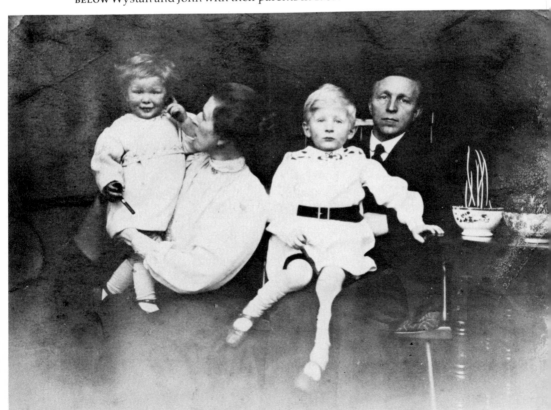

Wystan with his mother, 1911.

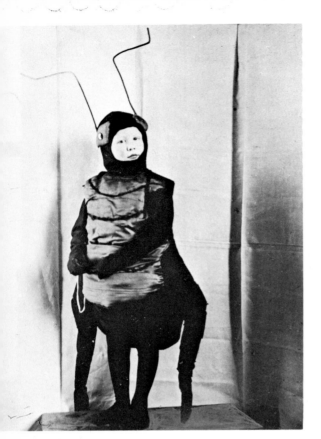

ABOVE St Edmund's School, Hindhead, Surrey: school photograph for 1915. Auden is sitting in the front row, at the feet of Mrs Ivo Bulley ('Miss Rosa'). Immediately behind her is Christopher Bradshaw-Isherwood. Auden's piano teacher, Bertha Lowe, is in the centre of the picture, and, on her left, is the headmaster, Cyril Morgan-Brown.

OPPOSITE BELOW The new boys for Michaelmas Term 1915 at St Edmund's: Auden is second from left in the top row.

BELOW The Library at St Edmund's where Auden worked when in Form IV (the 'Common Entrance' form) in 1919.

RIGHT Two pages from the holiday diary kept by the Audens in the Isle of Wight in 1917.
BELOW Apart from contributions to Gresham's school magazine, this is Auden's earliest published poem. It appeared in Heinemann's *Public School Verse*, Volume IV, 1923–1924.
OPPOSITE BELOW Speech day at Gresham's – to the right is Farfield, Auden's house from 1920 to 1925.

4 YARMOUTH (Isle of Wight). — High Street. — LL

Yarmouth, I. W., from the Bridg

WOODS IN RAIN

By W. H. Arden, Gresham's School, Holt

It is a lovely sight and good
To see rain falling in a wood.
The birds are silent, drunk with sound
Of raindrops kissing the green ground,
They sit with head tucked under wing
Too full of joy to dare to sing.
Flowers open mouths as wide I say
As baby blackbirds do in May;
While trees shake hands as grave and slow
As two old men I used to know,
And hold out smiling boughs to find
Whence comes this sweetest breath of wind.
But now the sun has come again
And he has chased away the rain.
The rain has gone beyond the hill,
But leaves are talking of it still.

a few hours and managed to get into Southampton under an escort. She was put into drydock and it was found that she was torn from the bows to beyond the middle of the ship, but the sand ballast acted as a sort of cement and so the ship kept afloat. The chief officer shot himself. We arrived at Freshwater to find oanly an old growler which was engaged, but the man who engaged it said we could come too.

31st   M, W & J went out shopping at Totland and then walked over by the fields to Freshwater Church (All Saints) to find out the services. Came back home in time for dinner. After dinner we walked onto Headon Hill and after we had seen the Tumulus we walked down into what looked like an old disused fort but when we got in there an Orderly turned us out saying that it was an Isolation Camp.* There were two large muzzle-loaded guns there. Then we walked down into Alum Bay but it was High Tide so we could not go and see the different coloured rocks. Then we came home. We had by that time almost discovered the shortcuts etc. It was a lovely evening and the sunset was beautiful. We saw some darks and Robins and several other birds. The rooms are very nice. For the sitting-room see drawing on the first page, Mothers room is a nice large one other the sitting room. J & W's room is a nice one also with 2 beds in it. B's room is a small one about the size of

*   M. heard it was cerebro-spinal meningitis. so felt anxious!

OPPOSITE Tom Gate, Christ Church – Auden's college.
ABOVE Oxford gasworks and the river at St Ebbe's. Walks such as this were thought by Auden to be the most beautiful in Oxford.
BELOW Cornmarket Street, Oxford, looking northwards, during Auden's undergraduate days.

OPPOSITE Auden in the broad-brimmed black felt hat that so irritated Christopher Isherwood.
BELOW Louis MacNeice while at Oxford.

LEFT John Layard. Both Auden and Isherwood became disciples of his for a short time in Berlin.
RIGHT Auden at twenty: a photograph by Stephen Spender.
BELOW The George, Oxford's most expensive restaurant during the 1920s.

him grow up', he said. He arranged for the girl and the room and was delighted at the sequel, as though he had accomplished some virtuous task.[1]

Gossip and interference in the lives of his friends were activities Auden continued to indulge in, whenever he could, throughout his life. It was eight years later that he broadcast for the BBC a talk entitled 'In defence of gossip':

Let's be honest. When you open your newspaper, as soon as you have made sure that England hasn't declared war, or been bombed, what do you look at? Why, the gossip columns. 'These Names Make News', 'Londoner's Diary', 'Behind the Headlines', 'Personality Parade' or whatever it is. And as for books, if you had to choose between the serious study and the amusing gossip, say, between Clarendon's *History of the Rebellion* and John Aubrey's *Scandal and Credulities*, wouldn't you choose the latter? Of course you would! Who would rather learn the facts of Augustus's imperial policy than discover that he had spots on his stomach? No one.

. . . Gossip has fallen under a cloud because of the people who abuse it . . . The person who ruins gossip is the person who repeats it back to its victim. That's every bit as bad as writing anonymous letters . . . There are some kinds of people in whose presence you should shut up like an oyster: people with strong moral views, members of Watch-Committees or Purity Leagues, natural policemen, schoolmasters.

. . . How often I have worked off ill-feeling against friends by telling some rather malicious stories about them, and as a result met them again with the feeling quite gone. And I expect you've done the same. When one reads in the papers of some unfortunate man who has gone for his wife with a razor, one can be pretty certain that he wasn't a great gossip.

. . . Gossip is creative. All art is based on gossip – that is to say, on observing and telling. The artist proper is someone with a special skill in handling his medium, a skill which few possess. But all of us to a greater or less[er] degree can talk, we can all observe, and we all have friends to talk to. Gossip is the art-form of the man and woman in the street, and the proper subject for gossip, as for all art, is the behaviour of mankind.[2]

In the autumn of 1929, Auden stayed for a time with Stephen Spender in Hampstead. He had submitted his charade, 'Paid on Both Sides' to T. S. Eliot at Faber & Faber, and one day was asked to call on Eliot to discuss its publication. On his return he told Spender that he had been made to sit for

[1] Margaret Gardiner: 'Auden: a memoir' (*New Review*, July 1976).
[2] Published in *The Listener* on 22 December 1937, having been broadcast in the BBC National Programme on 13 December.

an hour in a waiting-room before being admitted to the presence of the great poet-turned-publisher. The wait had been worthwhile, however, for Eliot had accepted the play and published it in the January 1930 issue of *The Criterion*, the quarterly literary review which he edited from 1922 until 1939. 'Paid on Both Sides' appeared with a dedication to Cecil Day Lewis. In a letter recommending E. McKnight Kauffer to read the play, Eliot referred to it as 'quite a brilliant piece of work' and said that its author was 'about the best poet that I have discovered in several years'.

Although he did not keep a diary or journal consistently throughout his life, Auden did make occasional journal entries in notebooks, as well as notes for poems. The contents of a Journal kept intermittently in 1929 consist almost entirely of *pensées* philosophical, psychological, and literary, ranging from the imponderability of 'Man is a product of the refined disintegration of nature by time' to the apparently simple hedonism of 'The only good reason for doing anything is for fun'. There is, however, a note obviously written while he was at work on *The Reformatory* or *The Enemies of a Bishop*:

> Do I want poetry in a play, or is Cocteau right: 'There is a poetry of the theatre, but not in it'? I shall use poetry in *The Reformatory* as interlude. Poetry after all should be recited, not read. I don't want any characters, any ideas in my play, but stage-life, something which is no imitation but a new thing.[1]

There had, of course, been poetry in 'Paid on Both Sides'; for Auden had interpolated previously composed poems into its prose dialogue at salient points. The publication of this almost impenetrably private charade in the January 1930 issue of T. S. Eliot's magazine brought Auden's name to a wider circle of readers than had previously been aware of it, and the apposite neatness of the fact that the poet who in due course was to be thought of as the literary voice of the thirties should have emerged onto the literary scene right on cue in January 1930, has been commented on in many a study of the period, which is now often referred to as that of 'the Auden generation'. Most of the early readers of 'Paid on Both Sides' found it obscure, but many of them recognized and responded to the tone of its voice, urgent, anxious yet unmistakably commanding. They sensed that, behind its flimsy plot of a strange feud between two families in the north of England, and between the lines of its dialogue, which veered from that of the blood feuds of the old sagas to the upper-class small-talk of the English public schoolboy, this odd charade exhibited a modernity which was not that of the inanely chic twenties at whose tail end it was written, but which

---

[1] *The English Auden.*

was authentically and essentially the voice of a present which already had its eyes fixed with a certain pessimism on the horizon of the future. The landscape in which the play's events are enacted is that already typically Auden country of flinty hills and limestone moors, the Pennine country of his childhood, familiar yet remote, like the known and experienced world translated into the focus of a dream, a dream forever trembling on the brink of nightmare.

'Paid on Both Sides' is susceptible of more than one interpretation. It can be seen, for instance, as a parable of growing up, as a study in types of strength and weakness, or as a demonstration of the important past weighing heavily and to devastating effect on the trivial present. Its obscurity may be a stumbling block to some, but its poetic ambiguity is really one of its strengths.

Neither obscurity nor ambiguity presented any problems to the distinguished poet and critic William Empson[1] who, writing in the spring 1931 issue of a Cambridge magazine, *Experiment*, provided his readers with a brilliant and authoritative explication of the play's action:

There is a blood-feud, apparently in the North of England, between two mill-owning families who are tribal leaders of their workmen; it is at the present day, but there are no class distinctions and no police. John, the hero of the play, is born prematurely from shock, after the death by ambush of his father; so as to be peculiarly a child of the feud. As a young man, he carries it on, though he encourages a brother who loses faith in it to emigrate. Then he falls in love with a daughter (apparently the heiress) of the enemy house; to marry her would involve ending the feud, spoiling the plans of his friends, breaking away from the world his mother takes for granted, and hurting her by refusing to revenge his father. Just before he decides about it, a spy, son of the enemy house (but apparently only her half-brother) is captured; it is the crisis of the play; he orders him to be taken out and shot. He then marries Anne; she tries to make him emigrate, but he insists on accepting his responsibility and trying to stop the feud; and is shot on the wedding day, at another mother's instigation, by a brother of the spy.

This much, though very confused and sometimes in obscure verse, is a straightforward play. But at the crisis, when John has just ordered the spy to be shot, a sort of surrealist technique is used to convey his motives. They could only, I think, have been conveyed in this way, and only when you have accepted them can the play be recognized as a sensible and properly motivated tragedy.

---

[1] Auden's senior by only a few months, he published an important volume of criticism, *Seven Types of Ambiguity*, in 1930.

Towards the end of February 1930, Auden entered hospital, and on 2 March underwent an operation for a rectal fissure: he was intermittently to suffer from the after-effects of this for several years. Isherwood, briefly visiting England from Berlin, went up to Birmingham twice to be with him during his convalescence. Auden had submitted a revised collection of poems to T. S. Eliot at Faber & Faber, who this time accepted it for publication. This first volume of Auden's verse to be commercially published was called simply *Poems*, and came out in September. By this time, Auden had found himself a job as a schoolmaster in Scotland. His allowance from his parents having come to an end, he had accepted a position as English teacher at the Larchfield Academy, a boys' preparatory school in Helensburgh, a resort town in Dunbartonshire at the entrance to Gare Loch on the Firth of Clyde. Auden succeeded his friend Cecil Day Lewis who had been teaching English there since the autumn of 1928. He took up his duties in April 1930, and was to remain at the Larchfield Academy for two years. At this period of his life, he expected that, probably for some years, he would have to support himself by teaching: but he also had a real feeling for the teaching profession. It was his opinion that, in the absence of a theory or orthodoxy of teaching, education had perforce to rely almost entirely upon the quality of the teacher. Having suffered to some extent from poor quality teachers in his own early school-days, he now had firm views as to what should be expected of someone entrusted with the education of the young:

> For a teacher to be of real value to his pupils, he must be a mature and above all a happy person, giving the young the feeling that adult life is infinitely more exciting than their own; he must be prepared to give them all his powers of affection and imaginative understanding when they want them, yet to forget them completely the moment they are gone, to be indifferent to them personally; and lastly he must have no moral bees-in-his-bonnet, no preconceptions of what the good child should be; he must be shocked or alarmed at nothing, only patient to understand the significance of any piece of behaviour from the child's point of view, not his own; to see in the perfect little ape his most promising charge, and watchful to remove as tactfully and unobtrusively as possible such obstacles to progress as he can.[1]

Auden enjoyed teaching at the Larchfield Academy. He told Margaret Gardiner, who came to Helensburgh to visit him, that it was as dotty as the school in Evelyn Waugh's *Decline and Fall* and that the headmaster was a caricature of a man, throwing his authority around while his dying wife lay listlessly all day on a chaise-longue in the summer-house on the lawn, in full view of the boys. Auden found that he had continually to startle his pupils

[1] *The Old School.*

into interest: he appears to have been a good and popular teacher from the beginning. Towards the end of Margaret Gardiner's stay, he told his class that he wanted whichever boy he pointed at to make up a rhymed couplet immediately on any subject of his own choice. He pointed at one small boy who, looking straight at Auden, declaimed: 'A charming man is Mr X/But far too fond of the opposite sex.' The entire class roared with laughter, and their teacher, too, was delighted: 'I told you that you were good for my reputation,' he said later to Margaret Gardiner. In a letter to Naomi Mitchison, Auden revealed that he really wanted to get a teaching job at Ottershaw College, 'the place started by the man who was sacked from Bryanston. Acording to Edward Upward, who is there, it's the bugger's dream; a cross between *Mädchen in Uniform* and *The Castle*.'

In pursuance of his infatuation with the language and the youth of Germany, Auden took a holiday in Berlin in late June, at the end of his first term. He stayed with Isherwood to whom he brought a present, a proof copy of his *Poems* which bore a dedication 'to Christopher Isherwood' and, as epigraph, the lines, 'Let us honour if we can/The vertical man/Though we value none/But the horizontal one.' This presentation copy also bore a personal dedication to Isherwood, full of private jokes in fractured German.

Isherwood had found himself a new lover (the model for Otto Nowak in *Goodbye to Berlin*), a young, good-looking bisexual German youth. To celebrate his friend's new relationship, Auden wrote him a poem which begins

> Dear Christopher, you old old bugger
> Here in this land of fear and rugger
> Where love is mostly hugger mugger
>   Your letters quoted
> By jealous ladies make us eager
>   To be devoted.

Auden was back in England by 18 September, the date on which *Poems* was published by Faber & Faber.[1] The volume contained about thirty short poems written between June 1927 and March 1930, and also the charade, 'Paid on Both Sides', which Eliot, having already published it in *The Criterion*, at first did not want to include, but which was added at proof stage. Published in blue paper covers at two shillings and sixpence, in an edition of one thousand copies, *Poems* was well received by the literary critics, and also sold quite satisfactorily, for a second edition of a thousand copies was published in November 1933, with seven new poems substituted for seven of the original ones. This second edition continued to be reprinted, and

---

[1] This is the publication date according to Faber & Faber. But Edward Mendelson, co-author of the Auden Bibliography, now thinks that 9 October, the date given to the US Copyright Office, is more likely to be correct.

during the following thirty years about eleven thousand copies of it were sold. At the rate of fewer than four hundred copies a year, this may not sound particularly impressive, but the sales of volumes of poetry have never been huge, and for a first book to stay in print and achieve a sale of eleven thousand was, and still is, highly unusual. Of course, it was joined by several other volumes by Auden throughout the thirties, forties and fifties, until it was eventually superseded by popular paperback editions of Auden's *Selected Poems* and *Collected Poems*.

Though only twenty-three, Auden had already found his individual voice as a poet. The opening lines of 'Consider', one of the finest poems in the volume, could have come from none of his contemporaries; though one can imagine it translated into the cinematic images of early Hitchcock:

> Consider this and in our time
> As the hawk sees it or the helmeted airman:
> The clouds rift suddenly – look there
> At cigarette-end smouldering on a border
> At the first garden party of the year.
> Pass on, admire the view of the massif
> Through plate-glass windows of the Sport Hotel;
> Join there the insufficient units
> Dangerous, easy, in furs, in uniform,
> And constellated at reserved tables,
> Supplied with feelings by an efficient band,
> Relayed elsewhere to farmers and their dogs
> Sitting in kitchens in the stormy fens.

Reviewing *Poems* in *The Listener*[1] along with volumes by Spender and Day Lewis, Bonamy Dobrée referred to 'the school of which W. H. Auden is leader, round whom are grouped in particular Stephen Spender and C. Day Lewis', and continued: 'They are, on the whole, communists, but communists with an intense love for England . . . They don't dwell in ivory towers; they are not in the least highbrow.' He found Auden sometimes a difficult poet, but felt that some poetry ought to be difficult, in order 'to challenge and to stretch our faculties', and concluded that Auden was sometimes 'as easy as you could wish'. The anonymous reviewer in the *New Statesman*[2] found the charade 'notable for the nervous tension it arouses', and thought that many of the poems in the book could 'be likened to wax dolls made by a childless man who loves children and knows all about how they should be brought up'. The *Poetry Review*[3] thought Auden syntactically reminiscent of

[1] 14 June 1933.
[2] 8 November 1930.
[3] November–December 1930.

Laura Riding and spoke of the 'Pennine bleakness' of his style. 'But there is anger too, and impatience with those who are "lecturing on navigation while the ship is going down", and sometimes he pauses . . . to indicate that which he finds valuable in life.' It was not only the critic of the *Poetry Review* who detected the influence of Laura Riding. Miss Riding's friend and publisher, the poet Robert Graves, wrote to Auden (who had subscribed to Laura Riding's *Love as Love, Death as Death*) to complain that the half-guinea he had paid for her poems did not give him 'the right to borrow half-lines and whole lines from them for insertion in his own verse'. Auden did not, in fact, borrow any phrases from Laura Riding, though her spirit is clearly present in several of his lines.

The sternly puritanical Cambridge lecturer and critic, F. R. Leavis, reviewed the second edition of *Poems* in his magazine *Scrutiny*.[1] He thought that 'Paid on Both Sides' represented Auden's talent at its most impressive, and asserted that, as a poet, Auden was 'too immediately aware of the equivocal complexity of his material, and too urgently solicited by it to manipulate it with cool insistence into firm definition and deliberately coherent elaboration'. He concluded that Auden had, nevertheless, 'achieved enough in the matter of technique to impress upon the reader a highly individual sensibility'.

Nine of the thirty poems in the 1930 volume are taken from the 1928 *Poems* privately printed by Stephen Spender; the remainder are post-Oxford. The earlier, younger poems tend to deal with love and landscape; in the other poems an awareness of politics begins to infiltrate into the landscape. Auden's politics were later to enter his poetry in a more direct, indeed a cruder manner. But in these poems of a young man, it is the manner which is revolutionary rather than the content: the manner of speaking, that is, not the poetic technique, for Auden, despite his technical brilliance, or perhaps because of it, never had cause to indulge in 'avant garde' posturings. The range of subject and feeling which he was able to display in this first volume is impressive, from the lyricism of

> I, decent with the seasons, move
> Different or with a different love,
> Nor question overmuch the nod,
> The stone smile of this country god
> That never was more reticent,
> Always afraid to say more than it meant.

to the urgent, dramatic message of

[1] June 1934.

Seekers after happiness, all who follow
The convolutions of your simple wish,
It is later than you think; nearer that day
Far other than that distant afternoon
Amid rustle of frocks and stamping feet
They gave the prizes to the ruined boys.
You cannot be away, then, no
Not though you pack to leave within an hour,
Escaping humming down arterial roads:

but the gift for memorable speech, for the phrase that stays in the mind, pervades the entire volume. 'It is later than you think' stands as an epigraph for the decade to follow, and the escape 'down arterial roads' is one which will be attempted again and again in Auden's verse throughout the thirties. A new generation had found its spokesman, and Auden's contemporaries, those who read modern poetry and fiction, not simply those who wrote it, recognized and responded to his voice and his message.

The voice was uniquely his, but the message was one which he had not formulated alone, and Auden himself acknowledged his debt to his circle of fellow writers: to Isherwood, of course, but not only to Isherwood. Sending a copy of *Poems* to Edward Upward, he wrote, 'I shall never know how much in these poems is filched from you via Christopher.' He had kept up his friendship with Upward, who was now teaching in Scarborough and who travelled up to Helensburgh to stay with him at the end of February 1931, during the half-term holiday. Upward remembers that when, on his first day there, Auden invited him to lunch at the school's expense, the headmaster's welcome seemed far from warm. Auden nevertheless invited Upward again the following day, and this time 'the head-master's expression of face was so undisguisedly angry that I was made to feel like a sponger and I would have walked out of the dining-room at once but for the fact that this might have seemed unfriendly to Auden'.[1]

Helensburgh is beautifully situated at the mouth of the Clyde, across from the industrial town of Greenock which Auden called 'the wicked city', and he and Upward explored as much of the surrounding country as they could during his friend's brief visit. One morning they were in a train travelling along the north shore of the Clyde when they noticed another train moving in the same direction along the south shore. The lumpy bursts of smoke trailing from its engine suggested to Auden an image which later turned up in one of his poems: 'the train's white excreta'. (Upward thought that it was on this journey that he discovered in the William Hickey column of the Daily Express the phrase 'awareness of Auden' used casually, as

[1] 'Remembering the earlier Auden' (*Adam*, 1973–74).

though the young poet were already a household name. But it must have been later, for Hickey was not invented until 1933. Whenever it was, Auden was pleased. 'Do you think it means that Auden has awareness, or that people are becoming aware of Auden?' he asked. 'It means both,' Upward suggested. Neither of them, probably, was aware that the columnist 'William Hickey' was Auden's Oxford friend and fellow student, Tom Driberg.)

It was while he was teaching at Helensburgh, early in 1931, that Auden began work on what was to be his next book *The Orators*, not a collection of separate poems but a curious kind of notebook in prose and poetry with a unified theme or series of themes. As published the following year, *The Orators* consisted of three parts or 'books', with a Prologue and Epilogue. Prose predominates in Book I, 'The Initiates' and Book II, 'Journal of an Airman', while Book III, 'Six Odes', is entirely poetry. With the exception of one of the odes, written the previous October, the whole of *The Orators* was completed during 1931.

In the notebooks he kept for jotting down ideas and phrases, and working on poems, Auden at this time and for many years later had the habit of writing little squibs or 'shorts', as he later called them, usually either two or four lines of epigrammatic wit, which give the lie to the frequently heard critical assertion that it was only in post-war, middle-aged decline that he resorted to such 'trivia':

> Schoolboy, making lonely maps:
> Better do it with some chaps.

> The pleasures of the English nation:
> Copotomy and sodulation.

> I'm afraid there's many a spectacled sod
> Prefers the British Museum to God.

> Love your cock
> Stand a shock.
> Hate your cock
> Soon a crock.

> Love is not a thing to understand:
> In love the cunt is better than the hand.[1]

In March there was, somewhat surprisingly, a staged production – as far

---

[1] The notebook containing these squibs was acquired in 1964 by the Arts Council of Great Britain, and is now housed by the British Library's Department of Manuscripts.

as is known, the first – of the charade, 'Paid on Both Sides', at Briarcliff College, New York. (The next known production was in England, at the Festival Theatre, Cambridge, for a week in February 1934.) Auden presumably knew of this American performance, though he had no connection with it. In the early summer he went to Scarborough to stay with Edward Upward. On the occasion of his arrival, Auden's sense of farce asserted itself, but mistimed dismally. Expecting Upward to meet him at the railway station, he had put on a red false beard before getting out of the train. However, due to a misunderstanding about the time of arrival, Upward was not there, and Auden had to walk along the platform and through the barrier in his ridiculous beard, too embarrassed to remove it in public. Finally he darted into one of the station lavatories, emerging clean-shaven again to hail a taxi.

Later in that same summer of 1931, Auden joined Isherwood, his friend Otto and Stephen Spender, at Sellin, a holiday resort on Ruegen Island off the German Baltic coast. While the others browned themselves in the sun, the determinedly pale-skinned Auden shut himself up in his bedroom, his blinds drawn against the daylight, and continued working on *The Orators*. But the holiday was, in general, not a wild success, mainly because Isherwood and his boy-friend quarrelled a great deal of the time over Otto's too lively interest in the girls at the local casino. Auden cut his visit short and returned to England, taking a brief holiday in the Orkneys, a trip that provided some of the scenery for *The Orators*. Back in Scotland at Larchfield in the autumn, he became friendly with Mrs Anne Fremantle, a twenty-one-year-old girl just down from Oxford, who was doing some literary research in the house of relatives. Later to make her career as an historical novelist and writer on religion, Anne Fremantle enjoyed talking about religion to Auden who, though formally not affiliated to any church, had never lost his interest in theological discussion. He liked teaching, he told her, and he liked teaching small boys best because they could be taught to concentrate, for 'one of the few things the human animal can learn to do is to learn to concentrate'. But he apparently found it a relief from teaching small boys to be able to discuss the Patripassian heresy (the belief that God the Father shared in the human sufferings of Christ), however unlikely it may seem that so arid a topic could engage the interest of anyone not professionally involved in religion. In Helensburgh, Auden also met another literary lady, a Scottish poet and ballad-writer called Marian Angus who was spending the winter there. She invited Auden to visit her, and read his poetry, but she wrote later to a friend that, though he had read 'yards and yards' of it to her, she was unable to understand a single line and thought it sounded like 'a voice from another planet'. At about this time, Auden explained in a letter to Naomi Mitchison that his only prejudice against women was a physical one: 'I am not disgusted but sincerely puzzled at what the attraction is. (Like watching a game of cricket for the first time.)'

Work on *The Orators* progressed, and Auden wove into it complex strands of thought and imagery from various sources. 'I've had a most important vision about groups which is going to destroy the church', he had written to Isherwood in October, without providing any details, and indeed the politics in *The Orators* is that of the visionary rather than the agitator. The politics of the 'Auden gang' were, in any case, far from clear in the immediately pre-Nazi years of the early thirties. It is, for instance, more than a little disconcerting to find Isherwood writing enthusiastically of the new German Youth Movement in the December 1931 number of Sir Oswald Mosley's Fascist magazine, *Action*: 'They are sombre, a trifle ascetic and absolutely sincere. They will live to become brave and worthy citizens of their country.' In fact, many of them lived to become Nazi thugs, which, in the context of the time, was the same thing. And Auden, looking back in middle-age on his twenty-four-year-old self (in his Foreword to a 1966 edition of *The Orators*), could see that he was, at that time, coming close to embracing a form of Fascism as the only way forward. It has to be faced that Auden's early voice is not a politically liberal one. Its vocabulary is that of the Leader; the 'truly strong man', to use the phrase which first occurs in a poem Auden wrote in April 1929 ('It was Easter as I walked in the public gardens': number XVI in *Poems*). However, Auden's aims in *The Orators* are as obscure as is occasionally his diction.

In August 1931, he wrote to a friend that, in Book II of *The Orators*, 'Journal of an Airman', he was attempting a kind of memorial to T. E. Lawrence ('Lawrence of Arabia'), and that its theme was 'the failure of the romantic conception of personality'. But, early in 1932, shortly before the book went to press, he wrote a Preface (discarded on the advice of T. S. Eliot) in which he apologized for the obscurity of the book, and stated that it was meant to be about a revolutionary hero. 'The first book describes the effect of him and of his failure on those whom he meets: the second book is his own account; and the last some personal reflections on the question of leadership in our time.'

Auden's engagement at the Larchfield Academy came to an end with the summer term of 1932, some weeks after the publication on 19 May of *The Orators*. Despite the now almost celebrated Auden obscurity, it was immediately acclaimed by its mainly young readers, who seemed able to penetrate to its meaning without difficulty, and who responded to its tone and manner with enthusiasm. *Poetry*, (Chicago)[1] said that in range and felicity of utterance Auden yielded to none among the poets of the day, and that he was 'the one man best equipped to write an epic of the "holy war" of

[1] May 1933.

the spirit against the combined stupidity and self-satisfied vulgarity of this age'. In the opinion of the *Poetry Review*[1] which, in the thirties, was a magazine of some stature, Auden was 'one of the four or five living poets worth quarrelling about' and *The Orators* a remarkable book 'which the poets of twenty years hence will know and discuss, no matter what revolutionary changes take place in society', though the reviewer thought that Auden had yet fully to master his medium. The general tone of the reviews of *The Orators* was one of praise, albeit occasionally qualified. A rare dissenting voice among Auden's contemporaries was that of John Sparrow (who, more than twenty years later, as Warden of All Souls College, was unsuccessfully to oppose Auden's election as Oxford's Professor of Poetry). Sparrow said in 1934 that *The Orators* was 'a work in which no single intelligible purpose is to be discerned, a jumble of images and jottings'.[2] One is tempted to comment that only the discerning can discern. Among the discerning not-so-young when *The Orators* appeared was John Hayward who wrote, in Eliot's *Criterion*:[3] 'I have no doubt that it is the most valuable contribution to English poetry since *The Waste Land*.'

The Orators, subtitled 'An English Study', was dedicated to Stephen Spender, with an epigraph which became one of the most quoted sentences in Auden's *oeuvre*: 'Private faces in public places / Are wiser and nicer / Than public faces in private places.' Eighteen years later, in the Preface to his *Collected Shorter Poems*, Auden was to refer to *The Orators* as a 'fair notion fatally injured'. Presumably he considered, in retrospect, that its fatal injury had been inflicted by the obscurity of its many private references, which could have been understood by no more than a small group of close friends. Curiously, however, the book appeared not to suffer unduly from this admitted defect at the time of its publication. Many readers who were not in the Auden circle found it moving and significant, among them a number who were to distinguish themselves in literature and the arts in later years. *The Orators*, almost despite itself, succeeded in communicating. T. S. Eliot, before publication, had told Auden not to worry about being thought obscure. Eliot was more concerned by what he considered to be certain improprieties of language: for instance, in Book II, 'Journal of an Airman', he insisted on one of the 'three kinds of enemy face' being changed from 'the fucked hen' to, curiously, 'the June bride', who, according to an American joke that Eliot liked, was 'sore but satisfied'.

A reading of *The Orators* today, after Hitler, Stalin, the cold war, and with Fascism creeping across the globe from left to right, clearly reveals Auden's airman to be a Fascist, and as clearly reveals the author's fascination with

---

[1] No XXIII, 1932.
[2] Quoted by Kenneth Allsop in *The Daily Mail* (15 June 1960).
[3] October 1932.

and admiration for his creation. Yet the ambiguous poet stepped back from that particular brink, and was perhaps helped to do so by the audacity and belligerence of his own book, by the manner in which its poetry triumphed over obscurity, irony and double irony, carefully insouciant incoherence and slightly diffident anarchism. The importance of *The Orators* remains. It was the poetic embodiment of ideas current at the time of its creation: perhaps a less original book than its author may at the time have privately thought it to be, certainly a work which spoke directly and reassuringly to its audience. It confirmed what they felt, and in terms congenial to them. Nevertheless, an ambiguity remains: to some it was a deeply disturbing book, even to some of the inner circle. In Stephen Spender's view, '*The Orators* is one of Auden's most vital, but also his most cynical, gangish and brutal work.'[1]

[1] In 'The Life of Literature', *Partisan Review* (November 1948).

Chapter Four

1932–1936

Young men late in the night
Toss on their beds,
Their pillows do not comfort
Their uneasy heads,
The lot that decides their fate
Is cast tomorrow,
One must depart and face
Danger and sorrow. [1]

Having by now quite clearly emerged onto the English literary scene, Auden found himself invited by several of the editors of leading magazines to contribute articles and to review books. Usually for either *Scrutiny* or *The Criterion*, occasionally also for the *New Statesman*, he began to review poetry and also books on education. He still expected that his professional career would continue to be in education, and indeed took on occasional teaching assignments until well after World War II. Throughout his life, he maintained his interest in education, although, after his reputation as a poet became an international one, his occasional articles tended more and more to be on literary subjects, especially those he contributed to American periodicals such as *The Nation* and *The New Republic*. He was prepared to communicate on any level, and the article on 'Writing' which he contributed in 1932 to a book called *An Outline for Boys and Girls and Their Parents* is no less impressive for being couched in simple language which the boys and girls could understand as easily as the parents. (The book, edited by Naomi Mitchison, also includes contributions by experts on physics, mathematics, astronomy, physiology, psychology, biology, chemistry, economics, music, painting and other subjects.) After dealing with speech, meaning and communication, Auden describes various kinds of writing, discusses why and how people both write and read, and ends by relating books to life:

> But whenever society breaks up into classes, sects, townspeople and peasants, rich and poor, literature suffers. There is writing for the gentle and writing for the simple, for the highbrow and the lowbrow; the latter gets cruder and coarser, the former more and more refined. And so, today, writing gets shut up in a circle of clever people writing about

[1] From 'The Witnesses'.

themselves for themselves, or ekes out an underworld existence, cheap and nasty. Talent does not die out, but it can't make itself understood. Since the underlying reason for writing is to bridge the gulf between one person and another, as the sense of loneliness increases, more and more books are written by more and more people, most of them with little or no talent. Forests are cut down, rivers of ink absorbed, but the lust to write is still unsatisfied. What is going to happen? If it were only a question of writing it wouldn't matter; but it is an index of our health. It's not only books, but our lives, that are going to pot.[1]

'A circle of clever people writing about themselves for themselves': no doubt that is how the 'Auden group' was described by some, by the ultra-conservative, by the aggressively philistine, or by those politically opposed to the direction these new voices appeared to be taking. But there is a sense in which one cannot begin to write for or to communicate with other people, unless one writes initially for oneself. One surely needs a special kind of arrogance to assume that one can make others interested in what does not interest oneself, or that one must deliberately talk down to one's audience. Or one needs to be an entertainer rather than an artist. The artist must, of course, be entertainer as well, if he is to interest anyone other than himself. If one were not entertained by *The Brothers Karamazov*, one would never finish reading it. If one were not entertained by *King Lear*, one would walk out of the theatre. Contained within Auden the poet was Auden the entertainer, the maker of aesthetically pleasing objects, constructed from words.

Auden took seriously his functions as poet, communicator, and teacher. When the English master at a public school in Buckinghamshire sent him a poem by a sixteen-year-old pupil, John Cornford, Auden wrote directly to the poet:

Dear Mr Cornford

A poem of yours has come to me with the suggestion that I shall say something about it. This, as you can imagine, is not easy, as I know nothing about you but your name and age. I think the only useful criticism is the personal kind – if I could say 'Get into the first XV' or 'Shoot your French master with a water-pistol', I might really be of use – but as I can't you must forgive me if anything I say sounds too like a governess.

First of all, I think your power of writing, of using words is very good indeed. Considered as a craftsman, you have nothing to fear. My only suggestion here (which I daresay is unnecessary, as I haven't seen anything else of your writing) is that you might do more with stricter verse forms. I think it is easier to find what it is that *you* want to say . . . as the

[1] *An Outline for Boys and Girls and Their Parents* (ed. by Naomi Mitchison; London, 1932).

very nature of the form forces the mind to think rather than to recollect. (Incidentally, while on this question of originality, of course being influenced by others doesn't matter. One damn well ought to be. And you must cheat and quote verbatim.)

The real problem though for you as for every other writer, but particularly for people like yourself who come of literary stock, and are intelligent and well-read, i.e. certainly developed, is that of the Daemon and the Prig. Real poetry originates in the guts and only flowers in the head. But one is always trying to reverse the process and work one's guts from one's head. Just when the Daemon is going to speak, the Prig claps his hand over his mouth and edits it. I can't help feeling you are too afraid of making a fool of yourself. For God's sake never try to be posh. I can't say anything more about this because I don't know you or your life. If it's a choice between reading and doing something else, do something else and remember that everything your housemaster says about the team spirit and all that (perhaps he doesn't but suppose it) is absolutely right but that it is the tone of his voice which makes it such a lie. He always forgets to put on the crown of thorns. May I anyway wish you every success and happiness.[1]

During 1932, Auden became involved in two new ventures, one literary and one theatrical. The literary venture was a project which had grown from talks between John Lehmann, then working for Leonard and Virginia Woolf at the Hogarth Press, and Michael Roberts, a young enthusiast for modern poetry: *New Signatures*, an anthology, edited by Michael Roberts, of the new young writers who had recently emerged. The key figures, of course, were Auden, Spender and Day Lewis, and others included William Empson, the American Richard Eberhart, William Plomer, and John Lehmann himself. In Lehmann's words, the anthology was intended to represent 'a reaction against the poetry that had been fashionable hitherto . . . a desire to assimilate the imagery of modern life . . . a new intellectual and imaginative synthesis that would be positive, not negative and pessimistic in its attitude to the problem of living in the twentieth century.[2]

Three poems by Auden appeared in *New Signatures*, which was published in February 1932. The anthology was immediately successful, selling out quickly and being reprinted within a few weeks; it also soon became thought of as a kind of manifesto of new poetry, and the poets within its pages found themselves lumped together in the imagination of readers and critics as 'New Signatures poets', though all that united them was the fact that they were

[1] Letter of 4 May 1932. Quoted in *Journey to the Frontier* by Peter Stansky and William Abrahams (London, 1966). John Cornford, the recipient of the letter, was killed on active service in the Spanish Civil War at the age of twenty-one.

[2] John Lehmann: *The Whispering Gallery* (London, 1955).

liked by Michael Roberts. *New Signatures* was followed up a year later by *New Country*, 'Prose and Poetry by the authors of New Signatures', which contained four poems by Auden. In due course, a magazine, *New Writing*, edited by John Lehmann, came into being from the fermentation of *New Signatures* and *New Country*. Michael Roberts' aims were avowedly political – his introduction to *New Country* called for a renunciation of monopoly capitalism – but John Lehmann's *New Writing*, when it appeared three years later, had a more literary slant without, however, foregoing any political awareness.

Auden's involvement in the theatrical venture, the Group Theatre, was greater and more immediate. The Group Theatre came formally into existence on 4 February 1932, founded by thirteen people, two of whom were Auden's old school-friend the painter Robert Medley and Medley's close friend Rupert Doone. Doone, who was, in fact, the real creator of the Group, had been an artists' model, a dancer for Diaghilev, had created ballets at Sadler's Wells Theatre in London and for Max Reinhardt in Berlin, and had worked as actor and director for the Festival Theatre in Cambridge. He founded the Group Theatre as a co-operative enterprise which, he hoped, would prove to be a social force and not merely a company for producing new plays of a calibre too rarified for the commercial theatre. For this purpose, he gathered around him a group of actors, designers, writers and musicians of varying standards and achievements, among them Tyrone Guthrie, Robert Speaight, William Alwyn, John Moody and Lydia Lopokova. The Group's headquarters were at the top of a building at 9, Great Newport Street in the West End of London, next door to the Arts Theatre, which is where meetings, discussions and occasional parties were held, and productions planned, and where weekly classes in speech, singing and movement took place.

Robert Medley and Rupert Doone wrote to Auden, inviting him to stay with them at their London flat in Fitzroy Street, and it was on this visit in the early autumn of 1932 that Auden agreed to associate himself with the Group Theatre and to write for it. He also helped to draft their policy statements, which were issued in April 1933 and January 1934. Doone is said by most people who knew him to have been a vain, arrogant man with a number of silly or pretentious ideas about theatre and an extraordinary ability to bully or charm others into accepting them. In its five active years in the thirties, the Group Theatre was to produce plays by Auden and Isherwood, Stephen Spender, Louis MacNeice, and T. S. Eliot's *Murder in the Cathedral*. (It flourished again, briefly, after the war, but to much less effect.) Doone's first suggestion to Auden was that he should write a play on the theme of Orpheus and Eurydice, which would be performed in modern dress, and which would include a role for a dancer or mime artist, which Doone himself would undertake. Accepting the brief, Auden began to work on the play in the winter of 1932–33.

Meanwhile, in the late summer months of August and September 1932, Auden saw a great deal of Isherwood, who had returned to London for the summer, and was now full of talk about the Nazi menace in Germany. Auden introduced Isherwood to Gerald Heard, the author, who was at this time Science Commentator for the BBC and was interested in psychical phenomena. Isherwood's mystical strain, however, was not yet developed, and he displayed considerably more interest in Heard's young friend, Chris Wood. In the autumn, Auden went to teach at the Downs School, Colwall, near Malvern, where he remained until the end of the summer term of 1935. In a letter to Naomi Mitchison he described the school as 'a mixture of *The Plumed Serpent* and the Church Lads Brigade. Lots of gags and thigh slapping. Also we have a Bach choir.'

In his spare time during his first term, when he was not working on his commission for the Group Theatre, Auden attempted to write a long poem, 'a dream vision in which Gerald Heard as Virgil led Auden as Dante through the hell of England',[1] but abandoned it after completing about a thousand lines of alliterative verse. To the September issue of *Scrutiny*, the young schoolmaster contributed a review of three books about schools and teaching, whose language seems to combine elements of the expository style of D. H. Lawrence and the cynical tone of early Noël Coward. 'Dearie,' he concludes,

> you can't do anything for the children till you've done something for the grown-ups. You've really got nothing to teach and you know it. When you have repapered the walls perhaps you will be allowed to tell your son how to hold the brush. In the meantime some of us will go on teaching what we can for a sum which even in its modesty we do not really deserve. Teaching will continue to be, not a public duty, but a private indulgence.

During the Christmas holidays, Auden spent ten days in Berlin with Isherwood. They discussed the scenario for the play Auden was writing for the Group Theatre, which had departed from the Orpheus theme. It was now to be called *The Dance of Death*. Isherwood made a few suggestions for it, though he did not formally collaborate with Auden on the play. In April 1933, Auden addressed a larger audience than he normally commanded, through the columns of a London newspaper, *The Daily Herald*. 'A Poet Tells Us How to Be Masters of the Machine', the headline proclaimed, but the poet did not, in fact, tell anything of the kind. Instead, he warned of the dangers of various kinds of machinery and ended with the assertion that the

[1] Edward Mendelson's Preface to *The English Auden*.

only way to master the machine was first to 'establish a Socialist state in which everyone can feel secure, and, secondly, have enough self-knowledge and common sense to ensure that machines are employed by your needs, and not your needs by the machinery.' A more socially useful piece of writing was his provision of some dialogue for a village play being produced by the wife of his recently married friend, John Betjeman, at Uffington in Berkshire. He also provided a prologue and an epilogue for the Group Theatre's programme, 'Songs, Dances and a Play', at the Croydon Repertory Theatre on 24 July.

In the early summer of 1933, Auden experienced one of those rare moments of visionary or mystical insight which, fleeting though they are, can strangely persist as a lifelong influence. A feeling of intense, unearthly serenity, a moment of enlightenment which passes, but which leaves behind it the knowledge that, if only for a moment, the universe *has* made sense. These experiences do not translate easily to words, not even to the words of so skilful a manipulator of language as Auden, and verbal accounts of such occasions require to be read with a special sympathy. Auden's account of his vision was written, or at any rate first published, a good thirty years later:

One fine summer night in June 1933 I was sitting on a lawn after dinner with three colleagues, two women and one man. We liked each other well enough but we were certainly not intimate friends, nor had any one of us a sexual interest in another. Incidentally, we had not drunk any alcohol. We were talking casually about everyday matters when, quite suddenly and unexpectedly, something happened. I felt myself invaded by a power which, though I consented to it, was irresistible and certainly not mine. For the first time in my life I knew exactly – because, thanks to the power, I was doing it – what it means to love one's neighbor as oneself. I was also certain, though the conversation continued to be perfectly ordinary, that my three colleagues were having the same experience. (In the case of one of them, I was able later to confirm this.) My personal feelings towards them were unchanged – they were still colleagues, not intimate friends – but I felt their existence as themselves to be of infinite value and rejoiced in it.

I recalled with shame the many occasions on which I had been spiteful, snobbish, selfish, but the immediate joy was greater than the shame, for I knew that, so long as I was possessed by this spirit, it would be literally impossible for me deliberately to injure another human being. I also knew that the power would, of course, be withdrawn sooner or later and that, when it did, my greeds and self-regard would return. The experience lasted at its full intensity for about two hours when we said good-night to each other and went to bed. When I awoke the next morning, it was still present, though weaker, and it did not vanish completely for two days or so. The memory of the experience has not prevented me from making use of others, grossly and often, but it has made it much more difficult for me to deceive myself about what I am up to when I do. And among the various factors which several years later brought me back to the Christian faith in which I had been brought up, the memory of this experience and asking myself what it could mean was one of the most crucial, though, at the time it occurred, I thought I had done with Christianity for good.[1]

This mystical experience which Auden shared with his three fellow-teachers at Colwall bore immediate fruit in a remarkable lyric poem which he wrote in the following days, and of which these are the opening stanzas:

> Out on the lawn I lie in bed,
> Vega conspicuous overhead
>   In the windless nights of June;
> Forests of green have done complete
> The day's activity; my feet
>   Point to the rising moon.

> Lucky, this point in time and space
> Is chosen as my working place;
>   Where the sexy airs of summer,
> The bathing hours and the bare arms,
> The leisured drives through a land of farms
>   Are good to the newcomer.

> Equal with colleagues in a ring
> I sit on each calm evening,
>   Enchanted as the flowers,
> The opening light draws out of hiding
> From leaves with all its dove-like pleading
>   Its logic and its powers.[2]

A new and more complex voice, and a richer awareness of the complexities of various layers of experience seem to enter Auden's poetry from this moment, co-existing and alternating with something almost as new, a deliberate simplification of diction and form in what was clearly an attempt to politicize and popularize his poetry. The arterial road now led in two

[1] Introduction to *The Protestant Mystics* (ed. Anne Fremantle, Boston, 1964).
[2] Four stanzas of the poem were set to music very beautifully by Benjamin Britten as part of his *Spring Symphony* (1949). Auden later revised the poem, deleting four of its sixteen stanzas.

directions. In February, Hitler had come to power in Germany, so it is not surprising that the political voice in Auden's work should begin to be heard more stridently on occasions. But the increase in warmth and sensitivity in his more personal poems is surely directly attributable to that prolonged moment of insight on a summer night in June.

It was at about this time, if not earlier, that Auden's taste in sex partners began to change from working-class youths to younger boys of his own social class. In some cases these relationships developed into enduring friendships.

Christopher Isherwood and his current German boy-friend Heinz were spending the summer with Francis Turville-Petre and an assortment of Greek youths on St Nicholas, a tiny Greek island rented by Francis, close to the mainland just north of Chalkis. Life on the island is described by Isherwood in *Christopher and His Kind*. Though Isherwood does not say so, Auden is thought to have visited his friend on the island during the summer, probably in August. During that summer, Auden also finished *The Dance of Death*, his play for the Group Theatre, and sent it to Rupert Doone at the end of August. He also sent a copy to his publishers, Faber & Faber, who published it in November, well before the play received its first performance early the following year by the Group Theatre, who began rehearsing it, however, in the autumn of 1933. Before the Downs School broke up for the Christmas holidays, Auden adapted Cocteau's *Orphée* for performance at the annual Christmas Songfest.

Christopher Isherwood was back from Germany and was busy trying to get Heinz into England. On 5 January 1934, during his school's Christmas holidays, Auden went to Harwich with Isherwood, to meet Heinz's boat. The boat arrived, and Heinz was on it. Auden waited with Isherwood outside the office where arriving aliens had to show their passports, but Heinz failed to emerge. Eventually, a smiling, bright-eyed immigration officer came out and asked Isherwood to come inside. Auden followed him. All was not well, for Heinz was carrying a somewhat compromising letter from Isherwood, which he had foolishly allowed the immigration official to see. 'I'd say this was the sort of letter that, well, a man might write to his sweetheart,' remarked the immigration official, as he refused permission for Heinz to enter the United Kingdom. Heinz left again on the next boat, and, in the train going back to London, Auden said to Isherwood: 'As soon as I saw that bright-eyed little rat, I knew we were done for. He understood the whole situation at a glance, because he's *one of us*.'

The Dance of Death, a very short, one-act play, was given two Sunday evening club performances at the Westminster Theatre on 25 February and 4 March, as part of a double bill with the medieval mystery play, *The Deluge*, which Auden had adapted. Later in the year, in October, it was produced again at the Westminster Theatre during the Group Theatre's season there. It received generally poor reviews. Derek Verschoyle in the *Spectator*[1] said that 'In the place of acting it offers a great deal of acrobatic posturing, some peculiarly tedious dancing by Mr Rupert Doone, whose talents do not seem to lie in the direction of choreography, and some Swedish drill in which most of the company participates, though with few signs of enjoyment.' Of the play itself, he wrote:

> The subject is the final struggles of a doomed middle-class, which pursues 'at first one Utopia and then another without really wanting new life because secretly they desire the old', and is ultimately dispossessed by a band of armed Communists – the methods which, with Mr Auden's approval, the Communists use to gain their object being precisely those whose employment by their victims he had previously condemned. The wide inconsistency is typical of the play. Hardly anywhere throughout it is there any evidence of acute observation or of independent thought. The satire is for the most part crude and jaded, and Mr Auden's verse is much too loose and dispersed to convey its points with economy or precision. The only parts of it which can be praised are the burlesque revue-sketches, but it seems unnecessary for the Group Theatre to have been formed with so much pomp merely to produce imitations of what has been much better done by Mr Cochrane and Mr Coward.

This was a review of the public performances in October, when *The Dance of Death* shared the evening with T. S. Eliot's *Sweeney Agonistes*, which 'macabre fragment' Derek Verschoyle found much more impressive. For this autumn Group Theatre season, Auden contributed to the programme a collection of aphorisms on the drama as he saw it. 'Drama is essentially an art of the body. The basis of acting is acrobatics, dancing, and all forms of physical skill.' This sounds more like Rupert Doone, who danced and mimed the role of Death, than like Auden with his active dislike of the ballet. More understandable, coming from Auden, are his assertions that drama should deal with the general and universal rather than the particular and local, and that it is 'not suited to the analysis of character, which is the province of the novel'.

The Dance of Death opens with an announcement: 'We present to you this evening a picture of the decline of a class, of how its members dream of a new life, but secretly desire the old, for there is death inside them. We show you that death as a dancer.' 'Our death,' mutters the chorus from behind the curtain. What follows is, it must be admitted, pretty arid stuff, glib Marxist propaganda alternating with doggerel, though, enlivened as it must have been by Herbert Murrill's spikily acerbic music and the 'small jazz orchestra'

[1] 11 October 1935.

down-stage, it was presumably a less lowering experience in the theatre than it is on the printed page. It is, perhaps, unfair to complain that the choruses are doggerel, for they were intended by Auden as parodies of popular forms, but this schematic Marxist allegory of a society on the rocks until rescued at the end by a beaming Karl Marx who enters with 'two young Communists' ('O Mr Marx, you've gathered/All the material facts/You know the economic/Reasons for our acts') can never have seemed very effective.

Even the literary magazines where Auden published his plays and reviews failed to find anything pleasant to say of *The Dance of Death*. Leavis, in *Scrutiny*,[1] adopted a dismissive tone. 'Auden can seldom have written more easily,' he admitted, 'but appears to know little better than the characters of his drama what the point of it is.' In *New Verse*[2] the young poet Gavin Ewart quoted the Announcer's opening two sentences, with the comment that 'there are very few passages in the rest of the play as good as these opening lines.' 'Indeed,' he continued, 'much of the verse that follows might have been written by Mr Coward or Mr Herbert, almost by any writer of dance lyrics.' Nearly half a century later, it hardly seems shaming to have been compared with Noël Coward or A. P. Herbert, whose lyrics were, to put it mildly, a cut above those of most other writers of 'dance lyrics'. *The Dance of Death* was not revived in later seasons of The Group Theatre. It was given its first performances in the United States by the Experimental Theater at Vassar College under the title *Come Out Into the Sun*, on 2 and 3 August 1935.

Auden's admiration for Communism ('the truly strong man' was now more Communist than Fascist, which is not all that much of a change) remained undiminished for some years to come. Reviewing a book on T. E. Lawrence, he wrote that Lenin and Lawrence 'seem to me the two whose lives exemplify most completely what is best and significant in our time',[3] and the poems he continued to write in the mid-thirties frequently revert to the search for a leader, for a direction. Auden's personal life at this time was curiously without direction. He enjoyed teaching at Colwall, was thought to be a good teacher and was certainly a popular one. But he was by no means entirely satisfied to go on teaching there. Restlessly, he looked about for other avenues to explore, and even contemplated seeking employment in the Soviet Union, for on 25 January 1934, he drafted a letter (whether or not he actually sent it cannot now be ascertained) to an unnamed correspondent:

[1] In June 1934.
[2] In February 1934.
[3] In *Now and Then* (Spring 1934).

> Downs School
> Colwall
> Nr Malvern
> England.

Dear Sir,

   Miss Galton[1] has written to me asking me to send you copies of my books. I have asked Faber & Faber to send you *The Orators* and enclose copies of the other two.

   Could you tell me if there are any possibilities of a job in Russia teaching English; I know no Russian.

> Yours truly
> W. H. Auden

That Auden still cared deeply about education and about the teacher's role in society is apparent from the essay that he contributed to *The Old School*, a book edited by Graham Greene in 1934. The essay appeared in the book under the title, 'Honour': Auden's original title had been 'The Liberal Fascist', an ironic but not totally inaccurate description of himself at the time. Significantly, when the magazine *New Verse*, in the summer of 1934, ran a questionnaire to poets which included the question, 'Do you take your stand with any political or politico-economic party or creed?', neither Auden, Spender nor Day Lewis replied. Significant of what? Cunning? Indecision? Lack of interest? Had Auden given a lead, many poets would have followed him, for his influence upon his younger contemporaries as poet and thinker was now at its highest. The poetry of Spender and Day Lewis resounded with echoes of Auden, and one unfortunate poet, Charles Madge, is remembered today virtually only as the author of the lines,

> But there waited for me in the summer morning
> Auden, fiercely. I read, shuddered and knew.[2]

Even Day Lewis, in a poem in *New Country*, was guilty of invoking Auden as 'Wystan, lone flyer, birdman, my bully boy!' no doubt to the lone flyer's embarrassment.

   Auden's literary reputation had by now spread beyond the shores of Britain and the Commonwealth, and in September 1934 an American edition of *Poems* was published by Random House in New York. This contained not only the poems from the English volume of that name but also the full texts of *The Orators* and *The Dance of Death*. There were reviews in the leading New York newspapers, the *Times* and *Herald Tribune*, as well as in a number of literary magazines throughout the United States. *Partisan Review*

---

[1] Miss Galton was the headmistress of Crichel School.
[2] 'Letter to the Intelligentsia' in *New Country*.

reviewed Auden's *Poems* along with Stephen Spender's first volume to be published in America, and considered that what was most interesting about both writers was that they were 'radical poets, that they present in poetry the same attraction for the middle and petty bourgeoisie, undergoing psychic as well as economic changes through the crisis, as the political analysis and the economic treatises of the middle-class intellectuals. It is the role of the prophet crying in the wilderness, the St John of the middle-class, prophesying inevitable doom and the day of reckoning.' The critic recognized *The Orators* ('probably the most brilliant piece of satirical writing in postwar poetry') as Auden's most considerable accomplishment and at the same time his most obscure work, and thought that Auden's principal talents would be found to lie 'in the field of satire, a weapon he controls with a gusto and an imaginative irony long absent from English verse.[1] *The Yale Review* also discussed Auden and Spender's volumes together, appreciated Auden's cleverness, but thought that Spender, 'with less cleverness, less show, and less trusting to form above content', was the better poet.[2] *Poetry (Chicago)* also voiced doubts, noting 'a certain vagueness or slipperiness of tone that sometimes leaves us in doubt of the final intention'.[3]

In the summer of 1934, Auden went off on a three-week motoring tour to Hungary, taking with him a boy from the school and Peter, the school's gardener and brother of one of the pupils. 'I'm off to the Carpathians,' he told Naomi Mitchison, 'stimulated I believe by childish memories of Dracula. I hope we get interred.' Extracts from Auden's holiday journal, from which the quotations below are taken, were published in the school magazine, *The Badger*,[4] under the title of 'In Search of Dracula'. The trio left the Downs School on 14 August ('Raced a quartet of beauties in dinky scarves as far as the Watford bypass'), stayed overnight in London, arrived in Dover the following day at about 2 p.m. 'and flirted with policemen till 4 when we managed to get on to the quay. New boat, the *Prince Baudouin*, very posh. Mutual photography. Went first-class out of bravado and to look at the splendid people in their soup plates. Sea calm unfortunately as I was looking forward to seeing Peter sick over a cocktail bar.'

Failing to find a hotel in Ostend, they spent their first night abroad in Gistelle, and the next day sped through Belgium, past Ghent, Brussels and Louvain, reaching the German frontier at tea-time. 'Pestered in Aachen by a German schoolmaster, probably a spy', they drove on to Cologne.

Friday, 17th. All rather subdued this morning and no wonder in this country which is being run by a mixture of gangsters and the sort of

[1] Alfred Hayes in *Partisan Review* (November–December 1934)
[2] December 1934.
[3] October 1935.
[4] In the issures of Autumn 1934 and Spring 1935.

school prefect who is good at Corps. Voting for the Reichkanzler on Sunday. Every house waves a flag like a baby's rattle. Private yachts for the flagmakers. Each shop has pasted a notice, 'We are all going to vote yes.' Slogans hang screaming above the cobbled streets of tiny hamlets, 'One Folk: One Leader: One Yes'. Photographs of the circus manager followed by a multitude of men and women showing their uvulas are pasted on the walls of barns, together with the information, 'The voting is absolutely free. DO YOUR DUTY.' Tea near Marburg where there were hornets. In a furious temper for some reason or other (O, Mr. Censor), skidding round corners on two wheels through pretty wooded hills. Reached Eisenach, Bach's birthplace, thinking of the Rector and Superbos. Talked to hotel proprietor who suddenly stopped and rushed to open the window. The Labour Corps were passing and one must be keen. After they had gone he closed it with a sigh of relief. Sat in a café in the market square listening to Hitler shouting from Hamburg. Sounded like a Latin lesson. Peter ate an ice out of his handkerchief.

On the 18th, they reached Dresden, via Weimar and Leipzig, and the following day had a 'pleasant drive over the Erzgebirge reaching a doll's house frontier village for lunch. Thank God we're out of the sight of flags at last.' In Czechoslovakia, they stayed for two nights with the Prince and Princess Lobkovics in their Schloss ('a seventeenth-century building the size of the Malvern Girls' school'), Auden having been armed with letters of introduction to the Princess, and they arrived in Prague in time for lunch on 21 August. The boys went off to bathe in the Elbe, and Auden 'went to bed with a detective story. Dinner on a restaurant boat. Ordered Bubbly which didn't suit our clothes but made us feel very on-the-Continong.'

Wednesday 22nd. Drove steadily all day through Broad and Jhilava but then lost the road and beached in a field. O Mummy. Started to sing 'Now the Day is Over', until Peter suggested getting out of the car and we managed to get her off again, careering like Puck over hill and dale till we found a road and reached Ur Hradista in the dark. Good and cheap but camera stolen.

The next day they crossed the Carpathians, travelling through Trenčin 'and thence through Salvator Rosa gorges to Poprad near the Tatras.' They had intended to continue through eastern Czechoslovakia to Transylvania, but Peter the gardener was suffering from a pain in his leg 'so magnanimously decided to give Dracula a miss and stay here for two days. Town full of peasants with their leathery everlasting faces.'

Friday 24th. Today, according to the others, we are going to camp. I don't see why we can't make up that part. Bought a sausage as big as a Michelin tyre and a bottle of local wine tasting like sanitary fluid, and set off for the Tatras. Real tourist resort, full of Tyrolese hats and peeks. Poured with rain so returned to hotel and cooked eggs in our bedroom. Went to see Conrad Veidt in *The Wandering Jew*, a sad come-down from his *Student of Prague* days, and then got off with the hotel band who by request played Hungarian music into the small hours, which always makes me feel like the exiled lover pulling on his snow boots in the middle of Siberia. To bed a little tiddley. 'Why am I a Schoolmaster?' I asked Peter, but he was asleep so now I shall never know.

Having given up their plan to drive further east to Transylvania, they now turned south, travelling through 'very wild country,' crossing the Hungarian border at Lucenec, and arriving on 26 August in Budapest, where they stayed for two nights. On their first evening they went to the elegant Café Hungaria 'to see and be seen by those who matter'. Auden spent the next day having difficulty getting the car repaired, while the schoolboy 'bought himself a pair of brown and white shoes, which means I shall have to go to the bank again tomorrow'. The following morning, they left Budapest on the first stage of their return home by a different route. Auden lost the way ('Much weeping but ran over a hen and felt better'), but they eventually crossed the Austrian border and reached Vienna in a thunderstorm. 'Went to the theatre to see a Viennese light opera, *The Princess on the Ladder;*[1] good. Had to speak to Peter very severely for pulling feathers out of the wrap of the lady in front.' On their second night in Vienna, they 'went to flicks in the evening to see Bela Lugosi in *The White Zombie*'. Then, with overnight stops in Salzburg and at a little *Gasthaus* outside Innsbruck, and after an unsuccessful attempt in Kitzbühel to see Auden's friend Hedwig Petzold, they crossed into Switzerland, stopping for the night at Pfäffikon on Lake Zurich. ('Hate Switzerland. Cooking rotten and architecture hideous. Tormented Peter by hiring a concertina player to play just behind him.') On Sunday 2 September they drove through Zurich and Basel into France. 'Reached Bar-le-Duc and had an epic meal. Champagne very cheap. Peter eclipsed all previous efforts.' Next morning they set out at 6 a.m. and drove via Rheims, where the coffee 'exceeded even that at the Winter Gardens, Malvern, in rankness and horror', to Ostend. By the time they reached London on 4 September, the travellers were down to their last fourpence.

Earlier in the summer, Auden had started to write another play, *The Chase*, which he completed in the weeks following his return from abroad. At the beginning of November he sent it to Isherwood for his friend's comment. *The Chase* was probably, in large part, a re-working of *The Fronny*,

[1] This must be Auden's mistranslation of Offenbach's *La Princesse de Trébizonde* which, as *Die Prinzessin von Trapezunt*, was being performed in Vienna.

of which no typescript appears to have survived. Isherwood made a number of suggestions for revisions and for new scenes, and gradually *The Chase* turned into a joint effort, a real collaboration between the two authors. Faber & Faber had already accepted for publication Auden's original typescript, but were now persuaded to advance him the fare to fly to Copenhagen (where Isherwood and Heinz were now living) to confer with his collaborator. Auden spent three days, from 10 to 13 January 1935, in Copenhagen, during which he and Isherwood made a few minor alterations to the play, and gave it a new title, *Where is Francis?* Its final title, *The Dog Beneath the Skin*, was decided upon later at the suggestion of Rupert Doone, who accepted it for production by the Group Theatre. The play was published in May by Faber & Faber, but the stage production, originally intended for the autumn of that year, was postponed, finally taking place in January 1936. At first, Auden's publishers were reluctant to add Isherwood's name to the title page, but Auden was insistent, and when the play was published it was 'by W. H. Auden and Christopher Isherwood', although Isherwood has always generously maintained that most of the play was written by Auden alone.

Still seeking to broaden his horizons and to find a way out of teaching as a full-time profession, Auden wrote in the spring of 1935 to Basil Wright, whom he had met years earlier at Oxford, and who was now working as a director of documentaries with John Grierson, the distinguished documentary film-maker, in the GPO Film Unit. Might there be, Auden wondered, an opening for him in the documentary film world? The GPO Film Unit was a social experiment which interested Auden. It had been receiving a good deal of publicity, and could well offer prospects for more exciting and influential work in education than continuing to teach at the Downs School. Basil Wright showed Auden's letter to Grierson, who encouraged Wright to offer Auden an engagement. The project Basil Wright was then working on was a film called *Coal Face*, which was devised by and was to be directed by the Brazilian Alberto Cavalcanti. The twenty-two-year-old Benjamin Britten had been engaged to write the music for the film, as a result of Grierson having asked the Royal College of Music if they had 'a bright young student who could write a little incidental music for a forthcoming film',[1] and on 4 July 1935 Basil Wright drove Britten down to Colwall to meet Auden at his school. Britten's diary entry for the day reads:

> Have a quick hair-cut before Basil Wright calls for me in his car at 10.00 and takes me down to Colwall near Malvern. Very lovely journey ie Maidenhead, Oxford, Tewkesbury. Arr. 1.45 – lunch at Park Hotel where we put up. We come here to talk over matters for films with Wystan

[1] From a letter written by Benjamin Britten to Paul Rotha, 15 July 1970.

Auden (who is a master at the Downs School here – incidentally, Bobby [Britten's elder brother, Robert] was a master at the Elms, another school in Colwall). Auden is the most amazing man, a very brilliant & attractive personality – he was at 'Fairfield', Greshams, but before my time. Work with him in aft. & then tea in Malvern. After that have a drinking party with most of the Downs' Masters (about 7) – but very boring.

The meeting was a success: Auden wrote the verse commentary for *Coal Face*, much of it taken from official reports of mine disasters and from lists of coal-mining job-names. The film also contains the first of Britten's settings of Auden, for the poem, 'Oh lurcher-loving collier, black as night', is sung on the soundtrack by the GPO Women's Choir, to tremendous effect, as the miners' cages come up from the pits.

As a result of the success of this first commission, Auden was offered a regular job (at £3 a week: 'starvation wages', according to Basil Wright[1]), as from the autumn of 1935, as a writer and general assistant with the GPO Film Unit. Auden left the Downs School at the end of the summer term. He also, very suddenly, married. Christopher Isherwood, temporarily living in Amsterdam, had met Erika Mann, the eldest daughter of Thomas Mann. Branded as a public enemy of the Third Reich, she was threatened with the loss of her German citizenship, and hoped to find an Englishman she could marry so that she could become a British subject. She asked Isherwood if he would be willing to marry her, but he refused and instead suggested that she write to his friend Wystan Auden, explaining the situation. She did so, Auden wired back 'Delighted', and Erika Mann immediately travelled across from Amsterdam and married Auden on 15 June at the Registry Office in Ledbury, Herefordshire, the nearest convenient location to the Downs School. Some months later, according to Erika Mann's brother Golo,[2] Auden visited his distinguished father-in-law at his house in Küsnacht on Lake Zurich, 'to indicate that he wished to take the relationship seriously'. Auden was, as usual, dressed in an extremely slovenly manner, and the Manns' housekeeper thought him 'nicht gerade schön' (not exactly attractive). He certainly took the relationship seriously enough to remain married to Erika and friendly with her family, though he and his wife never lived together.

In September 1935, Auden came to London to begin his full-time employment with the GPO Film Unit, but managed to find time for a weekend in Brussels with Isherwood in October. The GPO Film Unit had its offices in Soho Square and a sound-studio in Blackheath. It was at Blackheath that some of the Unit's finest films were completed, among them *Night Mail* with music by Britten and verse for the final section by Auden: 'This is the night

[1] In conversation with the present author.
[2] In an article in *Encounter*, January 1974.

mail crossing the border,/Bringing the cheque and the postal order . . .'

For several weeks at the beginning of his employment with the Unit, Auden stayed with Basil Wright who had a flat in a newly completed modern block in Highgate. Wright found him both an entertaining and an absolutely maddening guest: entertaining because of his quick mind and brilliant conversation, maddening because of his incredible untidiness and slovenly habits. He still loved playing the piano, and tended to rise early to play and sing hymns *fortissimo* on Wright's beautiful new Blüthner grand piano. He also used to leave lighted cigarettes on the side of the keyboard until they burnt into the wood. When his host remonstrated with him, Auden replied indignantly, 'It doesn't affect the *tone*.'

Auden's duties with the GPO Film Unit ranged from writing commentaries for the soundtracks to acting as assistant director and, on occasion, to such menial tasks as carrying cans of film. Auden used to say that he was once allowed to direct a brief shot of a railway guard, but since the guard dropped dead a minute later, he was thereafter considered an unsafe director. In fact, the 'guard' was a station manager who died some days later, which would seem to lessen the likelihood of the fledgling director being thought responsible.

Auden planned a film of his own, *Air Mail to Australia*, which would have involved him in taking the mail plane to Australia and supervising the filming of the stops *en route*, but this was never made. For *Calendar of the Year*, a film of which he was the production manager, he made an appearance before the cameras as Father Christmas, at a Christmas party staged for the film. But it was *Calendar of the Year* that brought Auden's career with the Film Unit to an end. As production manager, he was responsible for seeing that the budget was not exceeded. Unfortunately, he overspent by about £30, which was a heinous offence, and one for which Basil Wright, as producer-in-charge, had to reprimand him. Wright did this, as gently as possible, over dinner in his flat one evening, but the discussion triggered off a violent argument in which Auden's increasing disillusionment with the documentary film movement revealed itself. Auden left the GPO Film Unit in March 1936, after an association of about six months. He continued, occasionally, to write for documentary films made by the Strand Film Company and the British Commercial Gas Association. Another film project, *God's Chillun*, on the subject of the Negro and slavery, on which Auden and Benjamin Britten were keen to collaborate, was finally made in 1939, but not along the lines they had planned. It appears not to have been released.

William Coldstream worked for the GPO Film Unit at the same time as Auden, and when Auden moved out of Basil Wright's flat in Highgate, he lodged in Coldstream's house in Hampstead. Later, Coldstream painted his friend's portrait (see p. 168). They had both left the employment of the Film

Unit, Coldstream to devote himself to painting, and Auden to return temporarily to teaching. 'I went and stayed with him at the school, where he sat for me for his portrait,' Coldstream wrote later. 'His pupils would sometimes come and watch, among them a tall boy, then twelve years old, with a prodigious knowledge of the history of art, Andrew Forge. Wystan was always in very high spirits at this time and would particularly like to play and sing hymns to groups of boys and staff.[1]

Auden has left his own account of these days, and in particular of the beginnings of his friendship with Benjamin Britten, in a handwritten rough draft of a piece which was probably intended as a contribution to a volume, *Tribute to Benjamin Britten on his Fiftieth Birthday* (1963), though, in fact, it does not appear in that book, and is now published for the first time:

In the summer of 1935 Mr John Grierson, as he then was,[2] asked me to write a chorus for the conclusion of a GPO Documentary film called *Coal Face*. All I now remember about this film was that it seemed to have been shot in total darkness, and a factual statement in the commentary – the miner works in a cramped position. My chorus, he told me, would be set by a brilliant young composer he had hired to work for him, called Benjamin Britten. The following autumn I went myself to work for the GPO Film Unit. What an odd organization it was, Sir John Grierson had a genius for discovering talent and persuading it to work for next to nothing. There was Britten, there was William Coldstream, there was Cavalcanti, among others. Basically I loathed my job, but enjoyed the company enormously. The film which both Britten and myself worked on which I remember best was one about Africa which never got made because it turned out that there were no visuals. Our commentary was a most elaborate affair, beginning with quotations from Aristotle about slavery and introducing a setting of a poem by Blake. I wonder if Britten still has the score as there was some wonderful music in it. What immediately struck me, as someone who warms to languages, about Britten the composer was his extraordinary musical sensibility in relation to the English language. One had always been told that English was an impossible tongue to set or to sing. Since I already knew the songs of the Elizabethan composers like Dowland – and then I knew Purcell slightly – I knew this to be false, but the influence of that very great composer, Handel, on the setting of English had been unfortunate. There was Sullivan's setting of Gilbert's light verse, to be sure, but then his music seems so boring. Here at last was a composer who could both set the

[1] Sir William Coldstream in *W. H. Auden: A Tribute*.
[2] Auden appears to have thought that Grierson had been knighted. But he remained Mr John Grierson to the end of his life.

111

language [?and to whose music][1] it was a real pleasure to listen. Another collaboration I remember was a BBC programme about the Roman Wall which we were both rather proud of. It was from Britten, too, that I first heard the name of Alban Berg. We went together to a memorial concert just after his death.[2] I had a tummy upset and threw up in the street.

I have, alas, no talent for writing memoirs, but if I had I would devote a whole chapter to a house in Amityville, Long Island, the house of Dr William and Elizabeth Mayer, where Benjamin Britten and Peter Pears stayed in 1939–40; a house which played an important role in the lives of all three of us. It was during this period that Britten wrote his first opera, and I my first libretto, on the subject of an American folk-hero, Paul Bunyan. The result, I'm sorry to say, was a failure, for which I was entirely to blame, since, at the time, I knew nothing whatever about opera or what is required of a librettist. In consequence, some very lovely music of Britten's went down the drain, and I must now belatedly make my apologies to my old friend while wishing him a very happy birthday.[3]

Auden's fragmentary memoir of Britten has brought the narrative up to 1940. Returning to 1936 and the early days of their friendship and artistic collaboration, one finds Auden eagerly introducing the young composer to his friends such as Isherwood and Louis MacNeice. He also led Britten to an appreciation of several poets, ranging from Donne to Rimbaud. Auden's revolutionary opinions and anti-bourgeois behaviour appealed to Britten at the time, and the relationship progressed both personally and professionally. Britten thought Auden had 'some lively, slightly dotty ideas about music. He played the piano reasonably well, and was a great one for singing unlikely words to Anglican chants.'[4] Britten also once told the present author that he had been greatly influenced by Auden *personally* but never musically.[5]

Now having to support himself entirely by his writing, Auden began consciously to increase his output in various kinds of literary journalism. In 1935 he had edited an anthology of poetry with John Garrett, *The Poet's Tongue*; had contributed an essay on John Skelton to a book on *The Great Tudors*; and contributed essays on Christianity and on Psychology and the Arts to two other volumes. Writing to Geoffrey Grigson to thank him for a favourable review of *The Poet's Tongue* in the *Morning Post* – 'as the latter is

[1] Illegible in Auden's manuscript.

[2] Alban Berg died on 24 December 1935.

[3] The last four sentences of this draft have been published as a caption to a photograph of Auden and Britten in *Benjamin Britten: Pictures from a Life* (London, 1978).

[4] Quoted in an interview in *Music and Musicians*, November 1963.

[5] In a conversation in the autumn of 1963.

the paper of many reactionary Headmasters, it should do us a lot of good' – he asked, 'Did you see the wigging *The Dog Beneath the Skin* got in the *Spectator*?'[1] *The Dog Beneath the Skin*, which became known to its cast during rehearsals as 'Dogskin', had indeed had a wigging in the *Spectator*. The review was of the published text, for the play was not performed until several months later. The *Spectator*'s critic was I. M. Parsons, a contemporary of Auden's who was later to become a distinguished publisher. Parsons did not pull his punches. He thought *Dogskin*

> a shoddy affair, a half-baked little satire which gets nowhere. If it had been written by Mr Brown and Mr Smith instead of by two intelligent young men like Mr Auden and Mr Isherwood, nobody would have bothered to publish it, and nobody would have been the loser. For of all the dreary jokes imaginable it must surely be the dreariest, the flattest, and the stalest that has managed to get into print for some time. Dreary, because it is set out with a great deal of extravagant pretension; flat, because the satire is so crude that it completely misses fire; and stale, because the objects against which it is directed have been objects of ridicule for the last ten years or more . . . One wonders what fun an audience not entirely composed of morons could conceivably extract from so much knocking about of battered Aunt Sallies, and so much preaching to the converted.[2]

Scrutiny[3] was of the opinion that 'on the stage, parts of it might come off, but very little of the play stands up to cold solitary perusal'. Critical response was not noticeably more enthusiastic when the play was staged in January 1936, at the Westminster Theatre, in a production by Rupert Doone with music by Herbert Murrill and with a cast which, in typical Group Theatre fashion, was comprised of both established professional actors and actresses such as Veronica Turleigh and Robert Speaight, and also non-professionals such as Robert Medley who played a small role as well as, in his professional capacity, designing the scenery and the masks worn by some of the characters. There was a private Sunday performance on 12 January for Group Theatre subscribers: the public performances ran from 30 January. *New Verse*[4] said unkindly that 'the piece was not produced but thrown on the stage . . . the acting varied from very bad to quite good', while the *New Statesman*[5] thought that, 'Handed over to Messrs Cole Porter, Cecil Beaton

[1] Quoted in Catalogue number 114 (Alan Hancox, Cheltenham).
[2] *Spectator*, 28 June 1935.
[3] September 1935.
[4] February–March 1936.
[5] 12 February 1936.

and Oliver Messel with a cast of singers and a lavish production, something might be made of it. As it was, the bareness of the stage reflected the poverty of the lines.' *Punch*[1] complained of a lack of 'the humour which makes prolonged satire palatable. For this, wit alone is not enough, and here the irony is so terribly in earnest that even when comic relief is attempted the audience has an embarrassing feeling that it would be rude to laugh. And it can hardly be blamed, when it is treated in rapid succession and with vivid realism to a brothel, a lunatic asylum, and an operating-theatre where a major operation is in progress.' Writing in the *Spectator*,[2] Derek Verschoyle, who had been so scathing on *The Dance of Death*, gave a more balanced criticism:

> *The Dog Beneath the Skin* is in every respect a much more impressive work than Mr Auden's earlier play, *The Dance of Death*. It is more precise, and therefore more pointed, in its choice of subject-matter, more consistent and (for the most part) more mature in its satire, and, apart from its rather embarrassing conclusion, much less naïvely evangelistic in its political attitude. It takes its form from musical comedy and revue, and differs from everyday revue (which it occasionally challenges on its own ground) chiefly in its assumption of a comprehensive moral outlook. The choruses, in which the authors underline the purport of their satire, are eloquent and often moving, the dialogue has a competence of wit, and the prose scenes, which range from the burlesque to the gravely ironic, bear the mark of a genuine dramatic talent. Nevertheless, it is far from being a completely satisfactory play.

It is curious that, after a cursory mention of Isherwood at the beginning of his review, the *Spectator* critic assumes thereafter that Auden is solely responsible for all the verse speeches for the Chorus, and that Isherwood Auden's work, its final shape was to a large extent dictated by Isherwood, and many of the prose scenes were written by him. A letter from Auden to Stephen Spender in late June 1935 reveals that Auden was, not surprisingly, responsible for all the verse speeches for the Chorus, end that Isherwood wrote Act I, scene ii, except for the song; Act II, scene i, except for the leader's speech; Act II, scene ii, except for the song; the dialogue between the left and right feet in Act II, scene v; the Destructive Desmond episode in Act III, scene ii; the whole of Act III, scene iii, Act III, scene iv, from Francis's discovery on, and Act III, scene v, apart from the Vicar's sermon. Isherwood was also responsible, in outline, for the Ostnia Palace and Paradise Park scenes, and for several suggestions throughout the play.

The Dog Beneath the Skin is a very long play, and the Group Theatre

[1] 12 February 1936.
[2] 7 February 1936.

production made a number of cuts. The Lord Chamberlain's Office also required certain excisions to be made, but appears not to have been responsible for the staged ending, in which Francis is shot. This was an afterthought on the part of Isherwood: after the first production, the two authors agreed to revert to their published ending. The first real fruit of Auden and Isherwood's collaboration, *The Dog Beneath the Skin* is also the most successful. Its satire may be facile, but the play has great energy and pace, and a really imaginative production, with appropriate cuts, would very likely reveal it as still able to entertain audiences in the theatre.[1] Auden's choruses, forerunners of the kind of journalistic verse that today's poets write for themselves to perform at poetry readings, are so superior to today's products that they almost, but not quite, persuade one of the viability of a twentieth-century verse drama.

One of the songs in *The Dog Beneath the Skin* would certainly have been disallowed by the Lord Chamberlain if that gentleman had understood cockney rhyming slang. This is the nonsensical song sung by a drunken journalist in Act III, scene i:

> Alice is gone and I'm alone,
> Nobody understands
> How lovely were her Fire Alarms,
> How fair her German Bands!

> O how I cried when Alice died
> The day we were to have wed!
> We never had our Roasted Duck
> And now she's a Loaf of Bread!

The final words of the last two lines of each verse are examples of rhyming slang: for instance, 'Fire Alarms' are 'charms' (or perhaps 'arms') and 'German Bands' are 'hands'. The Auden notebook mentioned earlier (p. 89n) supplies a third verse which did not find its way into the play:

> At nights I weep and cannot sleep,
> Moonlight to me recalls
> I never saw her Waterfront
> Nor she my Waterfalls.

[1] The present author directed a staged reading of his own abridged version of the play at the Wigmore Hall, London, on 30 July 1977, under the auspices of the Poetry Book Society. The performers were William Squire, Christopher Benjamin, Jonathan Cecil, Tony Beckley, Rohan McCullough and Charles Osborne.

Chapter Five

1936

It is time for the destruction of error.
The chairs are being brought in from the garden,
The summer talk stopped on that savage coast
Before the storms, after the guests and birds:
In sanatoriums they laugh less and less,
Less certain of cure; and the loud madman
Sinks now into a more terrible calm.[1]

The success of the anthologies of new writing, *New Signatures* and *New Country*, in the early thirties had led John Lehmann to the belief that a literary magazine was needed, one which would publish the work of the younger writers, many of whom were united in a political stance, but a magazine which, unlike *Left Review*, would not place politics, as Lehmann put it, 'fatally first'. He wanted a magazine in which literature came first, 'with the politics only as an undertone'. Lehmann had consulted Christopher Isherwood who agreed to help him get Auden's active support, and Lehmann also proceeded to recruit a number of other young poets and prose writers, among them his sister Rosamund Lehmann, and several of his own friends such as Stephen Spender and William Plomer. At the moment when Lehmann was attempting to assemble the contents of the magazine's first issue, Auden was involved with the GPO Film Unit, and it looked as though he might be about to fly to Australia to make *Airmail to Australia*. 'However deeply Wystan A. may have involved himself with the Empire-builders and their film-hacks,' wrote the angry young editor to Isherwood, 'he must not be allowed to leave for our far-flung territories without producing something. He will probably write it while you stand over him one evening.'

New Writing, a twice-yearly magazine of contemporary imaginative writing, duly appeared in the spring of 1936, and was immediately successful. Auden did not appear in the first issue, though he was a regular contributor thereafter. *New Writing* No 4 contained two ballads by Auden, 'Victor' and 'Miss Gee'. 'Miss Gee', one of his best-known lighter poems of the thirties, is a piece of crudely effective Brechtian polemic on the dangers of repressed sexuality. Miss Gee dreams of a bull with the face of the Vicar –

> She could feel his hot breath behind her,
> He was going to overtake;

[1] From '1929'.

116

> And the bicycle went slower and slower
>   Because of that back-pedal brake

– but becomes ill, and bicycles to the doctor 'with her clothes buttoned up to her neck' –

> Doctor Thomas sat over his dinner,
>   Though his wife was waiting to ring;
> Rolling his bread into pellets,
>   Said: Cancer's a funny thing.

Miss Gee ends as a corpse on a slab, dissected by incompetent students.

Auden took leave from the GPO Film Unit in February 1936, probably in order to begin work on the next play which he and Isherwood had already begun to plan. The peripatetic Isherwood was now living in Portugal with his friend Heinz, where they had for some months been sharing a cottage in the village of Sintra, about fifteen miles from Lisbon, with Stephen Spender and his boy-friend Tony, an ex-guardsman from Cardiff (who is called Jimmy Younger in Spender's autobiography *World within World*). Spender and Tony left Portugal on 14 March for Spain, and on 16 March Auden arrived to begin work in earnest with Isherwood on their play, *The Ascent of F.6*. They had enjoyed their collaboration on *Dogskin*, and Rupert Doone and Robert Medley were keen for them to provide the Group Theatre with another play. From Sintra, Auden wrote his formal resignation to the GPO Film Unit. During the month that he spent in Portugal, he and Isherwood wrote, revised and typed the finished version of their play. Both were quick workers, and the division of labour was a neat one once the structure of the play had been plotted. Auden wrote the verse and Isherwood the prose dialogue. The one difference in their working methods was that Auden's first drafts were close to his final versions, whereas Isherwood usually found it necessary to write down the first nonsense that came into his head, in order to set his creative faculties in motion. Auden was appalled (and Isherwood embarrassed) when he came across one of Christopher's rough drafts, and read it. Their mornings were spent writing: characteristically, Auden worked indoors with the curtains drawn, while Isherwood wrote out in the garden and sunbathed at the same time. Work was quite frequently interrupted by play, and sometimes by play disguised as work. Auden insisted that, to get themselves under the skin of the mountaineers in their play, he and Isherwood should climb one of the steep hills near Sintra. But the playwrights were no mountaineers, and their climb 'was accompanied by laughter, lost footings, slitherings and screams.'[1] One afternoon, Isherwood and Heinz took Auden to the casino at nearby Estoril, to see the

---

[1] Christopher Isherwood: *Christopher and His Kind* (London, 1977).

hard-core afternoon gamblers: a result of this was Auden's poem, 'Casino', which begins 'Only their hands are living, to the wheel attracted'. Towards the end of Auden's stay, he and Isherwood were photographed by Heinz, sitting side by side on a sofa, and Auden murmured his suggested caption for the photo, a quotation from Yeats: 'Both beautiful, one a gazelle.' Shortly before Auden's departure, the German poet and playwright Ernst Toller, a refugee from Hitler's Germany, came to Sintra for a few days with his wife, and Auden was able to meet a man whose work he admired, and whose epitaph, sadly, he would write only three years later.

On 17 April, Auden left by train, taking with him the completed manuscript of *The Ascent of F.6*. Isherwood wrote in his diary that day:

> Wystan hasn't changed in the least. His clothes are still out at the elbows, his stubby nail-bitten fingers still dirty and sticky with nicotine; he still drinks a dozen cups of tea a day, has to have a hot bath every night, piles his bed with blankets, overcoats, carpets and rugs; he still eats ravenously – though not as much as he once did – and nearly sheds tears if the food isn't to his taste; he still smokes like a factory chimney and pockets all the matches in the house. But although I found myself glancing nervously whenever he picked up a book, fiddled with the electric light cord or shovelled food into his mouth while reading at meals; although I was often very much annoyed by his fussing and by the mess he made – still I never for one moment was more than annoyed. I never felt opposed to him in my deepest being – as I sometimes feel opposed to almost everyone I know. We are, after all, of the same sort.

Isherwood also noted in his diary that most of their play was written by either one or the other co-author, and that the only real collaboration was on the final scene. Elsewhere, they tended not to interfere with each other's work. Auden was responsible, according to Isherwood, for Act I, scene i; the dialogue between Ransom and the Abbot in Act II, scene i; Ransom's monologue in Act II, scene ii; the whole of Act II scene iv; all the songs and choruses, the speeches by Mr and Mrs A, and the other speeches between the scenes. It was understood throughout that Auden's speciality was to be what they called the 'woozy' bits, and Isherwood's the 'straight' bits, 'woozy' being taken to mean the lofty, grandiloquent, preacher-like style which Auden could adopt so easily in his verse. Auden was, at this time, generally regarded as a Marxist and thought to be a paid-up member of the Communist Party. Isherwood, who was as close to him as anyone, has implied that this was actually not the case, and that, though Auden outwardly supported Marxism, 'or at any rate didn't protest when it was preached',[1] his support was, at best, half-hearted and, in any case, under-

[1] *Christopher and His Kind.*

taken mainly to humour Isherwood and a few other friends who had stronger and firmer feelings about politics. In fact, unlike Spender, Day Lewis and others of his friends, Auden never joined the Communist Party and never showed any inclination to do so.

Isherwood discerned beneath his friend's dutiful anti-religious comment, a strong natural feeling for Christianity. No doubt the constant hymn-singing kept it alive. 'When we collaborate,' Isherwood wrote of Auden the following year, 'I have to keep a sharp eye on him – or down flop the characters on their knees (see 'F.6' *passim*); another constant danger is that of choral interruptions by angel-voices. If Auden had his way, he would turn every play into a cross between grand opera and high mass.'[1]

In England, Auden now began to see the distinguished novelist, E. M. Forster, regularly; frequently in Dover where Forster had begun to spend his summers. Having, the previous year, married Erika Mann in order to provide her with a British passport, Auden attempted to enlist Forster's aid in persuading other homosexuals to make similar marriages. 'After all,' he asked Forster, 'what are buggers for?' They did manage to arrange one such marriage, that of John Simpson, a friend of Forster's, to Therese Giehse, a German actress and friend of Erika Mann. The marriage took place in a registry office in Solihull, Birmingham, with Auden, in striped trousers and sporting a carnation, taking charge 'with great zest, answering all the clerk's questions on the bride's behalf and standing double brandies all round after the ceremony, declaring "It's on Thomas Mann".'[2] Early in May he briefly visited Erika Mann in Holland.

The year 1936 was an especially busy and productive one for Auden. In a book review he wrote for the April–May issue of *New Verse*, he said he could not believe 'that any artist can be good who is not more than a bit of a reporting journalist'. Certainly, he himself took his literary journalism seriously, even agreeing to undertake, in the summer, a journey to Iceland with Louis MacNeice, in order to write a travel book for Faber & Faber. *The Ascent of F.6*, the typescript of which Auden had delivered to his publisher in April, was published in September. He handed another typescript, his first book of poems since the 1930 volume, to Faber & Faber in June, and this was published in October. Throughout the year, Auden contributed articles and poems to *The Highway* (the magazine of the Workers' Educational Association), *New Verse*, *The Listener*, the *New Statesman*, *Time and Tide*, *Living Age*, *New Writing, 2*, *The London Mercury*, *The Times* and a few little magazines. Throughout his working life, Auden continued to maintain that the artist could only benefit from involvement in journalism, though he understood quite clearly that too deep an involvement could dull the sensibilities.

[1] In 'Some Notes on Auden's Early Poetry' (*New Verse*, November 1937).
[2] P. N. Furbank: *E. M. Forster: a Life* (Vol. 2, London, 1978).

Oddly, his assertion in 1936 that the only good artist is the one who is also something of a journalist was made in support of his contention that abstract art is inferior to figurative art. Auden liked plenty of news in his literature, and he wanted things, rather than ideas or pieces of abstract decoration, in his visual art. Symbolism, yes; pure abstraction, no. It must have seemed an eccentric position to take in the thirties, but now, after a decade or two in which the visual arts have been abstracting and trivializing themselves virtually out of existence, it appears as a fresh, engaging and sympathetic point of view.

Auden would have liked to teach at Bryanston School in Dorset, but ruined his chances of a position there when, hearing that Geoffrey Hoyland (the Downs School headmaster) was going to preach in the Bryanston Chapel, he wrote to a Bryanston boy (an ex-Downs School pupil of his) suggesting that an onion be placed in the chalice on the occasion of Hoyland's sermon. The boy was caught giggling, the letter confiscated, and Auden branded unsuitable as a Bryanston master. However, in the early summer of 1936, Auden paid a visit to Bryanston to see two friends. One was Michael Yates, whom he had taught at the Downs School, and who was now nearly seventeen. During Auden's weekend visit, they drove to Shaftesbury, about twelve miles away, for lunch. Michael Yates has related that, on another occasion, Auden in exasperation bumped a too leisurely cow into a ditch, but this time they reached Shaftesbury without incident, and over lunch Michael mentioned that, with three other boys and a master, he would be going to Iceland that summer. Auden did not immediately mention his and Louis MacNeice's intention to visit Iceland to write a book, but he referred to it in a letter to Michael a short time later, suggesting that he seek the master's permission for Auden to join the school party for part of their tour, so that he could include an account of it in the book.

Auden sailed to Iceland in June, and was there alone for six weeks before being joined by Louis MacNeice and, soon afterwards, the party from Bryanston School. (When the rest of the school party returned to England, Michael Yates stayed on with Auden and MacNeice for the last two weeks of their stay.)

After Auden had been in Iceland for a month on his own, he wrote a long letter to his wife Erika Mann, in which he confessed that he still hadn't 'the slightest idea how to begin to write the book. Gollancz told me before I left that it couldn't be done, and he's probably right. Still, the contracts are signed and my expenses paid, so I suppose it will get done. At present I am just amusing myself, with occasional twinges of uneasiness, like a small boy who knows he's got an exam tomorrow, for which he has done no work whatsoever.'

In due course, this and a second letter to Erika found their way into the book, *Letters from Iceland*. Auden had, he told her, not enjoyed the Icelandic capital, Reykjavik, very much, for it was the worst kind of provincial town, with nothing to do but drink, at ruinous expense, in the only hotel with a liquor licence. He made several excursions into the surrounding country, 'and had a nice time riding', and visited Thingvellir, 'the stock beauty spot, which is certainly very pretty, but the hotel is full of drunks every evening'. After about four weeks of meeting people and making notes for the section of practical tourist information in the book, he set out to see more of Iceland. His worst experience was with the cuisine of the country. He remembered with particular horror a soup which tasted of scented hair oil, and two kinds of dried fish which varied in toughness: 'The tougher kind tastes like toe-nails, and the softer kind like the skin off the soles of one's feet.' Meat, he found, was liable to be served in 'glutinous and half-cold lumps, covered with tasteless gravy', and there was also smoked mutton which was 'comparatively harmless when cold as it only tastes like soot, but it would take a very hungry man indeed to eat it hot'. Two Icelandic dishes are cautiously recommended by Auden in his chapter 'For Tourists':

> One is Hakarl, which is half-dry, half-rotten shark. This is white inside with a prickly horn rind outside, as tough as an old boot. Owing to the smell it has to be eaten out of doors. It is shaved off with a knife and eaten with brandy. It tastes more like boot-polish than anything else I can think of. The other is Reyngi. This is the tail of the whale, which is pickled in sour milk for a year or so. If you intend to try it, do not visit a whaling station first.

With Ragnar, an Icelandic guide, Auden travelled by bus to a farm near Hredavatn, where he did some riding and took a boat out on the lake. After a stay of a couple of nights, they continued to Saudarkrokur on the north coast, again by bus, on roads so bumpy that the Icelandic passengers were frequently sick, though Auden, rather surprisingly, was not. Saudarkrokur 'might have been built by Seventh Day Adventists who expected to go to heaven in a few months, so why bother anyway. I have no wish to see it again. The inn is dirty and smells like a chicken run.' They left next day for Holar which consisted of 'a church, a farm, and a large white agricultural school in the depths of a spectacular valley.' Here Auden played the harmonium in the church 'which is as ugly as most protestant places of worship', and at breakfast next morning exchanged the time of day with Goering's brother who was one of a visiting party of Nazis. His return to Saudarkrokur was by the slowest of milk carts which stopped at every farm to collect milk cans and took four hours to do twenty-five miles while Auden, who had run out of cigarettes, sulked.

From Saudarkrokur Auden and Ragnar proceeded by local bus to

Akureyri, with an overnight stay at a farm *en route*. Akureyri, the only town of any size on the north coast of Iceland, was much nicer than Reykjavik, despite the fact that there was a fish factory to the north of the town and 'today the wind is blowing from the north'. They continued on to Myvatn, a lake surrounded by little craters, where Auden enjoyed watching the haymakers on the farms. They made their way first north to Husavik and Asbyrgi, then south-easterly to the east coast, stopping overnight at a farm at Grimstadur, Auden by now nursing a heavy cold, and making a short stop the next day at another farm at Morduradalur, 'which is renowned for its home-made ale and a drunken clergyman'. At another large farm at Egilsstadur, Auden left the bus, parting company with Ragnar who was travelling further. Here he stayed for a few days, and began to write the long poem, 'Letter to Lord Byron', which is also included in *Letters from Iceland*. 'I suddenly thought I might write him a chatty letter in light verse about anything I could think of, Europe, literature, myself,' he told Erika Mann. 'He's the right person, I think, because he was a townee, a European, and disliked Wordsworth and that kind of approach to nature, and I find that very sympathetic.'

While he was at Egilsstadur, Auden borrowed the farmer's horse, 'the prize race horse of East Iceland':

> I didn't start too well, as when I mounted in a confined courtyard with a lot of other horses near, I clucked reassuringly at him, which sent him prancing round, scattering people and horses in all directions. I was rather frightened, but got on all right after that. The moment we got on the road, we set off at full gallop, and on the last stretch home I gave him his head and it was more exciting than a really fast car. The farmer said, 'You've ridden a lot in England, I expect.' I thought of my first experience at Laugavatn a month ago, and how I shocked an English girl by yelling for help. I thought of the day at Thingvellir when I fell right over the horse's neck when getting on in full view of a party of picnickers. This was my triumph. I was a real he-man after all. Still, Ronald Firbank was a good horseman. And what about those Scythians.

A few days later, he travelled about fifteen miles up the valley to Hallormsstadur, where he stayed at a girls' school which took in paying guests during the vacation. Here he wrote a cabaret sketch for Erika's actress friend, Therese Giehse, which was published that autumn in *New Writing, 2*. He also found himself listening a great deal to the radio, especially the broadcasts from England, from which he first heard about the civil war in Spain. Leaving Hallormsstadur, he returned to Egilsstadur and then drove over in the farmer's car to Seydisfjordur, where a primitive sportfest was being held. He stayed here for three days waiting for the coastal steamer,

Nova, on which he travelled back to Reykjavik around the north coast of the island.

The boat was almost empty, the only other passengers being a young American 'who had just taken his law finals and was having his last fling in Europe, one of those Americans who read everything from poetry to anthropology and economics, with apparently no preferences', and a twenty-four-year-old Norwegian fish merchant, 'looking nineteen'. The boat made several stops, which relieved the tedium of the voyage for Auden, who did not care for shipboard life, whether on small trading vessels or large passenger liners. One night during the voyage, 'after reading a silly book on spiritualism', he had a nightmare. He woke up in a sweat and wrote down what he could remember of it, incorporating his account in one of his letters to Erika and in the Iceland book. He also reprinted it thirty-four years later,[1] recalling that it was the only dream he had ever had which he thought, on conscious consideration, interesting enough to write down:

I was in hospital for an appendectomy. There was somebody there with green eyes and a terrifying affection for me. He cut off the arm of an old lady who was going to do me an injury. I explained to the doctors about him, but they were inattentive, though, presently, I realized that they were very concerned about his bad influence over me. I decide to escape from the hospital, and do so, after looking in a cupboard for something, I don't know what. I get to a station, squeeze between the carriages of a train, down a corkscrew staircase and out under the legs of some boys and girls. Now my companion has turned up with his three brothers (there may have been only two). One, a smooth-faced, fine-fingernailed blond, is more reassuring. They tell me that they never leave anyone they like and that they often choose the timid. The name of the frightening one is Giga (in Icelandic *Gigur* is a crater), which I associate with the name Marigold and have a vision of pursuit like a book illustration and, I think related to the long red-legged Scissor Man in *Shockheaded Peter*.[2] The scene changes to a derelict factory by moonlight. The brothers are there, and my father. There is a great banging going on which, they tell me, is caused by the ghost of an old aunt who lives in a tin in the factory. Sure enough, the tin, which resembles my mess tin, comes bouncing along and stops at our feet, falling open. It is full of hard-boiled eggs. The brothers are very selfish and seize them, and only my father gives me half his.

Auden was back in Reykjavik on 9 August, to find Louis MacNeice

[1] In *A Certain World* (New York, 1970).
[2] This is *Struwwelpeter*, which Auden had read as a child.

awaiting him. A few days later, Michael Yates and the other schoolboys from Bryanston turned up with their master, and Auden and MacNeice were on the quay to meet them. The object of the school expedition was to circle one of the central icefields, the Langjökull, on horseback, and the party had been told that an additional attraction was that they were to be joined by two poets, Messrs W. H. Auden and Louis MacNeice. Losing no time on arrival, the schoolmaster W. F. (Bill) Hoyland, the poets and the boys proceeded that same day to Gullfoss, the starting point of the expedition, where they found their two guides, Stengrimur and Ari, their provisions for a ten-day journey, and their seventeen horses, and where they camped on their first night. Auden and MacNeice shared a very small tent, with one piece of its central pole missing. It rained on the first night, the poets' tent subsided, 'Wystan declared he was going down with all hands; Louis merely hid deeper inside his wet sleeping bag'[1] and there they remained for the rest of the night, clammy canvas on their faces, whilst the rain fell and a strong spray from the waterfalls nearby blew steadily across them. At six o'clock the next morning, the school party at first saw only a flattened tent on the ground. 'Then the tent undulated and two wet cross faces appeared.'

The expedition's days followed a strict pattern. They would rise at six, saddle their own horses and set off, stopping briefly at noon to eat and to rest the horses. The landscape, consisting mostly of lava, and brown or grey rock, intrigued the others more than it did Auden, who thought it was untidy and uninteresting. He would have liked it even less had it looked tidy, for a comfortable untidiness was what he preferred in his surroundings. He got on well with the boys, teasing them when they complained, 'telling us that if we had come here to demonstrate our toughness, then, "children, it is time you did so, though heaven knows why you want to!"' When Bill Hoyland suggested that it would not seem so rough if they thought of the discomforts of the people climbing Everest, Auden tartly replied that he would much rather think of people dining at the Ritz.

Travelling across unexplored country, the guides using compasses to keep them on course, the party proceeded slowly to encircle the Langjökull. On three nights, they slept in primitive, turf-roofed huts, but most of the time they shivered in their tents. As they made their way across seventy kilometres of stony desert, Auden observed that 'anyone would be an optimist who expected to find anything as human as a dry bone in these parts'. 'Never again,' he said to MacNeice the night after they had crossed the desert, before going off to sleep with a cigarette in his mouth. But the next day, after twelve hours' riding, they reached a welcoming farm in the

[1] This and later quotations, unless otherwise identified, are from Michael Yates's 'Iceland 1936' in *W. H. Auden: a Tribute.*

midst of the wilderness. As they sat drinking decent coffee for the first time in days, with the rain beating against the window panes, Auden's spirits rose again. 'Isn't that a nice sound,' he said to Michael, 'just like the Lake District.'

The ten days' journey with the school party was described by Louis MacNeice in *Letters from Iceland*. He chose to write about it in the form of a long letter, headed 'Hetty to Nancy', an extremely 'camp' account of the expedition in which the four boys are transformed into a party of four girls with their mistress, Miss Greenhalge. MacNeice and Auden become two young spinsters, Hetty and Maisie:

Darling, *darling*, DARLING, it is very lucky your poor friend Hetty is alive. The worst night I have had since Aunt Evelyn walked in her sleep – you remember, the fire-extinguisher business. I had great difficulty to start with getting to sleep. For why? (1) Because we had pitched the tents with our heads running downhill, (2) because we had pitched it on bilberry bushes, which kept prickling me through the groundsheet, (3) because Maisie *would* get more and more foetal, so that in the end her feet were playing an absolute barrage on my tummy. All things, however, are possible and I did get to sleep in the end only to be woken by a clammy thing on my face like some very unpleasant beauty treatment – you know when they plaster you with eggs and whey and things – which turned out to be the tent or more precisely the inner cover of the tent because there are two. There was a frightful noise of rain outside and the whole tent was caving in under it, Maisie was swearing and saying she was going down with all hands. I took the ostrich's course and hid my head in my sleeping-bag. Not that that was unduly dry and the foot-end of it was sopping because that was where the door of the tent came. When I popped out my head again, the tent had become very much smaller (Heaven knows it was small enough to start with) and was closing in on us like something in Edgar Allan Poe. So I cowered round the pole in the middle and Maisie and I got entangled like a pair of wet tennis-shoes when one packs them in a hurry.

. . . After dinner Greenhalge opened a little case and, to Maisie's horror, began to offer the girls quinine pills and vegetable laxatives. Maisie has a bee in her bonnet about laxatives; she thinks her inside knows best . . . Greenhalge is a good sort really, always ready to lend you a knife or a cup and she does all the washing up. The girls don't do anything much in that line excepting possibly Anne [Michael Yates] who is going to be house-prefect next term. Anne is the best-looking though she will be better looking when she has learned not to pout. She probably has a nice little temper on occasions and does a power of grumbling. Her intonation and vowel sounds are just what you expect from a nice British schoolgirl.

'Some,' Michael Yates wrote later, 'may not find this amusing. Some, indeed, did not do so at the time of publication. However, it remains a fact that a mass of acute observation is incorporated in this spoofy account, not just of our progress but also more particularly of our individual characters and our reactions to rough conditions.'

On the party's return to Reykjavik, the other boys and Bill Hoyland sailed for England. Auden, MacNeice and Michael Yates spent one night as the guests of the Director of the local lunatic asylum, and Auden managed somehow completely to demolish the camp bed he slept on. After a further day's sight-seeing in Reykjavik, they sailed on the motor-ship *Laxoss* for Borganes and so by bus to the farm at Hredvatn where Auden had stayed several weeks earlier. They boated on the lake, and one day on one of its islands Auden 'launched into a lecture on the wickedness of some aspects of public schools, especially the power of the prefect, beating and fagging'. This was for the benefit of Michael, for Auden knew he was shortly to be made head prefect. 'All power corrupts,' he announced, and grinned with pleasure at Michael's anger.

They sailed to the far north of the island on another ship, the *Dettifoss*. At Patreksfjördur, where a stop was made to unload cargo, they decided to walk sixteen miles over the lava-strewn headland to a whaling station. Auden thought whales most beautiful creatures, and was distressed at the scene of carnage which greeted him there. 'It's enough to make one a vegetarian for life. It gives one an extraordinary vision of the cold, controlled ferocity of the human species.' They couldn't get a cup of coffee at the whaling station, and had to trudge back hungry, thirsty and exhausted. Michael sulked for three hours. 'Portrait of a person in a fucking awful temper,' said Auden, amused and clinically observant.

Isafjördur, which the ship reached the following day, was the place Auden thought the most beautiful he had visited in Iceland. Here they left the *Dettifoss* and, while waiting to find a motor-boat to take them further up the fjörd to Melgraseyri, stayed at the Salvation Army hostel, using the North Pole Café as their daytime base. They were unable to find anything to drink in the town, and in desperation approached the British Vice-Consul who produced a bottle of Spanish brandy. 'Almost kissing him we stumbled in our gum-boots as fast as we could to the Salvation Army where we behaved most disreputably. In one of our bedrooms, beneath a notice on the wall saying NO CARD PLAYING, we swiftly dealt our cards for rummy, the brandy in tooth mugs by our sides, "feeling like schoolboys hiding our sins from the maid".'

126

At last they found a motor-boat to take them to Melgraseyri, where they spent a blissful few days on a farm, enjoying warm hospitality in very beautiful surroundings. They were sad when the time came to return to Reykjavik and thence to England.

Among Auden's letters in *Letters from Iceland* is one which he described as 'a little donnish experiment in objective narrative', and which he addressed to William Coldstream, Esq. In one passage, he lists several of the more graphic moments of his tour, including some already mentioned:

Louis read George Eliot in bed
And Michael and I climbed the cliff behind Hraensnef
And I *was* so frightened, my dear.
And we all rowed on the lake and giggled because the boat leaked
And the farmer was angry when we whipped his horses
And Louis had a dream – unrepeatable but he repeated it –
And the lady at table had diabetes, poor thing
And Louis dreamt of a bedroom with four glass walls
And I was upset because they told me I didn't look innocent
(I liked it really of course)
And the whaling station wouldn't offer us any coffee
And Michael didn't speak for three hours after that
And the first motor-boat we hired turned back because of the weather
'A hot spot' he said but we and the vice consul didn't believe him
And that cost an extra ten kronur.
And it was after ten when we really got there and could discover a landing
And we walked up to the farm in the dark
Over a new mown meadow, the dogs running in and out of the lamplight
And I woke in the night to hear Louis vomiting
    Something like a ship siren
And I played 'O Isis and Osiris' on the harmonium next day
And we read the short stories of Somerset Maugham aloud to each other
And the best one was called *His Excellency*.
And I said to Michael 'All power corrupts' and he was very angry about it.
And he ate thirty-two cakes in an afternoon
And the soup they gave us on the last day tasted of hair oil
And we had to wrap the salt fish in an envelope not to hurt their feelings.

Auden was back in London for the publication on 24 September of *The Ascent of F.6* which he and Isherwood had dedicated to Auden's brother John. The following day, the first performance was given, at the Norwich Festival, of Benjamin Britten's *Our Hunting Fathers*, a song cycle for high voice and orchestra on which he had collaborated with Auden. Auden had chosen man's relationship with the animal world as his subject, and had selected three poems showing animals as pests, as pets and as prey – an anonymous prayer for deliverance from rats, an anonymous dirge on the death of a monkey, and a poem by Thomas Ravenscroft – and had framed them with a prologue and an epilogue which he himself wrote. The title of the cycle was derived from the opening lines of the epilogue, 'Our hunting fathers told the story/Of the sadness of the creatures'. The performance at Norwich 'amused the sophisticated, scandalized those among the gentry who caught Auden's words, and left musicians dazzled at so much talent, uneasy that it should be expended on so arid a subject, not knowing whether to consider Britten's daring style as the outcome of courage or foolhardiness.'[1]

Britten was now in his twenty-fourth year, and was beginning to make a real effect in the musical world. (The following year, his *Variations on a Theme of Frank Bridge* for string orchestra received its first performance at the Salzburg Festival, to great acclaim.) In the opinion of the 'Auden gang', the brilliant young composer was emotionally retarded. In a mock 'Last Will and Testament' which Auden and MacNeice jointly included, for no very clear reason, in *Letters from Iceland*, Auden wrote: 'For my friend Benjamin Britten, composer, I beg / That fortune send him soon a passionate affair.' And Christopher Isherwood and Basil Wright, dining one evening with Britten, said to each other while he was out of the room, 'Well, have we convinced Ben he's queer, or haven't we?'

In October, Auden's new volume of poems was published. The title he had given it, when he had delivered the typescript to Faber & Faber before sailing to Iceland, was *Poems 1936*, but the publisher's sales manager thought this unsatisfactory, and T. S. Eliot asked Auden to supply another title. Eliot's letter reached Auden in Iceland, and the poet replied with two alternatives, *It's a Way* or *The Island*, adding that 'On the analogy of *Burnt Norton* I might call it *Piddle-in-the-Hole*.' However, by the time Auden's letter reached London, Faber & Faber had had to go ahead with the printing, and had chosen a title, *Look, Stranger!*, taken from the first line of one of the poems:

> Look, stranger, on this island now
> The leaping light for your delight discovers,
> Stand stable here
> And silent be,
> That through the channels of the ear
> May wander like a river
> The swaying sound of the sea . . .

Auden was displeased, and wrote to his American publisher, Bennett Cerf

[1] Scott Goddard in *British Music of Our Time* (ed. A. L. Bacharach; London, 1946).

of Random House: 'As regards the latter [*Look, Stranger!*] Faber invented a bloody title while I was away without telling me. It sounds like the work of a vegetarian lady novelist. Will you please call the American edition *On this Island*.' *On this Island* was published in the United States four months later, in February 1937. In due course, Auden attached this title to the previously untitled poem, 'Look, Stranger . . .'

Auden spent much of the autumn and winter of 1936 putting *Letters from Iceland* together, in collaboration with Louis MacNeice. The result was something far removed from the conventional travel book. There is, it is true, a chapter of thirteen pages with reasonably practical information for travellers, but by far the greater part of the book consists of Auden's chatty letters in prose to Erika Mann Auden, in verse to Lord Byron, R. H. S. Crossman and William Coldstream, and in both verse and prose to Christopher Isherwood. (Auden's casual attitude to misprints is demonstrated in the poem at the beginning of his letter to Isherwood, which contains the line, 'And the ports have names for the sea'. What he had written was the more prosaic 'And the poets have names for the sea'. Rightly, he decided that the printed version was an improvement.) MacNeice contributed equally discursive verse epistles to his friends as well as the outrageous 'Hetty to Nancy' letter, and a chapter of extracts from earlier writers on Iceland is thrown in for good measure, as well as the jointly written poem entitled 'Auden and MacNeice: Their Last Will and Testament', and a number of excellent photographs taken by Auden.

With work on the book almost completed, Auden wrote on 8 December to an old teacher and friend of his family, E. R. Dodds, who had been Professor of Greek at Birmingham University for twelve years:

> I've decided to go out in the New Year, as soon as the book is finished, to join the International Brigade in Spain. I so dislike everyday political activities that I won't do them, but here is something I can do as a citizen and not as a writer, and as I have no dependants I feel I ought to go; but, O, I do hope there are not too many surrealists there. Please don't tell anyone about this. I shan't break it to my parents until after Christmas.[1]

Shortly afterwards, Auden enlarged upon his reasons for going to Spain, in a second letter to Dodds:

> I am not one of those who believe that poetry need or even should be directly political, but in a critical period such as ours, I do believe that the poet must have direct knowledge of the major political events. It is possible that in some periods the poet can absorb and feel all in his ordinary everyday life, perhaps the supreme masters always can, but for

[1] Quoted in *Missing Persons* by E. R. Dodds (London, 1977).

the second order, and particularly today, what the poet knows, what he can write about, is what he has experienced in his own person. Academic knowledge is not enough.

I feel I can speak with authority about *la condition humaine* of only a small clan of English intellectuals and professional people and that the time has come to gamble on something bigger.

I shall probably be a bloody bad soldier but how can I speak to/for them without becoming one?[1]

In other words, the time had come for Auden to translate his political beliefs into action. Since those beliefs had never been clearly formulated, it is hardly surprising that the action they led to should turn out to be confused and indecisive.

[1] Displayed at the 'Young Writers of the Thirties' Exhibition at the National Portrait Gallery, London, 1976, and quoted in *The New Review* (No 28, July 1976).

Chapter Six

1937–1938

Pick a quarrel, go to war,
Leave the hero in the bar;
Hunt the lion, climb the peak:
No one guesses you are weak. [1]

The Spanish Civil War, which had begun in July 1936 while Auden was in Iceland, acted upon the imaginations of young writers in a number of countries, and perhaps nowhere more strongly than in England. The struggle seemed unambiguous, the cause just. The battle between the forces of reaction and those of liberation, so often enacted in their poems and plays by the writers of the thirties, was now being waged in reality. The immediate response was a dramatic increase in writing about the cause, and specifically about the Spanish war, most of it propaganda and much of that fairly crude propaganda. By the end of the year, a number of stories and poems had appeared in literary magazines, and in March 1937 the Left Theatre Revue included a short play about the International Brigade which had been formed to come to the defence of the Spanish Loyalist government. As the months wore on, the conflict began to seem more complex, more real than the idealistic war it had at first claimed to be. Reports came back from those who had actually been to Spain and seen the reality behind the rhetoric.

A number of young men in Great Britain volunteered to fight against General Franco's forces in Spain. The majority of them were Communists, but there was a sizeable non-committed minority as well, who volunteered because they believed in freedom, and perhaps because they sensed that what was then happening in Spain could easily become the prelude to a wider European conflict. Also, it was an adventure, which was given a kind of respectability by its ideological nature: the old saga/public school world of 'Paid on Both Sides' brought to real life. John Lehmann, in his autobiography, described the atmosphere of the time:

> When the full significance of what was happening in Spain gradually became apparent, and all the political parties, organizations, the unattached liberals, intellectuals and artists who had become aware that their own fate was deeply involved in the battles developing in front of Madrid and Barcelona, had banded themselves together to organize the Inter-

[1] From 'Shorts'.

131

national Brigade and the Spanish Medical Aid, I think every young writer began seriously to debate with himself how he could best be of use, by joining the Brigade, or driving an ambulance, or helping the active committees in England or France, or in some other way. The pull was terrific: the pull of an international crusade to the ideals and aims of which all intellectuals (except those of strong Catholic attachment) who had been stirred by the fascist danger, felt they could in that hour of apocalypse, whole-heartedly assent.[1]

'I shall probably be a bloody bad soldier', Auden had predicted. He had, at least, intended to be a soldier, but by the time of his departure for Spain he had changed his mind, and now offered himself as an ambulance driver. Before Christmas he had written to Isherwood, 'I'm going to Spain in early January, either ambulance-driving or fighting. I hope the former. Is there any chance of seeing you in Paris on my way through? In case of accidents remember that you and Edward [Upward] are executors.'[2] On 11 January Auden travelled from London, seen off by a few friends including William Coldstream, to Paris, where Isherwood met him the next day at the Hôtel Quai Voltaire. They spent the day drinking with the indolent Brian Howard, one of Auden's Oxford contemporaries, a young man who devoted considerably more energy to the conduct of his social life and his homosexual affairs than to the development or use of his undoubted literary talents, and whose friends found him alternately amusing and, when he was drunk, impossibly boorish. In the evening Auden and Isherwood met up with several other people at the Café Flore where Auden was first introduced to James and Tania Stern, who were to become his close friends.

James Stern, the short story writer, and his German-born wife Tania were then living in Paris. Of his first meeting with Auden, Stern later remembered Auden's professed dislike not only of the French but also of their language, which he never learned to speak with any fluency. At the Café Flore that evening, Auden sat with a cup of coffee, his head buried in a book. 'Needless to say, all five or six of us had drinks. He didn't. He had a coffee. And should someone suggest a drink, he would shake his head and grunt. Pale, smooth-skinned, full-lipped, with a large brown mole on each cheek, he sat there, bent over, oblivious, absorbed.'[3] The following day, Auden's friends saw him off to Spain. He had a bad cold, but was generally cheerful, though anxious about his luggage which had already been sent on in error to the Spanish border, and which he feared he had lost.

Auden's departure for Spain had received a certain amount of publicity in

[1] *The Whispering Gallery* (London, 1955).
[2] Letter quoted in *Christopher and His Kind*.
[3] James Stern in *W. H. Auden: A Tribute*.

England. The day after he left London, the *Daily Worker* announced that 'W. H. Auden, the most famous of the younger English poets, co-author of *The Dog Beneath the Skin*, recently produced in London, and a leading figure in the anti-Fascist movement, has left for Spain. He will serve as an ambulance driver.'[1] Nine days later, the *Sunday Times* informed its readers, under a headline, 'Auden, on Eve of New Play, Goes to Madrid', that 'W. H. Auden, the poet, has left England for Spain to take part in the defence of Madrid. It is unlikely that he will be present to see his new play, *The Ascent of F.6*, written in collaboration with Christopher Isherwood, when it is produced at the Mercury Theatre at the end of February.'

In fact, Auden appears not to have got to Madrid, but only to Barcelona and Valencia. He found to his dismay that the Republican Government did not want him to drive an ambulance, and would not allow him to. Perhaps they had heard about his driving from other left-wing British poets. What he was allowed to do was to broadcast propaganda for their cause, but as his broadcasts were in English and were transmitted over a radius of not much more than fifty miles, they cannot have been of the slightest practical use. Auden's value to the Government lay in the publicity emanating from the announcement of his visit. It was not necessary for him actually to have made the visit. Disillusioned, he remained in Spain for several weeks, returning to England early in March. Among other English writers in Spain in 1937 were Stephen Spender, who had left his friend Tony and had married the previous autumn, and Cyril Connolly, both of whom were there as journalists. Connolly, who took his wife with him, later described meeting Auden at the poet's hotel in Valencia, having been given his whereabouts by Isherwood: 'Auden, who was working for the government radio, seemed overjoyed to meet us and ordered a bottle of Spanish champagne, a detail which delighted Isherwood, who said it would have convinced him that it was the real Auden and not some imposter.' Some weeks later they met again in Valencia, where,

> after a good lunch with much Perelada Tinto, we went for a walk in the gardens of Monjuich. By the remains of the old International Exhibition Auden retired to pee behind a bush and was immediately seized by two militia men – or were they military police? They were very indignant at this abuse of public property and it took several wavings of Harry Pollitt's letter[2] to set him free.[3]

Another comical view of Auden in Spain is provided by the journalist

[1] 12 January 1937.
[2] Pollitt was Secretary of the Communist Party of Great Britain.
[3] Cyril Connolly in *W. H. Auden: A Tribute*.

Claud Cockburn, a Communist Party member who was working for the Republican Government:

> At the outset Auden had the feeling that life could not be carried on at all without some kind of union with the Party. So he came to Spain; of course, what we really wanted him for was to go to the front, write some pieces saying hurrah for the Republic, and then go away and write some poems, also saying hurrah for the Republic; and that would be his job in the war – and bloody important at that. Instead of which, unfortunately, he took the whole thing terribly seriously; he wanted to *do* something . . . When Auden came out we got a car laid on for him and everything. We thought we'd whisk him to Madrid and that the whole thing would be a matter of a week before the end-product started firing. But not at all: the bloody man went off and got a donkey, a mule really, and announced that he was going to walk through Spain with this creature. From Valencia to the front. He got six miles from Valencia before the mule kicked him or something and only then did he return and get in the car to do his proper job.[1]

Cockburn may have embroidered his memories somewhat, but it must be admitted that his account of Auden's behaviour sounds plausible. It is almost certain that in his last weeks in Spain Auden did get to the front for a very brief period. The poet himself in later years was willing to remember no more than that he had wandered about Barcelona and Valencia with nothing to do, to speculate that perhaps he had not been given responsible tasks because he was not a party member, and to complain that sheer bureaucracy prevented him from being given an ambulance to drive. At the time, he obviously felt the entire episode to have been an embarrassing fiasco, and refused to speak in detail about it, even to his friends. He may not have seen much actual fighting, but he was disconcerted by much of what he did see; his disillusionment with the Communist cause began, not surprisingly, with his first glimpse of Communism in action. Twenty-five years later, he wrote to an enquirer: 'I did not wish to talk about Spain when I returned because I was upset by many things I saw or heard about. Some of them were described better than I could ever have done by George Orwell in *Homage to Catalonia*. Others were what I learned about the treatment of priests.'[2] Auden's disquiet is not apparent in the only article he sent back to England from Spain. He wrote it quite early in his stay, and it was published in *The New Statesman* on 30 January. Even allowing for the fact that descriptive prose was not Auden's metier, 'Impressions of Valencia' is a curiously

[1] Claud Cockburn, interviewed in *The Review, 11–12* (1964).
[2] Letter to Hugh D. Ford, 29 November 1962. Quoted in Ford's *A Poet's War* (Philadelphia, 1965).

muted piece, which could have been written by someone on the *New Statesman* staff, without leaving London:

The pigeons fly about the square in brilliant sunshine, warm as a fine English May. In the centre of the square, surrounded all day long by crowds and surmounted by a rifle and fixed bayonet, 15ft. high, is an enormous map of the Civil War, rather prettily illustrated after the manner of railway posters urging one to visit Lovely Lakeland or Sunny Devon. Badajoz is depicted by a firing-party; a hanged man represents Huelva; a doll's train and lorry are heading for Madrid; at Seville Quiepo el Llano is frozen in an eternal broadcast. The General seems to be the Little Willie of the war; in a neighbouring shop window a strip of comic woodcuts shows his rake's progress from a perverse childhood to a miserable and well-merited end.

Altogether it is a great time for the poster artist and there are some very good ones. Cramped in a little grey boat the Burgos Junta, dapper Franco and his bald German adviser, a cardinal and two ferocious Moors are busy hanging Spain; a green Fascist centipede is caught in the fanged trap of Madrid; in photomontage a bombed baby lies couchant upon a field of aeroplanes.

Today a paragraph in the daily papers announces that since there have been incidents at the entrances to cabarets, these will in future be closed at nine p.m. Long streamers on the public buildings appeal for unity, determination and discipline. Three children, with large brown eyes like some kind of very rich sweet, are playing trains round the fountain. On one of the ministries a huge black arrow draws attention to the fact that the front at Teruel is only 150km. away. This is the Spain for which charming young English aviators have assured us that the best would be a military dictatorship backed by a foreign Power.

Since the Government moved here the hotels are crammed to bursting with officials, soldiers and journalists. There are porters at the station and a few horse-cabs, but no taxis, in order to save petrol. Food is plentiful, indeed an hotel lunch is heavier than one could wish. There is a bull-fight in aid of the hospitals; there is a variety show where an emaciated-looking tap-dancer does an extremely sinister dance of the machine-guns. The foreign correspondents come in for their dinner, conspicuous as actresses.

And everywhere there are the people. They are here in corduroy breeches with pistols on their hip, in uniform, in civilian suits and berets. They are here, sleeping in the hotels, eating in the restaurants, in the cafés drinking and having their shoes cleaned. They are here, driving fast cars on business, running the trains and the trams, keeping the streets clean, doing all those things that the gentry cannot believe will be properly done unless they are there to keep an eye on them. This is the bloodthirsty and unshaven Anarchy of the bourgeois cartoon, the end of civilization from which Hitler has sworn to deliver Europe.

For a revolution is really taking place, not an odd shuffle or two in cabinet appointments. In the last six months these people have been learning what it is to inherit their own country, and once a man has tasted freedom he will not lightly give it up; freedom to choose for himself and to organize his life, freedom not to depend for good fortune on a clever and outrageous piece of overcharging or a windfall of drunken charity. That is why, only eight hours away at the gates of Madrid where this wish to live has no possible alternative expression than the power to kill, General Franco has already lost two professional armies and is in the process of losing a third.

But General Franco, unfortunately, was not losing; and by the time Auden left Spain at the beginning of March, although his detestation of what Franco stood for was as strong as ever, his admiration for international Communism and its intervention in the Spanish struggle was no longer uncritical. Oddly, his journey to Spain to support an anti-clerical government played its part in Auden's eventual return to Christianity. 'On arriving in Barcelona,' he wrote many years later,

> I found as I walked through the city that all the churches were closed and there was not a priest to be seen. To my astonishment, this discovery left me profoundly shocked and disturbed. The feeling was far too intense to be the result of a mere liberal dislike of intolerance, the notion that it is wrong to stop people from doing what they like, even if it is something silly like going to church. I could not escape acknowledging that, however I had consciously ignored and rejected the Church for sixteen years, the existence of churches and what went on in them had all the time been very important to me.[1]

The phrase 'liberal dislike' is significant. For all his talk about Marxism, Auden's attitudes were really never any further left than an uncommitted, radical liberalism. Day Lewis and Spender did become members of the Communist Party for a time in the thirties, but Auden never committed himself totally to the cause. And all three of them, indeed the English literary left in general, began to retreat from commitment to Communism, as they began to understand the difference between a sentimental, unthinking attachment to Marxist principles and a conscious assent to the methods employed by Soviet Communism under Stalin both in Russia and abroad.

[1] In his contribution to *Modern Canterbury Pilgrims* (ed. James A. Pike, New York, 1956).

Auden's visit to Spain, however, did produce a remarkable poem, 'Spain', which he wrote after his return in March, and which Faber & Faber published in May as a sixteen-page booklet, price one shilling, the poet's royalties being donated to Medical Aid for Spain.

A longish poem of nearly a hundred lines, 'Spain' was generally acclaimed as one of the finest poems Auden had written, and one of the best to have come out of the Spanish conflict. But it is not a piece of propaganda, and, read today, it does not seem totally devoted to the Marxist cause. It is a mature, complex and moving poem not so much about Spain as about political struggle and moral choice. To some extent, it is an abstract and rather cold examination of its subject; the Communist literary critics of the thirties certainly thought it at best lukewarm, but it was appreciated by critics not aligned to any political parties as a firm statement, made from Auden's own unideological position, of the agonizing difficulty of reaching moral decisions in the modern political world.

> 'What's your proposal? To build the Just City? I will.
> I agree. Or is it the suicide pact, the romantic
>   Death? Very well, I accept, for
> I am your choice, your decision: yes, I am Spain.'

> Many have heard it on remote peninsulas,
> On sleepy plains, in the aberrant fisherman's islands,
>   In the corrupt heart of the city;
> Have heard and migrated like gulls or the seeds of a flower.

> They clung like burrs to the long expresses that lurch
> Through the unjust lands, through the night, through the
>   alpine tunnel;
>   They floated over the oceans;
> They walked the passes; they came to present their lives.

The poem's final sentence, 'We are left alone with our day, and the time is short, and/History to the defeated/May say Alas but cannot help nor pardon', was condemned by Auden as a 'wicked doctrine' nearly thirty years later when he excluded the entire poem from his *Collected Shorter Poems*, but in its context it was an honest, if harsh, statement of fact. (In the fifties, Auden crossed out the last two lines in Cyril Connolly's copy of 'Spain', and scribbled in the margin, 'This is a lie.' Other friends' copies were annotated in similar fashion.)

Before going to Spain, Auden had written a commentary in verse for a documentary film, *The Way to the Sea*, produced by Paul Rotha for the Strand

Film Company. The subject of the film was the electrification of the Waterloo–Portsmouth railway line, and Auden's verse described the train journey. *The Way to the Sea*, with music by Benjamin Britten, was released early in 1937 while Auden was in Spain. An event of more importance to him, which also took place during his absence, was the opening night of the Group Theatre production of *The Ascent of F.6* at the Mercury Theatre, Notting Hill Gate, on 26 February. Isherwood had travelled to London to attend rehearsals, and had enjoyed watching Rupert Doone direct the production. He got on with Doone rather better than Auden had. Isherwood's own explanation for this was that 'being both small men and both prima donnas', they were natural allies. The natural allies were great admirers of the young Mickey Rooney, and the dress rehearsal of *F.6* was held up because Doone and Isherwood had taken themselves to see a new Mickey Rooney film, *The Devil is a Sissy* (retitled in England *The Devil Takes the Count*). 'Having once sat down in the cinema, they couldn't tear themselves away from this outrageous but potent tearjerker until it ended. By the time they reached the Mercury, the cast had been kept waiting for nearly an hour. Rupert, showing not the faintest trace of guilt and offering no explanations, started work immediately.'[1]

Doone offended the 'pale, boyish, indefatigable' Benjamin Britten by attempting to cut some of his incidental music at the final rehearsal, and Isherwood had to agree to cuts in the text as well, but the first night of the play was an immense success. Isherwood was in a state of such excitement that he kept repeating, 'Oh dear, what shall I do? I don't think I can sit down.' Britten wrote in his diary for that night: 'After the show we all have a good party at the theatre & then feeling very cheerful we all sing (all cast & about 20 audience) my blues as well as going thro' most of the music of the play! Then I play & play & play, while the whole cast dances & sings & fools, & gets generally wild.'

E. M. Forster, who was present, wrote to Isherwood immediately afterwards with criticisms of the play and the production, and, in consequence, Isherwood kept altering the end of the play, several endings being tried out in performance over the next week or two. Forster had already made several criticisms of the printed play in his review in *The Listener*,[2] and Stephen Spender in the *Left Review* had written that the hero, Ransom, was 'a colossal prig, a fact of which the authors seem insufficiently aware'.[3]

Critical opinion, however, was for the most part in favour of *The Ascent of F.6*. Although he found its morality questionable, C. Day Lewis thought the play showed a 'marked forward development' from *The Dog Beneath the Skin*,

[1] *Christopher and His Kind.*
[2] 14 October 1936.
[3] November 1936.

the construction firmer, and the verse no less fine.[1] The *New Statesman* considered that the authors had pumped life into a dead literary form and that, in the verse passages, Auden had written 'some of the best rhetorical poetry of this generation'. 'The play shows a more successful synthesis of literature and propaganda than anything Mr Auden, or Mr Auden and Mr Isherwood, have yet done', said the *London Mercury*. But a note of dissent was struck by Derek Verschoyle in *The Spectator*:

> The first act, which ends with Ransom's decision to lead the expedition, is remarkably good; but from that point the play decreases in coherence and force until it dies weakly in the muddle of the final scene. On the whole the production and performance were good. Mr Rupert Doone managed to restrain his liking for the flashier tricks of modernist staging until quite near the end, the settings were simple and appropriate, Mr William Devlin gave an admirable performance in the central part, and there was good acting from Mr Barry Barnes, Mr Edward Lexy and Mr Erik Chitty. The incidental music composed by Mr Benjamin Britten was both unnecessary and unpleasing.[2]

The version of the play performed at the Mercury Theatre differed somewhat from that published the previous autumn, for the authors had made some alterations in the light of the criticisms by Forster, Spender and others, and Auden had written to his American publisher: 'Isherwood and I are now altering it quite considerably. Faber published it early against our will and I shall be very glad if the American edition were to be the definitive one.' But their changes tended to obscure and, in some instances, to contradict the meaning of the passages replaced. Admittedly, meaning was never Auden's greatest interest. The changes Isherwood made during the play's run brought a further confusion to the proceedings. Auden returned from Spain on 4 March, unwilling to talk about his experiences there, even to Isherwood. On his first evening back he accompanied his co-author to a performance of their play, at which, to the amusement of many members of the audience, he turned to Christopher and said, in loud, reproachful tones, 'My *dear*, what have you *done* to it?'

The play continued to do well, and on 30 April the production was transferred to the Little Theatre. But a definitive text was not achieved for many years. Alterations were made from production to production, no two of which used exactly the same script. A version presented at the Arts Theatre, Cambridge, on 23 April differed from the Group Theatre's in several respects. Conscious of the fact that the ending, in particular, was not right, Auden and Isherwood went on worrying away at it, rewriting it for a

---

[1] *Poetry* (January 1937).
[2] 5 March 1937.

production by the Drove Players in New York in April 1939, for a projected production in August at the Bucks County Playhouse, Pennsylvania (which failed to materialize) with Burgess Meredith producing and playing Ransom, and for a London revival at the Old Vic in June 1939, with Alec Guinness as Ransom. Auden made a further revision of the ending for a college production in the United States in which he appeared himself as the cowled monk in Act II, scene i. But if the ending was never got right, this suggests that much that preceded the ending was also not right. The character of the hero, Ransom, whether one thinks him priggish or not, suffers from the co-authors' inability to decide upon their attitude to him. He seems to combine the Truly Strong Man so admired by them both, and a neurotic imitation of such a man, which, to a certain extent, is what the co-authors were. In a letter to E. M. Forster from Portugal, shortly after he and Auden had completed the play, Isherwood had written:

> *The Ascent of F.6* is about an expedition up a mountain and attempts to explain why people climb them . . . Which brings me to T. E. Lawrence . . . Please don't expect our *F.6* to cast a dazzling light on the subject. I only say the play's about him for shorthand-descriptive purposes. The whole conflict is entirely different and much clumsier, as it seems to have to be on the stage. It's only about Lawrence in so far as the problem of personal ambition versus the contemplative life is concerned.[1]

Auden's and Isherwood's difficulty lay in the fact that not only was Lawrence a more complex character than could easily be portrayed on stage, but also that Auden's attitude to Lawrence was constantly changing.

Shortly before he went to Spain, Auden had written one of his most beautiful lyric poems, 'Lay your sleeping head, my love,/Human on my faithless arm', addressed to a teenage boy:

> Lay your sleeping head, my love,
> Human on my faithless arm;
> Time and fevers burn away
> Individual beauty from
> Thoughtful children, and the grave
> Proves the child ephemeral:
> But in my arms till break of day
> Let the living creature lie,
> Mortal, guilty, but to me
> The entirely beautiful . . .

The poem appeared in *New Writing*, 3 in the spring, and Auden also transcribed it inside the front cover of Britten's copy of the first edition of their

---

[1] Quoted in *Christopher and His Kind*.

joint work, *Our Hunting Fathers*. He considered writing, in collaboration with Stephen Spender, a travel book about America, and actually signed a contract to do so. The book was never written. Living now partly in London and partly at his parents' house in Birmingham, Auden continued to publish poems and reviews. He was beginning now a habit, which continued for the rest of his life, of using drugs to set him up in the morning and to ease him into sleep at night: Benzedrine to start the day, and Seconal to end it. (It was only much later that he began to drink heavily as well.) He went back to the Downs School, Colwall, to teach for the summer term of 1937, but also continued to interest himself in the course of the war in Spain. In June, he allowed his name to be used as one of twelve signatories to a questionnaire which asked writers to declare themselves either for or against Franco and Fascism. The other signatories included Louis Aragon, Heinrich Mann, Pablo Neruda, Stephen Spender and Tristan Tzara. The replies, together with the questionnaire, were published by the *Left Review* in a booklet, *Authors Take Sides on the Spanish War*, at the end of the year. Auden's own cautiously worded reply read:

I support the Valencia Government in Spain because its defeat by the forces of International Fascism would be a major disaster for Europe. It would make a European war more probable; and the spread of Fascist Ideology and practice to countries as yet comparatively free of them, which would inevitably follow upon a Fascist victory in Spain, would create an atmosphere in which the creative artist and all who care for justice, liberty and culture would find it impossible to work or even exist.

Many of the other replies are predictable or characteristic (Evelyn Waugh: 'If I were a Spaniard I should be fighting for General Franco'; T. S. Eliot: 'While I am naturally sympathetic, I still feel convinced that it is best that at least a few men of letters should remain isolated'; Ezra Pound: 'Spain is an emotional luxury to a gang of sap-headed dilettantes'). Some are violent (Aleister Crowley: 'Franco is a common murderer and pirate: should swing in chains at Execution Dock'), others pacific (Aldous Huxley: 'To me, the necessity of pacifism seems absolutely clear'). Samuel Beckett was brief: '! Uptherepublic !'

It was during the summer that Auden met the novelist and poet Charles Williams, who worked for the Oxford University Press, and proposed to him that there should be an addition to the series of Oxford books of verse. The *Book of Modern Verse* edited by Yeats lacked authority, he claimed, and while the fifteenth-, sixteenth- and seventeenth-century volumes were adequate there was a need for an *Oxford Book of Light Verse*. Williams expressed the view that books of light verse were always very depressing when actually in front of one, but Auden insisted that light verse showed the differences between the sensibilities of various periods even better than what he called the more solemn stuff. Williams conscientiously reported Auden's proposal to the Delegates of the OUP who accepted it, and Auden was duly commissioned to edit *The Oxford Book of Light Verse*.

In the autumn Auden was awarded, and disconcerted some of his friends by accepting, the King's Gold Medal for Poetry, given for his most recent volume of verse, *Look, Stranger!* In August, *Letters from Iceland* had been published, and reviews now began to appear. Edward Sackville West in the *New Statesman*[1] noted that the authors had 'thrown loosely together everything that happened to occur to them in the course of their desultory journey, from serious poems to menus', and considered that the resulting extravaganza made very easy reading. He observed, however, that they had 'found a certain difficulty in making Iceland itself seem interesting.'

Goronwy Rees, in the *Spectator*,[2] was distinctly bad-tempered. 'It is extremely difficult,' he pointed out,

> to write a good travel book if you have no interest in your travels, a bad stomach, dislike of journeys, an eye obscured by rheum, and a liability to colds. Despite immense ingenuity, the authors have not overcome these handicaps . . . perhaps what the two authors would themselves most desire is that this book (apart from two poems, one by each of them, which give pleasure) should lapse into the oblivion from which the Book Society has so unkindly rescued it.

Other reviewers were politely dismissive. Even Christopher Isherwood, in *The Listener*,[3] complained that there was not much in the book about Iceland and the Icelanders, and added: 'Poets never seem to notice anything; it is a pity there was no novelist in the party.' One of the most favourable reviews was in the Chicago magazine, *Poetry*,[4] whose critic did not seem to mind that the authors told him more about themselves than about Iceland. He thought *Letters from Iceland* 'one of the wittiest, most entertaining books of recent years'. Perhaps the fairest comment of all is that of Louis MacNeice, who devoted only one sentence of his autobiography to *Letters from Iceland*. 'Our travel book,' he wrote, 'was a hodge-podge, thrown together in gaiety.'

While he was teaching the summer term at the Downs School, Auden was visited for a few days by Brian Howard whom he tried to encourage into a more professional attitude to writing. He even offered to collaborate on a book with Howard, or at least to advise him and perhaps write a Foreword;

[1] 7 August 1937.
[2] 3 September 1937.
[3] 11 August 1937.
[4] April 1938.

but Auden's description of his working methods, which involved rising at 8.15 every morning and working until 4 p.m., sounded far too exhausting to Howard. A much more engaging and productive collaborator was Benjamin Britten who, in 1937, composed a highly acclaimed song cycle, *On This Island*, using five poems by Auden, four of them from the volume, *Look, Stranger!* (or *On This Island*) and one from *The Dog Beneath the Skin*. Britten and Auden also worked together during the year on two radio programmes: 'Up the garden path', a recital of bad music and bad poetry which they chose jointly and which was broadcast in the BBC's Regional programme on 13 June; and 'Hadrian's Wall', which was commissioned by Auden's old school-friend John Pudney, who had now become a BBC producer. For 'Hadrian's Wall', Auden wrote an imaginative script about the Roman wall which stretches across the north of England, and about the Roman army of occupation. Britten composed original music with important parts for a chorus, and conducted it himself in the BBC's Newcastle studios. Auden's poem, 'Roman wall blues', was written for this programme, which was first broadcast on 25 November.

> Over the heather the wet wind blows,
> I've lice in my tunic and a cold in my nose.
>
> The rain comes pattering out of the sky,
> I'm a wall soldier, I don't know why.
>
> The mist creeps over the hard grey stone,
> My girl's in Tungria; I sleep alone.
>
> Aulus goes hanging around her place,
> I don't like his manners, I don't like his face.
>
> Piso's a Christian, he worships a fish;
> There'd be no kissing if he had his wish.
>
> She gave me a ring but I diced it away;
> I want my girl and I want my pay.
>
> When I'm a veteran with only one eye
> I shall do nothing but look at the sky.

Auden, Isherwood and Spender were among a number of writers invited to attend a Writers' Congress in Madrid to discuss the attitude of the world's intellectuals to the Spanish war. The Foreign Office refused them all visas, so only Stephen Spender went, entering Spain on a forged passport obtained for him by André Malraux, who travelled with him from the frontier to Madrid and explained that Ramos Ramos (the name on the passport) was a rare type of Spaniard, tall, blond and blue-eyed, who spoke a remote mountain dialect indistinguishable from English. When Spender returned from the Congress, he and his wife took a house near the Kentish coast for the rest of the summer, and here Auden visited them and wrote his ballad, 'James Honeyman'. The two friends talked of the Congress, and Spender described how it had been dominated by the fury aroused by André Gide's sharply critical account of the Soviet Union following his visit there. On his way back from Madrid, Spender had left a note for Gide in Paris, saying that he supported him in his desire to tell the truth about what he had seen in Russia. He reported this to Auden, who said, 'You were quite right. Exigence is never an excuse for not telling the truth.' Spender later recalled this conversation as a turning point in their attitude towards politics in the thirties.

In April, Auden had spent a few days in Paris. While there, he discovered that Christopher Isherwood's boy-friend Heinz was in trouble with the police and was about to be deported as an undesirable alien. Auden telephoned Christopher who was ill in London with a mouth infection, and Christopher sent another of his young admirers to Paris to escort Heinz to Luxembourg. In August, Heinz by this time having fallen into the hands of the German authorities and gone to prison, Isherwood and Auden took rooms in a house in Dover, at 9 East Cliff, on the harbour. Auden wanted to write a ballad, in the style of his 'James Honeyman' and 'Miss Gee', about Christopher's adventures with Heinz, but Isherwood objected to the idea, fearing that what he felt to be his private tragedy would be treated in the 'heartless comic style' of the earlier ballads. By the time he withdrew his veto, a year later, Auden had lost interest in the project. That summer in Dover, where they stayed until mid-September, Auden and Isherwood had two larger, joint projects to occupy them, a play and a travel book. The play was *On the Frontier*, of which they completed a first draft in Dover. (Auden wrote to his American publisher on 11 September to say that they had 'just finished a new play'; in fact, they did some more work on it *en route* to and from China the following year.) The travel book was one which, earlier in the summer, Faber & Faber in London and Random House in New York had jointly commissioned them to write. The commission was somewhat haphazard in that the choice of country or countries was left to the authors' discretion, though the publishers favoured somewhere in Asia. Auden and Isherwood discussed the project in Dover, and decided upon China, which was an exotic and unknown land, and had suddenly become, with the invasion of the Japanese Army in July, an extremely topical one. Also, unlike Spain, it was not, as Isherwood put it, 'already crowded with star literary observers'. 'We'll have a war of our very own,' said Wystan.

Frustrated in his desire to write a poem about Christopher and Heinz, Auden wrote instead a poem about Christopher. It is not a very good poem, for Auden rarely took much care with his informal pieces written for friends, but its tone of exasperated affection is engaging. The poem was never intended for publication, but was written into the preliminary pages of a copy of D. H. Lawrence's *Birds, Beasts and Flowers* which Auden gave to Isherwood on 3 September: hence, presumably, the style in imitation of Lawrence:

Who is that funny-looking young man so squat with a top-heavy head
A cross between a cavalry major and a rather prim landlady
Sitting there sipping a cigarette?
A brilliant young novelist?
You don't say!

Sitting in the corner of the room at a party, with his hair neatly
    brushed, quite clean,
Or lying on the beach in the sun
Just like the rest of the crowd
Just as brown, no, browner
Anonymous, just like us.

Wait a moment.

Wait till there's an opening in the conversation, or a chance to show off
And you strike like a lobster at a prawn
A roar of laughter. Aha, listen to that
Didn't you fool them beautifully,
Didn't they think you were nobody in particular,
That landlady
That major
Sold again.

With your great grey eyes taking everything in,
And your nicely creased trousers
Pretending to be nobody, to be quite humdrum and harmless
All the time perfectly aware of your powers
You puff-adder
You sham.

And your will, my word!
Don't you love to boss just everybody, everybody
To make all of us dance to your tune
Pied Piper
At an awkward moment.
Turning on your wonderful diplomacy like a fire-hose
Flattering, wheedling, threatening,
Drenching everybody.
Don't you love being ill,
Propped up on pillows, making us all dance attendance.
Do you think we don't see
Fussy old Major
Do you think we don't know what you're thinking?
'I'm the cleverest man of the age
The genius behind the scenes, the anonymous dictator
Cardinal Mazarin
Myecroft[1] Holmes
Lawrence of Arabia
Lady Asquith
Always right.'

And if anything goes wrong,
If absolutely the whole universe fails to bow to your command
If there's a mutiny in Neptune
A revolt in one of the farthest nebulae
How you stamp your bright little shoe
How you pout
House-proud old landlady
At times I could shake you.
Il y a des complaisances que je déteste.

Yet how beautiful your books are
So observant, so witty, so profound
And how nice you are really
So affectionate, so understanding, so helpful, such wonderful
    company
A brilliant young novelist?
My greatest friend?
Si, Signor.

---

[1] *Sic.* (Sherlock's elder brother spelt his name Mycroft.)

Standing here in Dover under the cliffs, with dotty England behind
  you
And challenging the provocative sea
With your enormous distinguished nose and your great grey eyes
Only 33 and a real diplomat already
Our great ambassador to the mad.

Use your will. We need it.[1]

Towards the end of November, Auden and Isherwood were both invited
to join a delegation of left-wing intellectuals and artists visiting Spain. The
invitation had already been accepted by Jacob Epstein, Paul Robeson and
several other celebrities. Auden felt that he ought to go, so a reluctant
Isherwood agreed to accompany him. 'The old war-horse will never again
desert its mate,' he said. But the delegation's travel permits were delayed,
and eventually Auden and Isherwood had to withdraw from the party, as
the time of their departure for China was drawing uncomfortably close.

Auden's literary fame had increased during 1937. His name was now
known to a wider circle of people, because of the plays and because of his
political pronouncements. But it was still in the smaller literary world that
his reputation was most secure, the world of the poetry magazines and little
reviews. At the beginning of the year, he and Michael Roberts had edited a
special English number of the Chicago magazine, *Poetry*, in which they had
included poems by Dylan Thomas, George Barker, William Empson, Edwin
Muir, Richard Church and Stephen Spender, as well as a review by Auden
of a volume of poems by William Plomer. Now, in November, the English
poetry magazine, *New Verse*, honoured Auden with a special 'Auden Double
Number', which in due course became a collector's item. The issue contained one new poem by Auden, the elegant, laconic 'Dover':

. . . The Old Town with its Keep and Georgian houses
Has built its routine upon such unusual moments;
Vows, tears, emotional farewell gestures,
Are common here, unremarkable actions
    Like ploughing or a tipsy song.

Soldiers crowd into the pubs in their pretty clothes,
As pink and silly as girls from a high-class academy;
The Lion, The Rose, The Crown, will not ask them to die,
Not here, not now: all they are killing is time,
    A pauper, civilian future.

[1] Quoted by Brian Finney in *Christopher Isherwood: A Critical Biography* (London, 1979).

Above them, expensive, shiny as a rich boy's bike,
Aeroplanes drone through the new European air
On the edge of a sky that makes England of minor importance;
And tides warn bronzing bathers of a cooling star
   With half its history done . . .

There were also a number of articles about the poet. Isherwood contributed 'Some Notes on Auden's Early Poetry', and Spender an account of Auden's progress from Oxford poseur ('he had a rather sinister public reputation for keeping a revolver in his desk') to quasi-Communist. Louis MacNeice wrote a 'Letter to W. H. Auden' which contained much sensible criticism and advice: 'I think you have shown great sense in not writing "proletarian" stuff (though some reviewers, who presumably did not read your poems, have accused you of it). You realise that one must write about what one knows. One may not hold the bourgeois creed, but if one knows only bourgeois one must write about them. They all, after all, contain the germ of their opposite.' MacNeice's letter ends: 'Poetry is related to the sermon and you have your penchant for preaching, but it is more closely related to conversation and you, my dear, are a born gossip.'

'Auden as a Monster' by the Editor, Geoffrey Grigson, is a splendidly belligerent piece, and there are less interesting articles by Kenneth Allott ('Auden in the Theatre') and Edgell Rickword ('Auden and Politics'). The issue is rounded off with 'Sixteen Comments on Auden' from Edwin Muir, George Barker, Frederic Prokosch (then a new young poet and novelist, and one of Auden's earliest American admirers), David Gascoyne, Dylan Thomas ('I sometimes think of his poetry as a great war, admire intensely the mature, religious and logical fighter, and deprecate the boy bush-ranger.'), Berthold Viertel (an Austrian film director: the 'original' of Friedrich Bergmann in Isherwood's novel, *Prater Violet*), C. Day Lewis, Allen Tate, Bernard Spencer, Charles Madge, Herbert Read, Ezra Pound ('I might be inclined to answer yr note IF I cd. discover why your little lot neglects to import cumming; W.C.W. and one or two other items of interest . . .'), John Masefield (who wrote simply 'All good wishes for the success of your tribute to Mr. Auden.'), Graham Greene ('to me Mr Auden is a long way the finest living poet'), Sir Hugh Walpole and W. J. Turner.

On 18 January 1938, the eve of their departure for China, a party was given for Auden and Isherwood. Arranged by Rupert Doone, it was held in the Hammersmith studio of another friend, the painter Julian Trevelyan, and the guests included the novelist Rose Macaulay, E. M. Forster and his friend Bob Buckingham, Brian Howard, Benjamin Britten and Louis Mac-Neice's future wife, Hedli Anderson. Hedli Anderson, accompanied by

Britten, sang three cabaret songs which Britten had just composed to words by Auden (including the haunting 'O tell me the truth about love', whose words and music are both in the manner of Cole Porter). People danced to a concertina, Forster and his friend enjoyed the party but detested the cheap wine-cup, and thought Rupert Doone 'an obvious crook', and an inebriated Brian Howard began a fight with someone (his host, perhaps?) by saying, 'I refuse to allow my friend to be insulted by the Worst Painter in London.' The following morning, the guests of honour took the boat-train for Dover, seen off by friends, journalists and cameramen. They spent the night in Paris, and then proceeded to Marseilles whence, on 21 January, they sailed for Hong Kong on the French liner *Aramis*, a ship of the Messageries Maritimes Line.

On board, they took it in turns to keep a travel diary, describing their social encounters with some of the passengers, among them a wealthy rubber merchant who was an admirer of Auden's poetry, and a young rubber planter returning from leave in England to his plantation near Singapore. When the ship docked at Port Said on 25 January, they were met by their old friend from Berlin days, Francis Turville-Petre, who was then living in Cairo and who insisted on showing them the city, although they wanted to explore Port Said which they had been led to believe was the sex capital of the world. Francis drove them to Cairo which they thought an 'immense and sinister Woolworth's where everything is for sale', showed them the Pyramids which Auden thought looked liked the tip-heaps of a quarry, and the Sphinx which impressed them. Auden wrote a poem about the Sphinx a few days later on the ship. A fellow-passenger assured him that the ancient Egyptians had foretold the future importance of America to the world, which was why the Sphinx faced to the west: this led Auden to include a line in the poem about the Sphinx 'gazing for ever towards shrill America'. But Auden then had doubts as to whether it did face west. Months later, back in London, he asked someone at the Egyptian Embassy, as a result of which he had to amend the line to read 'turning a vast behind on shrill America'.

Auden and Isherwood spent the night in Cairo with Francis, and rejoined their ship next morning at Port Taufiq, at the southern end of the Suez Canal. They were never to see Francis again, for he died in Egypt in 1942. The ship steamed on, calling at Djibouti on the Gulf of Aden, where they paid fifty francs to see three girls doing a very poor belly dance, Colombo which they thought 'an abandoned international exhibition', Singapore, and Saigon. At sea, they did a certain amount of rewriting of *On the Frontier*, and Auden wrote one or two more poems. On 16 February they reached Hong Kong where they stayed with the Vice Chancellor of the University for nearly a fortnight, meeting various local people, attending formal dinner parties, and finding the Victorian colonial atmosphere of the city not at all to their liking. 'The oxtail soup wasn't oxtail,' Wystan wrote in his journal, 'the women were cows and wore mermaid dresses; Sir Blank Blank, a squat red-faced toad, was reputed to have the Eighteenth Century Mind.' They met William Empson, on his way back to England from China where he had been Professor of English Literature at Peking University. Empson later wrote of his first meeting with Auden that 'he had the glamour of a correspondent. But he also had the glamour of Oscar Wilde; he was thick-necked and smoking big cigars and dining with the Governor of the Governor of Hong Kong, the Hong Kong-Shanghai Bank himself. He was very amusing.'[1]

On 28 February they left Hong Kong in the *Tai-Shan*, a river-boat, bound up-river for Canton. They were to spend the next fifteen weeks travelling around China, keeping a travel diary which in due course was to form the greater part of their book, *Journey to a War*. Although they passed close to a Japanese gunboat almost immediately upon leaving Hong Kong, the British-owned river-boats were being ignored by the Japanese so they were in no immediate danger. In fact, on only a very few days during their entire journey were they at all near the front-line fighting. For their stay in Canton, they were guests of an American and English missionary settlement in the village of Paak Hok Tung, half a mile down the river; their days were taken up with meeting the Mayor of Canton, dining with an americanized Chinese Colonel and his wife, lunching with the Governor of Kwantung Province, shopping, and wandering about the streets of Canton. They had visiting cards printed in English and Chinese, having been supplied by a friend in Hong Kong with phonetic Chinese names, Au Dung and Y Hsiao Wu. On their last evening in Canton they dined with the Captain of a British gunboat anchored in the river. Next day, they set out by train for Hankow, about four hundred miles to the north, undeterred by the fact that the railway line had been heavily bombed by the Japanese and that the journey might therefore take up to seven days. The train left at six in the evening, and by breakfast-time next morning it had reached the mountains. All that day, it pursued a cautious progress through the hot, fertile valleys of southern Hu-nan.

> The stewards hurried up and down the corridor with hot face-towels, bowls of rice, cups of tea. As the journey progressed the tea grew nastier, tasting increasingly of fish. The two armed guards in the corridor – one of them surely not more than twelve years old – peered into our compartment to watch the foreign devils screaming with laughter at mysterious jokes, singing in high falsetto or mock operatic voices, swaying rhythmically backwards and forwards on their seats, reading aloud to each other from small crimson-bound books. The swaying was an exercise which we

[1] In *The Harvard Advocate* (Vol. CVIII, Numbers Two and Three; Auden memorial issue).

invented, a vain effort to ward off constipation; the books were *Framley Parsonage* and *Guy Mannering*. Neither was a great success.[1]

The foreign devils caused the maximum amount of curiosity and amusement wherever they went in China, for Auden habitually wore a woollen cap and a huge overcoat, with carpet slippers instead of shoes, because of his corns, while Isherwood was usually attired in what he thought a war correspondent ought to wear, a beret, turtleneck sweater and riding-boots. The train journey took only three days, and by 8 March they were in Hankow, a fascinating old town almost all of whose clothing stores and restaurants were kept by White Russian emigrants. 'Their clocks,' said Auden, 'stopped in 1917. It has been tea-time ever since.' Here they met a number of interesting characters, among them Bishop Roots, the American Bishop of Hankow, Mr Donald, an Australian friend and advisor to Generalissimo and Madame Chiang Kai-Shek, and the Chiang Kai-Sheks themselves. They had tea with Madame who asked, in excellent, faintly American English, 'Please tell me, do poets like cake?'

'Yes,' replied Auden. 'Very much indeed.'

'Oh. I am glad to hear it. I thought perhaps they preferred only spiritual food.'

At the headquarters of General von Falkenhausen, Chiang Kai-Shek's chief German military advisor, the General's A.D.C. gave them some shattering news. 'Last night the German Army marched into Austria. Of course, it had to happen. And now I hope that England and Germany will be friends. That's what we Germans have always wanted. Austria was only causing trouble between us. A good thing the whole business is settled, once and for all.'

On one evening they went to a Chinese opera, on another they watched from the roof of one of Hankow's highest buildings as bombs fell out in the suburbs. Two days later, they proceeded further north by train to Chengchow, accompanied by a middle-aged Chinese servant, Chiang, whom they had acquired in Hankow. The seventeen-hour journey through a dry, bare landscape was uneventful, 'despite the usual prophecies of air-attack'.

At a single glance from the carriage window, one could seldom see less than two hundred people dotted over the paddy-fields, fishing with nets in village ponds, or squatting, on bare haunches, to manure the earth. Their gestures and attitudes had a timeless anonymity; each single figure would have made an admirable 'condition humaine' shot for a Russian peasant-film. What an anonymous country this is! Everywhere the labouring men and women in their clothes of deep, brilliant blue; everywhere

[1] *Journey to a War* (London, 1939).

151

the little grave mounds, usurping valuable square feet of the arable soil – a class-struggle between the living and the dead. The naked, lemon-coloured torsos, bent over their unending tasks, have no individuality; they seem folded and reticent as plants.[1]

As usual on their long train journeys in China, the two travellers indulged in arguments about literature, politics and religion. Auden, now sympathetic to religion, though still uncommitted, always found it easy to infuriate Isherwood to whom any religion was an anathema. When Isherwood on one occasion was especially violent in his denunciation of religious feeling, Auden cheerfully and prophetically exclaimed: 'My dear, one day you're going to have *such* a religious conversion!'

Well after midnight they arrived in Cheng-chow, which had been badly hit by air-raids, and managed to find themselves a hotel with an intact roof and an available bedroom. Through the window beside his bed, Isherwood could see the bomb-hole in the roof of the house next door. He lay awake, worrying about the possibility of a Japanese raid that night while, in the other bed, Auden slept soundly, 'with the long, calm snores of the truly strong'. At Cheng-chow they visited the American Mission Hospital, and then travelled east by train in the direction of the fighting. For no known reason, the train stopped for six and a half hours at a village called Min-chuan, which consisted of no more than a hut and a grove of willows in the middle of an immense mud plain. Auden christened it 'The Bad Earth'.[2] Eventually, having covered the last five miles in rickshaws, they arrived in Kweiteh, a walled town of great beauty. They called on the Roman Catholic Bishop, 'a rotund and cheerful pro-Franco Spaniard,' who looked forward to welcoming the Japanese whose attack on the city was thought to be imminent, and who would, he claimed, bring law and order to China. A Baptist minister told the visitors that he had a lot of bandits in his field. 'How very unpleasant for you,' said Auden sympathetically. 'Do they steal your vegetables?' It was then explained to him that the minister was referring to his mission-field.

On the train travelling further east to Sü-chow, they discovered that their servant Chiang had told everyone that they were doctors. Isherwood feared at any moment to be summoned to perform a major operation upon a wounded peasant or soldier. '"But at least", said Auden, "we'd be better than nothing." So we agreed, if called upon, to have a try.'

In Sü-chow, a city where the police were armed with flat swords which they carried slung on their backs in red sheaths, they met Dr Greer, a

[1] *Journey to a War*.

[2] The reference is to *The Good Earth* , a novel about China by Pearl Buck, who received the Nobel Prize for Literature in 1938.

seventy-year-old American lady and 'one of the great figures of the China Missions', who had spent the whole of her adult life in Sü-chow. The Japanese army was now about thirty miles to the north, and also advancing from the south-east. They asked a Chinese Major to provide a private car to take them to the front, but he discouragingly pointed out that the road was liable to attack by Japanese mobile units operating behind the Chinese lines. Undaunted, they instructed Chiang to hire rickshaws instead.

On 27 March a procession of four rickshaws set out for the front: two for the war correspondents themselves, one for Chiang and one for their luggage. At the north gate of the city they stopped for several minutes while Auden photographed, from every conceivable angle, a bronze ox which stood there as a charm against floods, and which was said to bellow when the water began to rise. A huge and amused crowd gathered to observe them, as well they might, for, as Isherwood admitted, 'Collectively, perhaps, we most resemble a group of characters in one of Jules Verne's stories about lunatic English explorers.' They eventually reached the front, but at a point which 'was only occupied by the Japanese at night, when almost all the real fighting and raiding takes place. During the daytime the Japs retire into Han Chwang village.'

'Over there are the lines to which we shall retreat,' said a Chinese officer. 'But you *mustn't* retreat,' Auden told him very severely, and received a polite but inscrutable Chinese smile in reply.

The train journey back to Cheng-chow and further west to Sian was both unbearably tedious and highly dangerous, for 'at Tung-kwan, where the line runs close beside the Yellow River, the Japanese had mounted guns on the northern bank'. The Chinese mind continued to elude Auden. Had the Chinese any guns? 'Certainly. Now we have some big guns.' 'I suppose,' said Auden, 'you shell the Japanese?' 'No, we don't do that. You see, we don't want the Japanese to know that we've got them.' One afternoon, a Japanese aeroplane suddenly appeared in the sky immediately above them, but the pilot, it seemed, was only on a reconnaissance flight. At Tung-kwan, they passed the Japanese guns, and were disappointed when they did not open fire:

> 'You see', said Auden. 'I told you so . . . I knew they wouldn't . . . nothing of that sort ever happens to *me*.' 'But it does to *me*,' I objected: 'and if it had this time you'd have been there, too.' 'Ah, but it didn't, you see.' 'No. But it might.' 'But it didn't.' There is no arguing with the complacency of a mystic. I turned over and went to sleep.[1]

After several days in Sian, where in 1911 the Chinese population had fallen upon the Manchus, slaughtering twenty-five thousand of them in a

[1] *Journey to a War.*

single night, on 10 April Auden and Isherwood left by train to make their
way back to Hankow, on the Yangtse Kiang, a journey of five days. The fine
spring weather in Hankow had brought an intensification of the air-raids.
('The Japs are now not only a danger but a positive nuisance. If Auden and I
go out shopping in different parts of the town, we have always to arrange an
emergency rendezvous – for there is usually no time to return to the Consu-
late, and the alternative may be an hour of solitary boredom standing in a
doorway or sitting in a café, waiting for the "all clear" to sound.') In Hankow
this time they met a number of Chinese intellectuals at a tea party at the
Terminus Hotel. At a reception given jointly by a British Admiral and the
Consul-General, they encountered a distinguished British group including
Sir Archibald Clerk-Kerr, the British Ambassador to China, who had arrived
from Japanese-occuped Shanghai, the journalist Peter Fleming, and his
wife, Celia Johnson, the actress. Auden and Isherwood stayed with Basil
Boothby, who was a member of the Embassy staff. One evening, the
Ambassador strolled over for an after dinner chat with Boothby, and was
told that, the previous day, Auden had written a marvellous poem about a
dead Chinese soldier ('Far from the heart of culture he was used:/Aban-
doned by his general and his lice,/Under a padded quilt he closed his eyes/
And vanished. . . .') 'Let him read it to us,' said the Ambassador, to which
Isherwood had to reply that Auden had already gone to bed. 'Go and tell
him to come down and read his poem to the British Ambassador,' Sir
Archibald commanded, whereupon Auden was quickly produced, 'blink-
ing at the light and looking more than usual like a big, mad, white rabbit,' as
Boothby recalled thirty-five years later. He began to read his poem, but after
the first line Isherwood interrupted to say that the Ministry of Information
had objected to the next line, as combining generals and lice in an
undignified way. Everyone laughed, but, when the poem was published in
the local newspaper a day or two later, Auden asked for an instant re-
translation and discovered that the offending second line had been altered
to read 'The rich and poor are combining to fight'.

Hankow was full of British residents; at a cocktail-party at the Race Club,
Auden was moved to observe that all traces of China had been lovingly
obliterated, not only from the Club premises but also from the surrounding
grounds. After a few more days and a few more visits – to the Orthodox
Easter service at the Russian church, attended by Hankow's huge colony of
Russian expatriates, and to a film studio where they saw work in progress on
a war film, *Fight to the Last*, the leisurely observers moved on, by river boat, a
few miles down the Yangtse Kiang to Kiukiang; but not before Auden had
managed to meet Chou En-lai briefly and by chance.

They stayed at a hotel called Journey's End, up in the hills a few miles
from Kiukiang. The idyllically situated hotel was run by a highly eccentric

Englishman named Charlton, whose staff of well-drilled house-boys was as famous in this part of China as the pornographic French literature he provided in the bedrooms.

> So we had tiffin under the camphor-tree, aware, in a trance of pleasure, of the smell of its leaves; of the splash of the stream over the stones; of the great gorge folding back, like a painting by Salvator Rosa, into the wooded hills behind the house. There were snipe to eat, and rainbow trout. It was all far, far too beautiful to be real. 'If I make the sign of the Hammer and Sickle,' I said, 'everything will disappear.' And Auden agreed: 'It's the third temptation of the Demon.'

After a couple of days at Journey's End, Auden and Isherwood attempted to move on to Nanchang, but missed the train at Kiukiang, and had to stay in the town overnight in a room in the China Travel Hotel which Auden, weak from the after-effects of an attack of dysentery, remarked would be a peculiarly suitable place to die in. They spent a gloomy afternoon talking about diseases and reading a depressing three-volume edition of Motley's *Rise of the Dutch Republic*, and a dull evening watching a trashy war film at the local cinema. Next morning, 3 May, they caught the train to Nanchang, where they stayed at the Burlington Hotel, and the following day they set off after breakfast to explore the town and to look for the headquarters of the New Fourth Army. They found the Army headquarters, but all the responsible officers were away somewhere near the front. At the American Mission Hospital, where Auden went to be examined, he fell into the clutches of a voluble lady missionary who, hearing that he wanted to get to the south-eastern war front, said: 'Are you insured with Jesus? Jesus has positively guaranteed eternal life. This life,' and she held up her thumb, 'is just a teeny span.' Auden regretted not having bitten the thumb.

Proceeding by train to Kin-hwa, they found themselves surrounded on arrival by a group of soldiers and police who escorted them to a hotel. This made them both nervous. 'Do you think that we're really under arrest?' Auden whispered. 'They'd probably be far too tactful to tell us so.' 'Perhaps they think we're spies,' replied Isherwood. 'Anyhow, we shall never know – until we're actually taken out to be shot.' 'Oh, they'd never shoot us. Far too crude. We shall simply disappear.'

The truth was that their fame had managed to precede them to Kin-hwa, for they were treated as people of great importance, and lavishly entertained. At an official luncheon, the two distinguished guests made it a point of honour to praise most warmly the dishes they liked least. '"Delicious", Auden murmured, as he munched what was, apparently, a small sponge soaked in glue. I replied by devouring, with smiles of exquisite pleasure, an orange which tasted of bitter aloes and contained, in its centre, a large weevil.' The Governor of the Province put at their disposal a large car to take them to the front. In addition to the chauffeur, their party included a civil servant, a Major and a freckled boy with projecting teeth whose presence, they were assured, was absolutely necessary. 'He had to carry a brandy bottle, he knew the road (this was untrue) and he "could find gasoline".' Auden suggested that perhaps the boy was a new kind of dowser. Isherwood's published account of the first part of their journey is hilariously vivid:

Beyond Lanchi the road leaves the river-valley and turns off into the hills. Soon we were hurtling round the curves of a mountain pass. The scenery was superb, but we were too frightened even to look out of the window. Instead, Auden tried to distract our thoughts from the alarming Present by starting a conversation about eighteenth-century poetry. It was no good: we could remember nothing but verses on sudden death. Meanwhile, the road twisted and struggled, and the car clung to it like a mongoose attacking a cobra. Pedestrians screamed, cyclists overbalanced into paddy-fields, wrecked hens lay twitching spasmodically in the dust-storm behind us. At every corner we shut our eyes, but the chauffeur only laughed darkly as befitted one of the Lords of Death, and swung us round the curve with squealing brakes. Neither Major Yang nor Mr. Liu showed the least symptoms of nervousness. 'The road is very difficult,' Mr. Liu observed peacefully, as we shot across a crazy makeshift bridge over a gorge, rattling its loose planks like the bars of a xylophone. 'It wouldn't be difficult,' I retorted, 'if we weren't driving at seventy miles an hour.'

We stopped at a small town for gasoline and a late lunch. In the square was an ambulance-truck full of wounded – the first we had seen that morning. Mr. Liu bought some tablets of Tiger Balm, the cure-all tonic which is advertised all over China. He was feeling in need of them because, as he explained, he had slept badly the night before. 'If I sleep well I am very strong. If I do not sleep I can do nothing.' Today he seemed actually to have shrunk into a little ivory-faced manikin, with a big wet baby's underlip. Nevertheless, he remained the perfect host. 'You are the guests of China,' he kept repeating. 'We must try to satisfy you. You are our friends.'

After this respite the D. H. Lawrence *Todesfahrt* continued. But we were braver now. With food inside us we ventured to admire the view. There were water-mills in the river far below. The hills were cultivated to their summits; the striped, wheat-covered folds of the mountains looked like yellow corduroy. 'Oh, my Gard!' exclaimed Mr. Liu, and was abruptly and violently car-sick. A few miles further on Major Yang, who had been looking very thoughtful, followed his example.[1]

After a day's travel, they reached Tunki, where they again encountered Peter Fleming. Finally, after a strenuous journey, partly on travelling-chairs and partly on foot, they reached Meiki and the army. Here they were closer to the fighting than they had been elsewhere: twelve hours after they left Meiki, it was taken by the Japanese. A couple of days later, they were all back in Kin-hwa, and on 20 May Auden and Isherwood travelled by bus to Wenchow on the coast. At Wenchow they took a Chinese coastal steamer, disguised as an Italian vessel complete with Italian Captain in order to fool the Japanese fleet, and proceeded up the coast to Shanghai. 'The Japs signalled to us to ask where we were going. "If they tell us to stop," said the Captain, "I shall refuse." "But won't they fire on you?" Auden asked. The Italian laughed: "I'd like to see the bastards try it! I should wireless to one of our warships. She could be here in two hours – and she'd send planes ahead of her."'

Japanese-occupied Shanghai was still an international port, with delights to suit all tastes:

> You can buy an electric razor, or a French dinner, or a well-cut suit. You can dance at the Tower Restaurant on the roof of the Cathay Hotel, and gossip with Freddy Kaufmann, its charming manager, about the European aristocracy or pre-Hitler Berlin. You can attend race-meetings, baseball games, football matches. You can see the latest American films. If you want girls, or boys, you can have them, at all prices, in the bath-houses and the brothels. If you want opium you can smoke it in the best company, served on a tray, like afternoon tea. Good wine is difficult to obtain in this climate, but there is enough whisky and gin to float a fleet of battleships. The jeweller and the antique-dealer await your orders, and their charges will make you imagine yourself back on Fifth Avenue or in Bond Street. Finally, if you ever repent, there are churches and chapels of all denominations.[2]

Auden and Isherwood stayed at the British Ambassador's private villa in the French Concession, met bandy-legged Japanese Generals at the Ambassador's garden party, and lunched with four Japanese civilians – a consular official, a business man, a banker and a railway director – at the Shanghai Club.

Shanghai, they discovered, was a city of violent contrasts; of luxury restaurants, and refugee camps; of elegant shops, and factories in which children were worked to death. Auden and Isherwood spent their last two

[1] *Journey to a War.*
[2] *Journey to a War.*

and a half weeks in China there, dutifully noting these contrasts in the travel diary which found its way into their book. What did not find its way into their book was an account of the many afternoons they spent in the bath-houses, being soaped and massaged by Chinese youths. Isherwood described the experience nearly forty years later, in *Christopher and His Kind*:

> You could pick your attendants, and many of them were beautiful. Those who were temporarily disengaged would watch the action, with giggles, through peepholes in the walls of the bathrooms. What made the experience pleasantly exotic was that tea was served to the customer throughout; even in the midst of an embrace, the attendant would disengage one hand, pour a cupful and raise it, tenderly but firmly, to the customer's lips. If you refused the tea at first, the attendant went on offering it until you accepted. It was like a sex fantasy in which a naked nurse makes love to the patient but still insists on giving him his medicine punctually, at the required intervals.

Every evening, over pre-dinner cocktails, Sir Archibald or his wife would ask their guests what they had been doing that afternoon, and Auden or Isherwood would invent suitable replies. When at last they tired of the delights of the bath-house, they left Shanghai and China on a Canadian Pacific liner, the *Empress of Asia*, having decided to travel back to England by way of the United States. They sailed from Shanghai on 12 June, calling at three ports in Japan. After China, Nagasaki surprised them with its cleanness. On a train to Tokyo, however, Auden was irritated when the porter kept flicking around his feet with brush and dustpan to collect his cigarette ash: he retaliated by dropping more of it than ever. In Tokyo, the sight of a screaming mob of Japanese seeing a troop train out of the station so shocked Auden that he dropped and broke his spectacles and had to travel on to America too short-sighted to see anything but the books he was reading. From Yokohama to Vancouver the voyage took ten days and the collaborators took the opportunity to complete their revision of *On the Frontier*. They travelled by train through Canada, entering the United States at Portal, North Dakota, through Minnesota and Wisconsin to Chicago and on to New York, arriving at a station which seemed to them like an oversized Roman temple. 'We ought to be wearing togas,' said Auden.

In New York, they were met by George Davis, novelist and literary editor of the fashion magazine, *Harper's Bazaar*, which had commissioned from them articles about their Chinese journey. Davis, whom they had met in London the previous year, showed them New York during their nine days' stay: the Rainbow Room, the night clubs of Harlem, Coney Island (on the Fourth of July), theatres, bars, parties. Through George Davis they met a number of celebrities, among them Maxwell Anderson, Orson Welles, Kurt

Weill and his wife Lotte Lenya. (Many years later, after Weill's death, Davis married Lotte Lenya.) Davis also offered to make sexual introductions for them, and, when Christopher requested 'a beautiful blond boy, about eighteen, intelligent, with very sexy legs', a boy exactly answering the description was produced. Both Auden and Isherwood fell in love with New York, and Auden promised himself that one day he would live there. On the Atlantic crossing back to England, he was uncharacteristically miserable, and on one occasion burst into tears, confessing to Isherwood that he could never find anyone to love him and that he believed himself to be a sexual failure. Arriving in London on 17 July, they went that evening to the theatre, to see their friend Beatrix Lehmann (John Lehmann's sister) in *The Telephone*, a translation of Cocteau's *La Voix Humaine*.

Chapter Seven

1938–1940

Heroes are buried who
Did not believe in death,
And bravery is now,
Not in the dying breath
But resisting the temptations
To skyline operations.
Yet glory is not new;
The summer visitors
Still come from far and wide,
Choosing their spots to view
The prize competitors,
Each thinking that he will
Find heroes in the wood,
Far from the capital,
Where lights and wine are set
For supper by the lake,
But leaders must migrate:
'Leave for Cape Wrath tonight,'
And the host after waiting
Must quench the lamps and pass
Alive into the house.[1]

In May, while he was in China, Auden's English publishers had brought out a volume of *Selected Poems* chosen from the earlier books of verse and from his contributions to the plays. Before going to China, he had completed his selection of poems for *The Oxford Book of Light Verse* after a fashion, though he had left most of the checking and sorting to his friend Mrs A. E. Dodds, wife of Professor E. R. Dodds. Auden now quickly wrote an Introduction, but left the proof reading of the entire volume to her, while he took a summer holiday. The book was published in October, and sold steadily for a quarter of a century. He also wrote, in 1938, his Introduction to an anthology, *Poems of Freedom*, which Victor Gollancz published in December. He and Isherwood lectured frequently on their China journey, and also began to assemble their book, *Journey to a War*, from their notes and travel diaries. In its final form, the book came to comprise half a dozen poems by Auden about the

[1] From 'Missing'.

Auden in 1930, by Cecil Beaton.

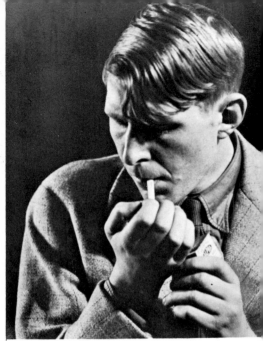

LEFT Christopher Isherwood.
RIGHT Auden at the time of the publication of *Poems* by Faber & Faber.
BELOW The 'Auden group' in 1930: Auden with Isherwood and OPPOSITE with Stephen Spender.

ABOVE Edward Upward, the novelist, who was at Cambridge with Isherwood, when they created the fictitious village of Mortmere. This fantasy later influenced the work of some of their friends, especially Auden, in the 1930s.
BELOW LEFT T. S. Eliot, Auden's publisher, and, as a poet, highly influential in the development of Auden's style.
BELOW RIGHT John Lehmann, editor of *New Writing*, in 1937.

LEFT Rupert Doone.

RIGHT John Grierson, for whom Auden worked in 1935 at the GPO Film Unit.

BELOW The painter Robert Medley putting the finishing touches to 'Talking and Playing' at the Royal Academy, 1937. He and Rupert Doone were two of the founder members of the Group Theatre.

Night Mail

This is the night mail crossing the border,
Bringing the cheque and the postal order,
Letters for the rich, letters for the poor,
The shop at the corner and the girl next door.
Pulling up Beattock, a steady climb—
The gradient's against her but she's on time.
Past cotton grass and moorland boulder,
Shovelling white steam over her shoulder,
Snorting noisily as she passes
Silent miles of wind-bent grasses;
Birds turn their heads as she approaches,
Stare from the bushes at her blank-faced coaches;
Sheep dogs cannot turn her course,
They slumber on with paws across.
In the farm she passes no one wakes,
But a jug in the bedroom gently shakes.
Dawn freshens, the climb is done.
Down towards Glasgow she descends
Towards the steam tugs, yelping down the glade of c
Towards the fields of apparatus, the furnaces
Set on the dark plain like gigantic chessmen.
All Scotland waits for her;
In the dark glens, beside the pale-green sea lochs,
Men long for news.

The first page of a leaflet issued in 1938 by the GPO, to commemorate the centenary of the Travelling P
Office. The text is the poem Auden wrote as part of the commentary for the film *Night Mail*.

ABOVE A poem by Auden accompanied this sequence from the film *Coal Face*, made in 1935. The score for the film was by Benjamin Britten.
BELOW Auden playing Father Christmas in the film *Calendar of the Year*.

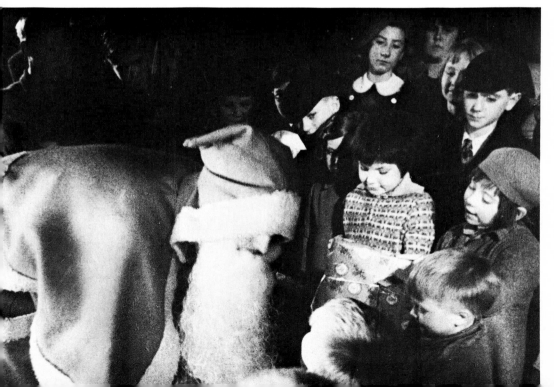

ABOVE William Coldstream, and the portrait he painted of Auden in 1937.
BELOW AND RIGHT E. M. Forster and Auden became close friends in the late thirties. The photograph of the two together at the seaside was sent as a postcard by Christopher Isherwood to Edward Upward in the summer of 1937.

below A scene from the first Group Theatre production of *The Dog Beneath the Skin*, at the Westminster Theatre in 1936: 'Have you seen Sir Francis Crewe?'
right The programme for the same production.

Three photographs by Auden from *Letters from Iceland* (1937) on which he collaborated with Louis MacNeice (RIGHT). Michael Yates (ABOVE), then a schoolboy, was one of the party who toured the country on horseback.

Nightly 8.30 ; Matinées, Fridays and Saturdays 2.30

In Association with the Group Theatre

THE ASCENT OF F.6

by W. H. AUDEN and CHRISTOPHER ISHERWOOD

Produced by RUPERT DOONE

Characters :

Michael Forsyth Ransom	William Devlin
Sir James Ransom	Raf de la Torre
Lady Isabel Welwyn	Ruth Taylor
General Dellaby-Couch	Erik Chitty
Lord Stagmantle	Edward Lexy
David Gunn	Barry Barnes
Ian Shawcross	Norman Claridge
Edward Lamp	Peter Ashmore
Dr. Williams	Philip Thornley
Mrs. Ransom	Dorothy Holmes-Gore
The Abbot	Evan John
Mr. A.	Will Leighton
Mrs. A.	Isobel Scaife
The Singer	Hedli Anderson
An Announcer	Stuart Latham
Blavek	Noel Woolf
Monks	Alan Aldridge, Michael Lane, Robert Newport

The Play is presented in Two Parts, with One Interval of 15 minutes.

SCENES IN PART I : Summit of the Pillar Rock, Wastdale ; A Room at the Colonial Office ; An Inn Parlour in the Lake District.

SCENES IN PART II : A Monastery on the Great Glacier of F.6 ; The Foot of the West Buttress ; Camp B ; The Arête ; The Summit.

The Music specially composed by BENJAMIN BRITTEN

Costumes, Masks and Scene by ROBERT MEDLEY

The Group Theatre production of *The Ascent of F.6* at the Mercury Theatre, February 1937. ABOVE, Mr and Mrs A. at breakfast; BELOW, the hero Ransom watches his companions reading their fortunes.

Isherwood and Auden about to board the boat-train on the morning of their departure for China, January 1938. They chose China because they wanted 'a war of their own' to write about.

RIGHT Auden in the trenches of the Chinese war
zone: a photograph published in *Journey to a War*,
1939. In fact, he and Isherwood saw very little
fighting during their trip.
BELOW Generalissimo and Madame Chiang
Kai-shek: photographs by Auden from *Journey to a
War*.

ABOVE Auden with William Coldstream and Benjamin Britten at the Downs School, Colwall, 1935.
BELOW On Coney Island in 1938. George Davis, the literary editor of *Harper's Bazaar*, is on the right.

LEFT Auden and Isherwood in Central Park, New York, in the summer of 1938.
BELOW Auden and Isherwood making a recording for the BBC after their return from China, 1938.

LEFT Benjamin Britten and Peter Pears, by Cecil Beaton.
RIGHT Cyril Connolly.
BELOW The Mann family at home in Princeton, New Jersey, April 1939, in a photograph taken for *Time* magazine. From left, Isherwood, Auden, Erika Mann Auden, Thomas Mann, his wife, his daughter Elizabeth and his son Klaus.

voyage from Marseilles to Hong Kong, a Travel Diary written up by Isherwood from the separate journals kept by Auden and himself, a selection of photographs taken by Auden and a final sequence of poems written by Auden in China. It was a much better organized, less scrappy affair than the Auden–MacNeice *Letters from Iceland*.

Auden returned from Belgium on 28 September, and was met at Victoria Station by Isherwood. It was a time of crisis, for the international situation had deteriorated rapidly since Hitler's annexation of Austria in March. Relations between Germany and Czechoslovakia were now seriously strained, Chamberlain and Hitler had had their conference at Berchtesgaden earlier in September, and only a few days before Auden's return to London Chamberlain had paid a second visit to Hitler at Godesberg. The demands made by Hitler at this meeting had not been acceptable, and a state of acute international crisis built up over the next few days. England, clearly, would help Czechoslovakia to resist Germany's demands, even if it led to war. On the 28th, special editions of the newspapers appeared at half-hourly intervals. Isherwood was miserably certain that war was imminent. 'The last shreds of hope are vanishing down the drain,' he wrote in his diary that evening. 'Wilson came back from Berlin, snubbed. The German Army mobilizes this afternoon. Parliament meets, to introduce conscription. Chamberlain spoke last night, like a wet fish, saying: How dreadful, how dreadful.'

The boat train drew in, and Wystan appeared, 'very sunburnt and in the highest spirits, wearing a loud, becoming check suit'. 'Well, my dear,' he greeted Isherwood, 'there isn't going to be a war, you know!' For a moment Isherwood imagined that his friend must have received some highly confidential information from a reliable source on the continent, but it transpired that at the British Embassy in Brussels Auden had met a lady who said she could read the future in cards. She had assured him that there would be no war that year. She was right. Hitler, Ribbentrop, Mussolini, Chamberlain and Daladier conferred in Munich on the following afternoon. Czechoslovakia, not represented at the conference, was sold out to Hitler, and Chamberlain came back waving his piece of paper and burbling of 'Peace in our time'. In England, some people were indignant, while others, the majority, were relieved. Auden and Isherwood were both indignant and relieved. They discussed seriously their already half formulated plans to return to the United States of America for an indefinite stay, and decided that they would go after they had seen their Chinese travel book to press and their play *On the Frontier* staged. Meanwhile, Isherwood was still busy assembling the final text of the book, and he and Auden were publicizing it. They also appeared on BBC Television on 12 October, discussing their most recent play, *The Ascent of F.6*, in a programme called 'Speaking Personally'.

During the autumn, Auden collaborated with T. C. Worsley in writing a pamphlet on education, which had been commissioned by a left-wing monthly called *Fact*. The pamphlet, *Education Today and Tomorrow*, proved to be insufficiently factual for *Fact*, who rejected it; it was then accepted by John Lehmann and published by the Hogarth Press in March of the following year, by which time Auden had left the country. Among the poems, reviews and articles which he published in the autumn of 1938, there is a curious prose piece, 'The Sportsmen: A Parable', which appeared in the autumn number of *New Verse*. This is the nearest Auden ever came to writing prose fiction: an odd little story about villagers and sportsmen, which is clearly a parable of the relation between poet and citizen, and between types of poet. The parable appears to be reminding the poet of his responsibilities as a citizen, which, in view of its author's imminent abrogation of his own responsibilities as a British citizen, is somewhat perplexing.

On 27 October *On the Frontier* was published, and on 14 November it was given its first performance by the Group Theatre at the Arts Theatre, Cambridge, in a production funded by the economist John Maynard Keynes, who had also paid for the Cambridge production of *The Ascent of F.6* the previous year. *On the Frontier* was produced by Rupert Doone with scenery and costumes by his friend Robert Medley, and the leading roles were played by Ernest Milton and Keynes's wife, the former dancer Lydia Lopokova. The music was provided by Benjamin Britten, who also accompanied the chorus for no fee throughout the run of the play, although he was rather hurt when Auden insisted that a song, 'Industrialists, bankers in comfortable chairs', in Act I should be sung, not to the music Britten had composed for it, but to the tune of 'Sweet Betsy from Pike'. (The chorus included a young tenor named Peter Pears who had become friendly with Britten in March of the previous year, and who was to live with the composer until Britten's death in 1976.) The reputations of Auden and Isherwood were now solid enough for the production of *On the Frontier* to be transferred to London, where it opened at the Globe Theatre, Shaftesbury Avenue, on 12 February 1939, although by then the general view was that the play was not a success. Its first night audience had been friendly enough, and had treated the play with polite respect, but as Isherwood was to recall, '*On the Frontier* wasn't a harrowing disaster; it passed away painlessly.' Guy Burgess, later to achieve notoriety as a Soviet spy, encountered John Lehmann at his Club one evening shortly after the première of *On the Frontier*, and exclaimed: 'The trouble about Wystan, Christopher and Stephen is that they haven't got the foggiest notion what politicians are really like!' Lehmann's comment, in his memoirs, was: 'They certainly hadn't got a clue to what Guy was really like.'[1]

[1] John Lehmann: *The Whispering Gallery* (London, 1955).

Reading some of the reviews cannot have been an entirely painless exercise for the authors. 'Messrs Auden and Isherwood continue to follow their principle of putting Marxist pap into bourgeois bottles,' Leavis's *Scrutiny*[1] announced, while *The London Mercury*[2] informed its readers that 'the dialogue is prosy and dull, and the poetry does not reveal the authors at their best'. *The Listener*'s anonymous critic (who was, in fact, C. Day Lewis) thought that it was 'not entirely the dwarfing effect of the recent crisis which makes *On the Frontier* seem the least successful of the Auden–Isherwood plays: it possesses neither the vitality and invention of *The Dog Beneath the Skin* nor the deeply realised moral conflict of *The Ascent of F.6*.'[3] Day Lewis was not the only member of 'the Gang' to give the play an unfavourable notice. Louis MacNeice in the *Spectator*,[4] found it disappointing: 'The theme again is vastly important, but the treatment is rather facile and seems to fall between two stools as if the authors could not decide whether they were writing a straight play or a crooked one. Compared with *The Ascent of F.6*, there is less sparkle, less poetry, less thought and even more embarrassment. The mystical love scenes of Eric and Anna made one long for a sack to put one's head in.' MacNeice thought the performance excellent, and Britten's music impressive and appropriate. It was left to the *New Statesman*[5] to rally around the cause. Referring to the first night as 'a great success', its reviewer continued: 'The play is precisely topical; for it deals not only with dictators and war, but boldly and sincerely with the problems which dictatorship and war have set for every member of the audience. The verse is admirable and the music effective.'[6]

It is not easy, today, to give a fair evaluation of *On the Frontier*, for its more immediate topicality has caused it to date more badly than the other Auden–Isherwood plays. Also, closer to the conventions of the pre-war West End play than *Dogskin* or *F.6*, it suffers by more direct comparison with such plays than the earlier *jeux d'esprit* were subjected to. According to Isherwood, Auden was responsible not only for the shape of the play but also for the poetry and a larger share of the prose than usual. Unfortunately, the poetry is off-hand Auden, and the prose dialogue too frequently stilted and unconvincing. The play's impact in 1938 must have been vitiated somewhat by the Lord Chamberlain's shameful insistence on Scandinavian names being substituted for German ones, in order not to offend Nazi

[1] December 1938.
[2] January 1939.
[3] 24 November 1938.
[4] 18 November 1938.
[5] 19 November 1938.
[6] The present author once asked Benjamin Britten if he thought any of the music he had written in the thirties for the Auden–Isherwood plays worth retrieving, and received the answer, 'Practically without exception – no.'

Germany, although audiences were well aware that the play's Leader was a caricature of Hitler. The day after the first night, T. S. Eliot wrote to the play's backer, Keynes: 'I am afraid that Hitler is not the simpleton that the authors made him out to be.'

According to Isherwood, the biggest laugh on the first night of *On the Frontier* had been achieved by Auden's curtain speech. He had been asked to make an appeal from the stage, for aid to children in Spain. Attempting to say that worse things were happening at that moment in the outside world than any of the events portrayed on the stage, he in fact said 'As you all know, worse things have been happening in the audience tonight than on the stage.' Perhaps, mentally, Auden was already in the New World. He seemed to have finished with the literary life of England: John Lehmann, attempting to recruit both him and Isherwood as literary advisors for his new series of *New Writing*, found that they were willing in spirit but weak in flesh, though he did receive some shrewd comments from Auden, who said of one young poet's work: 'I sometimes think that Hopkins ought to be kept on a special shelf like a dirty book, and only allowed to readers who won't be ruined by him.'

Cyril Connolly's book of criticism, *Enemies of Promise*, published in October, contained a highly laudatory reference to Auden:

> We have one poet of genius today, Auden, who is able to write prolifically, carelessly, and exquisitely, and who does not seem to have to pay any price for his inspiration. It is as if he worked under the influence of some mysterious drug, which gives him a private vision, a mastery of form, and of vocabulary.

On 15 November, from his parents' house in Birmingham, Auden wrote to Connolly: 'I think *E. of P.* is the best English book of criticism since the war, and more than Eliot or [Edmund] Wilson you really write about writing in the only way which is interesting to anyone except academics, as a real occupation like banking or fucking with all its attendant egotism, boredom, excitement and terror.'

Knowing Auden's and Isherwood's plans to go to America, Lehmann, in order to help them with money for the journey, commissioned from them a travel book about America, to be called *Address Not Known*. But, by Christmas, both authors had come to realize that this would be merely a repetition of the Chinese operation, whereas they were more interested in developing, separately, their own writing. The project was abandoned.

On 8 December, Auden lectured in Paris at the Sorbonne on poetic drama. Accompanied by Isherwood's current, temporary boy-friend, he and Isherwood went to Brussels for Christmas, where they joined Gerald Hamilton, a figure from their Berlin past, and the original of Isherwood's Mr

Norris in *Mr Norris Changes Trains*. On New Year's Eve, Auden gave a very lively party at which he read a poem he had written especially for the occasion, 'Ode to the New Year (1939)'. This consists of nine stanzas, addressed to friends present at the party, absent friends, and a few enemies. In 1970, Auden gave the present author a typescript of the poem. It was his wish that parts of it remain private: the stanzas printed below are numbers 1, 2, 4 and 5:

> O beautiful city of Brussels
>   With your parks and statues & boites,
> Where they really know how to cook mussels,
>   And there's fucking à gauche et à droite;
> For the sake of Breughel & Weyden,
>   For Rubens' wonderful cuisses,
> In the name of Gudila the Maiden,
>   On behalf of the Manneken Pis,
> Surrounded by glasses & dishes,
>   The pretty, the witty, the queer,
> I offer you first my good wishes,
>   I wish you a happy New Year.
>
> Dear Christopher, always a sort of
>   Conscience to which I'd confess
> In the years before Hitler was thought of,
>   Or the guinea-pig had a success;
> Now reviewers are singing your praises,
>   And lovers are scratching your back,
> But, O, how unhappy your face is,
>   So I wish you the peace that you lack;
> May your life in the States become better,
>   May the shadow of grief disappear,
> But – God – if you ever turn heter,
>   I won't wish you a happy New Year.
>
> Uncle Gerald, your charm is a mystery
>   I shall not attempt to define;
> It concerns your appearance, your history,
>   And your knowledge of servants & wine;
> Do you think if I summoned the waiter,
>   He could tell us instantly why
> The Embassy thinks you a traitor,
>   And Olive thinks you a spy?
> Now it's you that I raise my cup to,

Though I haven't the slightest idea
What on earth it is that you're up to,
    I wish you a happy New Year.

Petit Jacques, Ah do you remember
    – mais où sont les neiges d'antan? –
The Crisis weeks last September
    When you were my only amant?
When the touch of your hand made me bristle,
    And your lips made me hot as a coal,
Just after I learnt you could whistle,
    And before I realised you stole?
Sic transit gloria mundi,
    Now I would rather have Pierre,
But Do-as-you-would-be-done-by,
    I wish you a happy New Year.

In the poem's final stanza, a number of 'haters of man' are mentioned and wished 'a lake of brimstone to swim in/And a bloody nasty New Year'.

Auden was persuaded by Isherwood to undertake a brief journey to Berlin to help him cope with Heinz. They then returned to England on 9 January, having, during their Brussels holiday, completely finished work on *Journey to a War*, which they now delivered to Faber & Faber who published the book on 16 March. It was much more cordially received than *Letters from Iceland*. 'The title is mysterious,' the *New Statesman* review began, 'hinting at imaginary war and frontiers in the mind.'[1] It went on to express a fear that this new journey might easily have landed its readers 'no further away than Cheltenham or an Oxford common-room'. But surprised and delighted praise is showered upon the authors' 'personally truthful', necessarily partial view of China at war, for Isherwood's 'extraordinarily vivid diary' and for the 'remarkable achievement' of Auden's poems.

The press generally was favourable, though an acerbic note was struck by Evelyn Waugh in the *Spectator*. 'Poetry has always been a worry to the trade,' he wrote, and so 'Messrs Faber and Faber have hit on a new dodge of incorporating the slim volume [of verse] in a more solid and marketable work, and have attached 43 pages of Mr Auden's verse to a substantial travel diary of Mr Isherwood's, nearly 200 pages in length . . . it is impossible, hozever, to treat this publication as a single work; it is two books which for purposes of commercial convenience have been issued as one.' Waugh appreciated Isherwood's 'smooth and accurate kind of demotic language' and Auden's photographs, though not his poems:

[1] 18 March 1939.

The English public has no particular use for a poet, but they believe they should have one or two about the place. There is an official laureate; there is also, always, an official young rebel. I do not know how he is chosen. At certain seasons the critics seem to set out piously together to find a reincarnation of Shelley, just as the lamas of Tibet search for their Dalai Lama. A year or two ago they proclaimed their success and exhibited Mr Auden. It is unfair to transfer to him the reproach that properly belongs to them. His work is awkward and dull, but it is no fault of his that he has become a public bore.[1]

It is no fault of Evelyn Waugh's that he lacked an appreciation of poetry; he had a splendid ear for prose. His snidely amusing review is unfair to Auden in attributing the prose travel diary entirely to Isherwood, but this was a general assumption at the time (and perhaps still is), and one which was supported by the somewhat devious method Isherwood employed in conflating a text for publication from the two separate diaries of Auden and himself. He chose to incorporate passages from Auden into his 'first person' narrative, and by occasionally mentioning Auden as the author of a witty or perspicacious observation, contrived to give the impression that such quoted remarks were Auden's only contribution to the prose narrative.[2]

Journey to a War is a much more coherent whole than the Iceland book, and one which can still be read with interest and pleasure today. The travel diary, then grim reading, seems now like nostalgic escapism, and Auden's poems reveal him to be moving further away from side-taking, blame-imputing, socially conscious verse, towards a more philosophic stance. He no longer asks who is the attacker and who the attacked, but broods on the dehumanizing effects of war as seen from the viewpoint of an eclectic humanism instead of from the blinkers of a rigid political system, whether of the left or the right:

> As evening fell the day's oppression lifted;
> Tall peaks came into focus; it had rained:
> Across wide lawns and cultured flowers drifted
> The conversation of the highly trained.
>
> Thin gardeners watched them pass and priced their shoes;
> A chauffeur waited, reading in the drive,
> For them to finish their exchange of views:
> It looked a picture of the way to live.

[1] 24 March 1939.

[2] Waugh's *Put Out More Flags* (1942) has amusing references to Parsnip and Pimpernell, 'two great poets . . . Who had recently fled to New York.'

Far off, no matter what good they intended,
Two armies waited for a verbal error
With well-made implements for causing pain,

And on the issue of their charm depended
A land laid waste with all its young men slain,
Its women weeping, and its towns in terror.

On 16 January 1939, Auden broadcast a talk on his visit to China, in a programme called 'Midland magazine' on the BBC's Home service. Two days later, he and Isherwood left for America. The current Isherwood boy-friend (there was, at this time, a very quick turnover) and E. M. Forster came to Waterloo to see them off on the boat-train to Southampton in the late afternoon of the 18th. Waves of farewell were exchanged until the train had pulled out of the station. Then, settling back into their seats, the two friends grinned at each other. 'Well,' said Isherwood, 'we're off again.' 'Goody,' exclaimed Auden.

They spent the night on board the *Champlain*, which sailed the following day. The voyage was a stormy one, the ship tossed and slithered, and the collaborators were bored, for they had nothing to collaborate upon. Their inner journey must have been a stormy one, too, as each individually took stock of his position, and tried to plot a future course. Isherwood's thoughts were already tending towards California; Auden hoped to establish himself on the New York literary scene. Meanwhile,

Wrapped in rugs, they lay sipping bouillon, or they paced the deck, or drank at the bar, or watched movies in the saloon, where French tapestries flapped out from the creaking, straining walls as the ship rolled. They amused themselves by taking over the puppet-show in the children's playroom and improvising Franco–English dialogue full of private jokes and double meanings. Their audience of children didn't care what the puppets said, as long as they kept jumping about. Off the coast of Newfoundland, the ship ran into a blizzard. She entered New York harbour looking like a wedding-cake.[1]

When the quarantine launch arrived, on it to welcome Auden and Isherwood were Erika Mann (still Mrs Auden) and her brother Klaus. It was 26 January, the day that Barcelona was taken by Franco with the aid of the Italians, and the Spanish Loyalist cause collapsed. A month later, Britain and France recognized Franco's government, by which time both Auden and Isherwood were busy lecturing about China and promoting *Journey to a War*, whose American edition was published in New York in May, two months after the English edition had appeared.

[1] *Christopher and His Kind.*

Why had Auden and Isherwood decided in the middle of successful careers to leave the old world for the new? A year later, disgruntled voices were to be heard in England claiming that they and a few other intellectuals and writers had 'sold out', had turned tail and fled rather than actually fight for the anti-Fascist cause they had so vociferously espoused. But Auden and Isherwood did not flee from war, for what they had left, in January 1939, was an England optimistically convinced that there would be no war. This, however, did not stop the right-wing press in Britain from continuing to insist that the departure of Auden and Isherwood from England was some kind of cowardly betrayal of their country, and that they had in some way let the side down. This feeling took root and persisted even for some years after the war, to the detriment, unfairly, of the British reputations of both men. By this time, however, neither of them was professionally dependent upon his reputation in Britain. In a 1978 radio programme about Auden for the Australian Broadcasting Commission, in which the present author participated, Stephen Spender admitted, with engaging frankness: 'I pretended to feel shocked about it. And schoolboys whom [Auden] had taught would come and tell me that they were very disappointed, because Auden had taught them that the great thing in their lives was that they were going to be dedicated to fighting fascism; so, when the master who told them this went off to America, they either felt disappointed or pretended to feel disappointed. You know, in all these things one tends to exploit the possibilities of the situation a bit, doesn't one? And actually one doesn't care a damn. I don't think *they* cared a damn, or *I* cared a damn, really, or made any kind of moral judgment.'

Auden in later years would talk about having felt the need to free himself from English literary life in the way one speaks of a need to break away from the suffocating embrace of parents and family. Indeed, he tended to equate the literary scene in England with a cosy parish life of gossip and inconsequence. This is, no doubt, what kept him away from England for so many years after the war, but it is difficult to believe that it can have had much to do with his decision to go to America in 1939. Isherwood's feelings, though complex, are easier to understand: he wanted new worlds to conquer, and he was beginning to move towards the pacifist position in which, influenced by various Indian gurus, he has remained ever since. But Auden was motivated by a number of feelings, among which, surely, were boredom and curiosity. Also, he had been acting a multiplicity of roles for more than ten years, and he was finding it increasingly difficult to suspend his disbelief in them all. One morning in mid-Atlantic, as they were walking around the deck of the *Champlain*, Isherwood said to him: 'You know, it just doesn't mean anything to me any more – the Popular Front, the party line, the anti-fascist struggle. I suppose they're okay but something's wrong with me. I simply cannot swallow another mouthful.' 'Neither can I,' Auden replied.

At last they had learned that art and political slogans do not mix. It was a realization that Auden had been moving towards for some time. In leaving England, though no doubt at the time he would not have put it to himself in these terms, he was running away not from war but from politics. He was going to lead his own life in America. He also, though this too he was to become aware of only some time after his arrival in the United States, was beginning to move back to the church which, deep in his heart, he had never really left. In an article he wrote in 1938, which was published in *I Believe*, an anthology of 'the personal philosophies of certain eminent men and women of our time',[1] Auden was careful to discuss morality almost entirely in political terms, as though religion did not exist. But it was to be only a matter of months after writing this that he began going regularly to church again.

The voice of Auden lingered in Britain for some months after his departure in January. In the Spring number of John Lehmann's *New Writing* were eight of his recent poems, some of them written in Brussels over Christmas: 'Musée des Beaux Arts' which was to become one of Auden's most famous short poems ('About suffering they were never wrong/The Old Masters'), 'The Capital', and the oddly persuasive 'Brussels in Winter' with its memorable final lines:

> Ridges of rich apartments loom tonight
> Where isolated windows glow like farms,
> A phrase goes packed with meaning like a van,
>
> A look contains the history of man,
> And fifty francs will earn a stranger right
> To take the shuddering city in his arms.

A new work from Benjamin Britten, first performed in April, utilized lines by Auden. This was *Ballad of Heroes* for tenor (or soprano), chorus and orchestra, which Britten had composed in honour of those men of the British Battalion, International Brigade, who had been killed in Spain. Its first performance at the Queen's Hall was part of a Festival of Music for the People, organized by 'musicians of the progressive movement in Britain'. It was in three movements, the second of which was a setting of Auden's poem 'Danse Macabre', and the third a setting which combined part of the final chorus of *On the Frontier* with a mediocre propaganda poem by a communist poet, Randall Swingler.

If Auden's name was kept alive in England by his poems, reviews and other works, it was also kept alive by continued scurrilous references in the

[1] New York, 1939.

186

press to his 'desertion'. One anonymous reviewer wrote that Auden's admiration of Henry James was understandable, since they had both changed their nationality because England was at war! The debate was also conducted, at a slightly higher level of abuse, in the literary weeklies and periodicals, notably in the conservative *Spectator* in whose pages Harold Nicolson regretted that Auden, Isherwood, Aldous Huxley and Gerald Heard had all 'retired within the ivory tower' of the United States. 'It is not so much that the absence of these four men from Europe will cause us to lose the Second German War,' Nicolson wrote. 'It is that their presence in the United States may lead American opinion, which is all too prone to doubt the righteousness of our cause, to find comfort in their company . . . How can we proclaim over there that we are fighting for the liberated mind, when four of our most liberated intellectuals refuse to identify themselves either with those who fight or with those who oppose the battle?'[1] This led Stephen Spender to write to the *Spectator*:

A good many remarks have been made about the voluntary exile of Auden and Isherwood. I think that most of this criticism misses the point, because the arguments which apply to political actions do not apply to artists. Considered as a political gesture, Gauguin's renunciation of Western civilization and departure for the South Seas was impractical and irresponsible. Everyone would find it absurd if Monsieur Blum, for example, did it. However, in the history of painting it had enough significance to be justified. Similarly, if Auden and Isherwood say that they have left Europe because 'our civilization is done for' so that 'our culture must emigrate', they are being silly, because culture is not something that you can pack up in a bag and take away when a continent is at war. What does matter, however, is their writing. And if they succeed in writing better in America than they have done here they will be justified, in spite of the very sensible objections raised by Mr Nicolson.[2]

The level of debate took a nose-dive with the publication, some weeks later, of a scurrilous quatrain by someone who sheltered behind the initials W. R. M., but who was identified by E. M. Forster, in a letter to a friend, as W. R. Matthews, Dean of St Paul's:

> To Certain Intellectuals Safe in America
>
> 'This Europe stinks', you cried – swift to desert
> Your stricken country in her sore distress.
> You may not care, but still I will assert,

[1] 19 April 1940.
[2] 26 April 1940.

Since you have left us, here the stench is less.[1]

It rose again with E. M. Forster's contribution:

Sir, W.R.M.'s epigram in your issue of June 21st. impels me to ask whether there could not now be a close time for snarling at absent intellectuals. About half a dozen of them – not more – are away in America, and week after week their fellow-authors go for them in the newspapers. The attacks are highly moral and patriotic in tone, but their continuance raises the uneasy feeling that there must be something behind them, namely, unconscious envy; they are like the snarl of an unfortunate schoolboy who has been 'kept in', and is aggrieved because the whole of his class has not been kept in too, and therefore complains and complains about those stinkers out in the playground instead of concentrating on his own inescapable task.

And there is a further objection to this undignified nagging: it diverts public attention from certain Englishmen who really are a danger to the country. They, too, are few in number – perhaps again not more than half a dozen – but they have influence, wealth and position, which intellectuals have not, and they shelter not in the United States, but in the city and the aristocracy. Our literary lampoonists can here find a foe worthier of their powers. Let them leave their absent colleagues alone for the next fortnight, and denounce our resident Quislings instead. The consequences may be unpleasant to them, for Quislings sometimes hit back. But they will have the satisfaction of exposing a genuine menace instead of a faked one, and this should be sufficient reward.[2]

During his first months in New York, Auden worked on two projects for books, neither of which came to fruition. One of these was to have been a critical volume based on a number of essays and reviews he had already published in various magazines. He reshaped these into a completed manuscript, but it was not published and is now lost. The other book was a kind of philosophical quasi-autobiography which he intended to call *The Prolific and the Devourer*, its title drawn from the opposing categories of temperament postulated by William Blake in *The Marriage of Heaven and Hell*. Auden completed four parts of this, and probably intended to add more. Part I is in the form of short, self-contained, aphoristic paragraphs, with passages of autobiography inserted at random. His complete disenchantment with public and political life emerges clearly from this fragmentary work:

To be forced to be political is to be forced to lead a dual life. Perhaps this would not matter if one could consciously keep them apart and know

[1] 21 June 1940.
[2] 5 July 1940.

which was the real one. But to succeed at anything, one must believe in it, at least for the time being, and only too often the false public life absorbs and destroys the genuine private life. Nearly all public men become booming old bores.

Artists and politicians, he was now convinced, should not meddle in each other's worlds. Auden's unfinished manuscript comes to an end with these three paragraphs:

Artists and politicians would get along better in a time of crisis like the present, if the latter would only realise that the political history of the world would have been the same if not a poem had been written, not a picture painted nor a bar of music composed.

If the criterion of art were its power to incite to action, Goebbels would be one of the greatest artists of all time.

Tolstoi, who, knowing that art makes nothing happen, scrapped it, is more to be respected than the Marxist critic who finds ingenious reasons for admitting the great artists of the past to the State Pantheon.[1]

Auden's arguments here are illogical, simplistic and untenable. There is no way of telling whether the history of the world would have been different without art, because all we have to go on is the history of a world which is *not* without art. And Goebbels never claimed to be an artist. Whether or not art can incite to action, no one, surely, doubts that propaganda can, and Goebbels's profession was that of propagandist. *Pace* Tolstoy, art does not have to make anything happen, any more than a rose has to make things happen. Art happens. Art is. It is difficult not to feel that Auden's attitude to much of his earlier verse was illogical. Why should the poet place any other restraint upon his subject matter than that he deal with it in total honesty? Auden's 1972 poem, 'A Curse', about the modern automobile, was never likely to persuade Ford to produce 'an odorless and noiseless staid little brougham', but that did not stop the poet from writing it. Nor should his conviction that his protest poetry of the thirties had not saved one Jew from the Nazis have led him to repudiate it *en masse*. The simple 'Refugee Blues' (1939) and the complex 'Diaspora' (1940) do not have to produce evidence of their efficaciousness in order to prove their validity as poems. In any case, poetry moves in a mysterious way its wonders to perform: millions have read Auden's verse, and we cannot discover what its effect has been.

Weak and unconvincing though Auden's assertions about the nature of art may be, they reinforce the probability that, in leaving Europe in 1939, what he was really trying to do was to discover nothing so grandiose as the

[1] *The English Auden.*

nature of art but simply the nature of his own immense talent. He had been led along a path which, for him, was not the right one, and at last his metabolism rejected it. Fascist cant, Communist cant, that was for the merchants of cant, the politicians, to concern themselves with. Auden's gesture in turning his back on the public world of organized hypocrisy was a brave one. Understandably, the unbrave found it difficult to forgive him.

On their arrival in New York on 26 January 1939, Auden and Isherwood rented an apartment in the Yorkville section of Manhattan, and began to give immediate thought to the problem of earning their livings. Auden set about it in a straightforward manner by visiting the editorial offices of newspapers and magazines, identifying himself and asking for books to review. He also made it known that he was available to lecture and to give readings of his poems, and engagements soon began to trickle in. On 16 March he spoke on 'Effective Democracy' at the Foreign Correspondents' Dinner Forum. On 4 April he travelled down to the University of North Carolina to address the University's Institute of Human Relations on 'Integration and Freedom'.

During their first three months in New York, Auden and Isherwood renewed their friendship with Thomas Mann and his family, which included Auden's wife Erika Mann. The Manns at this time were living not far away at Princeton, New Jersey: on one occasion a photographer from *Time* was present, and Thomas Mann asked the two friends to pose for a photograph with the family. The photographer knew Auden was Mann's son-in-law, but asked what was Isherwood's relation to the Manns. 'Family pimp,' replied the great German novelist.

The final Auden Isherwood literary collaboration was on an article for *Vogue*[1] in which they selected and discussed the ten most promising British writers of the day. These were George Orwell, Ralph Bates, Arthur Calder-Marshall, Graham Greene, Stephen Spender, Rex Warner, Edward Upward, Henry Green, William Plomer and James Stern.

On 6 April, Auden and Isherwood took part in an event organized by the League of American Writers at the Keynote Club on West Fifty-second Street. This was a discussion of 'Modern Trends in English Poetry and Prose' which was also contributed to by Louis MacNeice, who had recently arrived in New York. Isherwood gave a talk about his visit to China, while Auden and MacNeice both read poems. In the front row of the audience were the twenty-two-year-old Harold Norse and his friend Chester Kallman, who was eighteen: both of them Jewish New Yorkers, poets, and both blonde and good-looking. They had come along in order to attract the attention of Auden, whom they both admired. Harold Norse later recalled that the room was overheated and that, while Auden was reading,

[1] 15 August 1939.

Somebody offered to open a window, and Auden screamed 'Oh, I would *love* that!' and we all broke up. He went on reading on the very edge of the platform and didn't see us at all. He was near-sighted. But Christopher did. We were winking and grinning, and Isherwood was grinning back while Auden and MacNeice read. After the reading we went up and said we were from the Brooklyn College *Observer*, and could we interview them. Auden kind of trumpeted, 'Oh, ah, see Mr Isherwood.' Christopher was very warm and sympathetic and wrote their address on a calling card and gave it to me saying he *hoped* I'd come and see them. I was all ready, but Chester took the card.[1]

Auden and Isherwood, who had stayed at the George Washington Hotel when they first arrived in New York, had now moved to an apartment at 237 East Eighty-first Street, and it was Chester who called there two days later. When Auden opened the door and saw him, he exclaimed involuntarily, 'But it's the wrong blonde!' However, he invited Chester in. If this was not, as one of their friends claimed later, a case of love at first sight, it was at least love at second sight. Auden made his *déclaration* a few days later when he presented Chester with a copy of Blake which he had inscribed with a quotation from his own poem, 'O tell me the truth about love':

> When it comes, will it come without warning
>   Just as I'm picking my nose,
> Will it knock on my door in the morning
>   Or tread in the bus on my toes,
> Will it come like a change in the weather,
>   Will its greeting be courteous or bluff,
> Will it alter my life altogether?
>   O tell me the truth about love.

It did alter his life altogether. He and Chester became lovers for some years, and friends until death. Kallman and Isherwood never got on very well, which is perhaps understandable. No doubt, at the beginning, each was to some extent jealous of the other. Auden once claimed that Isherwood's inherent anti-Semitism was the cause, which hardly seems likely. The Auden–Isherwood relationship began to cool, although they continued friends. Chester was a contributory cause to the cooling process, and another was Isherwood's growing interest in the Hindu philosophy of Vedanta, which Auden impatiently dismissed as 'mumbo-jumbo'. Soon, Isherwood was to flee to sunny California, to study Vedanta with Swami

[1] Harold Norse, in an unpublished interview quoted in *Isherwood* by Jonathan Fryer (New York, 1978).

Prabhavananda of the Vedanta Society of Southern California, and to work for M-G-M as a script-writer.

In an interview he gave to the *New York Times*, Auden said that he wanted to write a book about America, and that he planned to research it by spending eighteen months teaching at various schools. He was 'sure this will prove the best way in which to study the American scene'. The poet Richard Eberhart, who was then teaching at St Mark's School in South-borough, Massachusetts, happened to read the interview, and suggested to his headmaster that Auden be invited to join the teaching staff. As a result, at the beginning of May Auden spent about five weeks as a guest teacher, teaching English to the upper three forms. He wore his slippers, was popular with the pupils, tried to encourage Eberhart to take Benzedrine at breakfast, and was alternately shy and aggressively eccentric. A pupil recalls that

> the first assignment he gave to our class was to write a story or essay in which every sentence contained a lie . . . he was a consistently stimulat-ing teacher, and popular with his students. I have no doubt that he was possibly the best teacher any of us were ever to have at any point in our education, but we were not much aware of this at the time . . . we knew Auden was somehow a famous man, but we didn't think about it much. After supper Auden would often invite groups of boys up to his study, where talk was about 'books and men' and that kind of thing. . . .
>
> It is quite possible that the trustees of the school were unaware of Auden's sexual status. Blind spots abounded in that kind of society. But some of the faculty made no secret of their dislike for Auden, and I suspect this was because of his homosexuality and because he was leav-ing England at a time when others, including some St Mark's masters, were preparing to return and fight for England. At any rate, I recall the school chaplain – a 'hearty' who in other respects was a man of pro-foundly decent character – opening all the windows and waving the door back and forth after Auden had finished a class and left the room, as if to fumigate the place of Auden's presence.
>
> On our return to school the next year, both Eberhart and Auden had left. At the time I heard of no *chronique scandaleuse* concerning them, although there were inevitable rumours some of us heard later as adults. I doubt if the trustees or faculty ever had any idea of how lucky the school was to have had him, or of what he brought to his students. I hope that Auden had some sense of sympathy and gratitude from us, but I doubt if, in that schoolboy atmosphere, with a world war approaching, any of us had much time for thanking teachers for anything except in the various conventional ways boys say thank you when they leave school.[1]

[1] Letter from John Johnston Appleton to Charles Osborne, 8 June 1978.

Early in May, when Auden went up to Massachusetts to teach, Isherwood, accompanied by the boy-friend he had acquired through George Davis the previous year, departed by Greyhound bus for California. A few weeks later, Benjamin Britten and Peter Pears followed the example of Auden and Isherwood, and left England for America. Britten, in his own words, was 'a discouraged young composer – muddled, fed-up and looking for work, longing to be used',[1] and had decided to become a citizen of the United States, and to make his career there. He and Pears went first to Canada, and came down to New York later in the summer. Meanwhile, Auden, having finished teaching at St Mark's, took a long holiday with Chester Kallman, travelling by bus down to New Orleans, then west, first to Taos in New Mexico where they stayed for a month, and then on to California. It was this summer of travel together which consolidated the early stage of their relationship, and made them decide to live together permanently. Auden was now thirty-two years of age; Chester Kallman was eighteen. Born into a Jewish family in Brooklyn on 7 January 1921, he had been educated at Brooklyn College. He wrote poetry, and loved both opera, about which he became quite knowledgeable, and opera singers, about whom he accumulated a vast store of gossip. It was Kallman who led Auden to a deep and abiding interest in opera which was to become so important to him in his later years.

When Auden and Kallman returned to New York, Auden found a letter awaiting him from the American immigration authorities pointing out that he had violated the terms of his entry visa by undertaking paid employment at St Mark's School, and ordering him to leave the country by a date which was already one month past when Auden first saw the letter. Knowing of an official in Washington who might be able to help him, Auden flew down to the capital to seek his advice. At the suggestion of the official, he left the United States as ordered, travelled to Canada, and came back into the States as part of the ordinary quota for British immigrants. He was now able legally to earn his living in the United States: in addition to reviewing books for the leading intellectual weeklies, *The Nation* and the *New Republic*, he began teaching again, first for the Writers' School run by the League of American Writers, from October to December. But he was never happy with the hard Soviet line taken by the League and its administration, and, when he was castigated by his employers for having written for the 'Trotskyite' *Partisan Review*, he thought it wiser to stop teaching at the Writers' School. He continued to extend his freelance literary activities, calling on anyone whom he thought might possibly be able to help him with reviewing, journalistic assignments or broadcasting, and he continued to enjoy enormously the experience of living in New York. To a friend in England he wrote that

[1] Benjamin Britten: Speech 'On Receiving the First Aspen Award' (London, 1964).

America was proving the most decisive experience of his life:

> It has taught me the kind of writer I am, i.e. an introvert who can only
> develop by obeying his introversion. All Americans are introverts. I adore
> New York as it is the only city in which I find I can work and live quietly.
> For the first time I am leading a life which remotely approximates to the
> way I think I ought to live. I have never written or read so much.[1]

In another letter, Auden claimed that he wished never to see England
again, but instead wanted all his friends to join him in America when the
war was over. In a sense, Auden's English period, the Auden decade of the
thirties which had symbolically begun with the publication, in January 1930,
of 'Paid on Both Sides', can be said to have come to an end not when he and
Isherwood stepped aboard an ocean liner at Southampton, but in New York
when Auden sat in one of the dives

> On Fifty-second Street
> Uncertain and afraid
> As the clever hopes expire
> Of a low dishonest decade . . .

The date was 'September 1, 1939', the title of the poem which was
forming in Auden's mind as he sat over a drink. He began to write it that
day, and completed it the following day. It was published in October in the
New Republic, and it became one of his best-known, most quoted poems,
containing as it did Auden's most famous single line, 'We must love one
another or die'.

> . . . All I have is a voice
> To undo the folded lie,
> The romantic lie in the brain
> Of the sensual man-in-the-street
> And the lie of Authority
> Whose buildings grope the sky:
> There is no such thing as the State
> And no one exists alone;
> Hunger allows no choice
> To the citizen or the police;
> We must love one another or die.

Years later, Auden described 'September 1, 1939' as a hangover from his
English period: it was, he said, the kind of poem he had left England in order
to avoid writing. He came to object, in particular, to his most famous line. In
1945 he removed the offending stanza from the poem when it was included

[1] Quoted in Edward Mendelson's Preface to *The English Auden*.

in *The Collected Poetry of W. H. Auden*. In 1955 he allowed its reinstatement when the poem was included in an anthology of American verse, but altered the line to 'We must love one another and die'. Later he dropped the entire poem from his official *oeuvre*. When he came to justify, in print, his suppression of the poem, Auden got the sequence of events wrong:

> Rereading a poem of mine, *1st. September, 1939*, after it had been published, I came to the line 'We must love one another or die' and said to myself: 'That's a damned lie! We must die anyway.' So, in the next edition, I altered it to 'We must love one another and die'. This didn't seem to do either, so I cut the stanza. Still no good. The whole poem, I realized, was infected with an incurable dishonesty – and must be scrapped.[1]

In this case, the later Auden would seem to have read too literally or simplistically the Auden of 1939; but too much has already been written by too many about Auden's revisions. Clearly, an artist is entitled to alter his work, but if, as a reader, one dislikes the revision, one has the right to ignore it and prefer the original version. Poems are tougher than paintings, and much harder to destroy. Auden may have scrapped 'September 1, 1939', but it is safe to say that his readers have never done so, and that posterity is unlikely to, for it is a very moving poem. However, Auden was surely right when he referred to it as a hangover from his English period. It sums up the decade, and celebrates with a terse, elegant sadness the poet's farewell to it.

'September 1, 1939', is not only the title of a poem; it is also the date of Hitler's invasion of Poland. Two days later, on 3 September, Britain and France declared war on Germany. Benjamin Britten and Peter Pears were now in New York, and Pears had introduced Britten and Auden to his friend Mrs Elizabeth Mayer. Dr and Mrs William Mayer were refugees from Hitler's Germany. Dr Mayer had practised as a psychiatrist in Munich; his wife was a music lover with a unique talent for fostering and encouraging artists and musicians, who was later to collaborate with Auden in translations from German. Dr Mayer was medical director of an institution at Amityville on Long Island, and Stanton Cottage, their house in the grounds of the institution, became during the war years a centre for a number of creative artists, many of them European refugees. Britten and Pears stayed at Stanton Cottage for several weeks in the summer and autumn of 1939: the visitors' book reveals that Auden was there on 4 September, the day after the outbreak of war. It reveals too, that both he and Chester Kallman were present on 22 November, when a small family party was given for Britten's twenty-sixth birthday. Sir Peter Pears recalled that Auden and Kallman became frequent visitors to the house.[2]

[1] Foreword to *W. H. Auden: A Bibliography* (Charlottesville, 1964).
[2] In conversation with the present author.

At the end of 1939, Auden rented rooms in a house at 1, Montague Terrace, Brooklyn Heights, just across the East River from Manhattan. (Kallman was still living at home.) Auden was now able to adhere to a strict routine of writing, which was what he liked best, for he always insisted that a writer must keep regular hours, like any other worker. It now became his custom to rise at 6.30 and go straight to his desk, often without washing, for he was never the cleanest of individuals and his contempt for hygiene increased with age. After an interval for breakfast, he would continue to write until 10.30, when he would go to a cafeteria and continue working there until lunchtime. He would work again from 2 till 4, after which he relaxed. In the evenings he went frequently to the opera.

In 1940, George Davis of *Harper's Bazaar* took a lease on an old three-storey house in Brooklyn Heights at 7, Middagh Street, a short, tree-lined street, lurking in the shadows of the Brooklyn Bridge, only a few hundred yards away from the house in which Auden was living. Davis's purpose was to live in it himself and to invite a number of friends working in the arts to rent rooms at moderate cost. The first two to do so were Auden, on 2 October, and the young American novelist Carson McCullers. During 1940 and 1941, at one time or another, Davis had a number of distinguished tenants, and Auden took to managing the house and its occupants on Davis's behalf. Gypsy Rose Lee, the strip-tease artist, lived there while she wrote a murder mystery, *The G-String Murders*, with the help of George Davis. In the evenings, Auden, Davis, Gypsy Rose Lee and Carson McCullers often used to visit the nearby bars in Sand Street, much frequented by the U.S. Navy. When Gypsy Rose Lee moved out, the writer Paul Bowles and his wife Jane took over her rooms. Bowles described in his memoirs the congenial atmosphere of the place:

> To me the house was a model of *Gemütlichkeit*. It was furnished with what are now called antiques: examples of nineteenth-century American Ugly which George had picked up on Third Avenue and on Brooklyn's Fulton Street and combined with capricious perversity to make a comic facsimile of his grandmother's house in Michigan. It was well heated, and it was quiet, save when Benjamin Britten was working in the first-floor parlor, where he had installed a big black Steinway. George lived on the first floor, Oliver Smith, Jane and I on the second, Britten, Auden and Peter Pears, the British tenor, on the third, and Thomas Mann's younger son Golo lived in the attic . . . It was an experiment, and I think a successful one, in communal living. It worked largely because Auden ran it: he was exceptionally adept at getting the necessary money out of us when it was due. We had a good cook and an impossible maid (except that I doubt that any maid could ever have kept that house completely clean and neat), and

we ate steaming meals that were served regularly and punctually in the dim, street-floor dining room, with Auden sitting at the head of the table. He would preface a meal by announcing: 'We've got a roast and two veg, salad and savoury, and there will be no political discussion.' He had enough of the don about him to keep us all in order; quite rightly he would not tolerate argument or bickering during mealtime. He exercised a peculiar fascination over Jane, who offered to do his typing for him; astonishingly enough, he accepted, and she had to get up every morning at six o'clock and go downstairs to meet him in the dining room, where they would work for three hours or so before breakfast, calling out from time to time for more coffee from the kitchen.[1]

Golo Mann later recalled how effective Auden was as *paterfamilias*, supervising the black servants, cook and maid, expressing instant disapproval if anyone was late for a meal, announcing at breakfast, with a certain satisfaction, that it was rent-day, and later going from room to room extracting payment. Auden himself ate enormously at meal-times and drank impressive amounts of cheap red wine. He had also become a tough bargainer with publishers. 'Sie sind alle Verbrecher' ('They're all criminals') he said to Golo Mann.

The poet and critic Louis Untermeyer often visited his friend Carson McCullers at Middagh Street. He recalled one particular evening, 'a gay (in both senses of the word) occasion at which Auden and Gypsy Rose Lee were present. (Gypsy did not strip, but Auden did plenty of teasing.)'[2]

Chester Kallman moved into 7, Middagh Street, Louis MacNeice stayed for a time, as did Salvador and Gala Dali. George Davis accepted as lodgers only those who had Auden's approval. Peter Pears told the present author that, although he himself had rather liked the enormous room they shared, Britten never felt entirely comfortable there. 'Ben hated bohemianism,' he said, and 7, Middagh Street was nothing if not bohemian in its ambience. Nevertheless, they lived there from November 1940 to the summer of 1941.

On Thanksgiving Day, 1940, the company that assembled for mid-day Thanksgiving Dinner at Middagh Street included Auden and Kallman, George Davis, Gypsy Rose Lee, Britten and Pears, Louis MacNeice, Carson McCullers, and her estranged husband whom she had invited to dinner. Relaxing in the ground floor drawing-room after their meal, with brandy and coffee, they heard the approaching siren of a fire engine, and some of them, including Carson McCullers, rushed outside and tried to chase the fire engine for a few blocks. Carson McCullers said later that it was as she

---

[1] Paul Bowles: *Without Stopping* (London, 1972).
[2] Letter from Louis Untermeyer to Virginia Spencer Carr, quoted in V. S. Carr's *The Lonely Hunter* (New York, 1976).

was racing along the street that the *donnée* of her novel, *The Member of the Wedding*, suddenly came to her. It was only one of several important works that were first conceived among the bohemian frivolities of Brooklyn Heights: the first thoughts about an opera which was to become *Peter Grimes* occurred to Britten while he was living there, and Auden found it an extremely congenial place in which to work. Dozens of creative artists came and went, some staying only for short periods. At one time there was a long waiting list for permanent occupancy: among the short-term visitors was a trained chimpanzee and his keeper. The human occupants at one time or another included the composer Marc Blitzstein, the black American novelist Richard Wright, Christopher Isherwood who stayed for a few days in the summer of 1941, and the artist Pavel Tschelitchev who thought the wall of the drawing-room drab and enlivened it with a huge surrealist mural.

Auden's management of the house is remembered by survivors as having been exemplary. He devised menus, hired and fired servants and dealt with difficult tenants as to the manner born. As always, he was a stickler for punctuality, not only at mealtimes, but on all social occasions. When the household sent out invitations to a party, he added: 'The carriage will depart sharply at 1.00 a.m.', and he saw to it that festivities ceased, however abruptly, at the designated hour. Years later, Auden remembered that his rent, for a sitting-room and bedroom on the top floor, was twenty-five dollars a month, and that most of the other tenants paid about the same. There were two black servants. Eva, the cook, was paid fifteen dollars a week, and slept in the basement, while the maid, Susie, earned ten dollars and lived out. Auden remained proud, in retrospect, of his achievement in managing the household. 'Carson [McCullers] had absolutely nothing to do with housekeeping,' he said. 'She simply lived there, as did the other paying guests.'[1]

When Auden left for Michigan, the character of the house began to change, and gradually other occupants began to move out. Carson McCullers left in the winter of 1940–41, and when she visited George Davis in 1942 she noted that 7, Middagh Street was 'no longer campy but sedate and respectable'. In 1945, all the houses in Middagh Street were destroyed in the construction of a new automobile approach to Brooklyn Bridge. No trace of the street or the former atmosphere of the neighbourhood remains.

In England, Auden's defection was still a lively topic of discussion in literary circles. When friends asked him to answer some of the accusations that were being made, he was reluctant to do so. To his old friend and mentor E. R. Dodds who had written to ask why he could not come home, now that the fight against Fascism had actually begun, he replied that he would return only if he could find something special to do for the war effort

[1] Auden, in conversation with Virginia Spencer Carr, in 1971. Quoted in *The Lonely Hunter*.

as a writer. In his editorial in the February issue of *Horizon*, their friend Cyril Connolly referred to the departure of Auden and Isherwood to America rather ambiguously as 'the most important literary event since the outbreak of the Spanish War', and continued:

Auden is our best poet, Isherwood our most promising novelist. They did not suffer from lack of recognition in England where they received a publicity which they did everything to encourage, nor have they gone to America to animate the masses, for Auden has been teaching in a New England school and Isherwood writing dialogue in a Hollywood studio. They are far-sighted and ambitious young men with a strong instinct of self-preservation, and an eye on the main chance, who have abandoned what they consider to be the sinking ship of European democracy, and by implication the aesthetic doctrine of social realism that has been prevailing there. Are they right? It would certainly seem so . . .

Connolly always professed to be surprised when Auden and Isherwood complained to Stephen Spender about his comments, for he claimed that he had meant his editorial to be a defence of his two old friends. With friends like this, Auden and Isherwood must have thought, who needs enemies? They certainly had enemies, however, who managed to get a question asked about them in the House of Commons on 13 June 1940. *Hansard* for that day reports the following exchange:

Major Sir Jocelyn Lucas asked the Parliamentary Secretary to the Minister of Labour whether British citizens of military age, such as Mr. W. H. Auden and Mr. Christopher Isherwood, who have gone to the United States and expressed their determination not to return to this country until the war is over, will be summoned back for registration and calling up, in view of the fact that they are seeking refuge abroad?
Mr. Assheton: I have no information with regard to Mr. Isherwood. Mr. Austin [sic] gave an undertaking before leaving the country that he would return if called upon to do so; he is outside the age groups so far required to register under the National Service (Armed Forces) Act.
Mr. Mathers: On a point of order. There is no mention of Mr. Austin in this Question.
Sir J. Lucas: Is my hon. Friend aware of the indignation caused by young men leaving the country and saying that they will not fight? If they are not registered as conscientious objectors will he see that they lose their citizenship?

Louis MacNeice, who stayed at Middagh Street for some months, trying to write poems, with Britten and Pears rehearsing on one side of him and Gypsy Rose Lee ('like a whirlwind of laughter and sex') holding forth on the other, contributed an American Letter to *Horizon* in July, in which he tried to present Auden's case, which was, it must be admitted, essentially a selfish one, though no less valid for that: 'It is no question of *il gran refiuto*: he feels he can work better here than in Europe, and that is all there is to it.' MacNeice added that, speaking for himself, he too preferred, at the moment, being in America to being in England.

Having decided to stay in America and to apply for American citizenship, Auden registered in 1940 for the draft, but was turned down after his medical examination in 1942. Meanwhile, he continued to seek literary or teaching engagements, both in New York city and elsewhere. Early in the year, his new book of verse was published, the American edition preceding the English edition for the first time and by four months. The book was *Another Time*, which Auden dedicated to Chester Kallman, and which contains a larger number of his finest and best-loved poems than any other individual volume; mainly poems written between 1937 and the end of 1939. Among them are 'Brussels in winter', 'Lay your sleeping head, my love', 'Musée des beaux arts', 'Dover', the ballads ('Miss Gee', 'James Honeyman' and 'Victor'), the four cabaret songs which Britten had set to music, 'Refugee blues', 'Spain', 'In memory of W. B. Yeats' and 'September 1, 1939'.

Critical reception of *Another Time* in England was mixed. *The Listener*[1] divided the poems into three groups: 'the first serious and obscure because the author has telescoped so much thought into the verse, the second delightfully irresponsible but with some of the squibs a little damp, the third mainly elegiac and deeply moving.' T. C. Worsley in the *New Statesman*[2] wrote: 'The great merit of W. H. Auden's poetry is that it is written out of the centre of our cultural pattern . . . Reading Auden, even at his most obscure or his most silly, enlarges our understanding of what the life of our day is really like. . . . Most of the poems date from before the war and it is too early to say what effect migration will have on his work. I cannot believe that it will be detrimental, for he is the least provincial of poets.' However, Michael Roberts in *The Spectator*[3] thought the contents of the volume for the most part 'trivial or skilfully imitative'.

In February and March 1940 in New York Auden took part in a forum on Sound in Cinema, organized by the Association of Documentary Film Producers. Later in the year, he began to lecture once a week, for almost a year, first on 'Poetry and Culture' and then on 'The Language and Technique of Poetry', at the New School for Social Research whose faculty included a number of other distinguished European exiles. He wrote three scripts for radio, the first of which, 'The dark valley', was the most successful. Based on

[1] 22 August 1940.
[2] 27 July 1940.
[3] 26 July 1940.

the sketch, 'Alfred', which Auden had contributed to *New Writing* in 1936, it was broadcast on 2 June with Dame May Whitty playing the only role, and incidental music by Britten. The script was later published in a volume, *Best Broadcasts of 1939–40*. Auden's half hour (!) adaptation of *Pride and Prejudice* for radio had to be largely rewritten by the producer, John Houseman, before it was broadcast in November, but 'The rocking-horse winner', a dramatization of a short story by D. H. Lawrence, with which Auden was helped by James Stern who gave him information on betting procedures, was accepted and broadcast the following April.

On 17 June, Auden gave the Commencement Address at Smith College, a girls' college in Massachusetts, to an audience of two thousand. In his talk, which he called 'Romantic or Free?', he equated romanticism with a closed society, and told his audience that, 'whatever political label we may choose to wear, we have either to adapt to an open society or perish.' (Is not this a prose version of 'We must love one another or die'?) On 1 July he was with Klaus and Erika Mann (Mrs Auden), whose parents had just moved from Princeton to California. Later in July, he visited MacNeice, who was in a New Hampshire hospital, recovering from an operation for peritonitis. In August he spent a weekend at Bread Loaf Writers' Conference, a summer school for young writers and poets, in the Green Mountains near Middlebury, Vermont. He did some informal teaching, read his poems, talked and drank with Carson McCullers, and even joined in a softball game which he played as though it were cricket, under the captaincy of Robert Frost. In the autumn Auden and Britten worked on an operetta commissioned by Columbia University. This was *Paul Bunyan*, which was to have its first performance in May the following year. At the same time, Auden helped his friend to write a letter as well as an operetta. Britten had been approached to compose a symphony for the 2,600th anniversary of the foundation of the dynasty of the Mikado and had submitted to the Japanese authorities his outline of a *Sinfonia da Requiem* which they had approved. But when his completed score was handed over the composer received a furious protest through the Japanese Embassy, rejecting the work and complaining that its Christian dogma was a calculated insult to the Mikado. Britten called upon Auden to help him draft a reply, but the Japanese attack on Pearl Harbor the next year made a Japanese performance of the *Requiem* impossible.

Interviewed for the *Saturday Review*'s special number on the exiled European writers living in the United States,[1] Auden revealed that he had already taken out his first citizenship papers. 'The attractiveness of America to a writer,' he said, 'is its openness and lack of tradition . . . It's the only country where you feel there's no ruling class. There's just a lot of people.'

[1] 19 October 1940.

201

Chapter Eight

1940–1945

To throw away the key and walk away,
Not abrupt exile, the neighbours asking why,
But following a line with left and right,
An altered gradient at another rate,
Learns more than maps upon the whitewashed wall,
The hand put up to ask; and makes us well
Without confession of the ill.[1]

In 1940 Auden began to go regularly to church again, and by October he had rejoined the Anglican Communion. Commentators on Auden have made much of his conversion to Christianity, and the poet himself wrote about it in his contribution to the volume, *Modern Canterbury Pilgrims*,[2] in which he described his Anglo-Catholic upbringing, his gradual loss of interest in religion as he grew to manhood, and his realization that behind his devout phase 'lay a quite straightforward and unredeemed eroticism'. Growing away from a Christian family into an intellectual world where most people, certainly most writers, were atheists or agnostics, he had found himself ceasing to think about religion. But the beliefs of his childhood were still embedded within him, and it is hardly surprising that when, in his early thirties, he came to examine himself and his beliefs, he should discover that the faith drilled into him as a child had by no means died. He had, after all, helped to keep it alive with his playing and singing of hymns at every available opportunity, however ironically he may have thought he was behaving at the time, and he had never lost his taste for abstruse theological discussion. He had surprised himself by the extent to which he was disturbed at the treatment meted out to the church and its priests in Spain. Shortly after his Spanish visit, as he reveals in *Modern Canterbury Pilgrims*, he had met, in a publisher's office, an Anglican layman, 'and for the first time in my life felt myself in the presence of personal sanctity. I had met many good people before who made me feel ashamed of my own shortcomings, but in the presence of this man – we never discussed anything but literary business – I did not feel ashamed. I felt transformed into a person who was incapable of doing or thinking anything base or unloving.'

The man, whom Auden does not name in that essay, was Charles Wil-

[1] From 'Paid on Both Sides'.
[2] Ed. James A. Pike (New York, 1956).

liams, and the literary business they discussed was *The Oxford Book of Light Verse*. But, if Spain, Williams and, later, Kierkegaard had begun to lead Auden's thoughts back to the church, it was a mystical experience, apparently the opposite of the earlier experience of blissful communion on an English lawn in 1933, which brought a degree of urgency to his thoughts on the subject. This second experience, which he may have undergone some time during 1939, is recorded in a deliberately vague paragraph in the *Modern Canterbury Pilgrims* essay:

> So, presently, I started to read some theological works, Kierkegaard in particular, and began going, in a tentative and experimental sort of way, to church. And then, providentially – for the occupational disease of poets is frivolity – was forced to know in person what it is like to feel oneself the prey of demonic powers, in both the Greek and the Christian sense, stripped of self-control and self-respect, behaving like a ham actor in a Strindberg play.

What is most interesting about Auden's 'conversion' is that he remained very much as he had formerly been. He had been an extremely eccentric Marxist, and he now became an equally eccentric Christian, one in whom the Audenish outweighed the Christian elements. He was able to accept Christian dogma more easily than Marxist dogma, or at least to pay more lip-service to it, because it is, as dogma, less dangerous. It would seem that what Auden sought, after an experience which had frightened him, was a set of rules to which he could cling and which would protect him against unknown terrors. He had always, like most liberal humanists, accepted the moral tenets of Christianity. Now he was prepared to swallow its supernatural aspects as well for the sake, one might say, of a quiet life. Whether a quiet life produces better poetry than a turbulent life is debatable. Auden chose not to debate the issue, but to regard it as a challenge to his powers as a poet. If he changed at all as a result of becoming a Christian, it was a change in the direction of dogmatism and illiberality, though it would hardly be fair to lay the blame for this entirely upon the Church, for Auden encouraged the ageing and hardening process, and began to play the role of the inflexible old fogy years before he had any right to it.

Asked solemnly by a friend to state his theological position, Auden replied: 'Liturgically, I am Anglo-Catholic though not too spiky, I hope. As for forms of church organization, I don't know what to think. I am inclined to agree with de Rougemont that it will be back to the catacombs for all of us. As organizations, none of the churches look too hot, do they? But what organization ever does?'[1] He never allowed his religion to interfere with his pleasures, and was, for instance, quite happy both to consider homosexual-

[1] Quoted by Ursula Niebuhr in *W. H. Auden: A Tribute*.

ity a sinful state and to indulge in homosexual acts regularly for the rest of his life. He never finally or completely surrendered either to politics or to religion, but took from each precisely as much as he wanted, and no more. He liked having an official stance from which to view the world, and was certainly more content with the trappings of official Anglo-Catholicism than with those of Marxism. But, for all that he liked to indulge in theological and liturgical small-talk, no one who knew him at all well in the last twenty years of his life could truthfully call Auden a devoutly religious man. What he lost, in his teens, was not faith but childhood acceptance of what his elders had passed down to him; what he regained at the age of thirty-three, again, was not faith: he merely deliberately thought himself back into an organization with a reassuring ritual. If he jumped from the Marxist frying pan into the Anglo-Catholic fire, it was because he liked a hot climate. He also liked to be as tidy in large, abstract matters, as he was untidy in small, personal ones, creating thus a kind of balance.

In a letter to Stephen Spender, probably written during the autumn of 1940, Auden said of himself: 'As you know, my dominant faculties are intellect and intuition, my weak ones feeling and sensation. This means I have to approach life via the former; I must have knowledge and a great deal of it before I can feel anything. People imagine that I absorb things easily and quickly: this is true only in the most superficial way. On the contrary, I am really someone who has to grow very slowly; I develop slower than most people.' Further on in the same letter, he referred to the war: 'I wish you were over here, not because I don't support the allies – which, in spite of everything, I do – but because there doesn't seem anything that you cannot do just as well here as there (unless it be suffering) – and for selfish personal reasons.'

Throughout most of 1940, Auden had been a member of the Editorial Board of a little magazine, *Decision*, which was edited by Klaus Mann, and he was to remain actively connected with the magazine in 1941. Other members of the Board included Thomas Mann, Sherwood Anderson, Somerset Maugham and Robert Sherwood. Young poets began to write to Auden, sending their poems for comment. One, who called upon him in Middagh Street to say how moved he had been by Auden's poems, was told, 'That's why one writes them.' Early in 1941, Auden worked closely with Britten putting the finishing touches to their operetta, *Paul Bunyan*. In March, Auden's new book of verse, *The Double Man*, dedicated to Elizabeth Mayer, was published in New York by Random House. The poems in it had been written during most of 1940, and reflect something of his thinking about religion during that year. As he wrote later to an enquirer, '*The Double Man* . . . covers a period when I was beginning to think seriously about such things without committing myself. I started going to church again just about

October. It is therefore full of heretical remarks.'[1] The English edition, published two months later, had a different title, *New Year Letter*, and for an odd reason. Auden's title was suggested by a sentence from Montaigne ('We are, I know not how, double in ourselves, so that what we believe we disbelieve, and cannot rid ourselves of what we condemn.') He had offered the book to John Lehmann for the Hogarth Press, who announced it in their catalogues and publicity. Faber & Faber then pointed out that they possessed contractual rights to all of Auden's books, and T. S. Eliot negotiated a transfer of the book to his firm. However, not wanting to be seen to publish a book already announced by a rival publisher, Eliot changed the title to *New Year Letter*, the title of the book's central poem. This led him to alter, without consulting Auden, a phrase in another poem, 'Prologue', from 'a sorrow from the Double Man' to 'a sorrow from the invisible twin'.

Edwin Muir, writing in *Horizon*,[2] described *New Year Letter* as containing 'some of the best poetry that Mr Auden has ever written', claiming that 'the best poems have a clarity and depth . . . a fusion of the ordinary and the mythological which is as natural to him as it was to Kafka'. But other English critics were less convinced of the book's value. In the *New Statesman*,[3] G. S. Fraser said of 'New Year Letter' itself, a philosophical poem 1,707 lines long with a further seventy-nine pages of notes, that he had read it 'five times, with a mixture of astonishment, boredom, pleasure and increasing scepticism', and still had not been able to discover its author's philosophical position. Herbert Read in the *Spectator*[4] thought Auden was still in the process of digesting Kierkegaard: 'But he represents the modern intelligence in all its acuteness and confusion, and his present misuse of a medium (misuse rather than abuse, for it is fundamentally a failure in communication) does not affect our faith in his genius, and our expectation of its eventual expression either in verse that is "simple, clear and gay" (his own demand), or in prose that is clear, simple and serious.'

Some of the notes to the poems in this volume were reprinted later as 'Shorts'. They range from the flippant –

> To the man-in-the-street who, I'm sorry to say,
>   Is a keen observer of life,
> The word *intellectual* suggests right away
>   A man who's untrue to his wife.

to the seriously ironic –

> When Statesmen gravely say 'We must be realistic',
> The chances are they're weak and, therefore, pacifistic,

[1] Quoted by Kenneth Lewars in *The Quest in Auden's Poems and Plays* (M.A. thesis, Columbia University, 1947).
[2] August 1941.   [3] 5 July 1941.   [4] 6 June 1941.

> But when they speak of principles, look out: perhaps
> Their generals are already poring over maps.

On 5 March 1941, at the annual banquet of the *Yale Daily News* in New Haven, Auden delivered an address on the problems facing education, which was published in that newspaper later in the month. On the 13th, in a letter written from Brooklyn Heights to Stephen Spender, after berating his old friend for his review of *Another Time* he attempts once again to explain his own attitude to the European war:

> Dearest Stephen,
>
> People ring me up from time to time to ask me if I am going to answer what they describe as an attack by you in *Horizon*. As I have not read it and don't intend to, I can't.[1] I did happen by chance to see your review of my book . . . and was, I must confess, a little hurt.
>
> Your passion for public criticism of your friends has always seemed to me a little odd; it is not that you don't say acute things – you do – but the assumption of the role of the blue-eyed Candid Incorruptible is questionable. God knows it is hard enough to be objective about strangers; it is quite impossible with those whom one knows well and, I hope, loves. Personally, I will never write a review of a friend's work, nor even a review of a contemporary poet if I can possibly help it. As to your review of me, what you say is probably accurate enough, but the tone alarms me. 'One is worried about Auden's poetic future.' Really, Stephen dear, whose voice is this but that of Harold Spender M.P.[2] 'I hope, if I am bombed, he will write some sapphics about me' is funny and a good criticism, but for you to say it seems to be in shocking taste, suggesting that my only interest in you is as potential elegiac material. Your concluding sentence about being tired of receiving vague advice from America contains more than a trace of *suggestio falsi*. You know quite well that practically all the poems were written before the war; even the one you quote was finished the day before England actually entered the war, yet you suggest that the book is my American Message to the English People in their Hour of Peril . . .
>
> But what really alarms me is that in a crisis of this time, you should be so bothered about what other contemporary writers are up to. What has to be done to defend civilization? In order of immediate importance: (1) to kill Germans and destroy German property. (2) to prevent as many English lives and as much English property as possible from being killed

[1] This was the Editorial Comment, written not by Spender but by Cyril Connolly (see p. 198). But in a letter to Spender some months earlier, Auden had revealed that he had already read this: 'Of course I wasn't offended by the editorial which I thought very fair.'

[2] Spender's father.

and destroyed. (3) to create things from houses to poems that are worth preserving. (4) to educate people to understand what civilization really means and involves. Literary criticism is a very small and negative part of the last. With your gifts for creation and education there is more than enough for you to do. (Even in criticism there are the great figures of the past to illuminate.) For God's sake, Stephen, don't become a literary version of your uncle, or a Dorothy Thompson of the arts.

I dont see how my own attitude about the war can be of any interest except to myself, but here it is. If I thought I should be a competent soldier or air-warden I should come back tomorrow. It is impossible for me to know whether it is a reason or just cowardice that makes me think I shouldnt be of much military effectiveness. All I can do, therefore, is to be willing to do anything when and if the Government ask me (which I told the Embassy here). As a writer and a pedagogue the problem is different, for the intellectual warfare goes on always and everywhere, and no one has a right to say that this place or that time is where all intellectuals ought to be. I believe that for me personally America is the best, but of course the only proof lies in what one produces . . .

As to Christopher, I can only tell you what I think, which may not be what he would say or even authorize. What he is trying to do must seem meaningless unless one believes, and I do, firstly that there is such a vocation as the mystical contemplative life, and secondly that of all vocations it is the highest; highest because the most difficult, exhausting and dangerous . . . I have absolutely no patience with Pacifism as a political movement, as if one could do all the things in one's personal life that create wars and then pretend that to refuse to fight is a sacrifice and not a luxury. On the contrary, it is perhaps the only material reward that the contemplative gets in this world. That is why I respect Gerald [Heard] who really practices what he preaches, and have very little use for Huxley. I know that I am not fit for such a vocation; Christopher feels that he is called, and is certainly taking it very seriously. I think his friends should have enough faith in him to trust his judgment for himself. He never, as far as I know, tells others that they ought to do the same thing.

In New York on 5 May 1941,[1] *Paul Bunyan*, with libretto by Auden and music by Britten, was given the first of six performances in the Brander Matthews Hall of Columbia University, presented by the Columbia Theater Associates, an affiliation of all the acting groups in the University, with the co-operation of the University's Music Department and a chorus from the New York Schola Cantorum. The producer was Milton Smith, and the conductor Hugh Ross. The programme carried this description of the work:

[1] There had been a preview, the night before, for members of the League of Composers.

Paul Bunyan is the first operatic collaboration between Mr. W. H. Auden, one of the best-known young English poets, and Mr. Benjamin Britten, one of the most distinguished young English composers. The Columbia Theater Associates welcome the opportunity to present the world pre-miere of this interesting composition. The authors describe their work as a choral operetta, '. . . with many small parts rather than a few star roles.' They explain that they conceive of Paul Bunyan, the giant hero of the lumbermen, and one of the many mythical figures who appeared in American folklore during the Pioneer period, as '. . . a projection of the collective state of mind of a people whose tasks were primarily the physical mastery of nature. This operetta presents in a compressed fairy-story form the development of the continent from a virgin forest before the birth of Paul Bunyan to settlement and cultivation when Paul Bunyan says goodbye because he is no longer needed, i.e. the human task is now a different one, of how to live well in a country that the pioneers have made it possible to live in.'

In an article in the *New York Times* the day before the première, Auden had said: 'At first sight it may seem presumptuous for a foreigner to take an American folk-tale as his subject, but in fact the implications of the Bunyan legend are not only American but universal.' The New York critics appear to have thought it presumptuous of both librettist and composer, for *Paul Bunyan* received generally unfavourable reviews. 'Musico-Theatrical Flop' was the heading of Virgil Thomson's review in the *New York Herald Tribune*.[1] He thought Britten's music eclectic, witty at its best, but otherwise undistin-guished, and Auden's style 'flaccid and spineless and without energy'. *The New Yorker's*[2] view was that 'in the theatre *Paul Bunyan* didn't jell', and *Time*[3] complained that this 'anemic operetta put up by two British expatriates' was 'as bewildering and irritating a treatment of the outsize lumberman as any two Englishmen could have devised.' Olin Downes in the *New York Times*[4] was kinder to the work, but clearly *Paul Bunyan* was not a success. It was not performed again until it was revived in Great Britain in 1976, after the death of Auden and only six months before the death of Benjamin Britten.

From the summer of 1941, Auden was absent from New York for a year, teaching in Michigan, and by the time he returned Britten and Pears, having decided to go back to England, had already left America. Auden's Michigan engagements began with his participation in a Writers' Conference during the summer at Olivet College, a denominational college. To a friend, Ursula Niebuhr, he wrote: 'For a combination of reasons, personal, artistic and climatic, I have felt very lonely and low here. The truth is, I do not like the provinces, particularly in the USA where they are provincial by so many

[1] 6 May 1941.   [2] 17 May 1941.   [3] 19 May 1941.   [4] 6 May 1941.

thousand miles . . . The Middle West seems to me an Eliot landscape, where the spiritual air is "thoroughly small and dry". If I stay here any longer I shall either take to the mysticism that Reinhold [Niebuhr] so disapproves of, or buy a library of pornographic books.' But in the autumn he began teaching at the University of Michigan which he found more easily endurable, perhaps because Chester Kallman had moved to Michigan to be with him, and had enrolled at the University. The following spring Auden returned to New York.[1]

In August, 1941, his mother had died at the age of seventy-two: after the war Auden told his brother John that his distress at her death had been one of the factors contributing to his return to the religious faith of his childhood. He must have come to believe that this was so, although he had returned to the church a good ten months before his mother's death. Shortly after she died, Auden began to write a Christmas Oratorio called 'For the Time Being', for Britten to set. He worked on it while he was living in Ann Arbor and teaching at the University of Michigan, and finished it in New York in the following summer, dedicating it to the memory of his mother. Auden sent his typescript off to Britten, who pointed out to him that it was far too long to set to music complete, and suggested possible cuts. But, as Peter Pears remembers, Auden refused to cut a line of it, and the project foundered. (With Auden's approval, an American composer, Melvin Levy, many years later set an abridged version of 'For the Time Being', which was performed in New York in 1959. Auden's text is also quite frequently performed by religious groups as a spoken play.)

It was from this time that a certain coolness began to creep into the relationship between Auden and Britten. They seem not to have quarrelled, but rather to have drifted apart. To some extent, this was an inevitable consequence of their living on opposite sides of the Atlantic. When Britten returned to the United States for the American première of his opera *Peter Grimes* four years later, he and Auden met quite amicably, but as acquaintances: no longer as friends. Later still, both men tended to speak of each other as though there had been a real estrangement of some kind. Benjamin Britten once told the present author that he regretted being no longer friendly with Auden, and Auden on more than one occasion in the 1960s and early seventies mentioned in conversation that he had quarrelled with only one of his friends, Britten. Peter Pears did not remember that there was a decisive quarrel, but merely that their lives and attitudes began to diverge more sharply. He recalled that Britten was finding Auden an increasingly

---

[1] The misinformation that in 1950 Auden was appointed Assistant Professor of English Literature at 'Ann Arbor University', Michigan, a non-existent institution, was included in a chronological table in Richard Hoggart's *Auden: an introductory essay* in 1951, and subsequently found its way into other books and essays. Auden did not, in fact, teach in Michigan after 1942.

difficult professional collaborator, and also that he tended to disapprove of Auden's new young friend Chester. It is possible, too, that Auden was somewhat resentful of Britten's relationship with Pears. Britten still thought Auden a stimulating and exciting companion, but found him more and more overbearing where artistic collaboration was concerned. And so the Auden–Britten collaboration came to an abrupt end, in mid-project: the series of great operas which they might have written together was not to be. Britten composed the operas, but with other librettists. Only two minor works were still to come. The first of these was the 'Hymn to St Cecilia', the words written for Britten by Auden, and the music composed by Britten in a tiny cabin on a small Swedish cargo vessel crossing to Britain in March 1942.

Among the articles and reviews which Auden published during 1941 was an essay entitled 'Criticism in Mass Society', which he contributed to a volume called *The Intent of the Critic*, and in which he cited Langland, Dante and Pope as the major influences on his poetry. During the next three years he published fewer occasional prose pieces, perhaps because of the demands made upon him by his full-time teaching assignment at Swarthmore College, near Philadelphia. On 7 December 1941, Japanese sea and air forces launched a surprise attack on the United States naval base at Pearl Harbor, Hawaii, and on the following day the United States declared war on Japan. Auden spent a few days in California during the Christmas holidays, and visited the Mann family at Pacific Palisades, a suburb of Los Angeles. 'Auden was here to lunch with us, while Erika was home. He was boyish and nice as always, and to my mind it is to his credit that he could play with the baby so well,' Thomas Mann wrote to a friend.[1]

Early in January, Auden was back at Ann Arbor, where he and Chester had taken an apartment at 1223 Pontiac Street. On 8 January he wrote to Bennett Cerf suggesting that Random House publish a complete collection of his poems, although he did not want the volume to be called 'Collected Poems', since 'collected' conveyed to him an unwelcome suggestion of finality. The publisher was not enthusiastic, and it was only after several more letters from Auden that Random House eventually agreed to his proposal. (The book was published three years later.) On 16 January, Auden wrote to Stephen Spender, who had joined the Auxiliary Fire Service in London:

Dearest Stephen,

It was lovely to get your letter. I can well imagine how dreary the Fire-Brigade must be, when you can neither go away nor have anything to do. And I suppose they dont even let you wear one of those lovely brass helmets any more – You would look *such* a camp in one.

[1] *Letters of Thomas Mann* (New York, 1970).

I have thought of you a lot during the past year, as I have been having a great personal crisis, like you before me, of which I have reason to suspect that you have an inkling. Things are going to work out alright, I think, but it takes more faith and patience than is natural to me.

My plans are a bit vague. I have asked for deferment from the army until after the university year is over in May. In the meantime there is just a possibility that I may get a job in Washington: of course my request for deferment may be refused, in which case I suppose I shall presently be a quartermaster's orderly or something. Meanwhile I go on with my writing – an enormous oratorio.

Christopher is working in a refugee camp in Pennsylvania. After seeing him this summer, after a year, I feel quite happy that what he is doing is the right thing for *him* to do. (It wouldnt be for me.)

You mustnt judge him by rumours or even by anything he writes to you, because in what is a period of complete re-organization for him, he cant express himself properly. So please, Stephen dear, whether you write to him or not, do think of him warmly, because he needs it as we all do. In this period when we are all separated physically and all undergoing changes and doing different things, it is hard to write letters explaining what one is up to. Because of the lack of context words create more misunderstanding than otherwise, but deep down I have a firm conviction that we are not apart but all engaged on the same thing; and I do hope you feel the same. That is why I so distrust public statements of one's position, or criticism of other people's.

There have been practically no books of interest coming out recently in America. Two good volumes of poetry, one by Marianne Moore and one by Louise Bogan, which I'll try to send you as soon as I am over the financial crisis of the moment. The one really important book I read last year was published by the Oxford Press, so I expect you can get it over there, and if so, do read it. It is *Christianity and Classical Culture* by C. N. Cochrane. I have been reading St. Augustine a lot lately who is quite wonderful, only you must use Watt's translation, not Pusey's. Also, as a new camp, Disraeli's novels which must have been the inspiration for all of Harold Nicolson's books.

Did you hear that my mother died last August? It was a much greater shock to me than I expected.

Much love and happiness to you,
     Wystan.

Auden reviewed the three new books mentioned in his letter, in the *New Republic*, the *New York Times Book Review* and *Partisan Review*. Of Louise Bogan, a poet ten years his senior, who had reviewed his most recent two volumes of poetry in *The New Yorker*, he wrote that he fancied she would be paid, by future generations, 'the respect she deserves when many, including myself, I fear, of those who now have a certain news value, are going to catch it.'[1] He also began to write, in 1942, for the magazine *Commonweal*, contributing not only a superb appraisal of George Bernard Shaw (ostensibly a review of Hesketh Pearson's biography of Shaw) but also a number of religious essays, for which he used the pseudonym 'Didymus' (surname of the apostle Thomas, who first doubted and then believed: which is surely significant).

On 7 April 1942, the *New York Times* announced that Auden and a number of other writers, among them John Dos Passos and Carson McCullers, had been awarded Guggenheim Fellowships. 'It seems,' the *Times* commented, as though surprised by the situation of authors, 'that a writer of English can become quite famous and still need a scholarship in order to have leisure for creative work. More encouraging, it appears that some writers need help because they insist on writing to satisfy their own artistic rectitude and will not take formulas from editors or publishers.'

In the autumn of 1942, Auden took up an appointment as Lecturer in English at Swarthmore College. He remained there until the spring of 1945, teaching only part-time, writing part-time with the aid of his Guggenheim Fellowship grant. In the first semester or half-year he taught a course in Elizabethan Literature, and in the second held a seminar in Romantic Literature from Rousseau to Hitler. In his second year at the College he became Associate Professor of English and found himself teaching English Composition to students in a naval unit who were waiting to go to Officer Candidate School. He also attempted to teach spoken English to a group of Chinese naval officers who, for some reason, had been sent to Swarthmore.

Auden stayed for a much longer time at Swarthmore than at any of the other colleges at which he taught in the United States, and his involvement in the community life of the institution was whole-hearted. He contributed frequently to *The Phoenix*, the college newspaper, gave a number of extramural lectures, reviewed the plays performed by the students, served on committees, and made himself readily accessible to students seeking advice about writing. 'Rumors, Awe Surround Auden's Arrival Here' was the headline in *The Phoenix* on 20 October 1942, and though the awe may have diminished in the face of his amiability, the flames of rumour were fanned by his eccentricities. 'He is reported to have worn no socks, except occasionally on his head in bad weather, and no underwear; to have used a rope for a belt, worn bedroom slippers on the street, and often entertained in bathrobe and slippers.' As always, he was immensely popular with his students, for he treated them as adults and took their problems seriously, and in class he

[1] *Partisan Review* (July–August 1942).

encouraged them to think for themselves. 'Explain why the devil is (a) sad and (b) honest', was one of the questions he set his Elizabethan Literature students to answer; his composition class was asked to write the events of the day backwards. He preferred the 'ungodly but intelligent' to triumph in his classes, he told an interviewer from *The Phoenix*. He attended the Episcopalian church in Swarthmore regularly during his stay there, but always went to the early, eight o'clock service, in order to avoid the sermon. In all his years of church-going he listened to very few sermons. In a letter to Naomi Mitchison he said that he never knew, 'even in Germany, what anti-Semitism meant till I came to this country. All the same I like it here just because it is the Great Void where you have to balance without handholds.'

In his first year at Swarthmore, Auden took rooms in a house called Sunnybank, about a mile from the campus, and later moved to 16, Oberlin Avenue, where he occupied the first floor of a house where several families lived. The *Phoenix* interviewer gave a vivid description of the usual mess:

> An air of curious incompleteness pervades the household – phonograph records piled in albums and stacks along the left-hand side of the room, huge plush armchairs and sofas on the right. The entire rugless room, with its small table holding a large bottle of red wine and piles of cigarette packs, suggests the atmosphere of some temporary campaign headquarters of a political party, although Auden assures us it is to be improved. He plans to build a large record cabinet to house his collection, and will soon adorn his now bare walls with large contour maps of the countryside, which are his favourite wall decoration. 'I'm very disorderly myself, but that doesn't mean I like being disorderly. I don't. I would just prefer servants of my own,' he said. Taking us into the other two rooms, considerably neater, he showed us his prized possession: a monstrous centerpiece of wax flowers, carefully protected by a large glass cover ('Easily worth forty dollars, and I bought it for only ten dollars') and his large, low-set bed, once owned and slept in by Ehrlich, inventor of the syphilis cure.[1]

Auden's working schedule at Swarthmore involved him in rising early, writing all morning until two (he finally completed his Christmas Oratorio, 'For the Time Being', while he was at Swarthmore), then repairing for lunch either to a small restaurant called the Dew Drop Inn or to the Media Druggie. His classes usually met in the afternoon. After his first year he taught also at nearby Bryn Mawr College. He would make 'trips back and forth with a suitcase full of bottles, bringing in supplies to dry Swarthmore and returning empties.'[2] In addition to the amusingly iconoclastic lectures he prepared

[1] *The Phoenix*, 14 December 1943.
[2] Monroe K. Spears in *Swarthmore College Bulletin* (March 1962).

for his own students, he also found time to give public lectures at Swarthmore on such subjects as 'Vocation and Society', 'Education in the Democratic Society' and even 'Rimbaud's Influence on English Poetry'. A comic programme of bad music and poetry which he and some colleagues presented to the entire student body, and which Auden introduced in a variety of accents and invented languages, lived on in Swarthmore legend for many years. When the Little Theater Club of the college produced *The Ascent of F.6* in the spring of 1945, he gave his advice on interpretation and even played a minor, non-speaking role, that of the cowled monk in Act II. Christopher Isherwood had intended to come from California to see the production, but *The Phoenix* reported that he had changed his plans, and had left his monastery in order to write a script for Warner Brothers.

At Bryn Mawr, a young lady from the *College News* attempted to interview Auden shortly before he began to teach there. After telling her that anyone who asked him whether or not they should write would receive an unconditional 'No' for an answer ('If you are going to write, you won't have to ask someone else's advice before starting'), that literature courses were the worst possible preparation for a writer, and that the most important thing about poetry was the fun the poet himself got out of it, Auden decided he had had enough of the interview:

> 'Why people should feel that men who write always have something of great import to say is incomprehensible to me,' he said, explaining that one interviews explorers to the North Pole, or men just returned from the Italian campaign, but not a man who is merely carrying on the daily business of life. 'Most poets,' he concluded, 'are bad characters, vain and selfish, and interviews merely encourage them,' and so saying, he excused himself, and left the room.[1]

In February, 1945, Auden spoke to the graduating class at Swarthmore on 'The World of Flesh and the Devil', and ended with a few laconic words of advice to the students: 'Never forget you're a heel; read *The New Yorker*; don't wash too much.' He must already have been working on the poem 'Under Which Lyre' which he completed the next year and read at Harvard as the Phi Beta Kappa Poem of 1946, for it ends with these stanzas:

> Thou shalt not be on friendly terms
> With guys in advertising firms,
>   Nor speak with such
> As read the Bible for its prose,
> Nor, above all, make love to those
>   Who wash too much.

[1] *College News* (Bryn Mawr, 14 October 1943).

Thou shalt not live within thy means
Nor on plain water and raw greens.
   If thou must choose
Between the chances, choose the odd:
Read *The New Yorker*, trust in God;
   And take short views.

During the college vacation periods, Auden usually returned to New York City. In the winter of 1942, he lunched in New York with his old colleagues from the GPO Film Unit, John Grierson and Basil Wright, who wanted to persuade him to rejoin them and make films for the war effort in Canada. Auden agreed, out of politeness, to consider their offer, and later wrote to Grierson regretting he was unable to accept it. In 1943, he visited an old Oxford friend, Isaiah Berlin, who was working at the British Embassy in Washington, and through him he met the composer Nicolas Nabokov. Auden and Nabokov instantly got on well, and met again on several occasions, either in Washington, or in Annapolis where Nabokov was teaching, or at Swarthmore. At a dinner-party Auden gave for Nabokov at Swarthmore, a Frenchman was present, whom the anti-French Auden introduced as 'perfectly tame, my dear', meaning that he was sufficiently Americanized not to be referred to contemptuously as 'Frog'. However, Auden became embroiled in an argument with his French guest, during the course of the evening, on the merits of 'that dreary immoralist' André Gide. He rejected, with scorn, Gide's claim in *Si le grain ne meurt* that he had spent all night having sex with an Arab boy and had then taken him out to the sand dunes and continued until after sunrise. 'He's a conceited liar,' Auden declared. 'How could he have an orgasm after a night of fucking. I'll bet he couldn't even produce an erection!'

The dinner-party was not a conspicuous success. There was not enough to eat, and too much to drink. Nabokov was sick in the bathroom and then collapsed on a sofa. Next morning, Auden took him to the railway station. 'On the way in the taxi he chided me in the crankiest tone of his voice: "You shouldn't drink that much, Nicky . . . Russians never know their measure."'[1]

In the spring of 1943, Benjamin Britten composed 'A Shepherd's Carol' for a BBC radio programme, to words that Auden had discarded from an early draft of 'For the Time Being': 'O lift your little pinkie and touch the winter sky,/Love's all over the mountains, where the beautiful go to die.' It was the last of their joint works. (Thirty years later, there was a slight flurry of anxiety when Britten's carol was sung by the choir at a memorial service for Auden at Christ Church, Oxford, for the Dean's mind was not pure

[1] Nicolas Nabokov in *W. H. Auden: A Tribute.*

enough to refrain from suspecting some obscenity in 'pinkie', which is standard American colloquial usage for 'little finger', and by no means unknown in Great Britain.)

For the Time Being, Auden's new volume which consisted of two long poems, was published in America in September, and an English edition followed some months later. Both the title-poem (the Christmas Oratorio originally intended for Britten to set) and 'The Sea and the Mirror', a commentary on Shakespeare's *The Tempest*, contain prose passages as well as verse, and both are written in dialogue, so that they can be performed. ('For the Time Being' soon began to be performed by religious groups, but the only known performances of 'The Sea and the Mirror' were given in Oxford from 7 to 11 May 1968.) Critical reaction to the new volume was mixed. In the *Yale Review*[1] Louis Untermeyer called *For the Time Being* 'the most memorable book of poetry of the year and . . . the finest work yet composed by its extraordinarily gifted author'; however, the English critics were, in general, still resentful of Auden's absence from a beleaguered Britain, though Henry Reed, in *New Writing and Daylight*, after referring to the Christmas Oratorio as a failure, wrote of 'The Sea and the Mirror' that 'it is vivid, beautiful and vigorous'.[2] The philistine London *Evening Standard* did not review the volume but instead published, three weeks after the American edition had appeared, a silly paragraph under the heading, 'Too Audenish, My Dear': 'Poet W. H. Auden, now 37, has published a new book,' it began, and invited its readers to chortle over 'these astonishing lines put into the mouth of Joseph' in the Christmas Oratorio: 'My shoes were shined, my pants were cleaned and pressed,/And I was sitting down to wait/My own true love.'

Auden's selection of the poems of Tennyson also appeared in September, 1944. In his Introduction, he called Tennyson the stupidest poet in the language, which upset a number of Tennyson scholars, and led T. S. Eliot to remark to Stephen Spender that Auden was no scholar, for if he had been 'he'd have been able to think of some stupider poets'.[3]

In the spring of 1945, Auden came to the end of his time at Swarthmore and Bryn Mawr. On 29 March it had been announced that he was to be awarded the thousand dollar poetry prize of the American Academy of Arts and Letters, an award made to a poet only once every five years, in recognition of distinguished work. Auden was delighted but he was unable to be present at the ceremony on 18 May, for by then two things had happened: early in May the war in Europe had ended, and Auden had joined the US Strategic Bombing Survey and been sent to Germany.

[1] December 1944.
[2] 1945.
[3] Stephen Spender: *The Thirties and After* (London, 1978).

Chapter Nine

1945–1952

More even than in Europe, here
The choice of patterns is made clear
Which the machine imposes, what
Is possible and what is not,
To what conditions we must bow
In building the Just City now.[1]

Auden had offered his services to the United States Government in whatever capacity they thought he could be most useful, and had been given a job with the Morale Division of the US Strategic Bombing Survey, as a civilian research chief with the honorary or simulated rank of major. Major Auden astonished his friends Isaiah Berlin and Nicolas Nabokov by appearing in Berlin's Washington apartment one evening, in his smart military uniform, chuckling delightedly at his transformation into man of war, and announcing that he was being sent overseas within a few days. When Nabokov, who had been trying for some time to join the Allied Armed Forces overseas, asked how one got into the Morale Division, Auden replied, 'You just call them on the telephone and then go and apply for a job. Here, I'll give you the phone number.' He then produced a Pentagon telephone number, and a list of names of people to ask for, all of them Jewish names and beginning with the letter K. Within weeks, Nabokov, having sufficiently impressed Miss Katz, Mr Kohn and Mr Kalksteen, had also become a member of what he called the 'largely German-Kosher' Morale Division of USSBS (United States Strategic Bombing Survey) and was on his way to Europe.

Auden's assignment was to study the psychological effects of bombing on the civilian population in Germany, and to produce a report for the Pentagon. *En route* to Germany, he took some leave in England, visiting his father in Birmingham and several of his old friends in London. Many were disconcerted by the American Major who now confronted them, his English intonation clashing with his Americanized vowels, his attitude to them and to their wartime privations apparently so unsympathetic and clinical. John Lehmann's experience, as recounted in his memoirs, was typical:[2]

He arrived at my door one Sunday morning, complete with new Ameri-

---

[1] From 'New Year Letter'.
[2] *I Am My Brother* (London, 1960).

can officer's uniform and new American accent. A little overpowered by this, I was at a loss how to get the conversation going; but it did not matter, for without much beating about the bush, he launched into a long lecture, quoting detailed statistics of pig-iron production and the industrial man-power graph, on the world power position after the war. Great Britain, her Dominions and Empire had apparently been liquidated, while the two giants, the U.S.A. and the U.S.S.R., towered over the world. Britain, in fact, was lucky to have survived the war at all. There was no word from Uncle Sam Auden about what we had endured, the various skills, the faith, the unremitting industrial and military effort without which the fortress of Western civilization could never have been held; there was not even a personal word of sympathy to a former friend about the discomforts of flying bombs and flying glass and trying to work while a whole building shook and swayed about one, under the impact of high explosive. On the contrary, the second part of the lecture consisted of an exposé of the superiority of American culture, and a sharp calling to order of myself when, as a kind of desperate gesture of defence, I made some mild criticisms of recent American fiction.

Of course I was wrong to be so furious. Wystan's prognosis of the post-war situation was more than partly true; and I had forgotten how impersonal he was by nature, and how habitual it was with him to deal with a situation, when he felt uncertain or shy, by immediate attack. Stephen Spender told me later that he had had a violent row with him because of a similar lecture, but had made it up almost at once and found Wystan sympathetic and human as soon as the air was cleared: once the idea that we were going to be morally superior with him was out of the way. Indeed, I was disarmed myself when he told me at parting, with a pleasure that found an immediate response in me, that the American Navy had ordered 1,100 copies of his collected poems.

The distinguished American writer and critic Edmund Wilson was in London at the same time as Auden. In a letter to a friend in America, Wilson gave an outsider's view of Auden's reunion with his English friends:

. . . Stephen Spender, his old buddy, said to me that he thought it would be the hardest thing in the world for Auden ever to come back to England. A few weeks later, however, he turned up and, as Spender said, took the arrogant line when he might have taken the humble line. Without showing the least embarrassment, he complained about the coldness of English houses, and of other hardships of life in England, and told them that London hadn't really been bombed. They were speechless with indignation, having, they said, politely restrained themselves, when he explained to them the purpose of his mission, from remarking what a pity that he had

had no personal experience of the psychological effects of bombing. He also assured them – being a homosexual chauvinist – that General Eisenhower was queer. I love this story, because the English are such experts at putting other people down that it is wonderful to see an expatriate Britisher coming back and working out on the boys at home. . .[1]

In Germany, Auden embarked upon his tour of duty with much less compromise either of morals or of manner than one would have thought possible. He made no secret of his disgust at the political manoeuvres brought about by the end of the war, at General Patton's enthusiastic employment of ex-Nazis to run Bavaria, and at the forced repatriation to the Soviet Union of hundreds of thousands of refugees from that country. Together with the Major's uniform he still wore his carpet slippers, and not always a matching pair; he never learned about saluting, or how to address superior officers; and that his driving of a jeep was no less erratic than his pre-war driving is attested to by a reference to him in a poem by Lincoln Kirstein, who was at the time attached to General Patton's Headquarters: 'The fierce chauffeur will kill us if he can,/Cuts every corner, never honks his horn/And barrels wrongside down the autobahn'.

From 'Somewhere in Germany' (which was, in fact, Darmstadt), Auden wrote in May to Tania Stern:

> The town outside which we live was ninety-two per cent destroyed in thirty minutes. You can't imagine what that looks like unless you see it with your own eyes. We are billeted in the house of a Nazi who committed suicide and also poisoned his wife, children and grandchildren . . . The work is very interesting but I'm near crying sometimes . . . Good Rhine wine costs thirty-five cents a bottle and the weather is wonderful. The people, though, are sad beyond belief.

In Darmstadt he had met up with James Stern, who was even more terrified of Auden's driving than were most people:

> One morning in Nürnberg at the prospect of a long and complicated journey to interview a Nazi brewer, I couldn't stand it any longer. I simply got into the driver's seat ahead of him, waited until he was seated beside me, mentally closed my eyes and ears, held my breath, and moved off into the ruins. 'And without,' I heard him muttering between his teeth, 'without so much as a *by your leave* . . .' However, he did not explode. And I breathed not a word. Just drove on. And the subject was never mentioned again.[2]

[1] Edmund Wilson to Elizabeth Huling, 4 July 1945 in Wilson's *Letters on Literature and Politics* (London, 1977).
[2] James Stern in *W. H. Auden: A Tribute.*

When his investigations were completed, Auden found himself waiting about at the USSBS headquarters in Bad Homburg, near Frankfurt. He had nothing to do but attend debriefing sessions, and was delighted when Nicolas Nabokov turned up unexpectedly. The two friends exchanged grumbles. At the debriefing sessions, Auden complained, 'a lot of mid-witted folk talked mid-minded trash in bogus socio-political jargon with a most obscene German accent . . . What they want to say, but don't say, is how many people we killed and how many buildings we destroyed by that wicked bombing.' His colleagues were 'crashing bores', the desolation of the German cities was shocking, but even more so were the extermination camps which he had seen in the course of his tours. He had known, he said, that the 'obtuse Krauts' could be cruel, but he could never have imagined 'the horror of their meticulously systematic organization'. He tried to convince himself that the Nazis' mass-murder of Jews and others they thought undesirable made the Allies' mass-murder of German civilians morally defensible. And he was honest enough to admit that he simply did not know.

In the autumn of 1945, he was back in America. He moved into an apartment in New York, at 7, Cornelia Street, Greenwich Village, sharing it with Chester Kallman. Visitors to the apartment found it a cosy place, despite its almost unbelievable untidiness, and its permanent smell of cat piss. The cat, for from now on there would usually be a cat in Auden's dwelling-places, was very much in evidence, stalking across the table at dinner-parties, sniffing and occasionally sampling the food, and swishing its tail into the salad bowl.

The following spring, Auden taught for one semester at Bennington College in Vermont. On 20 May he took the oath of allegiance, and became a citizen of the United States. At the beginning of June, he stayed with Reinhold and Ursula Niebuhr at their country cottage about twenty-five miles from Bennington. Back in New York, he wrote the Niebuhrs a thank-you letter, in which he mentioned that he and Chester were 'all in a dither about tonight', for they were giving a dinner party for T. S. Eliot. 'It is the first real dinner party I've given. The menu is:

watercress soup (Chinese style),
cold salmon (will the glazing go right?),
Hollandaise sauce,
new potatoes,
kidney bean salad,
zabaglione,
Wisconsin blue cheese (a favourite of TSE's)

and as much Chilean white wine as we can stand. The rest is up to the

Comforter.' The party was a success, though Eliot wrote to the Niebuhrs that he did not get the impression Auden was 'settled, and I feared he was wasting his gifts in "adapting" *The Duchess of Malfi* for Elisabeth Bergner'.

For some time, Auden had been working intermittently on an adaptation of Webster's tragedy with Bertolt Brecht, who appears to have been making very heavy weather of something which had begun as a collaboration between him and H. R. Hays in 1942. Hays had dropped out when Auden joined the collaboration in 1943. When Elisabeth Bergner opened at the Barrymore Theatre, New York, in *The Duchess of Malfi* in October 1946, the version used was an adaptation by Auden alone, with music by Benjamin Britten. One wonders why Webster's play was ever thought to need adaptation, unless it was to explain away Bergner's Viennese accent.

On 6 August, Britten's opera *Peter Grimes*, which had first been performed with great success at Sadler's Wells Theatre, London in the previous year, was given its American première at the Berkshire Festival at Tanglewood, Massachusetts. Britten attended the opening performance, conducted by Leonard Bernstein, and Auden and Kallman were also present.

James and Tania Stern and Auden now jointly owned a holiday shack on Fire Island, a forty-mile strip of beach on the ocean side of Long Island. Tania Stern had purchased the shack on their behalf the previous year while Auden and Stern were in Germany. They named it Bective Poplars, Bective being the name of Stern's childhood home, and The Poplars a house owned by a relative of Auden. Auden lived in the Fire Island shack during the summers of 1946 and 1947. Beginning in the autumn of 1946, he taught a course, for two semesters, at the New School for Social Research, on the plays of Shakespeare, taking his students through all thirty-seven plays in chronological order. Cyril Connolly visited New York in November, and recorded a meeting with Auden in his diary: 'Wystan charming, though very battered-looking. More American than ever and much less self-conscious than in London . . . Much conversation about the USA and Wystan continues to propound his point of view . . . He always reverts to the same argument which I think is true for him – in the USA he receives anonymity, more money (he made ten thousand dollars this year and bought a mortgage) and his desire is gratified for a large, open, impersonal new country.'

It was at about this time that Auden began his custom of giving a champagne party on his birthday, 21 February, sending out formal invitations which included an admonitory phrase, 'Carriages at one'. These parties soon became events in the New York literary calender. Auden invited only those whom he genuinely liked, and was usually in radiant form on such occasions.

Ursula Niebuhr, who taught at Barnard College, persuaded Auden to lecture there for one term in the Department of the History of Religion. He gave a course of lectures on 'The Quest in Ancient and Modern Literature' in the spring term of 1947, for a fee of one thousand dollars. It proved a popular course, for he included a wide range of literature from fairy tales, through the *Aeneid*, the *Odyssey*, *Don Giovanni*, *Don Quixote* and *Faust* to *Alice in Wonderland* and Kafka. Before one of his lectures, he looked about him short-sightedly and held out his hand. Thinking that he wanted some chalk for the blackboard, Ursula Niebuhr handed him some. 'No,' said the distinguished lecturer with a beaming smile. 'Smackers! What about the smackers?' Unfamiliar with American slang, Dr Niebuhr did not understand that Auden was asking for his fee, but she was soon enlightened by her colleagues. Auden's Barnard students sometimes found his accent or his diction difficult to understand. He was often interrupted by requests to spell out on the blackboard something he had said. More than one student remembers that Auden usually complied, but with very clearly enunciated comments under his breath on the intelligence of his audience.

In 1946 and 1947, though he continued to live with Chester Kallman, Auden found himself involved in a heterosexual relationship as well. He had an affair with a very attractive blonde Jewish girl, Rhoda Jaffe, whom he had met through Chester. At the time of their first meeting, in the autumn of 1945, Miss Jaffe was married to a writer and critic, Milton Klonsky. She began to do secretarial work for Auden, mainly typing of manuscripts; by the spring of 1946 they were lovers, and she continued to do his typing. She obtained a divorce from Klonsky, and at one point the New York gossip columns were prophesying that she and Auden would marry. However, he does not appear to have seriously contemplated marriage. While he was teaching at Bennington College in Vermont, he spent as many weekends as possible with Rhoda in New York. The tone of his letters to her from Bennington is alternately playful and intimate: 'The weather is lovely but the bed is lonely and I wish you were in it. Aren't men *BEASTS*. No finer feelings. Much love. Wystan.' Beside his name he draws a male face peering at the sun rising between two breast-shaped hills or hill-shaped breasts.

On one weekend, they were unable to use his apartment:

(a) Can I stay at your place
(b) If not, could you book a room at a hotel for Mr and Mrs ———, Sayville, L.I. and in that case bring a little bag with you. The current rumour in N.Y. is not only that we are having an affair but that I was responsible for your abortion.

When he went to Tanglewood to hear *Peter Grimes*, he wrote to Rhoda that 'it was fine to see Benjy Britten again. The performance was terrible but the work made an impression just the same . . . Chester is in N.Y. and returns [to Fire Island] tonight. He seems to have found "something dreamy" across the road.' A few days later, he wrote: 'I'm so looking forward to your coming, and want to see you get a really good rest. The bar *is* going to be surprised.' (The clientele of the local bar was predominantly homosexual.)

Chester's infidelities were more frequent than Auden's. 'We had one *crise*,' Auden wrote to Rhoda, 'when we nearly parted for ever, but that passed off. The truth is, the bar here is a little too much for him. I call it Klingsor's magic garden, but you'll see for yourself. I'm wondering which of the heters are going to come hanging round the house when you come.' His loving concern for Chester is apparent from the frequency of Auden's references to him in letters to Rhoda from Bective Poplars. In the early summer of 1947, Chester was having an affair with a sailor: 'Chester came out on Saturday for one night, very fussed over his matelot and having to telephone constantly to N.Y. The latter, he tells me, is, what I suspected, *very* gentile and hard-drinking. I hope he won't get too involved, poor thing, as I don't believe he can have a serious relation with anyone who is interested in baseball.' Later, Auden writes that 'Work here has been rather difficult since Chester came but I think he is settling down now into a more regular life. The triple situation, of being sexually jealous like a wife, anxious like a nanny, and competitive like a brother is not easy for my kind of temperament. Still, it is my bed and I must lie on it.'

Auden was upset when one of his acquaintances said that it was all very well for him to call himself a Christian, but then why didn't he marry Rhoda: 'I have not treated you like a good Christian, darling, (or a good Jew) . . . Miss God appears to have decided that I am to be a writer, but have no other fun, and no talent for making others as happy as I would like them to be . . . I enclose an impersonal (honest) love poem which I defy you to say is obviously written by a queer. Lots and lots of love, darling. You are *so* good, and I'm a neurotic middle-aged butterball.'

When Stephen Spender stayed with Auden in his not unsqualid Greenwich Village room in the summer of 1947, he found his friend 'worse dressed, slightly more dishevelled, considerably stouter, but with the same pink skin and tow-coloured hair, the same angular alertness of movement. In manner he was perhaps gentler, though also more decided. On his mantelpiece a crucifix denoted the change in his beliefs.'[1] He still kept his curtains drawn to shut out the daylight. When Spender got up one morning and opened them, curtains and pelmet fell clattering to the floor, waking Auden who groaned sleepily, 'You idiot, why did you do that? No one ever draws them. In any case, there's no daylight in New York.'

[1] Stephen Spender: *World within World.*

Auden now began to give readings of his poems at universities and colleges. He was one of the first poets to do so on a regular and frequent basis, and could fairly be said to have played his part in bringing into existence that travelling circuit which gave employment to so many poets, British and American, during the fifties and the sixties. He also made it known that he was available to lecture, provided that the fee was right. The lecture he gave at Harvard in 1947 on *Don Quixote* as part of a series commemorating the quatercentenary of the birth of Cervantes, is still talked of, for he had consumed a few too many Martinis before lecturing, began by apologizing for his new set of dentures, and then launched upon *Don Quixote* by admitting that he'd never managed to read that novel through to the end, and doubting whether anyone in his audience had. When the noise of ruffling academic feathers had subsided, some years later Harvard offered Auden an impressive sum for a series of lectures. He refused because he had, at the time, no subjects on which he wanted to lecture. This unusual, one might say unacademic, frankness took the Harvard administration by surprise.

In the spring, Auden revised the text of *The Dog Beneath the Skin* for a production in July at the Cherry Lane Theater in New York. In this version, Francis is stabbed to death at the end of the play. On 11 July a new book, *The Age of Anxiety*, was published. Auden had been working intermittently on this long poem in dramatic form since the summer of 1944, and had completed it in November 1946. Subtitled 'A Baroque Eclogue', the poem is dedicated to John Betjeman, a volume of whose poems, with an introduction by Auden, was also published in New York in the same month. *The Age of Anxiety* was received by the American critics with no great enthusiasm; in the opinion of Randall Jarrell[1] it was 'the worst thing Auden has written since *The Dance of Death*; it is the equivalent of Wordsworth's "Ecclesiastical Sonnets".' The following year *The Age of Anxiety* was published in England, where it was not better received. 'The piece is persistently boring' wrote Patric Dickinson in *Horizon*;[2] the *New Statesman*[3] thought that, linguistically, it was by far the least attractive poem Auden had written, and found it 'difficult to believe that the intention and content of the poem justify its enormous length'; George D. Painter in *The Listener*[4] described it as 'a rheumatic crystal, a mainly descriptive pearl in a very sick oyster', thus implicitly demanding of the poet answers which philosopher and psychiatrist had failed to give. Despite this generally lukewarm reception, *The Age of Anxiety* has survived, to be seen now as a product of forties *Angst*, just as *The*

[1] In *The Nation* (Oct 18, 1947).
[2] May 1949.
[3] 30 October 1948.
[4] 7 October 1948.

Orators summed up that of the early thirties. John Bayley, writing ten years after its publication, called it 'Auden's greatest achievement to date, and the one which best shows the true nature of his scope and talent'.[1] It had some admirers, even in 1947. It won a Pulitzer Prize for Auden, and it inspired Leonard Bernstein to compose his symphony, 'The Age of Anxiety'.

Fire Island, especially in the summer months, was noted for its sophisticated homosexual community, and for the variety of entertainments organized by that community. Among these in the summer of 1947 was a carnival, which Auden attended as a bishop, 'mitre, cope and all', with Chester Kallman as 'a very rococo angel'. To 'Rhoda darling', Auden wrote: 'Chester looked wonderful as an angel and should have got the prize but for Cherry Grove intrigue which gave it to one of those extraverted queens who knows *every*one.'

Auden was now forty; in many ways a youthful forty, but beginning to ponder on his own mortality. 'I don't think I am over-anxious about the future,' he wrote to a friend in August, 'though I do quail a bit sometimes before the probability that it will be lonely . . . I shall probably die in a hotel to the great annoyance of the management, but I suppose when it comes to the point, one won't care so much.'[2]

In October, Auden was surprised to receive a letter from the composer Igor Stravinsky, who was then living in Los Angeles. Stravinsky, some months earlier, had looked at the Hogarth 'Rake's Progress' engravings in the Chicago Art Institute, and had thought they might provide the basis of an opera libretto, for he had wanted to compose a full-length opera in English ever since his arrival in the United States. He consulted his friend and neighbour Aldous Huxley who recommended Auden as the librettist. Stravinsky wrote, describing what he had in mind. Was the suggestion of interest to Auden? It was, and Auden wasted no time in skirmishing tactics. He replied immediately and practically:

Dear Mr Stravinsky,

Thank you very much for your letter of October 6th, which arrived this morning.

As you say, it is a terrible nuisance being thousands of miles apart, but we must do the best we can.

As (a) you have thought about the Rake's Progress for some time, and (b) it is the librettist's job to satisfy the composer, not the other way round, I should be most grateful if you could let me have any ideas you may have formed about characters, plot, etc.

I think the Asylum finale sounds excellent, but, for instance, if he is to

---

[1] *The Romantic Survival* (London, 1957).
[2] Letter to Ursula Niebuhr, quoted in *W. H. Auden: A Tribute.*

play the fiddle then, do you want the fiddle to run through the story?

You speak of a 'free verse preliminary'. Do you want the arias and ensembles to be finally written in free verse or only as a basis for discussing the actual form they should take? If they were spoken, the eighteenth-century style would of course demand rhyme but I know how different this is when the words are set.

I have an idea, which may be ridiculous, that between the two acts there should be a choric parabasis as in Aristophanes.

I need hardly say that the chance of working with you is the greatest honour of my life.

Yours very sincerely,
Wystan Auden

P.S. I hope you can read my writing. Unfortunately, I do not know how to type.

Stravinsky responded by inviting Auden to visit him and stay at his house in Hollywood. Auden wired his delighted acceptance, and arrived one night in mid-November, carrying a small bag and a huge cow-skin rug, a gift to Stravinsky from an Argentine friend. Stravinsky has left an account of this first meeting:

My wife had been anxious that our only extra bed, a studio couch, might not be long enough for him, but when we saw this big, blond, intellectual bloodhound on our front porch (before an hour had elapsed, however, we knew he was going to be a very gentle and lovable bloodhound, however super-intellectual) we realized that we hadn't been anxious enough. He slept with his body on the couch and his feet, covered by a blanket pinioned with books on a nearby chair, like the victim of a more humane and reasonable Procrustes.

Early the next morning, primed by coffee and whisky, we began work on the Rake's Progress. Starting with a hero, a heroine and a villain, and deciding that these people should be a tenor, a soprano and a bass, we proceeded to invent a series of scenes leading up to the final scene in Bedlam that was already fixed in our minds. We followed Hogarth closely at first and until our own story began to assume a different significance.

Mother Goose and the Ugly Duchess were Auden's contributions, of course, but the plot and the scheme of action were worked out by the two of us together, step by step. We also tried to coordinate the plan of action with a provisional plan of musical pieces, arias, ensembles and choruses. Auden kept saying, 'Let's see now . . . ah, ah, ah . . . Let's see . . . ah . . . ah . . .', and I the equivalent in Russian, but after ten days we had completed an outline which is not radically different from the published libretto.[1]

Composer and poet got on enormously well, each finding the other fascinating. All Auden's conversations about art, Stravinsky noted shrewdly, were 'so to speak, *sub specie ludi*', for creating poetry and music was a game with secret rules. Stravinsky recalled two events of Auden's visit, apart from their work together. One day Auden complained he had become deaf, and Stravinsky took him off to a doctor who cured him by syringing his ears from which he removed two huge globules of wax. And one evening poet and composer attended a production of Mozart's *Cosi fan tutte*, performed with an accompaniment of two pianos in the parish hall of a Hollywood church. Though Stravinsky may not have remembered, they also saw a performance of Lorca's *The House of Bernarda Alba*.

On his return to New York, Auden wrote to the Stravinskys on 20 November. 'The journey was a nightmare,' he told Mrs Stravinsky. 'I was transferred to an American Airlines local which left at 7 a.m., stopped *everywhere* and reached New York at 4 a.m. this morning. The meals, as usual, would have tried the patience of a stage curate, so you can imagine what I felt, after a week of your luxurious cuisine.' He enclosed a note to Stravinsky in French, with an English postscript: 'I can't tell you what a pleasure it is to collaborate with you. I was so frightened that you might be a *prima donna*.'[2]

Auden began immediately to write the libretto of *The Rake's Progress* on the basis of the synopsis he and Stravinsky had agreed; but, without informing the composer, he decided to ask Chester Kallman to collaborate with him in the actual writing. It was only when he mailed a completed Act I to California in January that he mentioned, as an aside, having 'taken in a collaborator, an old friend of mine in whose talents I have the greatest confidence'. Stravinsky was somewhat disturbed by this, but decided that there was no point in protesting at a *fait accompli*, and graciously accepted Chester. Auden was able to despatch Act II to the composer before the end of January, and he delivered Act III in person when he travelled to Washington to meet the Stravinskys on 31 March at the Raleigh Hotel where they were staying in the Lily Pons Suite. Robert Craft, Stravinsky's amanuensis, was also present and was able to note Auden's English horror of the Russian-style kisses with which both Stravinskys smothered him, his failure to notice Madame Stravinsky's cluster of gardenias over which he flung his coat, and his *ex cathedra* announcements, during lunch, on linguistic science as a key to thought structure, and on the influence of the British

[1] Igor Stravinsky: *Memories and Commentaries* (New York, 1959).
[2] Quoted in *Memories and Commentaries*.

nanny on that overrated pastime, philosophy. Auden and Stravinsky discussed *The Rake's Progress* in the afternoon, and Auden assured the composer that Chester Kallman was a better librettist than Auden himself, that 'the scenes which Mr Kallman wrote are at least as good as mine', and that 'Mr Kallman's talents have not been more widely recognised only because of his friendship with me.' Stravinsky replied courteously that he looked forward to meeting Mr Kallman in New York. When that meeting took place on 5 April the composer was immediately charmed by Kallman. By this time, he had read the entire libretto, and was able sincerely to tell both librettists how pleased he was with their work.

Two days later, Auden and Kallman sailed for Europe. 'I hope very much you will be in London to look after us,' Auden wrote to Cyril Connolly. 'It would be lovely if you could meet us at Victoria (you can be the town mouse this time). By the way, have you ever read *Tender is the Night*? I did for the first time this summer and found it magnificent – probably the best American novel since H.J.[1] It made me bawl like a baby.'[2]

In England Auden saw friends and family, before proceeding to Italy, to the island of Ischia where he had rented a villa for the summer. A few friends were encouraged to visit him and Chester on Ischia, among them Brian Howard, during whose visit Auden wrote a poem, 'Ischia', which he dedicated to Howard:

> . . . my thanks are for you,
> Ischia, to whom a fair wind has
> brought me rejoicing with dear friends
>
> from soiled productive cities. How well you correct
> our injured eyes, how gently you train us to see
> things and men in perspective
> underneath your uniform light . . .

In answer to Howard's frequently expressed criticism that he lacked visual sense, Auden later wrote: 'Never think that I don't know that your criticisms of my lack of visual attention are just . . . At the same time, as a poet, one of the most important lessons one has to learn is to recognize and accept one's limitations and, if possible, turn them into advantages.'[3]

Not surprisingly, Auden's affair with Rhoda Jaffe in New York had not survived his six months' absence in Europe, but he continued to correspond with her until she married again. In May, he wrote from Ischia to say that he

---

[1] Henry James.

[2] Quoted in *W. H. Auden: A Tribute*.

[3] Quoted in *Brian Howard: Portrait of a Failure* (ed. Marie-Jacqueline Lancaster; London, 1968).

found himself completely untroubled by sex, and that 'Chester, too, is quite changed, and in consequence our relationship is, for the first time, a really happy one.' But two months later,

> The sex situation in Forio is fine from my point of view, exactly what it ought to be, i.e. the women never go into the cafés or bars and if they do appear on the beach are covered up to the ankles, very few of the men and boys are queer . . . but all of them like a 'divertimento' now and then, for which it is considered polite to give 35 cents or a package of cigarettes as a friendly gesture. It is so nice to be with people who are never shocked or psychologically insecure, though half of them don't get enough to eat. (There is one small group who steal: this is disapproved of by the rest of the town. Everyone of course knows who goes with whom within 24 hours.)

In the autumn Auden and Kallman returned to New York, for Chester did not like to be too far away from the Metropolitan Opera at the beginning of the season, and under his influence Auden too had become a devotee of opera, that most comprehensive of the theatrical arts. During the year, in addition to a handful of new poems and occasional reviews, Auden had published three articles on things which gave him great personal pleasure: the detective story, opera, and music on gramophone records. For relaxation, he loved murder mysteries of the classical Agatha Christie variety, which he consumed in large numbers. In the May issue of *Harper's Magazine*, his article 'The Guilty Vicarage', subtitled 'Notes on the Detective Story, by an Addict', attempts to find intellectual justification for his addiction. His second addiction, opera, is the subject of 'Opera Addict' which he contributed to the July *Vogue*.[1] And in the *Saturday Review* of 27 November 1948, Auden's favourite records were listed. With two exceptions, they were operatic. No doubt the list would have been different, either earlier or later in his life. However, in November 1948 Auden now chose to contribute the following list:

Bach: 'St. Matthew Passion'. The Leipzig recording, with Günther Ramin conducting, Lemnitz and Hüsch as soloists.
Bellini and others: An operatic Recital by Claudia Muzio.
Donizetti: 'Don Pasquale'. The La Scala recording with Tito Schipa.
Donizetti: 'Lucia di Lammermoor'. The version on Parlophone, with Pagliughi and Malipiero, Tansini conducting.
Mozart: 'Cosi fan tutte'. The Glyndebourne recording, Fritz Busch conducting.

[1] American edition: it also appeared in the English edition in March, 1949.

Verdi: 'Ritorna vincitor' from *Aida*. Rosa Ponselle.
Verdi: 'Un ballo in maschera'. The Rome recording with Gigli and Caniglia, Serafin conducting.
Verdi: Requiem. The Rome recording with Caniglia, Stignani, Gigli and Pinza, Serafin conducting.
Wagner: Quintet from *Meistersinger*. Schumann, Schorr et al.
Wagner: 'Herzeleide' scene from *Parsifal*. Flagstad and Melchior.
Wagner: *'Die Walküre'*. Acts I and II. The composite Vienna–Berlin recording with Lehmann and Melchior.
Weber: 'Und ob die Wolke sie verhüllt' from *Freischütz*. Tiana Lemnitz (Polydor version)
Weber: 'Gebet des Hüon' from *Oberon*. Helge Roswaenge.

The autumn found Auden teaching again for one term at the New School for Social Research. On 9 November, along with virtually every other poet or writer of any eminence who happened to be in New York, he attended a reception at the Gotham Book Mart for Edith and Osbert Sitwell. At one point, the poets present were ushered into the back room to be photographed with the Sitwells. Elizabeth Bishop recalled that 'Auden was one of the few who seemed to be enjoying himself. He got into the picture by climbing on a ladder, where he sat making loud, cheerful comments over our heads.' (See page 261.)

Stravinsky had for months been at work on the composition of *The Rake's Progress*. When he came east to give concerts in New York and elsewhere, Auden met the composer at Pennsylvania Station on 3 February 1949, at the distinctly un-Audenish hour of 6.55 a.m., and explained that he could not listen to the completed scenes of Act I that morning, as had been arranged, for he was on jury duty. The audition was postponed until the evening when Auden was able gleefully to inform Stravinsky that he had 'hung the jury and obstructed injustice in the trial of a taxi-driver who would have been a victim of the prejudice of car-owners'. After hearing most of Act I of their opera, Auden told Stravinsky not to take such trouble to make every word audible, and asked him to change the soprano's final note to a high C. Stravinsky thought the word to be sung was unsuitable for a high note, so Auden wrote a new last line on the spot, standing behind the composer as he played, and attempting to follow the music over his shoulder, much to Stravinsky's annoyance. Later in the month Stravinsky conducted an afternoon concert in New York, and invited Auden to appear on the programme to read a group of his poems. Among the poems Auden chose to read was the beautiful 'In praise of Limestone', which he had written in May of the previous year when revisiting the landscape of his childhood. In his later years, he was known to refer to it as perhaps his favourite of all his poems:

> . . . In so far as we have to look forward
> To death as a fact, no doubt we are right: But if
> Sins can be forgiven, if bodies rise from the dead,
>   These modifications of matter into
> Innocent athletes and gesticulating fountains,
>   Made solely for pleasure, make a further point:
> The blessed will not care what angle they are regarded from,
>   Having nothing to hide. Dear, I know nothing of
> Either, but when I try to imagine a faultless love
>   Or the life to come, what I hear is the murmur
> Of underground streams, what I see is a limestone landscape.

On three consecutive days in March, Auden delivered the Page–Barbour lectures at the University of Virginia. When these were published the following year as *The Enchafèd Flood*, E. M. Forster wrote: 'He elicits a response which I cannot always explain. Because he once wrote "We must love one another or die", he can command me to follow him . . . *The Enchafèd Flood* is itself a poem. Though its tone is critical, it is not constructed like a lecture-house or a thesis. Brooding in it is the ruined or unbuilt city, and we must either build it or die'.[1]

In the spring, as Auden and Chester Kallman were preparing to depart for another Ischian summer, a controversy developed over the Bollingen Foundation's award of a prize, the first of an annual series, to Ezra Pound for *The Pisan Cantos*. The judges, among them Auden, T. S. Eliot, Allen Tate Robert Penn Warren and Robert Lowell, had made it clear that they were honouring Pound's poetic achievement and that they had been influenced by no other considerations. In other words, they did not wish to be thought of as condoning Pound's Fascism and anti-semitism. The magazine *Partisan Review* criticized the judges' decision, quoted lines from *The Pisan Cantos* (e.g. 'the yidd is a stimulant, and the goyim are cattle'), asked how far it was considered possible, in a lyric poem, 'for technical embellishments to transform vicious and ugly matter into beautiful poetry', and invited the judges to answer. Auden's answer, it has to be admitted, was both silly and evasive. He said that he shared *Partisan Review*'s concern over the extensive preoccupation of contemporary criticism with form and its neglect of content, but thought that everyone, surely, had had the experience of reading a book which he was aware was bad for him personally, whatever its artistic merit, or however harmless it might be for others. *The Pisan Cantos* was no doubt such a book for some people, perhaps even the majority of people:

> Anti-semitism is, unfortunately, not only a feeling which all gentiles at
> times feel, but also, and this is what matters, a feeling of which the

[1] *The Listener* (26 April 1951).

majority of them are not ashamed. Until they are, they must be regarded as children who have not yet reached the age of consent in this matter and from whom, therefore, all books, whether works of art or not, which reflect feeling about Jews – and it doesn't make the slightest difference whether they are pro or anti, the *New York Post* can be as dangerous as *Der Stürmer* – must be withheld.

If it were to seem likely that the *Pisan Cantos* would be read by people of this kind I would be in favour of censoring it (as in the case of the movie, *Oliver Twist*). That would not however prevent me awarding the *Pisan Cantos* a prize before withholding it from the public. But I do not believe that the likelihood exists in this case.

One can only charitably assume that, mentally, Auden was already anticipating his summer atrophy in a blend of Italian sun and martinis.

Among the book reviews Auden published during 1949 was a perceptive and sympathetic article in the *New York Times Book Review*[1] on Somerset Maugham's *A Writer's Notebook*. Auden had always read Maugham with pleasure, and was to re-read some of his novels during his last years. Without ignoring Maugham's limitations, Auden made it clear that he valued highly what the novelist had to offer: 'Thank you for having given us so much pleasure for so long, for having never been tedious.'[2]

Stravinsky, having difficulty with Act II of the opera, wrote to Auden in November, asking him to come to California again. But Auden had a busy schedule of lectures and readings, and eventually Stravinsky travelled to New York to confer with his librettists. Robert Craft has described Auden and Stravinsky, in the composer's room at the Lombardy Hotel, trying to work out how long it would take to wheel the bread machine onstage in Act II:

Auden, responding swiftly, and as if he had had a great deal of experience with baby carriages, jumped to his feet, extended his arms and crossed the room pushing an imaginary vehicle of that sort, while Stravinsky held his stopwatch like a starter at a track meet. But this somnambulistic exercise could not have had much validity since no one knew the dimensions of the stage on which the opera was to be performed, and as a result the music here is generally found to be too short.[3]

The following March, 1950, Stravinsky was again in New York for concerts and recordings, and he and Auden spent a day together working on

[1] Issue of 23 October 1949.

[2] A good ten years later, Auden was delighted when the present author drew his attention to Verdi's remark 'The boring is the worst of all styles'. Thereafter, he was often heard to quote it.

[3] *W. H. Auden: A Tribute.*

their opera. On 9 March, Auden returned to Swarthmore College, where he had taught during the war years, to lecture under the auspices of the Department of English and the Cooper Foundation on 'Nature, history and poetry'. In the spring and summer, he and Chester departed for Ischia, again renting the villa, at Via Santa Lucia 22 in the village of Forio, that they had taken the previous year. They were to rent a villa on the island every summer until 1958. Auden continually sought to impose patterns upon his life, daily, weekly, annual patterns, and was always at his happiest and most relaxed when following a routine. His summer routine on Ischia is described by the American poet, Anthony Hecht, who visited him there in 1950:

> He was remarkably myopic and could rarely recognize anyone at a distance of more than ten feet. His clothing, even in the licensed atmosphere of an Italian beach resort, resembled, in his own words, "an unmade bed". His work habits were fixed and inflexible, though set aside on Sundays. He rose around six in the morning and worked for a while before a breakfast of coffee, and continued to work, with a brief interruption for a light lunch, until around three in the afternoon. The rest of the day and the early evening was for diversion, dinner and drinks. But he had a fixed hour of retirement at, I think it was, 10.30, so that he could be up and at work at six the next morning.[1]

Auden told Hecht, that summer, that he had never been able to work after three in the afternoon, but that it was only after his adult acceptance of the Christian faith that he understood the reason for the sense of indolence, loss and depression that overcame him at that time: it was the canonical hour of the crucifixion! He also lectured Hecht and his other guests on their musical tastes. Indeed, one could say he hectored them. 'Anyone who seriously maintains that his favourite music is Beethoven's last quartets is simply a snob who is putting on airs,' he insisted, in his concern to separate music from religion. Music thought to be in any degree 'spiritual' was highly suspect: he was shocked to hear that Anthony Hecht intended to hear Bach's *Magnificat* in Rome on an evening when there was also to be a performance of Bellini's *Norma*. He enjoyed devising games involving lists or choices. For instance, if you had a month left to live, after which you were assured of a heavenly afterlife, with what works of art would you wish to spend your final month on earth? Auden's own choices, in July 1950, were the novels of Firbank, the paintings of Caravaggio, the lyric poetry of Tennyson and the overtures of Rossini. (Playing a variant of that game with the present author about ten years later, Auden opted for a sumptuous production of Strauss's *Der Rosenkavalier* with 'the only Marschallin' Lotte Lehmann, a multilingual

[1] 'Discovering Auden' by Anthony Hecht in *The Harvard Advocate*.

anthology of poetry mainly by Goethe, Dryden and Leopardi, the Brueghel room in the Kunsthistorisches Museum in Vienna, and an adequate supply of detective stories.)

Stravinsky wanted *The Rake's Progress* to have its première in America, since it was an English language opera, and preferably in a small theatre in New York where it could be given a run of performances. However, by the autumn of 1950, when Auden was teaching for one term at Mount Holyoake College, negotiations were in progress with the Teatro La Fenice in Venice, and early in 1951 agreement was reached that *The Rake's Progress* would be performed at the Fenice in September. On 16 February Auden wrote to Robert Craft who, by this time, was playing, amongst other roles, Boswell to Stravinsky's Johnson:

Dear Bob,

It's wonderful news about Venice. But there are one or two matters which – strictly *entre nous* – Chester and I would like to know about.

It seems to us that, if there is, as I understand, a *large* sum of money being paid for the première rights, we are entitled to ten per cent thereof. What do you think?

As the contract is not being negotiated through Boosey Bean,[1] we are completely in the dark as to the facts.

Could you use your discretion, and if circumstances are propitious, mention the matter to *Il Maestro*?

Hope Cuba is fun.

Love,

Wystan

The matter was mentioned, and eventually a fee was negotiated which covered the librettists' travel to Venice and their involvement in rehearsals. Meanwhile, other projects engaged Auden's attention. In England, the Group Theatre, quiescent during the war, had become operative again, and Rupert Doone had asked Auden to translate Cocteau's play, *Les Chevaliers de la Table Ronde*, for a proposed production at the Edinburgh Festival in 1952. Auden translated the play, but the Edinburgh Festival production never took place. *The Knights of the Round Table* was first performed on radio by the BBC in May 1951, and eventually produced by the Group Theatre, three years later, at the Playhouse Theatre, Salisbury, with Ernest Milton as Merlin.

On 2 February a new Auden volume of poems, *Nones*, was published in New York. (The English edition followed a year later.) Securely established now as a leading poet, Auden had therefore to expect niggling reviews in the literary pages of the newspapers and magazines. David Daiches in the *Yale*

[1] Betty Bean, of Boosey and Hawkes, Stravinsky's publishers.

Review[1] described *Nones* as 'a mixed bag of poems, some lyrical, some argumentative, some ironic, some didactic, and some merely clever', as though it had been written by one of that year's undergraduates; of 'In Praise of Limestone', one of the finest poems, not only in the volume but in Auden's entire *oeuvre*, he wrote that it 'bores before it comes to an end'. Enjoying the volume more than most reviewers, G. S. Fraser, in the *New Statesman*, explained the double meaning of the title, 'Nones', a daily office of the Church originally said at the ninth hour, the canonical hour at which Christ hung on the cross and darkness covered the earth, and also 'nones' as an old spelling of 'nonce', many of the poems in the book being nonce-pieces or poems inspired by unrecurring occasions. He called 'In Praise of Limestone' 'the loveliest poem here', and thought that Auden had 'never written with more confident ease' than in this volume.[2]

In March 1951, Auden allowed himself to be persuaded to take part in a Congress for Cultural Freedom in India. But he did not enjoy the platitudinous waffle that is obligatory on such occasions, nor did he take delight in the customs of cultures other than his own. 'We had to sit on the floor, my dear, and were given lukewarm tea,' he complained later to Nicolas Nabokov. 'A female in costume, with donkey-bells around her ankles danced, jerking and jiggling her head, making eyes at everyone and fanning out her fingers. Preposterous nonsense! And imagine, all that boredom and not a drop of drink! I got up and told the Prime that it "wasn't my cup of tea" and that I'd like to go back to my hotel . . . His daughter, a glum-looking young lady, took me to the door and sent me back packing.'[3]

Auden's summer villa at Forio d'Ischia from 1951 to 1956 was at Via Santa Lucia 14, a few doors away from the villa he had taken in the previous two years. His summer stay on Ischia in 1951 was enlivened by his suspected involvement in the case of the two senior members of the British Foreign Service, Guy Burgess and Donald Maclean, who defected to the Soviet Union that year. Burgess and Maclean were both homosexuals but not, as was widely assumed at the time, lovers. (Indeed, Burgess was horrified at the suggestion: 'The idea of going to bed with Donald!' he exclaimed to Tom Driberg when they met much later in Moscow. 'It would be like going to bed with Edith Evans.') On 25 May, the day Burgess and Maclean disappeared, after having been warned by Kim Philby that the Foreign Office had discovered they were Soviet agents, Auden had been breaking his journey from New York to Ischia by staying with Stephen Spender in London. On the previous evening, Burgess had attempted to phone Auden, but he was out and Spender characteristically forgot to mention the call to Auden. (In some

[1] *Yale Review* (September 1951).
[2] *New Statesman* (1 March 1952).
[3] Nicolas Nabokov: 'Excerpts from Memories' in *W. H. Auden: A Tribute.*

respects, the Spender–Auden relationship resembled that of Laurel and Hardy, Auden's exasperated affection coping with Spender's gaffes in a manner not dissimilar to that of Ollie in the face of Stan's innocence.) Auden departed for Ischia, only to find some days later that he had become an object of great interest to the Italian security police. Even worse, he was interviewed by a *Daily Express* reporter, with the result that, accompanied by a photograph of Auden, the following appeared in the *Express* on 13 June:

POET AUDEN TELLS EXPRESS MAN

BURGESS KNEW ATOM SPY
'He talked about Nunn May'
From DON SEAMAN: Ischia (off Naples) Tuesday

W. H. Auden the poet, whom Guy Burgess – the missing diplomat – wanted to contact, spoke up tonight. He said Burgess was a Communist and a friend of Alan Nunn May, the atom spy, before joining the Foreign Office.

Auden has known Burgess 20 years, since his undergraduate days at Cambridge – and he went to school with Donald Maclean, the other missing diplomat.

Twice security police from Naples have questioned Auden because it was rumoured that his white-painted home on this sun-seared island was to have been the end of the line for Burgess.

The police are still watching discreetly.

In the Spanish civil war anti-Fascist Auden drove an ambulance. In 1939 he went to America and he is now a U.S. citizen.

Tonight, sitting amid the purple bougainvilia and the blaze of geraniums of that colourful house of his on the Via Santa Lucia, he said:

'All my sympathies with the Communists ended with the Nazi–Soviet alliance in 1939. I have nothing to do with the Communists now.

'Burgess was an open Communist in the late 1930's.

'In New York – where I spend six months of the year – we met several times.

'While he was at the Embassy in Washington Burgess was still pro-Communist.

'We met last in March this year. We talked about Fuchs and Nunn May – he was Burgess's close friend.

'I asked him if he had been "screened", and Burgess spoke of diplomatic immunity.'

Auden believes that Burgess and Maclean were forced to leave England on May 25.

At that time Auden was staying in St. John's Wood, London, with his friend Stephen Spender, the poet and former Communist.

Burgess phoned there on the night of May 24 and asked for Auden.

Auden said: 'I was out and Spender forgot to pass on the message. In fact, I did not know about the phone-call until this week.'

Now, Auden believes that Maclean – 'he knew quite a lot about the atom bomb' – and Burgess were kidnapped in France.

He thinks they were contacted at St. Malo, told they were wanted officially, and a car was waiting.

The baggage they left behind? 'They could have been told: "It will follow later." They would accept that.

'I feel sure that if Burgess was at large in Europe he would have contacted a friend, someone like myself; he was a prolific newspaper reader and must have known he was wanted.

'He would never have sent that telegram to his mother. Never. It is totally alien to his nature.'

No English security police have called on Auden. Local police will not say if any English police are still on the island, but close watch is kept on English visitors.

Five minutes after I arrived in Forio today the local caribinieri sergeant questioned me. Who was I and where was I from? Why was I here?

Armed police are still scrutinising the gangways of each tourist ship that docks on Ischia, and all have seen photographs of Burgess and Maclean.

The following day, Auden wrote to Spender:

Stephen, dear,

Well! The combination of that phone call and some lady who thought she saw La B. in the train on his way to Ischia has turned this place into a mad-house. The house watched night and day by plain-clothed men etc. etc. The climax has been the interview with me published in the *Daily Express* which I dare say you've seen. The rather nice young reporter who came suffers from that form of deafness characteristic of reporters which hears what it wants to hear instead of what is actually said. Reuter's came today and I've tried to straighten the story out, but the whole business makes me feel sick to my stomach. I still believe Guy to be a victim, but the trouble though about our age is that one cannot be certain.

How is everyone? If you could get one of the servants to pack up my camera and post it, I should be grateful.

Much love to all,
        Wystan.

The approaching première of *The Rake's Progress* diverted Auden's attention from the Burgess–Maclean affair. On 17 August, he and Chester dined with the Stravinskys and Robert Craft at the Pappagallo in Naples. 'Italian and English are the languages of heaven,' Auden told the assembled company. '"Frog" is the language of hell . . . The Frogs were expelled from heaven in the first place because they annoyed God by calling him *cher maître*.' (This petulant outburst was brought on because some French visitors had just annoyed Auden by calling Stravinsky *cher maître*.)

Stravinsky's doctors in Naples forbade him to take a trip to Ischia, much to Auden's disappointment. However, Robert Craft visited the island, staying overnight with Auden and Kallman in their pleasant little villa which was kept reasonably clean and tidy by 'a handsome Neapolitan Ganymede with a manner like his not quite believable name, Giocondo'. Craft recorded the visit in his diary:

> We walk to a beach in the afternoon, Wystan at high speed (he is now wearing plimsolls) in spite of the heat, and, himself excepted, universal indolence; but the water is bathtub warm, and only Moses (the household dog), still starting at every false throw, is aquatically inclined. On the return to Forio we meet Chester Kallman, just back from a visit to another part of the island. Wystan is always happier in tandem with Chester, and the best of his former good spirits now seem like doldrums in comparison. He dotes on the younger poet, in fact, listening admiringly to his talk, calling attention to jewelled bits of it, and supplying helpful interpretations for rougher gems, though as a rule if Chester appears even to be on the verge of speaking, Wystan will remain quiet. When the younger poet goes to the kitchen for a moment, Wystan says of him that 'He is a very good poet and a far cleverer person than I am.' Whatever the truth of these assessments, Chester most certainly *is* a very good cook. By some oversight, however, the spinach has not been washed tonight, and after what sounds like a painfully gritty bite, Wystan reports a considerable presence of sand; then, lest we think him persnickety, he quickly adds that he doesn't in the least mind, and even manages to suggest that he has become quite fond of it.

Composer, librettists and entourage moved to Milan for the first rehearsals of *The Rake*. Stravinsky was not amused when Auden reported a story that Britten, on looking at a score of the opera, had remarked that he liked everything about it but the music. However, relations between Auden and Stravinsky remained cordial throughout a trying rehearsal period, despite Auden's constant disparagement of the producer, Carl Ebert, and the designer, Gianni Ratto. ('It could hardly be worse if the director were Erwin Piscator and the singers were climbing and descending ladders.') Auden was also upset because he and Chester, having failed to make hotel reservations, at first had to reside in a *bordello* where 'the girls were very understanding, but the rooms could be rented only by the hour and so were terribly expensive'. The highlight of the Milan sojourn was a dinner party which Auden and Kallman gave for the Stravinskys, after which the assembled company all went off to a performance of Giordano's *Fedora*, an opera which failed to live up or down to Chester's hilarious account of it in advance. The 'lowlight' of the rehearsal period in Milan was the failure of Auden, who attended rehearsals in a Chianti-stained white linen suit, to carry out successfully the one task with which he had been entrusted, namely to coach the Italian chorus in their English enunciation. At the Venice première, not one word they sang could be understood.

On 5 September, the cast, chorus, orchestra, composer and librettists of *The Rake's Progress* travelled by train from Milan to Venice. At Verona, an American in Auden's compartment said to his companion, 'Hey, didn't Shakespeare live here?' at which Auden observed loudly, 'Surely it was Bacon.' At the Hotel Bauer in Venice, discovering that the room allotted to him was small and shabby, Auden was so upset that he rushed to Stravinsky's luxurious suite and burst into tears. It was only after Madame Stravinsky had informed the management that Maestro Auden was a modern equivalent of Guglielmo Shakespeare, who had been received at Buckingham Palace by the King, that a better room was provided for him. There was a rehearsal of *The Rake* at the Fenice that evening. The chorus's unintelligible English drove Auden afterwards to take refuge in drink and a midnight gondola ride with the Stravinskys, the poet's drunken rendering of passages from *Die Walküre* leading Stravinsky to recollect that Colette had once sung Wagner to him when they got drunk together on the train from Paris to Nice. When Auden's song was interrupted by the appearance of a large rat running along a wall two feet from the gondola, the startled singer declared 'It's the D.T.'s.'

Among Auden's admirers was an American woman who, not content to worship the poet from afar, or on the printed page, was constantly seeking opportunities to meet him and begin a closer relationship. To his horror, this woman turned up in Venice during *The Rake's* rehearsal period. On more than one occasion, in order to escape her, he was forced to leave his friends precipitately and jump into a passing gondola; once, he missed his footing and nearly landed in the canal.

On the day of the première, 11 September, Auden was, according to Stravinsky, 'as nervous as an expectant aunt'. But the performance at the Teatro La Fenice that evening was well received, though by all accounts Stravinsky did not conduct very impressively, and of the singers only Elisabeth Schwarzkopf was liked by all. *The Rake* survived its first, unsatisfactory production to establish itself in due course as one of the two or three most successful post-Straussian operas.

In Venice, Auden made the acquaintance of his Italian translator, Carlo Izzo, who asked him to explain a line in an early poem, 'Song of the Beggars' in which six beggared cripples 'follow the delicious breeze like a tantivy pig'. Why, wondered Signor Izzo, should a tantivy pig follow the breeze? 'Why not?' was the only answer he got from the poet.

Back in New York for the autumn and winter of 1951, Auden found several chores awaiting him. The previous year, together with Lionel Trilling and Jacques Barzun, he had been instrumental in setting up a high quality book club, the Reader's Subscription. Among his duties was the choosing of books, some of which he reviewed in the club's periodical, *The Griffin*. He was to continue his association with the Reader's Subscription and its successor, The Mid-Century Book Club, until 1962. He also allowed himself, in 1952, to be talked by Nicolas Nabokov into attending another event organized by the Congress for Cultural Freedom, this time in the heart of Frogland, Paris. But when Nabokov tried to persuade him to lecture in Japan for the Congress, Auden dug his heels in: 'It's so far away . . . and then you have to eat all that raw fish, drink tepid rice wine and live in cardboard houses . . . And someone told me that the toilet seats are much too small for my bottom . . . Besides, I can't distinguish one Japanese from another . . . Let Stephen go, he likes that sort of thing.' Instead, he and Chester went off to Ischia for the spring and summer as usual. The year ended, in New York, with a couple of splendid evenings, both involving the Stravinskys. On 26 December Auden and Chester gave a Christmas dinner party for Igor and Vera Stravinsky and Robert Craft. 'The apartment,' wrote Robert Craft in his diary,

> is imaginatively decorated for the Yuletide, with empty bottles, used martini glasses, books, papers, phonograph records, all realistically strewn about to create a marvellously lifelike impression of randomness. And the decorators have achieved other, subtle touches of picturesqueness as well, such as, in lieu of frankincense, filling the flat with stale, boozy air. We compete for the most recently occupied, and hence dusted, chairs – the furniture looks as if it had been purchased with Green Stamps – then choose drinks, tipping out cigarette butts and ashes, dregs of earlier drinks and other detritus from the glasses in which they seem most likely to be served. But, shortly before dinner, the fine line between decor and reality momentarily confuses V! Visiting the lavatory and finding shaving utensils and other matter in the sink, a glass containing a set of snappers (store teeth), a mirror in which it would be impossible even to *recognize* oneself, a towel that would oblige the user to start over again, and a basin of dirty fluid on the floor, she unthinkingly empties the basin and fills it with fresh water. Not until dessert time do we discover, with

mixed emotions, that she has flushed away Chester's chocolate pudding.

Auden entertained the Stravinskys with stories of the mouse which ran about the apartment and of which he had become fond. 'There are usually scraps enough lying about for the poor dear to eat,' he said, as his guests uneasily surveyed the greasy plates upon whose hardened remnants of earlier meals the excellent food they were offered was piled. After dinner, they listened to bits of opera on the gramophone: Purcell, Verdi, Wagner. Auden's Yule-tide merriment diminished only once during the evening when his persistent female admirer telephoned.

The following evening, 27 December, Auden had drinks with the Stravinskys at their hotel: his fellow-guests were Edith and Osbert Sitwell. Auden had warned his hosts that Edith drank 'like a fish', and had also informed them that she was 'as bald as a coot'. But Dr Edith's head remained swathed in black silk throughout her visit, and the heavy drinking was done by Auden and Stravinsky, watched by the narrowly squinting eyes of the intimidating poetess.

Chapter Ten

1953–1964

Yes, these are the dog-days, Fortunatus:
  The heather lies limp and dead
On the mountain, the baltering torrent
  Shrunk to a soodling thread;
Rusty the spears of the legion, unshaven its captain,
  Vacant the scholar's brain
  Under his great hat,
Drug though She may, the Sybil utters
  A gush of table-chat.[1]

It was in 1953 that Auden and Kallman moved to another apartment in Greenwich Village, at 77, St Mark's Place, the house in which Trotsky had once worked for *Novy Mir*, as Auden delighted to tell visitors. There Auden stayed for nearly twenty years, continuing to spend the spring and summer of every year in Europe. Early in the year, Auden's harrassment by his female admirer came to an abrupt end. 'She finally had to be taken to the coop,' he told Robert Craft. 'She was ringing up every few minutes, hammering at the door in the middle of the night, even bribing the manager of the building to be let into my apartment; though once inside she did no more than take measurements of my old suit in order to buy me a new one.' She had also, to Auden's horror, begun shouting in public that she and he had had sexual intercourse together. In fact, he had met her only once, and that at the request of her psychiatrist.

For the spring semester beginning early in February, 1953, Auden taught as the William Allan Neilson Research Professor at Smith College, in Northampton, Massachusetts. While there, he took part in the faculty play, *Rosina*, on 17 April, playing the role of Pa Greenseed. According to the programme, 'the recitative of the Ghost was composed by the song team of W. H. Auden and W. A. Mozart'. He also sponsored a student competition to rewrite the end of *The Dog Beneath the Skin*. On 25 May, he was appointed to the poetry advisory committee of the National Arts Foundation (which later became the National Endowment for the Arts): the other appointments announced on the same day were those of Walter Gropius to the committee on architecture and Basil Rathbone to the drama committee.

The following January Auden was awarded the Bollingen Poetry Prize for

[1] From 'Under Sirius'.

242

1953. This was the prize which, funded by the Bollingen Foundation, a philanthropic trust set up by Paul Mellon, had been given for the first time in 1948 when a number of judges, Auden among them, awarded it to Ezra Pound. Following that highly contentious choice, the administration of the Prize had been handed over to Yale University, and a committee appointed by the University Library awarded it to Wallace Stevens in 1949, John Crowe Ransom (1950), Marianne Moore (1951) and Archibald MacLeish and William Carlos Williams jointly in 1952. Announcing the award of the Bollingen Prize to Auden for 1953, the Yale librarian said: 'A tough thinker, Auden is a man who expresses himself acutely and with poetic vivacity. In his identity as an American, he has become a permanent part of American poetry.'

In February 1954, Auden was momentarily involved with Spain for the first time in many years, when, along with nineteen other prominent American citizens, he signed a message to General Franco condemning the use of military courts in Spain to try civilians charged with political offences. This gesture was made in consequence of a Madrid court-martial having sentenced eighteen civilians to prison for terms of up to fifteen years. In March, the Living Theater Studio in New York presented the first staged performances of Auden's *The Age of Anxiety*. (Bernstein's symphony, based on Auden's poem, had been used for Jerome Robbins's ballet, *The Age of Anxiety*, in 1950.) One of Auden's now rare meetings with Christopher Isherwood occurred when Isherwood came to New York for the publication of his novel, *The World in the Evening*. Auden criticized his old friend for not having made the sexual scenes a little more explicit. 'We have to know who was fucking whom,' he said, 'and you never make that clear in the book.' At the end of the year, Auden was one of four new members elected to the American Academy of Arts and Letters: announcing this, the *New York Times*[1] quaintly described the poet as 'one of the chief influences against the standards of nineteenth century poetry'.

The Shield of Achilles, Auden's next book of verse, was published in New York early in 1955 and in England towards the end of the year. Reviews this time were generally respectful. 'My first and lasting impression, with this book, is of dealing with a master, a poet of such technical authority that he is always touching accomplishment and doing it, moreover, without much struggle,' wrote Howard Nemerov in *The Kenyon Review*;[2] in John Lehmann's *London Magazine*,[3] a fair and balanced review ended with the sentence, 'As long as he can couple verbal perfection with a sense of disquiet like this, Auden will remain among the finest living poets.' This volume won Auden a National Book Award.

[1] 17 December 1954.
[2] Summer 1955.
[3] March 1956.

In the autumn, at the invitation of his friend Professor Ursula Niebuhr, Auden lectured again at Barnard College as part of a course on religion. He and Kallman had been commissioned by NBC (the National Broadcasting Company) to translate the libretto of Mozart's opera, *Die Zauberflöte*, for a television production, and by October they had finished their translation which was performed on television on 15 January 1956, and subsequently published.

Auden had allowed his name to be put forward as a candidate for the Oxford University Professorship of Poetry, the holder of which is chosen, every five years, by a ballot of those graduates who have taken their Master's degree in Arts. Any two Oxford MAs can nominate a candidate, and all the University's MAs are entitled to vote, though they must travel to Oxford to cast their vote in person. The retiring Professor was Auden's old friend, Cecil Day Lewis: those competing to succeed him included Auden, Harold Nicolson and the Shakespeare scholar, G. Wilson Knight. The position is one of some prestige, or at least it remained so in Auden's day. The Professor was required to give one lecture in each term for a period of five years, for the not exactly princely emolument of £300 per year. On 9 February, those of Oxford's MAs who were interested and lived close enough to Oxford to register their votes there, did so. Auden was declared the winner, with 216 votes, a majority of twenty-four over Harold Nicolson. He arranged to give his inaugural lecture in June.

Before leaving New York on his spring migration to Europe, Auden received some unsought publicity as a result of one of his many acts of charity, which he liked to perform as anonymously as possible. A woman called Dorothy Day, who ran a 'House of Hospitality' for the poor on the lower East Side of Manhattan, had found herself in trouble with the fire laws, and was fined two hundred and fifty dollars as the landlord of a firetrap. The Magistrate heard that Miss Day was doing her best to comply with the regulations with the help of donations from well-wishers, and, deciding to discover what extenuating circumstances there were, asked Miss Day to appear before him again the following day. A report appeared in the *New York Times*, under the heading, 'Poet and Judge Assist a Samaritan: Dorothy Day's Hostel Gets Auden's Gift – Fine is Lifted':

> As Miss Day left the house on her way to court, there was a group of needy men about the door, awaiting the distribution of clothing. From their midst a man, who looked much like the rest, stepped out and pressed a piece of paper into her hand.
>
> 'I just read about your trouble,' the man said. 'I want to help out a little bit towards the fine. Here's two-fifty.'
>
> Miss Day, elated over having $2.50, as she thought, of the total,

thanked her benefactor and hurried on. In the subway on her way to Upper Manhattan Court, she looked at the check.

It was for the full amount of the fine, $250. And it was signed by one of the leading poets of the United States, British-born W. H. Auden. Miss Day was apologetic for not having recognized him.

'Poets do look a bit unpressed, don't they?' she said.

Mr Auden had read about Miss Day in the paper at breakfast and had rushed out to do what he thought ought to be done.[1]

In April, Auden and Chester left for Ischia. This year, they rented a different villa in Forio, at Quarto San Giovanni, Vico 4. Exceptionally, they did not return to New York for the winter, but lived abroad until the autumn of the following year. A friend who was in their apartment, helping with last-minute packing, remembered Auden looking about his rooms, in tears at leaving his familiar surroundings, even though, unlike Chekov's Madame Ranievskaya, he would be returning to them eighteen months later. In Oxford, Auden gave his inaugural lecture on 11 June. It was his only Oxford lecture that year. For future years, the authorities had agreed to his giving all three lectures in the one term, to save him travelling time and expense. So he would usually spend the month of May in Oxford, delivering his lectures on a vast range of subjects including Robert Frost, D. H. Lawrence, the dramatic use of music in Shakespeare's plays, Byron's *Don Juan*, Marianne Moore, *Pickwick Papers*, and the hero in modern poetry. The lectures were subsequently revised for publication, and most of the material appeared in due course in a volume of essays by Auden, *The Dyer's Hand*.

It was Auden's habit, while he was in residence at Oxford, to make himself accessible to students every morning. At eleven he would shuffle off in his slippers to the Cadena Café in the Cornmarket, where, he said, the only decent coffee in Oxford was to be found. Having let it be known that students who wished to talk or to show him their verse could simply sit down and join him, he was usually to be found holding court to a group of students crowded into his booth, while others stood around, straining to catch his words. The more serious poets were invited to visit him in his rooms which in 1956 were in the Christ Church annexe in Brewer Street. Here his comments on their work, unfailingly sympathetic but always shrewdly practical, could be made in private. He was invariably courteous to the young, and sometimes to the not so young. When a student brought the visiting American beat poets, Allen Ginsberg and Gregory Corso, to meet him, Auden received them tolerantly, though privately he dismissed their work as rubbish. Perhaps in order to cut short the visit, he showed them

---

[1] 2 March 1956.

both round Christ Church Cathedral, and was horrified when, as they parted, both Ginsberg and Corso knelt and attempted to kiss the turn-ups of his trousers.

In addition to his lectures, it was the duty of the Professor of Poetry to deliver every second year, the Creweian Oration or *Oratio Creweiana*, in Latin, 'in commemoration of Benefactors to the University, according to the intention of the Right Honourable Nathaniel Lord Crewe, Bishop of Durham'. Auden prepared his texts for these orations in English, which was then translated or paraphrased for him by a tutor in Classics. During the five-year term of his Professorship, Auden took his duties seriously for the few weeks of each year that he spent in Oxford; preparing his lectures with great care: but what he enjoyed most, he told a number of his friends, was his informal contact with students at the Cadena.

Auden's father, Dr George Auden, died on 3 May 1957, at the age of eighty-five. Auden, who was with him at the end, later told friends that he had said cheerfully to the old man, 'Well, father, you're dying you know.' In June, it was announced in Italy that Auden had won the Feltrinelli prize, which carried with it a cash award of approximately £1,200. It was this money which helped to enable him, the following year, to buy a small farmhouse in Lower Austria. His first intention had been to purchase the villa in Forio d'Ischia which he had been renting; but the landlord, hearing about the prize, asked such an unreasonable sum for what was a quite small house that Auden changed his mind and began to seek not just another villa but another country.

In any case, life on Ischia in the village of Forio was less enjoyable than it had been. 'Forio has been invaded by Limey lushes,' Auden told the novelist Robin Maugham when he visited Ischia in company with Michael Davidson, who had befriended Auden when he was a schoolboy. 'You see,' Auden continued, 'I don't like sunshine. I would like a Mediterranean life in a northern climate.' He also confided to his visitors that returning to Oxford had brought back to him all that he disliked about England: 'In America I won't open my mouth for less than three hundred dollars. In England I found people expected me to speak for five pounds. I found them provincial. A don at the House asked me whether Eisenhower was a Democrat or a Republican. So I gave him a little lecture on the American electoral system. But I feel he ought to have known, don't you? England *is* terribly provincial – it's all this *family* business. I know exactly why Guy Burgess went to Moscow. It wasn't enough to be a queer and a drunk. He had to revolt still more to break away from it all. That's just what I've done by becoming an American citizen . . . I also find criticism in England very provincial. In the literary world in England, you have to know who's married to whom, and who's slept with whom and who hasn't. It's a tiny jungle. America's so much larger. Critics may live in New York, but the writers don't.'[1]

Auden's disillusionment with Ischia was exacerbated by what one might call the Giocondo affair. Giocondo, his handsome young Neapolitan houseboy, was well aware that he created interest and perhaps even stirred some passion in Auden's coterie. There was even a certain amount of jealousy between Auden and Chester Kallman over Giocondo's affections. Sex had for some years played a diminishing role in the Auden–Kallman relationship, and by the late 1950s they were no longer lovers but companions. Chester enjoyed a series of affairs with younger lovers, while Auden's interest in sex had become spasmodic and perfunctory, though he was still capable on occasions of being stirred to action by male beauty.

In the winter of 1955–56, while Auden and Kallman were absent from Ischia, Auden had sent Giocondo a cheque to cover his salary and petty cash expenses. Auden claimed that the cheque was for 60,000 lire, but he filled in the amount only in figures, leaving the space for the amount in words blank, his Italian not being equal to the task of writing 'sixty thousand' as 'sessanta mille'. But, when the cheque was presented for payment, it was for the sum of 600,000 lire, and the bank refused to pay since Auden did not have that much money in his account. He returned to Ischia in the spring of 1956, to find that the row had reached colossal proportions involving not only most of Auden's friends in Forio but also all of Giocondo's numerous relations. Auden claimed that Giocondo had added a nought to the cheque, while Giocondo claimed that he had been given a cheque for 600,000 lire as a gift in return for favours rendered, but that Auden was unable to admit it for fear of Kallman's jealous wrath. A restaurant in Forio which was owned by Giocondo's brother-in-law, and patronized by most of the foreign colony, among them Sir William Walton and Prince Henry of Hesse, became a centre for discussion between the feuding groups until Giocondo, having become a barman there, refused admission to the pro-Auden faction. Visitors to the restaurant, even those who neither knew nor cared about the dispute, were startled to be regaled by its barman with stories of the famous poet's personal hygiene or lack of it and of the litter of soiled underpants, broken egg shells, crumpled newspapers and cigarette ends which Giocondo had been required to clear away every morning. The general opinion among the populace was that Giocondo had been hard done by.

Clearly, it was time for Auden and Kallman to move on from Ischia. In choosing somewhere else to live, Auden used to say later that he bore several considerations in mind: it should be a German-speaking country but not Germany, it should produce drinkable wine, and it should give him access to an opera house of high standard. This last consideration was

[1] Quoted in Robin Maugham: *Escape from the Shadows* (London, 1972).

particularly important since he had virtually given up going to the Metropolitan Opera in New York because he disapproved of the 'absolutely ghastly' Rudolf Bing regime. On his last visit to the Met, he had embarrassed his host by waiting until the enthusiastic applause had died down at a performance of Tchaikovsky's *Eugene Onegin*, and then shouting 'Shame!'

It was inevitable that those requirements of wine, opera and German should have led Auden and Kallman to inspect properties in Austria, in the countryside around Vienna. They were helped in this by the daughter of Auden's old Kitzbühel friend, Hedwig Petzold. In the spring of 1958, they agreed to purchase, for the sum of ten thousand dollars, a converted farmhouse and three acres of land in the village of Kirchstetten, on the edge of the Vienna Woods, twenty-nine miles west of Vienna. They lived in Ischia through most of the summer of 1958 until the Kirchstetten house, which was to be their spring and summer home until Auden's death fifteen years later, was ready for them to occupy. From the very beginning, the villagers of Kirchstetten were proud that a distinguished man of letters had come to live among them. Auden had seen the house advertized in a Viennese newspaper, had taken the train from Vienna, a journey of about forty minutes, and, 'providence-led' as he wrote in a poem some years later, had 'first beheld Kirchstetten on a pouring wet October day' and fallen in love with the landscape, village and house. Kirchstetten is not an Austrian tourist village with a frothy head of *Gemütlichkeit*, but a quiet farming community whose charm is no less palpable for not being instantly on display. Its surroundings, rolling wooded terrain and lush green fields, charmed Auden instantly: his enjoyment of the regular, settled life he and Chester were now able to live was obvious to the friends who visited them there. The routine they established was that they would spend spring and summer in Austria, and autumn and winter elsewhere. At the end of October, the village farmhouse in Austria would be exchanged for city life. Auden would return to the Greenwich Village apartment in New York, while Chester Kallman would spend his winters in Athens where, for years, he had a Greek lover, Yannis Boras. In April, Auden and Kallman would converge again upon Kirchstetten.

The house always remained what it was, a small country farm-house, with peasant-style Austrian furniture, whitewashed walls in the cosy living-room, and the small bedrooms comfortably but simply furnished. Chester had insisted, however, upon the installation of a modern American kitchen. Auden's study, an attic room, access to which was by an outside staircase, contained a desk near the window, with a splendid view over the countryside, an untidily stacked bookcase and a couch for day-time naps. The Auden–Kallman collection of gramophone records was kept downstairs in the living-room. To the *New York Times* interviewer who visited him in

October, some months after he and Chester had moved in, Auden said he was proud of the house. (He also said that they were completing an English translation of Brecht's *Die sieben Todsünden* and added that, though a remarkable writer, Brecht had been a most unpleasant man.)

From Vienna to Venice is a comfortable overnight train journey of eight hours. In September, Auden took the night train from the Südbahnhof for Venice, where he was lecturing during a Contemporary Music Festival. Here he literally bumped into the Stravinskys in a side street one evening, and a day or two later lunched with them. At lunch, openly contemptuous of the array of pill bottles on the table in front of the composer, he muttered to Robert Craft, 'The steadiest business in the world would be a pharmacy next door to Stravinsky.' Later, in discussing a certain opera with Stravinsky, he suggested that perhaps one should study it. 'No,' replied the composer, 'one should just steal from it.' While he was in Venice, Auden wrote his poem of farewell to his years of Italian semi-sojourn, 'Good-Bye to the Mezzogiorno' which contains a reference to Monte, the landlord who had tried to fleece him:

> . . . Go I must, but I go grateful (even
>   To a certain *Monte*) and invoking
> My sacred meridian names, *Vico, Verga,*
>   *Pirandello, Bernini, Bellini,*
>
> To bless this region, its vendages, and those
>   Who call it home: though one cannot always
> Remember exactly why one has been happy,
>   There is no forgetting that one was.

Auden and the Stravinsky *ménage* met again at the end of the year when Auden came to dinner in New York on 28 December. On that occasion, Stravinsky said that he, Vera and Robert Craft hoped to attend a performance of the Brecht-Weill *Seven Deadly Sins*, in the Auden-Kallman translation, to which Auden cattily replied, 'Better hurry and get tickets or you'll never get in. Samuel Barber's *Vanessa* is on at the Met that night.'

On 23 January 1959, at the annual dinner of the Poetry Society of America at the Waldorf-Astoria Hotel at which he read several of his most recent poems, Auden was awarded the Society's gold medal 'for distinguished service to poetry'. In the spring, together with Jacques Barzun and Lionel Trilling, he resigned from the Readers' Subscription Book Club whose Editorial Board they comprised, and the three of them formed the Mid-Century Book Society. Auden was quoted in the *New York Times*[1] as saying, 'Poets and professors and all those whose love of books exceeds their love of automobiles will welcome a chance to save in excess of 50 per cent on their

[1] 1 April 1959.

book purchases.' The Book Club also published a magazine, written almost entirely by Barzun, Trilling and Auden until all three withdrew from the Club in 1963. Auden's contributions included review-articles on Betjeman, James Agee, Marianne Moore, Robert Graves, Philip Larkin, Cesare Pavese, Van Gogh, Kafka and Leonardo.

In April, Christopher Isherwood came from California to discuss with Auden and Chester the possibility of collaborating on a stage musical version of Isherwood's Berlin stories, *Goodbye to Berlin*. The proposal was that Auden and Kallman would be responsible for the lyrics. (A straight play, *I am a Camera*, based on the stories, had been written by John van Druten and staged with great success in 1951.) Both Auden and Kallman were enthusiastic, though, when he was asked about the project some weeks later by a journalist, Auden denied rumours 'that he was to write the lyrics for a musical of Christopher Isherwood's *Goodbye to Berlin* with Marilyn Monroe as its star. He said he was "furious" about the reports.'[1] The project did not get off-the ground for some time, due to the difficulty of finding a financial backer. When it eventually did go forward, Auden and Kallman were not connected with it. With a script by Joe Masteroff, lyrics by Fred Ebb, and music by John Kander, *Cabaret* opened on Broadway in November 1966.

Before he departed for Europe, Auden was interviewed in St Mark's Place by BBC Television for the programme *Monitor*, shown some weeks later. It contained some shrewd comment on readers and poets:

> People are always saying that modern poetry is so difficult – presumably they mean in comparison with poetry of the past. I wonder, first of all, when people say this, how much poetry of the past they know. Sometimes I think that what they regard as obscurity shows that they take poetry a little too seriously; one of the elements in poetry is the riddle, that you do not call a spade a spade. It is evident that people enjoy solving riddles, because otherwise crossword puzzles would not have the popularity they have. It is odd that some of the people who spend hours doing crossword puzzles, and love doing them, are the first to raise objections because they do not understand a line of poetry . . .
>
> . . . In reading poetry I look for originality in this sense, that if I read a volume of poems by somebody I want to feel that this person has a unique perspective on the universe; that it is from his point of view, and not somebody else's. Secondly, I look for a real love and reverence for the medium itself – that is to say, for language . . . Sometimes I think people do not even think about 'making' [a poem] at all, but about 'expressing themselves' – which is something very different, and which can be a boring idea – as opposed to trying to tell truthfully what one sees.

[1] Sunday Times (10 May 1959.

During his Oxford weeks each year, Professor Auden had got into the habit of throwing the occasional party in his rooms in Christ Church. At a party in 1959, one of the undergraduates who was drunker than his colleagues was sick all over the notebooks and papers on Auden's table. Auden appeared not to mind, and a comparatively sober undergraduate who was present thought that the mess would probably have been left had not an American Air Force Sergeant cleaned it up. It was in this year, too, that an inebriated Christ Church rowing eight, celebrating the successful outcome of a race, raged about the college in search of someone to throw into the pond in the centre of Tom Quad. When they appeared on Auden's staircase with the apparent intention of selecting him as their victim, he invited them in, gave them more to drink and told them they were gorgeous boys. Disconcerted, they eventually left to search for a more conventionally unconventional victim.

Auden had by now become something of an Oxford institution. His lectures, given to crowded audiences, were described in *Isis* as both entertaining and provoking: 'We are told of the Good Life and the Just Life, of Antonio's homosexuality and Caliban's innocence, of Falstaff's tummy and his moral beauty, and on at least one occasion, we have been sung to.' Few other Oxford Professors of Poetry, before or since Auden, have been so popular. His informal seminars at the Cadena Café made him seem like a latter-day Socrates among the ladies resting from their shopping. He was moved, to some extent by self-interest, to present the Christ Church Senior Common Room with a refrigerator, so that dry martinis could be served as an alternative to port. (Having once been served a sufficiently dry martini – which, for him, required the vermouth bottle merely to be passed over the gin in an incantatory gesture – by a barman in Leicestershire, Auden used to say, for years afterwards, that the only place one could get a decent martini in England was in Ashby-de-la-Zouche.)

The previous autumn, Auden and Kallman had been asked by the German composer Hans Werner Henze to write an opera libretto. They had corresponded about this, and now, in the summer, Henze visited the two poets at Kirchstetten to discuss it further. Auden and Kallman had planned an original libretto, set in the Austrian alps in 1910, about a monstrous old Viennese poet, Mittenhofer, and the final details of plot and form were now agreed. By December, the libretto of *Elegy for Young Lovers* was ready, and was sent from New York to Henze in Naples.

During that summer at Kirchstetten, Auden and Kallman had also worked on a translation of Lorenzo Da Ponte's Italian libretto for Mozart's *Don Giovanni*. This, like their earlier translation of Schikaneder's *Die Zauberflöte* libretto, was commissioned by NBC; it was used in a broadcast performance in April 1960. This time, however, the collaborators relied more heavily on cribs than they had with *The Magic Flute*, for neither partner's Italian was equal to the task of translating directly from Da Ponte. In the autumn, they began another translation, of Brecht's text for the Brecht-Weill *Aufstieg und Fall der Stadt Mahagonny* (Rise and Fall of the City of Mahagonny), a translation which has not yet been published or, it seems, performed.

In April 1960, a new volume of poems, *Homage to Clio*, was published in New York. Auden having now attained the status of a living 'classic' author, a man widely regarded as among the few really great poets of the century, reviewers felt free to be as rude about him in print as if he were dead. '*Homage to Clio* is probably his worst book since *The Dance of Death*' wrote the young poet Thom Gunn in *The Yale Review*.[1] In his view, High Church snobbery had repressed the poet's active intelligence, 'replacing it with the habit of continual trifling' and had led Auden to write 'poetry that is both morally and technically frivolous'. In a bad book, Gunn thought a poem called 'There Will Be No Peace' was 'perhaps the worst of Auden's poems I have seen in book form.' The *New Statesman*[2] offered faint praise: 'one must admit at the very least that he has an interesting mind and that his language is adequate to it.' In the *Spectator* in a long article 'What's Become of Wystan?', Philip Larkin, in whose view Auden's most valuable work had been done in the thirties, arrived at the conclusion that 'in some way Auden, never a pompous poet, has now become an unserious one. For some time he has insisted that poetry is a game, with the elements of a crossword puzzle: it is "the luck of verbal playing". One need not be a romantic to suspect that this attitude will produce poetry exactly answering to that description.'[3]

There is a certain amount of light verse in *Homage to Clio*, for instance:

> As the poets have mournfully sung,
> Death takes the innocent young,
> > The rolling in money,
> > The screamingly funny,
> And those who are very well hung.

There are also some very beautiful lyric poems, amongst them 'The More Loving One':

> Looking up at the stars, I know quite well
> That, for all they care, I can go to hell,
> But on earth indifference is the least
> We have to dread from man or beast.

[1] September 1960.
[2] 9 July 1960
[3] 15 July 1960.

How should we like it were stars to burn
With a passion for us we could not return?
If equal affection cannot be,
Let the more loving one be me.

Admirer as I think I am
Of stars that do not give a damn,
I cannot, now I see them, say
I missed one terribly all day.

Were all stars to disappear or die,
I should learn to look at an empty sky
And feel its total dark sublime,
Though this might take me a little time.

While he was in London in June on his way from Oxford to Kirchstetten, a party was given for Auden by his London publishers, Faber & Faber, at their premises which were then in Russell Square, Bloomsbury. Their edition of *Homage to Clio* was about to appear. Mr and Mrs T. S. Eliot were the hosts, and other guests included such figures from Auden's past as Stephen Spender, A. L. Rowse, Isaiah Berlin, Louis MacNeice and Tom Driberg, as well as some younger poets from the Faber list, among them Ted Hughes and his wife Sylvia Plath. A week or so earlier, still in Oxford, Auden had been interviewed for the *Daily Mail* by one of the more intelligent and knowledgeable literary journalists, Kenneth Allsop, to whom he confessed that being a Professor of Poetry was 'rather like being a Kentucky Colonel. It's not really a subject one can profess – unless one hires oneself out to write pieces for funerals or the marriages of dons.' Less frivolously, he spoke of poetry as a defender of language: 'Language is always being corrupted and today the corrupters have more efficient machinery, with television and mass communication, than they ever had. We live in a technological world, and there it is. My personal view is that every poem written today is important, because it is a blow struck for the personal outlook on behalf of all those who are being robbed of a personal outlook.' He gave his usual reasons for preferring to live in America, although he loved coming back to the 'nice, cold leathery toast for breakfast, and the ghastly climate', adding that in America there was 'much less nose-wrinkling about how a literary gent earns his living. I lecture, give readings of my poetry for quite reasonable sums, do a job for a highbrow book club and do occasional TV. Although one has to work hard, it's easier to make money there than here.'

In the last week of October, Auden gave his final two lectures at Oxford as Professor of Poetry. Back in his adopted country for the winter he turned up in Washington in January for the inauguration of John Kennedy as President, standing with Richard Eberhart and his family outside the White House to watch the parade, and displaying his most affable social behaviour at a Georgetown party in the evening. Like so many people, he expected the Kennedy administration to herald a bright new era for America.

Henze's opera was given its first performance at the Schwetzingen Festival on 20 May 1961, in a German translation as *Elegie für junge Liebende*. Kallman attended rehearsals first in Munich and then in Schwetzingen – 'Needless to say, all seems to be chaos and fury,' Auden wrote to Stephen Spender from Kirchstetten a week before the première – and both librettists were present on the first night which was, at best, a *succès d'estime*. Immediately afterwards, Auden gratified 'a life-long day-dream' by paying a three day visit to Hammerfest in Norway, the most northerly town in the world, and then stayed for a few days with Spender in London. Spender, who was then co-editor of *Encounter*, asked his old friend to contribute to a symposium, but met with a refusal: 'As to poets and universities, I am bored with the subject.'[1]

The first performance of *Elegy for Young Lovers* in its original language was given on 13 July at Glyndebourne, in Sussex, during the annual summer opera festival. Again, Auden and Kallman were present. Strolling in the beautiful gardens at Glyndebourne during the rehearsal period, they encountered John Christie, the Festival's eccentric 'onlie begetter' who asked them who they were. On being answered, he was no better off, for he had not heard of them. What were they doing there? They explained that they had written the libretto of *Elegy for Young Lovers*. 'Oh dear, you shouldn't have, really you shouldn't,' murmured Christie sorrowfully, as he walked away. Perhaps he was right, but one hopes that he expressed himself in stronger terms to the composer. There was some booing to be heard on the first night, after which the word was passed around and audiences stayed away in droves from the remaining seven performances. One can but speculate as to whether Glyndebourne is blessed with audiences of unusually refined taste and perception, or whether they would also have rejected a modern masterpiece. Auden always referred to the opera as 'Allergy for Young Lovers', since that was the title with which it came back from his typist: within a few years, he was talking about the work to friends as though he himself were allergic to it.

Before returning to Kirchstetten for what remained of the summer, Auden took part in a television programme with Stephen Spender, Christopher Isherwood and Cyril Connolly, in which they were interviewed by the journalist and 'TV personality' Malcolm Muggeridge in his most self-caricaturing manner:

[1] Letter to Stephen Spender, 13 May 1961.

Muggeridge: Christopher, you, after all, have been in the most curious position, when you watched this very successful play, *I am a Camera*, I imagine you did watch it, when you could see on the stage the young Christopher Isherwood, actually in the flesh.

Isherwood: Yes it was spooky, of course. The only thing was that they insisted on – in the States, unfortunately I didn't see it here – on having a juvenile lead, a romantic lead instead of a character actor, and this of course made it seem very different to me from what I personally am.

Muggeridge: You didn't feel in those days you were a junior lead?

Isherwood: No, no, definitely not, I would have scorned that –

Auden (interrupting): Always the performer!

Muggeridge: Wystan, what do you, I mean, looking back at yourself, when you were writing those poems on Spain, and all that kind of thing, what do you feel about it?

Auden: Well, a merciful curtain descends, really. I mean I can remember extremely little, because, personally, of the kind of things I wrote between about 1932 and 1939, the things that I like now I sort of wrote by accident. I mean I was writing –

Muggeridge: So that you don't really have a sort of picture of yourself as you were, writing all those things.

Auden: No.

Muggeridge: Do you like those poems better than the ones you're writing now, or not?

Auden: No.

Muggeridge: You like the ones you're writing now better?

Auden: Well, I won't say – it's not a question of whether they're better or worse, but whether you feel they're in your own handwriting.

Muggeridge: And the earlier ones don't really seem . . .

Auden: Well, at a certain period, I think some of them were, some of them weren't, but for better or worse one thinks one knows what one wants to do now.

Muggeridge: Which is the one that you'd sort of bank on if you had to choose one?

Auden: Oh, that I couldn't say.

Muggeridge: You couldn't say.

Connolly: Well, 'About suffering the Old Masters . . .' that one, I think.

Muggeridge: Stephen, you're, after all, connected with this, with Cyril's magazine, *Horizon*.

Spender: Yes.

Muggeridge: A literary magazine, a very difficult thing to run in this country.

Spender: Yes.
Muggeridge: And now running another one, *Encounter*. Is it very different?

This, one cannot help but remark, is the kind of cosy, familiar (in its meaning of family-like or domestic) literary gossip which kept Auden away from England for so long.

Asked by the *Sunday Times* to contribute to a Christmas feature in which a number of well-known writers and critics listed their favourite books of the year, Auden mentioned *The Correspondence between Richard Strauss and Hugo von Hofmannsthal* as having interested him enormously, but claimed that the single piece of literature which had given him the greatest pleasure in 1961 was an article in *The Scientific American* called 'Cleaning Shrimps', which was not about how to clean shrimps, but about a kind of shrimp which lives by cleaning fish!

It was from about this time, a period when the Gay Liberation Movement was beginning to make its presence felt in America, that Auden began occasionally to let slip in public the mask behind which he had tended to hide his own sexual nature. Too fastidious to join any of the activist groups, and too well-bred to thrust knowledge of his sexual tastes upon people who might have reacted with shock, or boredom, or the former pretending to be the latter, he had nevertheless got to a stage in life and in fame where he felt less vulnerable than formerly. There were, for instance, times when he clearly thought it not only a duty but a pleasure to jolt the young. In the autumn of 1962, travelling from New York to New Haven by train to lecture at Yale University, he sat in the club car and was eyed furtively for some time by two Yale students who finally sent a note to him which read, 'We can't stand it a minute longer: Are you Carl Sandburg?' Auden sent a note in reply: 'You have spoiled mother's day.' Although he was never to make any public pronouncement about his homosexuality, in the later nineteen-sixties he was always willing to talk to homosexual student societies at universities where he was lecturing or giving poetry readings. He saw no reason to pretend, but he also saw no reason to proclaim. Nevertheless, towards the end of his life, Auden refused to allow one of his poems to appear in an anthology of 'gay' verse, for the reason that he had written his published love poems to be read without reference to the sex of the person addressed.

He enjoyed best, now, those months he spent each year in Austria. The winters in New York became something of an endurance test, for he felt lonely without Chester whom he usually did not expect to see again until the spring. His Manhattan friends and acquaintances were no real substitute for the domestic companionship he valued so highly. But he enjoyed dining out, and was always good value on such occasions. Dining with the

Auden in his Tolkien sweater.

ABOVE LEFT The English novelist and poet, Charles Williams. His Christian faith was one of the influenc
that led to Auden's return to the Anglican communion in 1940.
ABOVE RIGHT The novelist Carson McCullers, who shared Auden's house in Middagh Street, Brooklyn
Heights.
BELOW LEFT Gypsy Rose Lee, the stripper – another inmate of 7 Middagh Street.
BELOW RIGHT Auden and Britten in New York in May 1941, when the first performances of their operett.
Paul Bunyan were being given at Columbia University.

LEFT Auden with James Stern in Bad Nauheim, 1945, when they were both members of the United States Strategic Bombing Survey.
RIGHT May 1945: Auden amongst the ruins of Nuremberg.
BELOW On Fire Island, 1946. Auden wrote that he 'Arrived to find the *Life* photographer waiting who made me do the most absurd things like wading into the water and gazing soulfully out to sea. What will appear I daren't dream of.'

LEFT Auden and James Stern with Rhoda Jaff close friend of Auden's and his secretary for years, sitting outside 'Bective Poplars', the holiday shack on Fire Island shared by Aude the Sterns in the summers of 1946 and 1947.
BELOW Auden, Spender and Isherwood on F Island.
BOTTOM With Rhoda Jaffe on Fire Island.

LEFT Lecturing at the New School for Social Research, New York, in 1947.

BELOW With Cecil Day Lewis and Stephen Spender in Venice for a PEN Club conference, autumn 1949.

BOTTOM A reception at the Gotham Book Mart for Edith and Osbert Sitwell, seated in the centre, on 9 November 1948. Auden is sitting on a ladder, and clockwise from him are Elizabeth Bishop, Marianne Moore, Delmore Schwartz, Randall Jarrell, Charles Henri Ford, William Rose Benet, Stephen Spender, Marya Zaturenska, Horace Gregory, Tennessee Williams, Richard Eberhart, Gore Vidal, and Jose Garcia Villa.

TOP With Chester Kallman in Venice, 1949.
LEFT Auden during one of the summers he spent on Ischia.
ABOVE Auden in 1951.

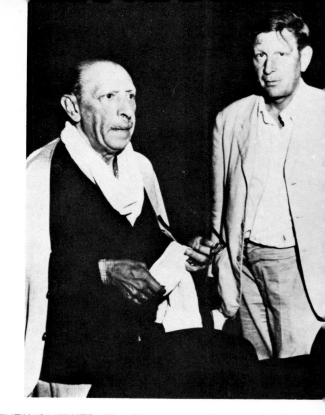

RIGHT Stravinsky and Auden during rehearsals for *The Rake's Progress*, Milan, 1951.

BELOW The first American performance of *The Rake's Progress* at the Metropolitan Opera, New York, 1953. From left to right: Norman Scott (Trulove), Mack Harrell (Nick Shadow), Hilde Güden (Anne), Eugene Conley (Tom), Stravinsky, Auden, Fritz Reiner (the conductor) and Kallman.

ABOVE With his friend Ursula Niebuhr and her poodle Winnie.
BELOW In Oxford, 1957, with Robert Frost.

ABOVE The Faber party given in 1960 preceding the British publication of *Homage to Clio*. From left, Louis MacNeice, Ted Hughes, T. S. Eliot, Auden, and Stephen Spender.
BELOW Moran Caplat (General Administrator of Glyndebourne), Auden, Kallman and Hans Werner Henze, during the rehearsal period for *Elegy for Young Lovers*, 1961.

ABOVE At an Oxford garden party in 1968 with Jean Cocteau.
BELOW Auden dining with the Stravinskys, George Balanchine, Robert Craft, and Lincoln Kirstein, in December 1969.

ABOVE In the garden of his home in Kirchstetten, Austria.
BELOW LEFT At a reception in London during the 1971 *Poetry International.* Auden was, as usual, wearing his carpet slippers.
BELOW RIGHT Caricature by David Levine, 1972.

THIS PAGE AND OPPOSITE ABOVE The farmhouse at
Kirchstetten, near Vienna, which Auden and
Kallman bought in 1958, and which remained
their summer home until Auden's death in 1973.

BELOW Packing books in his New York apartment at 77 St Mark's Place. Auden left America for good in February 1972.

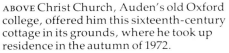

ABOVE Christ Church, Auden's old Oxford college, offered him this sixteenth-century cottage in its grounds, where he took up residence in the autumn of 1972.

RIGHT A pause during a poetry reading at the Oxford Union, 1972.

BELOW In Peck Quad, Christ Church, in 1972. The fourth and fifth windows in the middle row to the left of the corner are those of his old rooms when an undergraduate.

ABOVE Allen Ginsberg and Auden during *Poetry International* in 1973, the last such festival Auden was to attend.
BELOW Shortly before his death in September 1973, Auden in the garden at Kirchstetten with Chester Kallman and Charles Osborne.

TOP The funeral at Kirchstetten, 4 October 1973.

LEFT John Betjeman standing over the memorial stone, which he unveiled in October 1974, in Poets' Corner, Westminster Abbey.

ABOVE Advertisement in the *Harvard Advocate* Special Auden Memorial Issue, 1974.

Stravinskys at the Pierre Hotel in November 1962, he cheerfully informed
them that Cardinal Spellman could have become a saint 'but thought it too
fruity to do a miracle', then launched into one of his monologues about
opera, describing the beginning of Act II of *Die Walküre* as 'a Victorian
breakfast scene, Wotan meekly cracking his morning egg behind *The Times*
while Fricka furiously rattles the teacups' and *Pelléas et Mélisande* as 'an
underwater opera. Nobody can be that refined; the piece succeeds because it
flatters the audience. But imagine devoting an opera to people with manias
for losing things.'

The Dyer's Hand, a volume of essays based largely on those which Auden
had given as Oxford's Professor of Poetry, was published in November
1962, in New York. Earlier in the year he had been elected a Fellow of Christ
Church. He ended 1962 unacademically, by appearing on Christmas Eve on
the Merv Griffin Show on NBC Television. He was now famous on several
levels, as a poet internationally, as a critic in England and America, as a
performer of his own poetry on the American University circuit, and on
radio and television in the United States as an all-purpose intellectual. At
the heart of all this was his poetic achievement. Translated into more than
thirty languages, among them Bengali, Icelandic, Korean and Slovene, he
had also been the subject of a number of critical studies, and many more
were to follow.[1]

Hans Werner Henze, keen to do another opera with Auden, had suggested that they collaborate on a tragedy, and Auden had suggested *The
Bacchae* of Euripides. Auden and Kallman worked on their libretto in the
autumn and winter months of 1962–63, Kallman this time spending part of
the winter with Auden in New York. 'The other night we had Harold
Nicolson to dinner and invited the Niebuhrs to meet him,' Auden wrote to
Spender in January. 'It turned out that both H. and Reinhold N. have
bladder trouble, and the two old gentlemen did a ballet all evening to
the loo and back . . . O, by the way, *Time* is doing a cover-story on me. I'm
terrified.'

In April, Auden took part in a symposium on 'Symbol and Myth in
Contemporary Art' in West Berlin, and attended the première there of
Darius Milhaud's opera, *L'Orestie*. At a luncheon party given by Nicolas
Nabokov for the crippled composer, Auden was at his crankiest. The meal
had to wait until Milhaud could be seated, but this produced a croak from
Auden of 'You're twenty minutes late, Nicky.' 'Quelles manières,' whis-
pered Madame Milhaud to their host.

In June, Auden wrote a poem, 'On the Circuit', which casts an ironic eye
upon the poetry-reading circuit and his own involvement in it. He soon

[1] The 1972 Bloomfield-Mendelson *Bibliography* lists 577 books, articles and theses but makes
no claim to be exhaustive.

added it to his own repertoire of poems to read in public, which only very rarely included any of his poems from the thirties. As 'On the Circuit' brings the world of the touring celebrity poet to vivid life, its sixteen stanzas of autobiographical Auden verse are quoted in full, as a temporary respite for the reader from non-Auden biographical prose:

Among pelegian travelers,
Lost on their lewd conceited way
To Massachusetts, Michigan,
Miami or L.A.,

An airborne instrument I sit,
Predestined nightly to fulfil
Columbia-Giesen-Management's
Unfathomable will,

By whose election justified,
I bring my gospel of the Muse
To fundamentalists, to nuns,
To Gentiles and to Jews,

And daily, seven days a week,
Before a local sense has jelled,
From talking-site to talking-site
Am jet-or-prop-propelled.

Though warm my welcome everywhere,
I shift so frequently, so fast,
I cannot now say where I was
The evening before last,

Unless some singular event
Should intervene to save the place,
A truly asinine remark,
A soul-bewitching face,

Or blessed encounter, full of joy,
Unscheduled on the Giesen Plan,
With, here, an addict of Tolkien,
There, a Charles Williams fan.

Since Merit but a dunghill is,
I mount the rostrum unafraid:
Indeed, 'twere damnable to ask
If I am overpaid.

Spirit is willing to repeat
Without a qualm the same old talk,
But Flesh is homesick for our snug
Apartment in New York.

A sulky fifty-six, he finds[1]
A change of mealtime utter hell,
Grown far too crotchety to like
A luxury hotel.

The Bible is a goodly book
I always can peruse with zest,
But really cannot say the same
For Hilton's *Be My Guest*,

Nor bear with equanimity
The radio in students' cars,
Muzak at breakfast, or – dear God! –
Girl-organists in bars.

Then, worst of all, the anxious thought,
Each time my plane begins to sink
And the No Smoking sign comes on:
What will there be to drink?

Is this a milieu where I must
How grahamgreeneish! How infra dig!
Snatch from the bottle in my bag
An analeptic swig?

Another morning comes: I see,
Dwindling below me on the plane,
The roofs of one more audience
I shall not see again.

[1] The change to the third person here may be confusing if the reader does not realize that 'he' refers to 'Flesh' in the previous stanza, in which 'our snug apartment' is occupied not by Auden and Kallman but by Flesh and Spirit.

God bless the lot of them, although
I don't remember which was which:
God bless the U.S.A., so large,
So friendly, and so rich.

The following month, Auden wrote a poem, 'The Common Life', addressed to Chester Kallman. It is, in its way, a love poem, though the love is not *eros* but *agape*. There are, one could say, three central love poems in Auden's *oeuvre*: 'Lay your sleeping head, my love', written to a teenage lover; 'The Common Life', written to his companion of many years, now following him into middle-age; and 'Glad', which Auden would write two years later, addressed to Hugerl, a Viennese call-boy. From *eros* to *agape* and back to *eros*. The strongest feeling is that aroused by Chester or, perhaps more accurately, aroused by life with Chester. Reading the celebrated 'Lay your sleeping head' one catches, as the poem progresses, a certain air of 'I could not love thee dear, so much, loved I not poetry more'. And 'Glad', one feels, ought to be retitled 'Sad', in its making-the-best-of-it acceptance of a relationship which exists only in bed and which, while it does not exclude affection, is basically a commercial operation:

How is it now between us?
Love? Love is far too
Tattered a word. A romance
in full fig it ain't,
Nor a naked letch either:
Let me say we fadge,

And how much I like Christa
Who loves you but knows,
Good girl, when not to be there.
I can't imagine
A kinder set-up: if mims
Mump, *es ist mir Wurscht*.

But 'The Common Life', is moving and not at all sad:

It's a wonder that neither
has been butchered by accident,

or, as lots have, silently vanished into
History's criminal noise
unmourned for, but that, after twenty-four years,
We should sit here in Austria

as cater-cousins, under the glassy look
of a Naples bambino,
the portrayed regards of Strauss and Stravinsky,
doing British crossword puzzles,
is very odd indeed.

Their common life was one of real companionship, from which the sexual element had departed years before. A New York friend, interviewed in a Boston 'gay' magazine, *Fagrag*, a year after Auden's death[1] said that Chester used to remember 'to the very day, the last time they had sex, which had been years ago before 1953'. He also revealed that, in New York, Chester's way of life had produced problems:

I remember once he and Chester had a disagreement because Chester liked to cruise a lot and liked rough trade. Wystan himself tended to prefer highbrow queens or smart college boys. Wystan finally put his foot down about Chester bringing crowds and dangerous types into the house. That changed their lifestyle considerably. That was the right thing to do; they were always getting ripped off. Chester was once arrested during the Wagner years when they used to send agents provocateurs around picking people up.[2] Chester got one of those and was arrested. This was when it happened. Wystan pulled strings to get him out of the mess. It was not so much that he did not want these people in his house, it was for Chester's own good. Wystan loved Chester who imperilled himself repeatedly.

The *Fagrag* interview also gave a couple of examples of Auden's camp habit *en famille*, amusing to some, irritating and silly to others, of quoting famous lines but substituting 'Your mother' for the original noun or pronoun:

In one of Spender's poems, he would change 'I' to 'your mother' and alter 'I think continually on those who are truly great' to 'Your mother thinks continually on those who are truly great'. He loved doing this with the Bible, which shows something of his lack of piety. I remember him saying once, 'Your mother is the resurrection and the life. If she be lifted up, she will lift up all men unto her.'

That Auden's relationship with Chester Kallman endured to the end of his life was due to many things: to their shared interests, to their professional collaboration and to their very real knowledge of each other's strengths and weaknesses. Also, of course, as partners in any marriage of long standing must, they simply got used to being together, and to making

[1] *Fagrag* (September 1974): 'Remembering Auden', an interview with John Button.
[2] Wagner was Mayor of New York from 1954 to 1965.

allowances for each other. They enjoyed working together on their opera libretti. Now, having finished *The Bassarids*, based on *The Bacchae* of Euripides, they were keen to find another project. It did not have to be opera, for they had no objection to making some money out of a Broadway musical. Having been edged out of the project which in due course produced *Cabaret*, they now became involved in a scheme to turn Cervantes' *Don Quixote* into a musical. They prepared some lyrics, but Auden told the London *Evening Standard*[1] that 'Nothing is settled yet. I don't want to talk about it until I am certain we can do it. I have read the first draft of the book, but I am afraid that will have to be rewritten.' One of Auden's lyrics, for a song to be sung by Don Quixote, ends with the lines:

> It shall not be! Enchanters, flee! I challenge you to battle me!
> Your powers I with scorn defy. Your spells shall never rattle me.
> Don Quixote de la Mancha is coming to attend to you.
> To smash you into smithereens and put a final end to you.

Eventually the producer of the show came to the conclusion that the Auden-Kallman lyrics were not quite what he wanted. When *Man of La Mancha* finally reached Broadway two years later, its lyrics were by one Joe Darien.

When his old friend Louis MacNeice died, Auden flew from Kirchstetten to London on 16 October, stayed with the Spenders, and delivered an address at a memorial service at All Souls Church, Langham Place, opposite the BBC where MacNeice had been employed as a producer of radio features. 'In this age,' Auden said, 'to die at fifty-five is, statistically speaking, to die early, but worse things can befall a poet than an early death. At least Louis MacNeice was spared that experience which some poets have had to endure, and for many years: the experience of being condemned to go on living with the knowledge that the Muse has abandoned them.' He praised MacNeice's refusal ever to 'fake feelings' in his verse. Of all the poets of their generation, MacNeice, he felt, had the least cause for self-reproach.

On 22 November 1963, Benjamin Britten celebrated his fiftieth birthday. Auden had neither spoken to nor seen his old friend for many years, but he wrote a tribute to Britten which, for some reason, perhaps because it was received late, did not find its way into the volume which Faber & Faber published on Britten's birthday.[2] On the same day, President Kennedy was assassinated in Dallas. Auden, in company with millions of others, was profoundly shocked: like hundreds of artists all over the world, he tried later to shape his response into a work of art in his own medium. Dining with the Stravinskys in New York two months later, in January 1964, he found that

[1] 18 September 1963.
[2] See p. 111.

Stravinsky wished to compose an elegy to Kennedy's memory, and began to discuss ways of doing it. 'I'm an old hand at this sort of thing,' he told the composer, as he worked out a form in which to write words for Stravinsky to set. (After Auden had left, the composer said to Robert Craft: 'Wystan is wholly indifferent to J.F.K.; what he cares about is the form. And it is the same with his religion. What his intellect and gifts require of Christianity is its form – even, to go further, its uniform.')

Auden was in good spirits at Stravinsky's dinner party despite, or perhaps because of, having drunk 'a jug of Gibsons before, a bottle of champagne during, a bottle (*sic*) of Cherry Heering (did he think it was Chianti?) after dinner.'[1] He trotted out several of his party pieces, among them his view that the time had not yet come to admit that 'Shakespeare was in the homintern, or, for that matter, that Beethoven was queer'; and his descriptions of Rilke as 'the greatest Lesbian poet since Sappho' and of Yevtushenko as 'the poor man's *Howl*.' Before leaving, he forbade his hosts to attend a poetry reading he was soon to give: 'I never allow anyone I know to come to those things. First of all, I want to keep my tricks to myself, and second, I'm always afraid someone in the back of the hall is going to shout something like "We've heard all that before" or "Get her!"'

The following month, Auden wrote his 'Elegy for J.F.K.' and sent it to Stravinsky, whose setting for baritone voice and three clarinets was composed in Hollywood in March, and was given its first performance at a concert in Los Angeles conducted by Robert Craft on 6 April. But, by then, Auden had fled to Europe: not, as usual, to Austria, but first to Iceland, where he had not been since his visit with Louis MacNeice in 1936.

[1] Robert Craft: *Stravinsky* (London, 1972).

Chapter Eleven

1964–1973

Yet, at this very moment when we do at last see ourselves as we are, neither cosy nor playful, but swaying out on the ultimate wind-whipped cornice that overhangs the unabiding void – we have never stood anywhere else, – when our reasons are silenced by the heavy huge derision, – There is nothing to say. There never has been, – and our wills chuck in their hands – There is no way out. There never was, – it is at this moment that for the first time in our lives we hear, not the sounds which, as born actors, we have hitherto condescended to use as an excellent vehicle for displaying our personalities and looks, but the real Word which is our only raison d'être.[1]

It was at the invitation of the Government of Iceland that, in April 1964, Auden returned to the country that he liked to think of as the land of his ancestors. He was officially entertained at luncheons, dinners and receptions, met both the President and the Prime Minister of Iceland, and stayed with the British Ambassador, Basil Boothby, whom he had first met in China in 1938. The unflattering comments on Iceland that Auden and MacNeice had made in *Letters from Iceland* a quarter of a century earlier had been forgotten, or at least were not referred to, and some of the friends Auden had made on that earlier visit called at the Ambassador's house to renew acquaintance with him. Before leaving Iceland, he went off alone to the north-west of the island, where he, Michael Yates, and Louis MacNeice had spent very happy days during their tour in 1936, and there he wrote a poem, 'Iceland Revisited', a succession of fourteen *haikus*. ('Twenty-eight years ago/Three slept well here./Now one is married, one dead.') He stood for a time on the exact spot where he, Michael and Louis had stood to say farewell to their hosts, and gazed across the fjord to the sea, remembering. But, all too soon, it was time to fly back 'to hot baths, cocktails, habits', away from the 'Fortunate island,/Where all men are equal/But not vulgar – not yet.'

In May, a query from Stephen Spender, who was teaching at an American University, elicited from Auden an interesting remark about Yeats in relation to his own work: 'I am incapable of saying a word about W. B. Yeats because, through no fault of his, he has become for me a symbol of my own devil of authenticity, of everything which I must try to eliminate from my own poetry, false emotions, inflated rhetoric, empty sonorities.

[1] From 'The Sea and the Mirror'.

> No poem is ever quite true,
> But a good one
> Makes me desire truth.

His make me whore after lies.' He added that Spender's daughter had made him read 'Jack [*sic*] Lennon's book which, to my amazement, I thought rather good and funny!',[1] and that he would be flying to and from the United States for three days in June, 'to get an Hon. degree from Swarthmore'.

At Stephen Spender's urging, he attended an International PEN Conference in Budapest in October, driving from Kirchstetten on 15 October and returning on the 18th. Auden always found such conferences boring and pointless, but Spender had told him that his presence in Hungary would help to boost the morale of Hungarian writers. He was dismayed when he learned the name of his co-delegate, a female poet from the English branch of PEN, 'Entre nous', he wrote to Spender, 'the prospect of ―― ―― as a co-delegate does not fire me with enthusiasm.' However, he went, albeit unwillingly.

In the autumn, Auden moved to Berlin for six months, as a participant in an artists-in-residence project sponsored by the Ford Foundation. This involved him in taking part in a Congress of African and European writers, despite the fact that, as he informed Stravinsky who came to Berlin for a week in September, he was himself 'unable to follow nigritude'. He was also irritated at having to endure discussions in French at the Congress: 'Why should I be compelled to listen for hours at a time to Pierre Emmanuel's rhetorical frog effusions?' His behaviour at a Stravinsky dinner party in Berlin, as reported by Robert Craft, is typical of Auden's public form in his later years:

> He talks about the film that the Austrian government has been making of his life in Kirchstetten. 'One scene is in church – not terribly appropriate, perhaps (a naughty bar might have been more suitable) but you can hear me singing. Besides, the priest loved being photographed and got all dolled up for it. You can also hear me speaking *Kraut*, ungrammatical, no doubt, but chatty, and I get in some *echt* expressions.'
>
> Switching to poets, he expresses admiration for Robert Frost, 'in spite of his mean character, for he was jealous of every other, and especially every younger, poet. So was Yeats a jealous old man, who behaved abominably to younger poets. But Yeats was untruthful, too, which is the reason I dislike his poetry more and more. Why can't people grow dotty gracefully? Robert Graves is aging well, by the way, except that he has become boastful, implying he's the oldest poet still fucking. Now

[1] John Lennon: *In His Own Write* (London, 1964).

obviously it is normal to think of oneself as younger than one is, but fatal to want to *be* younger.'

He condemns Shelley ('a thoroughly uninviting character') for shareholding in cotton mills, but may be seeing the poet in the light of Dickens's 'Merdle' as he condones Wordsworth's similar investments in railroad stocks, adding, however, that 'I'm fond of trains.' As for Byron he was 'a master, not of language, but of speed. If Goethe had been able to understand him in English, he wouldn't have liked him at all.' Goethe's love-life, he goes on, shocks and bores him. 'He moves along so smoothly, then every once in a while along comes one of those awful outbursts of "*Mein Liebchen*".' He mentions a desire to translate the *Römische Elegien*, but says that so far the task has seemed impossible. 'I also want to do a poem explaining why photography isn't an art' he says, 'and of course any claim for the cinema as an art is rubbish. For the moment I have a medieval anthem in the works, one of those the-latter-half-is-the-mirror-of-the-first-half things. I promised it to Willie Walton at a party when I was in my cups.'

Is he in his cups now? He chews out a waiter for bringing him a glass of water: 'I haven't had any of that for thirty years and don't propose to start now.' (When Stephen Spender joins us later and I.S. asks him what *he* would like to drink, Auden whispers to me, 'Cocoa, I should think.') There is no mental fuzziness, in any case, though diction is less distinct, and though, with the ebb and flow of *alcools*, as 'frogs' say, conversation becomes more and more of a one-way street. His memory is unfailing when it comes to quoting poetry, which he spouts as if he had been struck by the hoof of Pegasus. But when he is obliged – as who isn't? – to rummage for a name or date, his twill-weave facial integument (with a wiggly wen) contracts while his right hand stirs what might be an unseen pancake batter. These, however, are the only outward signs of the throes of thought.[1]

Auden left the dinner party with a final salvo fired at the 'frogs', whose 'famous *clarté* is thicker than the thickest *Wiener* treacle', and a foreboding that the next day's conference would be 'a day among the Laestrygones. But if anybody brings up the subject of literary criticism, I will bolt. After all, we were put on this earth to make things.'

While he was in Berlin, Auden had a brush with the police, who picked him up on suspicion of inebriety in public. Telling friends of this later, he complained that the Berlin police paid members of the public to inform on those they had reason to believe were drunk. 'I was a victim of the snooping Kraut mentality,' he would say.

[1] Robert Craft: *Stravinsky* (London, 1972).

Early in the New Year, still in Berlin, Auden learned of the death of T. S. Eliot, and told Reuter's correspondent that the news had been a shock to him. Eliot 'was a great poet and a great man,' he said. 'I knew him since 1929, and we were very good friends.' In March he returned to Kirchstetten, and it was during that month that he wrote the third of his key love poems, 'Glad', to Hugerl, that Viennese call-boy with whom he had a business relationship which did not preclude a degree of affection. They had met in a bar in Vienna nearly ten years earlier when, to paraphrase the poem, Hugerl was in need of money, and Auden wanted sex. 'For how much and how often/You have made me glad,' he wrote:

> Glad that I know we enjoy
> Mutual pleasure:
> Women may cog their lovers
> With a feigned passion,
> But males are so constructed
> We cannot deceive.

Auden was glad, too, that their interests, outside of sex, diverged: 'I cannot tell a Jaguar from a Bentley/And you never read.' Glad, even, 'for that while when you stole/(You burgled me too),/And were caught and put inside:'. Some may think these are strange things to be glad for: evidence of the emptiness of life for Auden in his sixties. But 'Glad', which Auden did not publish during his lifetime, is the poem of a realist, a man as concerned not to deceive himself as he was concerned not consciously to deceive others.

He had, many years earlier, probably in 1948, written for his own amusement and the erotic stimulation of his friends a pornographic poem which he called 'The Platonic Blow'. For years, this circulated in typescript copies; in March 1965, to Auden's embarrassment, it appeared without his authorization in a New York little magazine, *Fuck you: a magazine of the arts*, in which it was described as having been 'snatched from the notebooks of W. H. Auden'. In public he usually denied authorship of the poem whenever he was asked about it, though privately he was quite proud of it, and even wittily acknowledged the stylistic influence of Charles Williams. (Three years later, interviewed for the London *Daily Telegraph* magazine,[1] Auden admitted he had written the poem and complained that it had been pirated by a New York press which didn't have the grace even to pay him.) Some weeks after its publication in *Fuck you*, 'The Platonic Blow' was issued separately in 'a Trade edition' of 300 copies and 'a Rough Trade edition of 5 numbered copies, each with beautiful slurp drawings by the artist Joe

[1] 9 August 1968.

283

Brainard'. Two further limited editions, one of three copies, and one of two, are described in the preliminary pages of the 'Trade edition', but since the descriptions themselves verge on the pornographic, the present (and prudent) author refrains from quoting them here.

The poem itself, a not unimpressive example of pornographic art, was soon pirated by an English publisher, and began to appear in a multiplicity of unauthorized, usually Xeroxed editions, sometimes under the title, 'The Gobble Poem'.[1] It consists of thirty-four stanzas of which this is the first and most innocuous:

> It was a Spring day, a day for a lay, when the air
> Smelled like a locker-room, a day to blow or get blown;
> Returning from lunch I turned my corner and there
> On a near-by stoop I saw him standing alone.

'A Platonic Blow' was not, of course, Auden's only excursion into pornographic or erotic verse. Artists in most media like to amuse themselves by producing *erotica*, and he was no exception to the general rule. He was also adept at producing unpornographic but slightly indecent limericks, and always appreciative of his friends' efforts in this genre. One of Auden's most popular limericks went thus:

> The Bishop elect of Hong Kong
> Had a dong that was twelve inches long.
> He thought the spectators
> Were admiring his gaiters
> When he went to the gents'. He was wrong.

In July 1965, a collection of somewhat more respectable poems by Auden was published in New York (and, the following January, in London). This was *About the House*, containing many domestic poems about the house at Kirchstetten and the way of life he and Chester had perfected there; poems about the trivia of domesticity, which led some of Auden's critics to complain that he appeared to have succumbed to Austrian *Gemütlichkeit*. ('Why not?' one can almost hear him grunt.) However, many of the poems in this volume are not 'about the house' but about other people, about language, about the erosion of values and the importance of clinging to the personal in an increasingly impersonal world. 'The Common Life', addressed to Chester Kallman, exemplifies both kinds of poem:

[1] The various editions are described fully in *W. H. Auden: A Bibliography, 1924–1969* (Charlottesville, 1972). There are copies of one edition or another in a number of American libraries (see the National Union Catalog) and in Great Britain in the British Library, the Bodleian, and the Arts Council Poetry Library.

A living room, the catholic area you
   (Thou, rather) and I may enter
without knocking, leave without a bow, confronts
   each visitor with a style,

a secular faith: he compares its dogmas
   with his, and decides whether
he would like to see more of us. (Spotless rooms
   where nothing's left lying about

chill me, so do cups used for ashtrays or smeared
   with lipstick: the homes I warm to,
though seldom wealthy, always convey a feeling
   of bills being promptly settled

with checks that don't bounce.) There's no *We* at an instant,
   only *Thou* and *I*, two regions
of protestant being which nowhere overlap . . .

By now deeply encrusted in habit, Auden seemed to find it necessary to run his life according to a strict time-table, from which deviations became fewer. Punctuality, always high on his list of virtues, assumed an ever-increasing importance in his life, while lack of it in others made him extremely irritable. He was no longer willing to consider projects which would interfere with his routine of six months in New York, six months in Kirchstetten, no longer interested in visiting places he had not seen, or revisiting scenes from his past. Once, when a friend asked him if he would like to go back to the landscape he had loved as a child, he replied sadly, 'Oh no, that was Paradise. I could never go back.'

Within the routine there was some scope for variation. In January 1966, in Brooklyn, Auden addressed the Tolkien Society of America, on 'Tolkien as a Man'. 'Well,' he began. 'Tolkien is a man of average height, rather thin. He lives in a hideous house – I can't tell you how awful it is – with hideous pictures on the walls. I first encountered him in 1926, at a lecture at Oxford. He read a passage from Beowulf so beautifully that I decided Anglo-Saxon must be interesting, and that has had a great influence on my life.' He assured the members of the Tolkien Society that the Elvish language used in Tolkien's *The Lord of the Rings* had affinities with Finnish.

In the summer, he and Chester drove from Kirchstetten along the auto-bahn to Salzburg, where Henze's *The Bassarids* was given its première during the Salzburg Festival, in a German translation. (The Auden-Kallman libretto was not heard in its original English until the opera was produced at

Santa Fé, New Mexico in August 1968.) In October, Auden preached from the pulpit of Westminster Abbey, at a service for people working in science, technology, and medicine. 'It looks as if traditional morality is to be succeeded by fashionable morality,' he told his congregation. 'Heroin and Sade will be in one year, cocoa and virginity the next.' A few days after his Westminster Abbey sermon, he was awarded in Vienna the Austrian State Prize for European literature, an amount of about two thousand American dollars. In the winter, back in his snugly untidy Greenwich Village apartment, he talked to a London *Evening Standard* journalist. 'I spend six months of every year in this flat. It suits me perfectly. I can shop for Polish and Jewish food in the markets, and cabs are plentiful. I start work at six in the morning, and every Sunday I go to church at St Mark's in the Bowery.' He said that he hoped to translate the whole of Wagner's *Ring* operas: the interviewer quaintly referred to this as 'a monumental project which could give Auden the immortality which has eluded him for so long'. (When the present author some months later drew Auden's attention to this reference to his elusive immortality, he replied: 'Ignorant and illiterate pricks, the lot of them!') The poet confessed, in the same interview,[1] to having once taken LSD: 'It was an absolute frost, since I'm completely pickled in alcohol, anyway. After about an hour, I thought I saw a vision of my postman waving his arms through the window of a restaurant. The next day the postman knocked on my door. "I waved at you yesterday and you ignored me," he said.'

In February 1967, Auden celebrated his sixtieth birthday. There was the usual party at St Mark's Place, and the occasion was also marked by a special issue of *Shenandoah*, the quarterly magazine published by Washington and Lee University in Lexington, Virginia. Under the title, 'A Tribute to W. H. Auden on his Sixtieth Birthday', the Winter 1967 issue contained articles and poems about Auden by Stephen Spender, Geoffrey Grigson, Roy Fuller, Lincoln Kirstein, E. R. Dodds, Julian Symons and others. In the spring, in Kirchstetten, Auden received the news that he had won the 1967 National Medal for Literature, an award given annually in America by the National Book Committee, an association of private citizens, to an author for his total contribution to American literature. The citation stated that Auden's poetry had 'illuminated our lives and times with grace, wit and vitality'.

It was in 1967 that the Poetry Book Society in Great Britain mounted for the first time its Festival of spoken poetry, *Poetry International*, a week of readings in London, featuring the world's leading poets. Auden was invited to participate, and agreed to do so, although it meant interrupting his Austrian summer. On the opening night, 12 July, at the Queen Elizabeth Hall, Auden shared the platform with a number of other distinguished poets

[1] London *Evening Standard*, 14 December 1966: an interview by Jeremy Campbell.

who included Pablo Neruda, John Berryman, Stephen Spender and William Empson. The following night, he appeared again. Other poets who took part during the week included Hugh MacDiarmid, Anne Sexton, Yehuda Amichai, Allen Ginsberg, Ingeborg Bachmann and Robert Graves.

Auden stayed with Stephen and Natasha Spender in London for the duration of *Poetry International*, and Spender took the opportunity to enlist his friend's support in an attempt to start a new literary magazine. For some years, Spender had been co-editor of *Encounter* with Melvin Lasky, but when it became publicly known that *Encounter* was subsidized by the American CIA, Spender resigned, angrily announcing that Lasky had kept him in ignorance of the provenance of a large part of their funds. Together with a group of friends which included Isaiah Berlin, Stuart Hampshire, Frank Kermode and Karl Miller, he drafted proposals for a new, independent review. Auden agreed to add his name to the signatories of the proposal, withdrew poems in proof from *Encounter* and, misunderstanding the political position of Nigel Dennis, Lasky's new co-editor, wrote to Dennis expressing 'shocked surprise' at his having accepted the co-editorship, which he held until 1970. Spender's project foundered, since he and his associates found it impossible to raise sufficient funds to launch a new magazine.

In the autumn, Carson McCullers died, and on 1 October, together with Gypsy Rose Lee and other survivors from their shared Brooklyn past, Auden attended her funeral service at St James' Episcopal Church on Madison Avenue, New York. Later in the month he returned to England to give the inaugural T. S. Eliot lectures at the new Eliot College of Kent University, and was visibly pleased by the warm, affectionate welcome he was given by the students. While he was in England, a book was published there which was a kind of parallel to *Authors Take Sides on the Spanish War* with whose publication Auden had been involved in 1937. This was *Authors Take Sides on Vietnam*. Auden had not, this time, been concerned in the compilation of the book; he was merely one of the authors who answered the questions 'Are you for, or against, the intervention of the United States in Vietnam?' and 'How, in your opinion, should the conflict in Vietnam be resolved?' Authors being no wiser than any other professional group of people, there were a good many simplistic replies, most of them against American involvement in Vietnam, but some for it. There was also, however, a large group of replies which showed at least some understanding of the moral and political complexity of the issue. Auden's was one of these:

Why writers should be canvassed for their opinion on controversial political issues I cannot imagine. Their views have no more authority than those of any reasonably well-educated citizen. Indeed, when read in

287

bulk, the statements made by writers, including the greatest, would seem to indicate that literary talent and political common sense are rarely found together.

If, as a social human being, I am asked my opinion about some political issue in England, Europe, or the United States, my answer, however stupid or prejudiced, is at least in part based on personal knowledge. I have travelled in the countries concerned, I know something about their inhabitants, their history, their language, their ways of thinking. But what do I, or any other writer in the West, know about Vietnam, except what we can glean from the newspapers and a few hurriedly written books? We know far more, even, about China.

It goes without saying that war is an atrocious corrupting business, but it is dishonest of those who demand the immediate withdrawal of all American troops to pretend that their motives are purely humanitarian. They believe, rightly or wrongly, that it would be better if the communists won.

My answer to your question is, I suppose, that I believe a negotiated peace, to which the Vietcong will have to be a party, to be possible, but not yet, and that, therefore, American troops, alas, must stay in Vietnam until it is. But it would be absurd to call this answer *mine*. It simply means that I am an American citizen who reads *The New York Times*.[1]

Early in November, while Auden was in New York and Kallman in Athens, their Kirchstetten housekeeper, Emma Eiermann ('Frau Emma') died. Sudete German refugees from Czechoslovakia, she and her brother had looked after the Kirchstetten house and garden for years. After her brother Josef died, Frau Emma carried on alone, a woman of strong character, grumpy, suspicious of many visitors to the house, and absolutely devoted to her employers. When he returned to Kirchstetten the following spring, Auden expressed in a poem something of his affection for her:

> *Liebe Frau Emma,*
> *na, was hast Du denn gemacht?*
> You always made
> such conscience of our comfort,
> oh, how could you go and die,
>
> as if you didn't know
> that in a permissive age
> so rife with envy,
> a housekeeper is harder
> to replace than a lover,

[1] From *Authors Take Sides on Vietnam* (ed. Cecil Woolf and John Bagguley. London, 1967).

> and die, too, when we
> were thousands of miles away. . . .

The poem goes on to describe some of Frau Emma's eccentricities and characteristics, and ends with a benediction: *'Du gute, schlaf in Ruhe.'*

The National Medal for Literature which Auden had won (a commemorative bronze medal accompanied by a cheque for five thousand dollars) was to be presented to him at a ceremony in the Smithsonian Institution, Washington DC, on 30 November. Auden drafted an acceptance speech in advance, and sent a copy to Washington so that a press release could be prepared. On the day, he drove down to Washington from New York but, delayed by a snowstorm which that morning blanketed the eastern seaboard of the United States, did not arrive in time to participate in the ceremony. His acceptance speech was read by Leo Rosten, and Auden eventually turned up during the reception that followed. In spring of the following year, 1968, Auden was honoured with another award, the Gold Medal for Poetry, given by the US National Institute of Arts and Letters. Again his acceptance speech had to be read for him, for his spring migration to Austria was not to be interrupted for the accumulation of honours. On his first day in Kirchstetten in April, he drove his Volkswagen into a telephone pole and broke a shoulder-blade. And so the following month, instead of driving, he and Chester travelled by train to Florence to attend the wedding of Auden's niece Anita, and to see a performance of Meyerbeer's rarely staged opera, *Robert le Diable*. Back in Austria by the end of May, Auden gave the opening address at the Salzburg Festival on 25 July, and, together with Kallman, attended some of the Festival's opera performances, among them Mozart's *Don Giovanni*, conducted and produced by Herbert von Karajan.

In August 1968, an acute international crisis was created when Czechoslovakia was occupied by Warsaw pact forces which overthrew the apparently too liberal Dubček regime. Auden, who had frequently expressed his disillusionment with political protest poetry, who had exclaimed bitterly that no poem of his in the thirties had helped to save a single Jew from the gas chambers, was moved to protest in the only way that a poet can: he wrote a poem. He may no longer have believed this to be an efficacious act, but the true poet writes when he has to, and so Auden wrote 'August 1968':

> The Ogre does what ogres can,
> Deeds quite impossible for Man,
> But one prize is beyond his reach,
> The Ogre cannot master speech.
> About a subjugated plain,
> Among its desperate and slain,

The Ogre stalks with hands on hips,
While drivel gushes from his lips.

The household split up as usual at the end of October, Wystan making his way back to the New York apartment while Chester went off to Athens for the winter. (Chester suffered a bereavement when, on 13 December, his Greek friend Yannis Boras was killed in a motor accident, at the age of twenty-six.) Among Wystan's chores during the winter was the writing of a libretto for a short opera or musical play, which he undertook at the request of Charles ('Chuck') Turner, the head of the music department of Wykeham Rise School, a girls' school in Washington, Connecticut. Auden based his poem, 'The Ballad of Barnaby', on the medieval French legend of 'Le Jongleur de Notre Dame'. The music was composed by the school's pupils, and the work was performed at the school on 23 and 24 May 1969.

One of Auden's minor ambitions was to get into the Oxford English Dictionary as the first person to have used a new word in print, or to have extended the meaning of an existing word. In a review of J. R. Ackerley's *My Father and Myself*, which he contributed to the *New York Review of Books* before leaving for Austria in the Spring, he included two expressions which he hoped the OED would notice. 'Plain sewing' and 'Princeton-first-Year', New York slang for two types of homosexual behaviour.

Part of the spring and summer in Austria was spent, with Kallman's help, preparing a libretto based on Shakespeare's *Love's Labours Lost* for an opera to be composed by Nicolas Nabokov.

In July, Auden flew from Vienna to London to take part again in *Poetry International*. This, formerly a biennial event, had now become an annual one, and Auden was to participate in it every summer, building it into his regular timetable. In 1969, his fellow participants were Ogden Nash, Robert Bly, Janos Pilinszky, Edward Brathwaite, Anthony Hecht and Vasko Popa: on the eve of the opening performance a reception was given for the poets on the roof of the Arts Council building in Piccadilly. Auden greatly admired Ogden Nash, and always maintained that it was at his suggestion that Nash had been invited to take part in the festival. (It was not.) But his lack of admiration of Robert Bly was also great and became increasingly and embarrassingly vocal during the course of the evening's drinking.

Throughout the festival week, Auden seemed in good form, more relaxed now, in his sixties, than he had been for some time, according to his friends. Interviewed by the *Sun*[1] he admitted as much. 'I don't want to lose *any* of my past,' he said. 'No. But then I've had an exceptionally lucky life. I got a decent education. I was loved by my parents. I was sometimes unhappy, but

[1] 12 July 1969.

I was never bored. I've been allowed to do what I wanted to do. Why the hell should I complain?' When he was asked the usual question about his repudiation of his left-wing verse of the thirties, he made the reply which he had already given on countless other occasions:

It's not that I go back on my opinions. But I've become very sceptical about *engagé* poetry. Political social history would be no different if Dante, Michelangelo, Byron had never lived. The arts can't do anything about this. Only political action and straight journalistic reportage can.

I feel a little guilty about some things I wrote in the thirties. Nothing I wrote against Hitler prevented one Jew being killed. Nothing I wrote made the war stop a minute sooner.

The most a writer can do is what Dr. Johnson once said: 'The aim of writing is to enable readers a little better to enjoy life or a little better to endure it.'

He predicted a swing of the pendulum away from the permissive society 'because it's got to the point where it's self-destructive and boring. All the pornographic books show such a *hatred* of sex. They never make it sound any fun. And they are so monotonous. Unless you get very eccentric indeed, you are limited in the number of sexual actions you can describe.' This is fair comment on run-of-the-mill pornography; Auden's own pornographic poem, 'The Platonic Blow', not only communicates enjoyment but is also quite inventive.

Auden was now inclined to trot out the same remarks, often in exactly the same words, whenever interviewed. When he visited Sweden in September, to participate in a symposium arranged by the Swedish Nobel Foundation, he talked on Swedish television with Göran Bengtson, and produced his by now familiar *bons mots*: Shelley was wrong, it is not poets who are the unacknowledged legislators of the world, but the secret police; poetry is an enjoyable game, and the player, the poet, must not overestimate his importance; the poet has much to learn from the scientist. But at the end of the interview, asked if he considered himself to be part of a continuing literary tradition, Auden uttered an unhackneyed and moving reply:

Yes, and the wonderful – the other nice thing about the arts, the invaluable thing about them, is that they're almost the only means we have of breaking bread with the dead. That is to say, all right, Homer is gone, his society is gone, but you could still read the Iliad and get a lot from it. And I do. I personally think that, without communication with the dead, we'd be entirely enclosed in the present, and it's not a fully human life. There's a good remark of Chesterton's about tradition. He said: 'Tradition is the democracy of the dead. It means giving votes to that remotest and obscurest of classes, our ancestors. It refuses to submit to the arrogant oligarchy of those who simply happen to be walking around.' It's a good remark.

It is widely thought in Swedish literary circles that one reason why Auden never won the Nobel Prize for literature was that he showed too clearly his eagerness to win it: indeed, that his pursuit of it during his visit to Sweden was quite blatant. Whether or not this is so, it is true that an influential member of the Swedish Academy (which selects the Nobel Prize winner in literature) who considered Auden's poetry too lightweight for consideration came also to dislike Auden personally during his brief visit to Sweden.

When Auden left Stockholm, his Swedish publisher Georg Svensson saw him off from the Grand Hotel:

> I went up to his room where he was packing. This certainly was something to watch. I have never seen anything like it, he just shovelled everything topsy-turvy into two enormous suitcases: clothes, shirts, books, underwear, toilet articles, without caring to straighten anything out. I was particularly fascinated by noticing that all his shirts were torn, with big holes at the elbows. His travel reading consisted of crime paperbacks, and two of them he gave me. I have forgotten which they were, but he thought them 'rather good'. When we eventually had managed to close the suitcases by sitting on them, I suggested we should call the hall porter to get somebody to fetch them, but this he refused most emphatically. 'No,' he said, 'we will carry them ourselves, otherwise there will be heaps of people to tip.' So we carried the heavy luggage to the elevator, and rushed through the lobby to the waiting taxi, where he took a hasty farewell of me.[1]

City Without Walls, published in England in September, contained recently written poems, among them 'Prologue at Sixty', with its description of Auden's Austrian home and its list of his sacred places:

> . . . Though the absence of hedge-rows is odd to me
> (no Whig landlord, the landscape vaunts,
> ever empired on Austrian ground),
> this unenglish tract after ten years
> into my love has looked itself,
>
> added its names to my numinous map
> of the *Solihull* gas-works, gazed at in awe
> by a bronchial boy, the *Blue John Mine*,
> the *Festiniog* railway, the *Rhayader* dams,
> *Cross Fell*, *Keld* and *Caldron Snout*,

[1] Letter from Georg Svensson to Charles Osborne, 30 August 1978.

of sites made sacred by something read there,
a lunch, a good lay,[1] or sheer lightness of heart,
the *Fürbringer* and the *Friedrich Strasse*,
Isafjördur, Epomeo,
Poprad, Basel, Bar-le-Duc,

of more modern holies, *Middagh Street,*
Carnegie Hall and the *Con-Ed* stacks
on *First Avenue*. Who am I now?
An American? No, a New Yorker,
who opens his *Times* at the obit page,

whose dream images date him already,
awake among lasers, electric brains,
do-it-yourself sex manuals,
bugged phones, sophisticated
weapon-systems and sick jokes . . .

It was really only with Chester Kallman in their *Wienerwald* farmhouse that Auden felt happy and secure. For some time he had ceased to enjoy his winter months alone in the Greenwich Village apartment, and now he began to put out feelers to his old Oxford college, Christ Church, in the hope that he might be invited to spend his declining years there. 'After all,' he said to a New York interviewer, 'Cambridge did as much for Forster. Next time I'm there, I think I'll broach it to them.' He was genuinely worried that, if he were to suffer a heart attack in New York, it could be days before he was found. He wanted to be part of a community again: understandably, his thoughts tended towards his old university. But he professed to be highly embarrassed and 'absolutely furious' when his remark about Christ Church was published,[2] resulting in a London paper telephoning the Dean of Christ Church, who could only say that Mr Auden was 'a person the college is always glad to see', but that there was extreme pressure on college accommodation.[3] 'I was merely discussing the problems of living alone when one gets very old,' Auden told the London *Daily Telegraph*,[4] 'and in fact I am not even thinking of returning to England at the present time.' He admitted that 'it might be rather nice' to have rooms in Christ Church, but denied any intention of trying to bring pressure to bear on the college. Having thus sown, or inadvertently dropped, the seed, he sat back and waited for it to bring forth fruit. Meanwhile, he got through the New York winter as best he

---

[1] Auden was amused when in French translation, 'a good lay' became 'un bon poème'!
[2] In *Esquire*, January 1970.
[3] The Guardian, 11 December 1969.
[4] 13 January 1970.

could, with the aid of his split-second daily routine. To Stravinsky's 'How are you?' when Auden arrived for dinner one evening in December, he replied, 'Well, I'm on time, anyway.' Drink now affected him more noticeably than in the past, causing some disconnected and, occasionally, startling remarks to emerge from the great poet's lips. 'Everyone knows that Russians are mad,' he suddenly announced at the Stravinskys' dinner table.

Loneliness in New York led him to accept more engagements to give poetry readings than were good for his now uncertain health. He was in average condition for a man in his sixties who drank far too much, was overweight and did no physical exercise, but average condition should not lug itself about the United States by plane on a tightly crowded schedule. Still, 'They loved me,' he told Stephen Spender delightedly when he dined with his old friend in New York in February, and indeed he loved their loving him. Despite his talk about the writer's essential privacy, he increasingly enjoyed displaying himself to audiences, and not only in person but in print. He rarely refused an interview to a journalist, whether in New York, Kirchstetten or London, and often commended to the attention of friends the resultant articles in *Life, Esquire* and other magazines. At the 1970 *Poetry International* in London, he shared a platform with Tennessee Williams, Pier Paolo Pasolini, Allen Tate and others, and flew up to Scotland for an additional performance in Edinburgh. He returned to England from Austria again in October to give a poetry reading in Leeds, in his native Yorkshire.

December in New York found Auden holding forth to a group of medical students and physicians at the Downstate Medical Center in Brooklyn, during a two-day visit he made to the Center as part of a visiting scholar programme which was designed to give those engaged in the necessarily narrow disciplines of science a chance to range more freely in fields of thought. Auden discussed with the physicians a wide range of topics including the necessity of mathematics, the nature of the Italian male, the character of national cultures, poetry, education, political history, and Catholic liturgy. 'I like to think,' he told them, 'that if I hadn't become a poet I might have become an Anglican bishop. Politically liberal, I hope; theologically and liturgically conservative, I know.'

Early in December he dined *chez* Stravinsky, who now lived all the year round in New York, and whose health was rapidly failing, 'I've just done Igor's obituary for *The Observer*,' Auden announced cheerfully over dinner, to the Stravinskys and Robert Craft. 'I talk about him as the great exemplary artist of the twentieth century, and not just in music.' He assured his host that he loved him, while he merely admired Wagner, 'who was indisputably a genius, but apart from that an absolute shit'. He also confessed that he had given up sleeping pills, as the kind he was used to was too difficult to procure in Austria. 'Instead, I keep a glass of vodka by my bed, which tastes better.' He boasted of his current income from the sales of his poetry, and said wittily that 'Henze wears a Mao tunic now, but with lots of money in the pockets.' At nine o'clock, he muttered his ritual 'It's way past my bedtime' and fled from the dinner table and the apartment. He was not to know that he would never speak to Stravinsky again.

In the previous twelve months or so, three people with whom Auden had been associated in the thirties had died: Gerald Hamilton, on whom Isherwood had largely based his Mr Norris; E. M. Forster, the novelist whom both Auden and Isherwood loved and admired; and Erika Mann, to whom Auden was still married when she died. Auden was now at that age when one's friends begin, disconcertingly, to die off. In February 1971, he happened to be in St Louis, Missouri, on his birthday, during the course of a poetry reading tour. Expecting to have to spend his birthday, his sixty-fourth, alone, he was delighted to find that a New York friend who was in St Louis on business had arranged a party *à deux* in their rather seedy hotel, with plenty of champagne and English crossword puzzles. The next morning, a Sunday, he attended the service at the St Louis Episcopal Church and bellowed out the hymns with a lusty enthusiasm.

Auden and Chester had just got together again in the spring at Kirchstetten when they heard the news that Stravinsky had died in New York on 6 April.[1] Auden can hardly have been surprised, for he had visited the barely conscious composer the previous week and embraced him (saying to Robert Craft, 'You never know when it's the last time'), but he was saddened and unsettled by the composer's death which, some months later, he would keep referring to in conversation with friends and colleagues in London. He came to London for the annual *Poetry International* in July, and enjoyed meeting poets from Eastern Europe, and two Israeli poets whose work he admired, T. Carmi and Yehuda Amichai. But when one of the directors of the festival suggested that he join some of the other poets in a poetry reading in Cardiff the following week, his response was simply, 'Now don't be silly, dear.' He later explained that he might have had to meet Welsh bards in Cardiff, and that one had to draw the line *somewhere*.

His London appearances were, as usual, favourably received. 'Auden comes along,' noted *The Guardian*,[2] 'gets lots of love and applause from the audience, and reads familiar poems.' A *Financial Times*[3] critic wrote: 'His control of the audience is phenomenal: no rounds of applause within his allotted fifteen minutes; no encores, no poems written before 1960. He reads

[1] The obituary tribute that Auden had written several months earlier duly appeared in the *Observer* on 11 April.
[2] 12 July 1971.
[3] 12 July 1971.

his intricately constructed later works with a disciplined but pedantic respect for their metre. A bad fit of coughing on one night and a failure of the microphones on the next hardly ruffled him. He read, or rather recited for he rarely needed to consult his text, two characteristically speculative elegies for doctor friends, and on the following evening the marvellous sequence, "Talking to Dogs", "Talking to Mice" and "Talking to myself".'

As always, he enjoyed talking to the press, though his limited repertoire of stories was now suffering from over-exposure, and the same references to the thirties, to the course of history being unchanged by Dante, Goethe or Shakespeare, the same paraphrased quotation from Dr Johnson kept appearing in published interviews. In private conversation, too, he would often repeat himself, sometimes within minutes. When the Americans landed a man on the moon, Auden was scathing on the subject: 'The moon is a desert. I have seen deserts.' It was a good remark the first time round, but two years later, like a comedian playing the same circuit once too often with stale material, he would produce it again, and look around for the applause. He had already said the same thing most effectively in his 1969 poem, 'Moon Landing':

> . . . Worth *going* to see? I can well believe it.
> Worth *seeing*? Mneh! I once rode through a desert
>   and was not charmed: give me a watered
>   lively garden, remote from blatherers
>
> about the New, the von Brauns and their ilk, where
> on August mornings I can count the morning
>   glories, where to die has a meaning,
>   and no engine can shift my perspective.

Auden was now really desperate to find somewhere other than New York to spend his Chesterless winters. He did not mind the numerous phone calls from strangers who merely wanted to talk to the famous poet whose work they admired: one such phone call was from Bette Davis, who called from Hollywood at ten in the evening to tell Auden how much she was enjoying something of his that she was reading, apparently unaware that it was 1.00 a.m. in New York, and way past Auden's bedtime. He was more disturbed when, just before he left New York for Kirchstetten in the early spring of 1971, the phone rang and a voice said: 'We are going to castrate you and then kill you', but at least he had the presence of mind to reply, coolly, 'I think you have the wrong number.'

In October, on his way back to America from Austria, Auden stopped over in London to stay for a few days with the Spenders and to inaugurate a series of discussion programmes at the Institute of Contemporary Arts.

Announcing the ICA event, *The Times*[1] said that 'Charles Osborne, an old friend of Auden and newly appointed Literature Director of the Arts Council, is taking the chair, ready he says, to act as arbiter, referee or bystander as occasion demands.' In fact he was required to be little more than bystander. Auden and Spender did a kind of intellectual Laurel and Hardy act. Auden, playing Hardy to Spender's Laurel, dominated the proceedings. Poets could change and affect the world, insisted Spender, citing William Blake. 'What did he change?' cried Auden, to which his old friend replied mildly that one could hardly give statistical answers, but, for instance, there was Shelley. 'That detestable poet,' interjected Auden. But surely, suggested Spender, the Labour party had acquired a number of ideas from him? 'Then that's what's wrong with the Labour party,' Auden replied. The discussion was in full flight when, to the astonished amusement of the audience, at 9.30 p.m. Auden consulted his watch, announced that it was way past his bedtime, and walked off the stage, leaving Messrs Spender and Osborne to smile sheepishly at the audience and follow him.

During this autumn visit, Auden met again several people whom he had not encountered for many years. One of these was an ex-lover, Richard Crossman, now a leading member of the Labour party, and editor of the *New Statesman*. The meeting was not a success, for Crossman professed to be nauseated by Auden's return to the religion of his childhood and also expressed disappointment that his ex-lover was no longer producing the kind of verse which Crossman most enjoyed. 'What I want from Auden,' he exclaimed later to a member of the *New Statesman* staff, 'is good homosexual love poetry, like "Lay your sleeping Head". Show me any good homosexual love poem from the later poetry. That's what I want!'

A luncheon party given, at Auden's instigation, for Miss Winnie and Miss Rosa from his old prep school, St Edmunds, was much more successful. This was held at Odin's Restaurant, in Devonshire Street, just off Marylebone High Street, and was attended not only by the two daughters of Auden's old headmaster, now elderly ladies, but also by several of Auden's contemporaries from the school's Literary Society, the fiftieth anniversary of whose founding the luncheon was also intended to honour. Auden was in fine convivial form on this occasion, and felt close to his schooldays of half a century earlier.

In November his new book, *Academic Graffiti*, appeared, a disappointing collection of clerihews: disappointing not because clerihews are trivia, but because too many of these are not very good trivia:

> My first name, *Wystan*,
> Rhymes with *Tristan*,

[1] 8 October 1971.

> But – O dear! – I do hope
> I'm not quite such a dope.

In New York, he and Chester, who was paying a comparatively rare winter visit to the United States, dined in January with Vera Stravinsky and Robert Craft, when the talk was of older and happier times. This was Auden's last winter in New York, for he had now concluded an arrangement with his old Oxford College, whereby he would spend his future winters in Oxford. He had accepted the offer of a small cottage in the grounds of Christ Church, for which he would pay a moderate rent. On his sixty-fifth birthday, 21 February 1972, a combined birthday and farewell party was given for him in New York, at the Coffee House on West Forty-Fifth Street. When a toast was proposed, and the speaker began with the words, 'I don't know what genius is –' the querulous voice of the guest of honour interrupted with, 'Well, who does?' He was returning to England, Auden told his friends, not because he was in any way disillusioned with the United States of America, but because he had become nervous of muggers in New York (though he had never been mugged), and because he had reached the age at which he felt he needed not to be quite so alone as he was for six months of each year in New York. He hoped to act as a kind of informal writer-in-residence at Christ Church, where he would from now on spend his winters, but he would continue to live in Austria from April to October with Chester Kallman. 'In Oxford,' he said, 'I shall be part of the college community. I should be missed if I failed to turn up for meals, especially as they are provided free. Pity that doesn't apply to the drinks also . . . Anyway, why shouldn't I spend my second childhood in the country where I spent a happy first childhood?'[1] But he did not plan to change his citizenship again: he would remain an American. He sublet his New York apartment to Michael Newman, a young poet and journalist.

On 15 April, two of Auden's New York friends drove him to the airport. One of them, Dr Oliver Sacks, wrote an account of the scene of farewell:

> Wystan and Orlan and I arrived early then, and whiled away the hours in a meandering conversation (it was only later, when he left, that I realized that all the amblings and meanderings returned to one point: that the focus of the conversation was farewell – to us, to America, to those thirty-three years – an entire half of his life – which he had spent in the USA; a trans-Atlantic Goethe, he would half-seriously, half-jokingly say). Just before the call for the plane, a complete stranger ceme up to us, a quintessential (almost allegorical) American, intensely shy, sincere and effusive; he stuttered 'Gee! You look like, you are Mr. Auden . . . We

[1] Interview in *The Daily Telegraph*, 8 February 1972.

298

have been honoured to have you in our country, Sir. You'll always be welcome back here as an honoured guest – and a friend. Goodbye, Mr. Auden, God bless you for everything!' – he stuck out his hand, and Wystan shook it with great cordiality. He was much moved – there were tears in his eyes. I turned to Wystan and asked him whether such encounters were common to him: 'Common,' he said, 'but never common. There is genuine love in these common encounters . . .'[1]

In May, Auden's old friend Cecil Day Lewis died. Since the death of John Masefield in 1967, Day Lewis had been Great Britain's Poet Laureate, and the question which began to be asked was: who would the Queen appoint to succeed Day Lewis? Various names were mentioned in the English press, among them those of Stephen Spender, Philip Larkin and, surprisingly, in view of the fact that he had been an American citizen for a quarter of a century, W. H. Auden. Stephen Spender was quoted in *The Guardian*[2] as saying that Auden 'would always have liked to be Poet Laureate . . . You see, he's a very good occasional poet. What we really want from a Poet Laureate is high camp, which is high artificiality but great fun. Auden has that fun.' But, from Kirchstetten, Auden wrote angrily to scotch rumours that he might be interested in becoming Poet Laureate: in a letter published in *The Times* on 31 May he said that he was amazed and distressed to read

> that my New York agent is reputed to have conjectured that I would not mind becoming a British citizen again if, thereby, I could become Poet Laureate. Even if I coveted the post, which I don't, to do such a thing for such a motive I should regard as contemptible.

On 4 June he published in *The Sunday Times* a farewell salute to Day Lewis which, after a more formal assessment of Day Lewis's poetic achievement, ends with these more personal paragraphs:

> I don't remember exactly how I first met Cecil, but it was certainly very soon after I came up to Oxford in 1925. At that time he was sharing digs with Rex Warner, whom, incidentally, I have never quite forgiven for losing his excellent translations of Maximian's Elegies. Cecil introduced me to the later Yeats, and I introduced him to Hardy, Frost and Edward Thomas. I can't recall who first discovered Emily Dickinson or Gerard Manley Hopkins. Much as we admired him as a man, an editor, a critic and a poet, neither of us was poetically influenced by Eliot, but, then, who has been? I am always surprised when students in the States want courses in Contemporary Literature. That we regarded as our business

[1] Oliver Sacks, in *W. H. Auden: A Tribute*.
[2] 26 May 1972.

and would never have dreamed of asking our tutors to tell us about it.

Another interest we had in common was music. Cecil possessed a good tenor voice and I used to accompany him in Elizabethan songs. In company, then and later, he could be most amusing and witty but, so far as I know, he never wrote a comic poem. Humour, including black humour, he reserved for his fiction.

When I went down in 1928, I went to Berlin and, during the next twelve years, travelled extensively. Cecil was much more insular and did not cross the channel, I believe, until after the war. Neither of us had private means and could not yet hope to earn our living by our pens, so we both became schoolmasters. That I did so was largely his doing. Cecil had been teaching at a prep school in Scotland, but in 1930 moved to a school in Cheltenham. Thanks to his recommendation, I succeeded him. When, twenty-six years later, I succeeded him as Professor of Poetry, I'm sure he had a hand in it.

I happen to be both a lover of poetry and a Whodunit addict, but it must have been a source of enormous satisfaction to Cecil to know that, as Nicholas Blake, he could give pleasure to thousands who would never dream of reading Day Lewis. In his early days, his detective Nigel Strangeways exhibited certain traits of behaviour which, I am proud to believe, were taken from me.

In later days we did not see as much of each other as I should have liked. The Atlantic is a wide ocean. It was sheer bad luck that, the only time when Cecil was in the States, to deliver the Charles Eliot Norton lectures, should have been the one winter when I was not in New York, but in Berlin. When we did meet, however, it was just as if we had seen each other yesterday.

Thank you, Cecil. It was a great privilege to have been permitted to know you.

Having succeeded Day Lewis twice, Auden was not to do so a third time. The Prime Minister's office, after due consultation with the appropriate bodies, among them the Arts Council, advised the Queen on her choice. It was announced that another of Day Lewis's and Auden's Oxford contemporaries, John Betjeman, was to be the new Poet Laureate. Meanwhile, in more than one interview, Auden had made it clear that he regarded suggestions that he was interested in the post as 'a load of bosh'. He conceded that 'one of the reasons why people have said I might be in the running is because they think I have a talent for occasional verse. In fact I do not find it very difficult. Last October I wrote the words for the official Hymn for the United Nations which was composed by Pablo Casals. I managed to sit down and write it straight off.' Indeed, the Hymn sounded as though both

Auden and Casals had done precisely that. On 22 June, the *Evening Standard* told its readers that 'Mr Auden is in London to take part in *Poetry International* directed by Charles Osborne. In October he will return to take up permanent residence in a cottage in the grounds of Christ Church, Oxford, his old college. He will pay £3 a week rent, will have no official title, but will be there to give advice and inspiration.' He was quoted as saying that he would miss New York, that he looked forward to spending his winters in Oxford, but that 'London is becoming very ugly. The new architecture is dreadful. But I find the suggestive advertizing on the Underground the most shocking development.'

Poetry International that year occupied the third week in June: Auden participated in it fully and with evident enjoyment. He attended a programme of readings from his *Commonplace Book* which had been published two years earlier, made a number of audible comments, not all of them complimentary, during the performance, and afterwards congratulated the participants, Diana Rigg, Dudley Moore, Paul Hardwick and Malcolm Muggeridge. He made private and unprintable comments on the poetry and person of R. D. Laing, the eccentric and, at that time, fashionable psychologist who had been invited to read his poems, and he arranged not to have to appear on the same programme as Robert Lowell whom he refused ever to meet again, since he considered Lowell had behaved badly in leaving his wife, Elizabeth Hardwick. He also drew the attention of the present author to the fact that Chester Kallman had, the previous year, published his third volume of poems, and that he, Auden, had reviewed it favourably in *Harper's Magazine*.[1] 'If you like the poems, Charles, do please invite Chester to next year's festival,' he said. 'If you don't like them, I'd deem it a very great personal favour if you would invite him in any case.' In September, back in New York very briefly, Auden stayed for two weeks with his tenant Michael Newman in his old apartment and allowed Newman to interview him for the *Paris Review*, of which the young journalist was an associate editor. Being interviewed by a friend, he was at his most relaxed, and offered, as well as opinions on poetry and poets, an unusual amount of small talk about himself and his way of life:

. . . in the old days people knew what the words meant, whatever the range of their vocabulary. Now people hear and repeat a radio and TV vocabulary thirty per cent larger than they know the meaning of. The most outrageous use of words I've ever experienced was once when I was a guest on the David Susskind TV program. During a break he had to do a

[1] Auden's review, in the March 1972 issue of *Harper's Magazine*, begins, disarmingly: 'I can see no reason why the fact that Mr Kallman and I have been close friends for over thirty years should debar me from reviewing him. In my experience, one's feelings about a writer as a person and one's aesthetic judgment of his work affect each other very little, if at all.'

plug for some sort of investment firm, and he announced that these people were 'integrity-ridden'! I could not believe my ears! . . . I never write when I'm drunk. Why should one need aids? The Muse is a high-spirited girl who doesn't like to be brutally or coarsely wooed. And she doesn't like slavish devotion – then she lies . . . I was brought up believing that you should not buy anything you cannot pay cash for. The idea of debt appals me, I suppose our whole economy would collapse if everyone had been brought up like me . . . I'm very fond of my food. I'm lucky when I'm in Austria because my friend Mr. Kallman is an expert chef, so I'm rather spoiled in the summer . . . Sometimes when one is cooking for oneself, one gets a craze for something. Once I had a craze for turnips. But with solitary eating one doesn't like to spend much time and simply gobbles it up fast . . . I couldn't imagine going mad. It's simply something my imagination cannot take. One can be dotty – but that's different! . . . One of the great things about opera singing is that you cannot pretend it's naturalistic . . . I don't like the phone very much and never stay on long if I can help it. You get some people who simply will not get off the line! I remember the story of the man who answered the phone and was kept prisoner for what seemed an age. The lady talked and talked. Finally, in desperation, he told her, 'Really, I must go. I hear the phone ringing!' . . . I think the first prerequisite to civilization is an ability to make polite conversation . . . personally, I don't see how any civilized person can watch TV, far less own a set. I prefer detective stories . . . I'm not very interested in other planets. I like them where they are, in the sky . . . Charlie Chaplin and the Marx Brothers were quite funny . . . I'm not very good on Joyce. Obviously, he's a very great genius – but his work is simply too long. Joyce said himself that he wanted people to spend their life on his work. For me, life is too short, and too precious . . . I suppose my favourite modern novelists are Ronald Firbank and P. G. Wodehouse – because both deal with Eden . . . my stock went up last year, I know. There was a feature on me in the *Daily News* – which everyone here seems to read. After that they figured I must be somebody. It was very nice to get all that attention . . . I've told people I'm a medieval historian when asked what I do. It freezes conversation . . .[1]

When Michael Newman asked Auden which living writer he thought had 'served as the prime protector of the integrity of our English tongue', his unhesitating reply was 'Why me, of course!'

In September, a volume of his recent poems, *Epistle to a Godson*, was published, poems whose tone and manner echo those of the elderly Goethe. The following month, Auden was in London, staying with his brother John

---

[1] Extracts from interview in *Paris Review*.

in Thurloe Square while he waited for his Oxford cottage to be got ready. He seemed to have got heavier and, if possible, scruffier, since his summer visit, and was drinking, if not more heavily, then at least with a more determined regularity. 'I have a fairly regular schedule,' he admitted. 'Before lunch I have a vermouth, with lunch I have a beer. At ten to six I start on vodka martinis, at dinner I have wine. After dinner I have more wine.'[1] And, he forgot to add, a large vodka to induce sleep. 'I drink because I love it. I never work after dinner, I'm glad to say. I have been drunk, but I can stand it pretty well. The only effect alcohol has on me is to make me a little inclined to hold forth.'

Questioned by a journalist about his health, he said that his heart was perfectly sound but that what he feared was a lingering and debilitating illness. 'When life is becoming a burden you should let go. The nicest way, I think, would be a heart attack, it's cheap and it's quick.' He talked a good deal now about illness and death, punctuating his phrases with sudden chasms of silence, or with 'ums' and 'ahs' which led nowhere. His world seemed even more enclosed than before, and it was not always easy even for his closest of friends to enter. Once, he had been given to saying he intended to live until he was eighty-four (probably in order to outlive Goethe who died at eighty-three), but in this first and, as it was to prove, only winter of his discontented return to England, he seemed not to expect so much either of his body or of his spirit. His mood was more akin to that of the poem, 'Talking to Myself', which he had written the previous year, and which ends:

> Time, we both know, will decay You, and already
> I'm scared of our divorce: I've seen some horrid ones.
> Remember: when *Le Bon Dieu* says to You *Leave him!*,
> please, please, for His sake and mine, pay no attention
> to my piteous *Dont*'s, but bugger off quickly.

The return to Oxford was not a success. He was lonely in his sixteenth-century cottage, and though at four in the afternoon he dutifully shuffled along in his carpet slippers to St Aldate's coffee house (the Cadena, scene of his earlier triumphs, was no more) as often as not no students came to sit with him. The Christ Church after-dinner atmosphere had changed, too, since the fifties. Dinner was now a less leisurely affair than it had been, and frequently there would be no one to sit with him as he determinedly lingered over his port. In any case, by that stage in the evening Auden was no longer at his most sober. The cottage itself, for which, incidentally, he paid something closer to an economic rent than the '£3 a week' mentioned in the press, was a former brewhouse in the garden of one of the Canon-Professors, and

[1] *Daily Mail*, 14 October 1972.

303

it offered him both privacy and accessibility to society. But he was no longer flexible enough to adjust to a way of life which was not only remote from what he was used to in New York, but also unaccountably different from what he had remembered it as being or from what he had anticipated it would be. An Oxford friend[1] described the failure of Auden's attempt to establish his *Stammtisch* at the St Aldate's Church Bookshop and Coffee House:

> It may be that, by comparison with about fifteen years earlier, there were fewer young men in Oxford of sufficient talent and taste to interest him and be interested in him. A number of those who visited the café came for the wrong sort of reasons. He seems chiefly to have been beset by post-graduates from overseas, some perhaps seeking thesis material, others having read little or nothing of his work but anxious to view him as tourists might view a curious monolith. Too often, looking rather formidable, he would be sitting by himself, watched from other tables. Some sensitive undergraduates felt inhibited from approaching him by the mere fact that it had become the craze and fashion to do so. Then there were the representatives of experimental trends in writing with which Wystan was entirely out of sympathy, and his condemnations of which tended to be dogmatic rather than tactful.

There were occasions when he seemed happy and contented, usually at lunch with one or two old friends. But his evenings more often than not were spent alone, for the inflexibility of his time-table militated against his being invited to dinner parties. Everyone knew that at nine, whether fed or not, he would tap his watch, mutter that it was way past his bed-time, and totter off home. He did meet a few young poets whom he felt were worth encouraging: there is a small group of them, still young, who remember Auden's last winter in Oxford with affection and gratitude. Auden himself enormously enjoyed a production by the Christ Church and St John's Dramatic Society of *The Dog Beneath the Skin*, and was delighted when the director interpolated a scene in which 'a corpulent poet with a heavily lined face shambled on in bedroom slippers, sat down and in a comically elaborate manner lit a cigarette'. But, in general, he tactlessly and ungratefully complained about most aspects of Oxford life. The traffic was worse than in New York. The streets were becoming as dangerous as those of New York. The intellectual atmosphere was, in comparison with that of New York, intolerably provincial. Clearly he was homesick for New York in winter! He became embarrassingly involved in prosecuting a twenty-seven-year-old labourer who, he claimed, had stolen his wallet containing £50. For some reason, he had also given the young man a cheque for £50. The labourer was found not

[1] David Luke in *W. H. Auden: A Tribute*.

guilty at Oxford Crown Court, and the real facts of the matter are probably best left in obscurity.[1] Early in January, however, he wrote to Michael Newman in New York, '. . . am settled into my cottage . . . but Oxford city is sheer hell. Compared with N.Y., it's five times as crowded and the noise of the traffic is six times louder. Ironically enough, I had to leave New York and come to Oxford in order to get robbed . . .'

After a poetry reading at a church in Bloomsbury, Tom Driberg took Auden, Stephen and Natasha Spender and their son Matthew, to supper upstairs at the Gay Hussar, an excellent Hungarian restaurant in Soho. To diversify the company, Driberg had also invited Marianne Faithfull and Mick Jagger's younger brother, Christopher. Auden distinguished himself by saying to Marianne Faithfull, 'When you're smuggling drugs, do you pack them up your ass?'

On 7 February, the company of West Berlin's Deutsche Oper gave the première of Nabokov's opera, *Love's Labour's Lost*, at the Théâtre de la Monnaie in Brussels. Auden and Kallman were present, to hear their libretto sung in its original English. (The same company gave two performances of the opera in West Berlin in September, and three further performances during their 1973–74 season, since when it has neither been revived nor performed elsewhere.) The opera was received respectfully rather than enthusiastically, and Auden later complained that music and text had been swamped by a misguided production. In the spring, Auden and Kallman saw a performance of a much more successful Shakespeare opera, Benjamin Britten's *A Midsummer Night's Dream*, which Auden denounced in a letter to Spender as 'dreadful – pure Kensington.'

When he came to London for his annual appearance in *Poetry International* in June, Auden seemed in better form than he had been the previous year, though he confided to friends that 'a defective ticker' had been diagnosed. He was accompanied this time by Chester Kallman, who had also been invited to participate in the poetry festival. Auden made three appearances during the festival week: the first was in a symposium on 'The Poet as Librettist', in which he joined a panel of composers and librettists which included Elisabeth Lutyens, Nicholas Maw, Myfanwy Piper, Ronald Duncan and Chester Kallman, under the chairmanship of the present author, who was standing in at short notice for an indisposed J. W. Lambert; the second was a poetry reading in company with five other poets; his third and last appearance was at the Young Vic, in a special *Poetry International* performance for television, in which his co-stars included Sir John Betjeman, Mr Allen Ginsberg, Mrs (now Dame) Edna Everage, and Sir John Gielgud.

[1] Auden's own account of it to the present author some months later was so disjointed and, frankly implausible that he has mercifully failed to retain the details in his memory.

At the beginning of July, Auden and Kallman returned to Kirchstetten for the summer. Auden wrote a few slight, pleasant, conversational poems which were collected in his posthumous final volume, *Thank You, Fog*, and he and Kallman worked on a verse text, 'The Entertainment of the Senses', which had been commissioned for an antimasque with music by John Gardner. Late in September they mailed to the Director of the Redcliffe Concerts of British Music a first draft of their text, which ends with the lines:

> The moral is, as they have said:
> Be with-it, with-it, with-it till you're dead.

The day after the text for the antimasque was received in London, W. H. Auden died, suddenly and unexpectedly, in Vienna. He had, after all, told his spirit when the time came, to 'bugger off quickly', and so it did. He and Chester had locked up their Kirchstetten house for the winter, and were spending a few days in Vienna before going their separate ways until the spring, Auden to Oxford, Kallman to Athens. They had planned one or two visits to the Vienna State Opera, and Auden had written on 27 September to his brother John in London announcing his intention of flying to London on 2 October, and asking to be met at Heathrow and put up for the night. Auden and Chester had separate rooms at the hotel they regularly used for overnight stays in Vienna, the Altenburgerhof, an inexpensive establishment in the Walfischgasse, which had the advantage of being less than a five-minute walk from the Opera House.[1] On the evening of Friday 28 September, Auden gave a poetry reading at the Palais Palffy, to members of the Austrian Society of Literature. Chester and a Greek friend did not accompany him, preferring instead to go to the Staatsoper where another Greek friend, the baritone Kostas Paskalis, was singing the title-role in Verdi's *Rigoletto*.[2] Auden seemed tired and not in good spirits but, after asking Chester to call him at nine the next morning, went off to the Palais Palffy where, by all accounts, he gave a successful performance. When Chester knocked at Auden's door at nine on Saturday morning, he could get no answer. The door was locked, which one might think not unusual in a hotel, but it disturbed Chester who knew that Auden never bothered to lock his door at the Altenburgerhof. He called the hotel management, and had the door broken open. Entering the room, he could see at once that his friend was dead. 'He was lying on the wrong side. He never lay on his left side. He thought it was bad for his heart. He was cold when I touched him.' An inquest held in Vienna on 1 October found that Auden had died of heart

---

[1] Now turned into offices, it was a hotel which Auden had often attempted to recommend to the present author: 'I dont know why you stay at these expensive places. Of course, if you *must* have a bathroom . . .'

[2] This account is based on the author's conversations with Kallman some months later.

failure, early on the Saturday morning. 'No,' said Chester. 'He died on the Friday night. Wystan would never have died after midnight.'

'Chester, why did you mention just now that the door was locked? Do you suspect that Wystan may have hastened his own death?'

Chester Kallman was silent for several seconds, and then answered: 'No. I mentioned it to you because it was odd, and I still can't explain it. But, no, I don't think that. He might have had difficulty getting to sleep, perhaps some drunk was raging around in the corridor. The door was locked, that's all. Wystan would have been perfectly capable of easing his exit, but he would have found a way of letting me know. He was tired. He was so tired.'

The last poem Auden wrote was one of his 'Shorts',

> He still loves life
> But O O O O how he wishes
> The Good Lord would take him.

On Sunday 30 September, the world learned of Auden's death from the newspapers. In London, the Dean and Chapter of Westminster Abbey offered his family a place for the poet's ashes in the precincts of the South Transept of the Abbey, Poet's Corner. But Auden had expressed a wish to be buried in the village churchyard in Kirchstetten: it was, of course, a Catholic church, but he had been a member of its congregation for years. And so, in the presence of his brother John, a few friends, a number of villagers, and representatives of the governments of those three countries which meant most to him, England, America and Austria, the body of W. H. Auden was laid to rest at Kirchstetten on Thursday 4 October 1973.

I was present in Kirchstetten that day. A year later, requested by a Harvard University magazine to contribute something to its Auden memorial issue,[1] I wrote the following account of the day of the funeral:

I first met Auden sometime in the 'fifties, and I remember that our conversation on that occasion, at the restaurant Chez Victor in London, was predominantly not literary but musical. We agreed enthusiastically that Leontyne Price, who had just emerged onto the international opera scene, was the best young soprano around. At subsequent meetings, we found it less easy to agree on who were the best young poets, for he would produce American names I had never heard of, while dismissing the new young English poets *en bloc*. I suspect this was not a game he took too seriously. Many of our meetings took place in and around Vienna in the summer, and I would usually visit him and Chester Kallman at their

---

[1] *The Harvard Advocate* (Volume CVIII: Numbers Two and Three).

house in the village of Kirchstetten, about thirty miles from Vienna on the other side of the *Wienerwald*. In 1967, when we began in London our series of poetry festivals, *Poetry International*, Wystan Auden was one of our star performers. From then on, he never missed a festival, taking part in each of them up to and including *Poetry International 73*. In that final summer in London, he seemed, if anything, to be in sprightlier health than he had been for some time. At lunch in my apartment, before an afternoon we were to spend filming for TV, he gossiped easily and indiscreetly about his adolescence and youth. Weeks later, I stood at his graveside in Kirchstetten, flinging my spadeful of earth onto his coffin.

I am not a great attender of funerals, in fact I have managed to avoid those of members of my own family who have died; Wystan's was my first. I flew to Vienna that autumn evening, not only as a friend but also as a representative of two British cultural organizations. Three friends and colleagues of mine, I discovered, were also flying from London that evening to attend the funeral the following day, so we arranged to meet in Vienna and travel out to Kirchstetten together. They were Edward Mendelson, Wystan's literary executor, Charles Monteith, his English publisher, and Stephen Spender. That evening in Vienna, I went alone to the Volksoper to see an opera, *Der Evangelimann* by an Austrian composer, Kienzl. I'd never before had an opportunity to see it, and I was sure Wystan would have approved. At nine o'clock the following morning, Ed, Charles, Stephen and I piled into a taxi and asked the driver to take us to Kirchstetten. A slight confusion arose immediately, for there are two Kirchstettens within striking distance of Vienna and the driver needed some persuading that the one we wanted was where we said it was. Eventually, however, we set off in the right direction. It was a crisp, clear sunny morning in early October.

We were on the outskirts of Vienna when Stephen, who as the tallest was allowed to sit in front with the driver while the rest of us squeezed into the back, suddenly remembered that we ought to take wreaths with us. He himself had a long list of friends in London who had commissioned him to lay wreaths on the grave. He produced his list, which looked alarmingly like Leporello's catalogue. We consulted the driver, whose advice was that we should try the flower market in the Linke Wienzeile, near the Theater an der Wien. Back we drove, and conscious now that time was pressing, we fanned out when we arrived at the Flower Market, and simultaneously assaulted four separate flower stalls to give our orders for instant wreaths, or at least bundles of appropriate flowers tastefully packaged. As Stephen and I could make our arrangements in German, while Charles and Ed could not, this took longer to finalize than it might otherwise have done. But in due course we set off again, a dozen or so cellophaned bouquets of flowers now stowed away in the boot of the taxi. The driver wondered audibly whether we would get to Kirchstetten by eleven, the time of the funeral. I began to think of *Bye, Bye Braverman*.

The drive, skirting the Vienna woods, was a pleasant one. We talked, each contributing affectionate anecdotes about Wystan, until, as we neared the village of Kirchstetten, our mood was lightly wistful rather than mournfully solemn. In the village, it was obvious that some momentous event was imminent, for at every corner we saw officials, policemen perhaps, *en pompe funèbre*, in important-looking uniforms with lots of braid, and plumed helmets. We had a slight altercation in the taxi as we attempted to direct our driver to the Auden house. I had been there frequently, and I'm not sure that any of the others had been, so I was presumed to know the way. But I had usually been met by Wystan at the station, and driven in his beaten-up Volkswagen to the house, a drive so fraught with danger, thanks to Wystan's erratic steering, that I had never really noticed what direction we were taking. I was certain only of one thing: that, although there was now a street in the village named after Wystan, the house was not itself in Audenstrasse. As I was adamant on this point, some minutes were added to our travelling time, for the house *is*, in fact, in Audenstrasse.

The lane outside the house and the small garden were full of newspaper reporters and TV men with cameras. We made our way through them, while our now drooping flowers were unloaded from the taxi, and entered the house to find Chester Kallman and six or seven other people sitting in the living-cum-dining room, partaking of the Austrian version of funeral bak'd meats, which consisted of a huge *Wurstplatte* and flagons of *heurige* white wine. I knew some, but not all of the mourners. Three or four of them, including Sonia Orwell, had come from London, and most of the others were Austrian. There was a good-looking young Viennese couple whose presence in this middle-aged assembly was never clearly explained.[1] Chester, understandably in a state of distress, was not making much sense; we newcomers sat with the others and partook of the refreshments offered, making polite subdued bi-lingual conversation with our neighbours. I could hear Charles Monteith speaking Greek to the man he was sitting next to. Out of embarrassment or nervousness, I found myself drinking two or three glasses of the sharp new wine rather too quickly. I decided to fill my glass with water, and went to the kitchen to do so, where I was disconcerted to find the coffin containing Wystan on the kitchen table. I murmured my farewell to him, and returned to the other room. A few moments later, I glimpsed through the window the coffin being taken across the garden to a hearse waiting outside the front

[1] They were in fact, Hugerl and his wife.

gate. Someone from the staff of the *Bestattungsunternehmer* came in to inform Chester that the funeral procession was now ready to move off, but Chester said 'There's something I have to do first, but I want only Wystan's friends here. Please ask the newspapermen to leave the grounds.' The newsmen removed themselves from the garden, and Chester addressed those of us who were still sitting around the dining-table. 'Wystan wanted a certain piece of music by Wagner, Siegfried's Funeral March from *Götterdämmerung*, to be played at his funeral', he said, 'so I'd like you all to stand while we play it'.

For a moment I thought he might have had the Vienna Philharmonic Orchestra hidden in the woods outside, but it soon became apparent that we were to listen to a gramophone record, for Chester now began feverishly to search for it among the hundreds of records stacked along one wall of the room. I had been present at a luncheon party in that same room a year or two earlier at which Wystan had indeed made his request for Siegfried's Funeral March, but I was by no means convinced that he was serious about it. We had been telling one another what music we wanted played at our funerals – I seem to remember I had opted for the 'Aufersteh'n' movement from Mahler's Second Symphony – and Wystan had said 'Nothing less than a hero's funeral music will do for me.' But there it was, Siegfried's Funeral March was about to be played, and I was suddenly aware that Chester was asking my advice as to which recording he ought to put on the gramophone. 'There's Knappertsbusch and the Vienna Philarmonic,' he said, 'That's quite good, isn't it?'

'Yes, by all means.'

'Or do you think the Karajan is better?'

'I'd play the Knappertsbusch, Chester.'

'There's always this Solti, but that's part of a complete recording, so I'd have to find the right place to begin.'

'Play the Knappertsbusch, Chester.'

After a false start, the needle found the right groove, and we stood as Wagner's portentous drum beats came crashing out at us. But I had barely risen to my feet before I felt myself knocked in the solar plexus by the sheer emotive force of Wagner's genius. 'You bastard,' I apostrophized the great composer under my breath as I felt the tears suddenly well up into my eyes. Then I heard the sound of loud sobbing, and looked up. It was the young Viennese girl. By this time, I could scarcely see through my tears, but before the watery curtain quite shut out my vision, I glanced across at Stephen down whose cheeks the tears were also rolling. 'Bloody Wagner,' I murmured, while the great hero's funeral march proceeded inexorably onward. As soon as it had finished, we filed outside to take up our positions behind the hearse and walk in procession to the village

310

church. No wonder the newspapers next day spoke of our faces ravaged with grief.

In front of the hearse stood the village band. When they struck up, it was with a distinctly sprightly Austrian dance tune, to which we walked at a pace decently funereal but far too slow for the music. (I subsequently learned that Wystan had specifically asked – but how, where, whom, when? – for joyful music to be played at his funeral. So much for Siegfried.) Photographers and cameramen lined the route, and when we reached the village square the coffin was taken out and carried up the hill to the church. At this point, a cry of grief burst forth from Chester who was being half-supported by Stephen and someone else. Inside the church, the choir sang a pretty hymn that sounded like minor Schubert. Wystan was an Anglican, and so the Anglican priest had come from Vienna to bury him. But he was also a regular church-goer, and, since the only church in an Austrian village is a Catholic one, he had become a member of the congregation there, and a friend of the local priest. So he was buried by two priests in a joint Anglo-Catholic service, partly in English, partly in German. When we followed the coffin out into the churchyard, the sun was shining and the birds singing. The effect was Mahlerian, or would have been, had the media men not been so much in evidence. As I moved forward to drop my earth into the grave, I could see out of the corner of my eye, Stephen, under a tree, being interviewed by BBC Television.

We filed out of the churchyard, leaving Wystan lying in a suitably commanding situation at the head of the gently sloping hill. At the exit, Wystan and Chester's housekeeper directed us to the village inn where a luncheon was laid on for thirty or forty of the hundred or more who had attended the ceremony at the graveside. More cold meats, and more *Weisswein*. What I remember most clearly about lunch is meeting Count Colloredo, descendant of the Archbishop Colloredo who literally kicked Mozart out of his service. After lunch, the hard core of us accompanied Chester back to the house. There were stories of a former secretary of Wystan's from America who had turned up in Kirchstetten a day or two early for the funeral, had been seen crawling out of a window at the inn early one morning, and had not been observed since. He certainly didn't make it to the cemetery. Back at the house, there was more to drink. The Viennese wine was abandoned in favour of harder stuff. There were twelve of us. I had earlier arranged to give dinner to Charles, Stephen and Ed in Vienna that evening, and now one of them, Stephen I think, suggested to me that I should perhaps ask Chester if he'd like to join us. I did so, and yes, he would like to come into Vienna and dine. Unfortunately, due to some misunderstanding which I now can't recall in detail, the word got about that I was inviting the entire party to dinner. I could hardly say that had not been my intention, so I thought hard about where to take them all that would be reasonably lively, to disperse the funeral gloom, and not too expensive. The *Weisser Rauchfangkehrer*, I decided, was the appropriate place. But I couldn't just turn up there at eight o'clock with a party of twelve, I would have to order a table. There was no phone in the villa Auden, so I would have to go to the Burgermeister's house and phone from there. The man to whom Charles had earlier been speaking Greek, and with whom I now discovered I had no language in common, took me to the Burgermeister. The restaurant at first said no, they couldn't manage a table for twelve that evening, but I was too distrait to suffer defeat, so I bullied them into accepting us. By now it was late afternoon. Back at the house, someone tentatively suggested ordering taxis to take us to Vienna, but, fearful that I would find myself paying for these too, I found myself insisting that we take the train, and led the entire party down to the railway station before they could rebel.

Dinner began quietly, but soon became gayer, and by the dessert course, when people were coping valiantly with both the taste and the pronunciation of *Brandteigschokoladencremekrapfen* or whatever, the company, under the influence of yet more of the heady Viennese wine, became positively lively. It was, I thought, the proper way to celebrate Wystan. We separated noisily after dinner in the Kärntnerstrasse, and broke up into smaller, quieter units. I walked back to my hotel on the other side of the Donau Kanal, stopping on the bridge to murmur a few words of drunken sentiment down into the swiftly flowing water.

Next morning, the survivors dispersed. Ed, who had made good use of his time at the Auden house, was probably gloating over manuscripts somewhere; Stephen decided to stay on for a day or two and look at pictures in the Kunsthistorisches and the Albertina; only Charles and I boarded the plane for London. He seemed to have recovered from the emotional and gastronomical buffetings of the previous day, but I was still feeling far from well when we landed at Heathrow.

Chapter Twelve

Ave atque vale

Now for oblivion: let
the belly-mind take over
down below the diaphragm,
the domain of the Mothers,
They who guard the Sacred Gates,
without whose wordless warnings
soon the verbalising I
becomes a vicious despot,
lewd, incapable of love,
disdainful, status-hungry.
Should dreams haunt you, heed them not,
for all, both sweet and horrid,
are jokes in dubious taste,
too jejune to have truck with.
Sleep, Big Baby, sleep your fill.[1]

When I first encountered Wystan Auden he had not fully developed that extraordinary network of lines which connected up the remotest outposts of his features, and which led Stravinsky to remark, 'Soon we shall have to smooth him out to see who it is.' I remember thinking that at moments he looked like Danny Kaye. Looking back now, however, at photographs of Wystan in the fifties, I can see more than a little of Jonathan Miller as well. I already knew many survivors from the English literary scene of the thirties, and at that time within the period of a few months I found myself meeting several characters from the pre-war Berlin which Wystan had known: Herr Issyvoo himself, as well as Jean Ross – Isherwood's 'Sally Bowles' – and Gerald Hamilton ('Mr Norris'). Wystan was not only comparatively unlined – he was still in his forties – but also had not yet begun to affect that geriatric shuffle which characterized his last years and into which he grew slowly. The slippers, however, were already in evidence, though not invariably.

I was working for *The London Magazine* which was edited by John Lehmann who had founded it in 1954 (and named it after a literary magazine of the 1820s), and I thought it would be a good idea to interview Wystan at some length (as they say nowadays, 'in depth' or, even worse, 'in-depth')

---

[1] From 'A Lullaby'.

for the magazine. Wystan was agreeable, but for some reason the interview never got off the ground, and when John sold the magazine to Alan Ross in 1961, and I remained with it as Assistant Editor, I had only the notes of a number of conversations consisting almost entirely of gossip: not even literary gossip, most of it, but operatic. Wystan was going to the opera frequently in Vienna at the time, and spoke with passionate enthusiasm of many of the new young singers he had heard there. He seemed to know a lot about their private lives, which impressed me, but I thought I might surprise him with the news I had recently heard, that a certain soprano was having an affair with a well-known conductor in Vienna. 'Don't be silly,' Wystan said, 'there are two good reasons why that's highly unlikely: one, she's black, and two, she hasn't got a cock.'

The interview was never completed: after sessions at the house in Kirchstetten and the apartment in New York (both, I think, in 1962), I decided to abandon it because the copious notes I had made were mostly indecipherable, and also because, unless pressure was being applied by a deadline imposed by a commissioning editor, my natural sloth usually prevented me from completing most projects. One day, I showed Wystan a roneoed copy of *The Gentle Planet*, a collection of poems I had written in the early fifties. There were twenty poems, and he instantly dismissed sixteen of them as being 'not properly finished'. Three he thought were good, and one, a short poem of three stanzas, he made me rewrite. 'The first two lines,' he said, ' "The poet's vacant/and engaging smile" promise one a poem about a poet's vacant and engaging smile, and then you go traipsing off into a pallid imitation of some minor Georgian.' He struck out the rest of the poem, and handed it back to me. 'Describe the smile, interpret it, if you like. But just do that, and nothing else. And it hasn't got a title. I like poems to have titles. Call it "The Smile". And keep it metrically regular. All those weak endings must go.' He jabbed a finger at 'betrayal', 'shadow' and 'reflection'. 'You can get rid of those for a start.' I went away and did what I was told. Next time I saw him, I showed him 'The Smile', and he read it through twice. 'There you are,' he said. 'It's perfect now. It's small, but it's perfect. Well, almost. If you change the punctuation in the last stanza, and turn some of those commas into full stops, to get a more *staccato* effect, that would do it.' I changed the punctuation:

> The poet's vacant
> and engaging smile
> is even falser now
> than once it was.
>
> Ingredients: love,

mirror, hate and cold.
(Amused self-pity
is an added spice.)

He's bored and fretful,
lazy, gentle, proud.
And anxious. Frightened.
Scared to death of life.

After 1962, I never visited Wystan again in New York. I saw him when he came to London, or when I went to Vienna, which was usually in May or June for the *Festwochen*. My first meeting with Chester Kallman was at the Vienna State Opera House. He and Wystan had driven in from Kirchstetten to attend a performance of *Don Giovanni* conducted by Karajan. The cast was high-powered: Leontyne Price, Elisabeth Schwarzkopf, Irmgard Seefried, Eberhard Wächter, Walter Berry, Anton Dermota. Afterwards, Wystan and Chester took me to a louche bar which they frequented – the Piccadilly, in the Annagasse – and we argued for hours about singers. Chester was always good company, and fun to argue with. I liked his New York-Jewish humour, his wry pessimism, his Oscar Levantish presence. He drank even more than Wystan did, and after Wystan's death he accelerated the pace: he survived his friend by no more than sixteen months, and died in Athens at the age of fifty-three.

Wystan was not such fun to argue with, for he would often bulldoze you into accepting his opinions unless you stood up to him, in which case he often backed down. 'Charles and I have had an interesting conversation about Wagner,' he announced to Chester who was emerging from hours in the kitchen. 'We have not,' I said. 'I've simply been listening to a series of unsupported assertions.' (In Berlin, Wystan interrupted a distinguished English music critic who was defending Debussy's *Pelléas et Mélisande*: 'No, dear, you take it from mother, *Pelléas* is shit.') There were occasions, however, when he was prepared to be more flexible, and it was fascinating then to watch him actually thinking, considering, rather than merely repeating a formula he had accepted at some time in the past and was no longer prepared to re-test. Once, we talked about his revision of his pre-war poetry, and he defended his right to make what alterations he wished to make. He was fond of quoting Valéry's 'A poem is never finished, only abandoned'. I refused to be pushed into the opposing stance, the romantic view that the finished poem is a sacrosanct object which not even its creator can tamper with. Instead, I tried to reconcile both viewpoints. 'Yes, Wystan,' I admitted, 'of course the poet can do what he likes with his own poems. But, unless he manages not only to destroy every copy of the text he

315

wishes to suppress, but also to erase it from the memories of other people who may love it and cling to it, then he must accept that it will continue to have its own life and its own validity.' 'No,' he said, 'you must believe one thing or the other. I repudiate the rubbish I've written.' 'But after you're dead – ' 'Oh, I don't care what happens after I'm dead.'

With Chester's help, on one occasion at Kirchstetten I attempted to persuade Wystan to alter a line in one of his poems of the thirties, a line which it had not previously occurred to him to revise. This was the slighting reference to Richard Tauber in 'Letter to Lord Byron': 'There may be people who hear Tauber twice.' In fact, on his next visit to London I played Wystan records of Tauber singing Schubert and Schumann *Lieder*, and arias by Mozart, Bizet and Weber, and finally wore him down. He admitted he had been wrong about Tauber, and said he would consider altering the line when the opportunity arose. I suggested amending it to 'There may be some who think McCormack nice.' 'That *sounds* all right,' he agreed, 'but I'll have to see what Chester thinks of McCormack.'

Crosswords were always much in evidence at Kirchstetten, for Chester was as much addicted to them as Wystan was. Hopeless at solving even the easiest crossword, I was forced into a pose of superiority. But I enjoyed Wystan's enjoyment of words, and his virtuoso way with them. He was adept at composing palindromes, and was proud of having written what may be the longest one in English, a sentence of eighty-five letters which reads the same backwards as forwards: 'T. Eliot, top bard, notes putrid tang emanating, is sad, I'd assign it a name: gnat dirt upset on drab pot toilet.' I put Wystan's admiration for Tolkien's *The Lord of the Rings* on that level, and wished I'd had a Marx Brothers T-shirt to match his Tolkien sweater which he wore with pride. There came, thank goodness, a time when he seemed to have got bored with Tolkien.

Snatches of Kirchstetten conversation come to mind. Wystan boasting of his earnings from the sales of his poetry: I forget whether, one year, it was fifteen or thirty thousand pounds or dollars – fifteen and dollars, I imagine – but one was expected to be impressed, and one was. Like many people who are capable of extraordinary generosity where large sums of money or large investments of emotional energy are required, he could sometimes be absurdly mean in small matters. Stephen Spender tells the story of arriving to visit Wystan on Ischia, and being greeted with drinks on the terrace of the villa. Reaching out to take a cigarette, he was sharply told by Wystan to buy his own.

'But, Wystan, I haven't got any Italian money. I haven't had a chance to change any.'

'What have you got? Travellers' cheques? I'll change one for you, and you can buy some cigarettes at the corner store.'

Stephen signed a travellers' cheque, and Wystan disappeared into the house with it. When he returned, he held some Italian currency in one hand, and waved the international edition of the New York *Herald-Tribune* in the other. 'I'm afraid the exchange rate is against you today, dear,' he exclaimed gleefully, as he counted out a rather measly number of *lire* into Stephen's hand.

Though he used to tease Stravinsky about his interest in money – he once suggested the composer should set the German word 'millionen' to music: 'Think how you could aspirate the final syllable, Igor, and keep it going, page after page, like the compounding of interest.' – Auden was capable of boasting of his own holdings of, for instance 'tax-deductible Dominion oil stocks, an arrangement that looks a little louche to me, but my lawyer seems to know what the traffic will bear.'[1]

One day, a friend and I arrived at Kirchstetten to find Wystan in a state bordering on nervous exhaustion. 'I have an American fan, a mad woman,' he said, 'who's always writing to me and pestering me. I'd no idea she was in Europe, but she actually turned up here this morning on the train from Vienna. She said she was going to stay. I had a dreadful time getting rid of her, because she said she had no money and nowhere else she could stay. I finally drove her to the station and made sure she got the train for Vienna. Fortunately we had a lot of cash in the house, because I had to give her her fare back.'

We sympathized, and I said that the fare to Vienna, whatever it was (a train journey of no more than thirty miles), was a small price to pay for being rid of the lady. 'Vienna?' said Wystan. 'I gave her the airfare back to New York.'

Whenever I planned to be in Vienna, I always let Wystan know in advance. Usually I would spend a day with him and Chester at Kirchstetten. There would be martinis in the garden, but not before noon. Wystan always insisted on bottle and glass being chilled, which meant that the first drink was decently cold; but then the bottle would be left standing in the sun, and for the next hour our refills became warmer and warmer. These were 'straight' martinis: vodka or, if one insisted, gin appeared only at the evening cocktail hour. Lunch was served by Chester punctually at one, and was usually followed by an audition of the latest opera records they had acquired. I remember Wystan urgently commending to me a recording of a rare early nineteenth-century opera, *Medea in Corinto* by Giovanni Simone Meyr, the teacher of Donizetti. After about half-an-hour or so, Wystan would shuffle off to his study to work, or read, or sleep, while Chester would continue to play his records of old singers. The current Viennese favourites were fine, but we usually finished up listening to Lotte Lehmann.

[1] Both quotes are from Robert Craft's *Stravinsky*.

If Tolkien indicated one area into which I could not follow Wystan, religion was another. We once talked about the Bible, and I trod warily, remembering his dislike of those who 'read the Bible for its prose'. When he asked me my favourite book of the Bible (he was strong on favourites) I answered truthfully, 'Ecclesiastes', and he shook his head. An acquaintance of Wystan's told me of having been present at a dinner party in New York in the fifties, *chez* Jennie Tourel, at which Wystan had held forth at some length about his religious feelings. After he had left, the composer Marc Blitzstein remarked: 'Wystan doesn't love God; he's just attracted to him.'

After Wystan had lived in Kirchstetten for some years, the local council honoured him by changing the name of his street (straggling lane, rather) from Hinterholz to Audenstrasse. He was proud of this, but was not brash enough to change the address on his writing-paper, so one continued to get letters from, and to write to, 'Hinterholz, 6', which, I suppose, is why I got it into my head that it was some other street in the village which had been named after him. On religious feast days, instead of putting a date on his letters, he would put the name of the day, either in German or in Latin, such as *Corpus Christi* or *Karfreitag* (Good Friday). He once wrote to T. S. Eliot, dating his letter 'Mariae Himmelfahrt', the day of the Assumption of the Virgin Mary. Eliot, who was in hospital, gave the letter to his secretary to acknowledge, as a result of which Wystan received a communication in Kirchstetten addressed to Fräulein Maria Himmelfahrt, delivered by a puzzled if not shocked postman.

I often wondered why there was no piano in the Kirchstetten farmhouse, but I didn't like to ask. I suspected that Wystan might have become self-conscious about his piano-playing when music came to mean more to him, and that he had simply put it behind him. I entered his attic study only once, shyly invited to see it. I have no clear memory of the kitchen: that was Chester's domain. The living-room, where one ate, listened to records, talked, or read books, and the garden, where one had drinks and tea on sunny summer days, are what remain in my memory of Kirchstetten. The living-room was the essence of Austrian-Jewish *Gemütlichkeit*: 'cosy' and 'fun' are the words that come to my mind as I think of it, and they are words that Wystan used a lot. ('You're really Goethe, disguised as Herr Biedermeier,' I said to him once, or perhaps I merely thought it.) It was very much a lived-in room, just as Wystan's was a lived-in face. As a non-smoker, I was always conscious that the room smelt of stale cigarette smoke, for not even Frau Emma dared to open a window. Litter, in the form of old newspapers, bills paid or unpaid, food-stained cookbooks, was, one felt, kept at bay, but only just. There were drawings on the walls. I have forgotten what they were, if ever I knew, but am told they included an Augustus John (of Yeats) and a Munch (of Richard Strauss). The presence, in some form, of

Stravinsky I recall. Could that have been another drawing? Perhaps a signed photograph.

Auden would never have written an autobiography, people say. No, I don't imagine he would have. But then, he did. His commonplace book, *A Certain World*, is as close as he got to it in prose, but in verse, his 'Letter to Lord Byron' is unashamedly autobiographical, and a strong vein of auto-biography runs through his entire poetic *oeuvre*. His love of gossip made him an avid reader of biography and autobiography: the trivial, anecdotal memoirs of musicians and actors as much as 'serious' biographical studies of famous authors. And he loved reading the correspondence of the famous, the *Letters of Thomas Mann*, *The Correspondence Between Richard Strauss and Hugo von Hofmannsthal*. Reviewing the memoirs of J. R. Ackerley, he com-plained that Mr Ackerley was never quite explicit 'about what he *really* preferred to do in bed'. He ended his review of Tchaikovsky's diaries:[1] 'After all, he wrote the most beautiful ballet music in the world and detested Brahms. He is our friend. And who does not enjoy reading a friend's diary?' Wystan often said we should not want to read other people's letters, but he apparently enjoyed my translation of Verdi's letters, which he reviewed very favourably in the *New York Review of Books*.[2] 'I don't think,' he wrote, 'that [Verdi] would have any objection to our reading this selection of his letters, admirably translated and edited by Charles Osborne.' True, he went on to say that he was glad I had included 'no embarrassing "human" documents, no love letters', but knowing Wystan I think he would have been no less glad if I had. I don't want to labour the point. He did leave instructions with his executors that his friends were to be asked to destroy his letters after his death. Kafka went further: he asked Max Brod to destroy all his manuscripts. Fortunately, Brod disregarded his friend's request. I do not think that many of Wystan's friends have destroyed his letters. Surely, one day, they will be collected and published.

In 1965, in a preface to my own prose translation of *Die Zauberflöte*, I reviewed existing singing translations, among them the one which Wystan and Chester had done for American television. I thought it was pretty awful, and after making the general point that its main faults were 'its appalling vulgarity, and its lack of contact with the style of the original', I went on to give examples. For instance, of Papageno's entrance song, I wrote:

> The Auden version is a failure, and a mouthful of a failure at that. Each line has far too many syllables, it has recourse to the verb 'to ken' which is neither German nor English, and some of its adjectives are ill-chosen. Papageno should surely not refer to himself as a '*tall* bird-catcher'. It isn't

[1] In the *New York Times*, 2 December 1945.
[2] 9 March 1972.

in the German, and he's most appropriately played as of slight, bird-like, stature. In Auden, the third line, for instance, changes from 'Ich Vogel-fänger bin bekannt', to 'In vain do all the pretty little creatures fly' which alters the smooth, sinuous line of the original to an impossible gabble. Papageno, of course, is a lovable fraud. He doesn't really know the names of different birds, they are all 'Vögel' to him. The erudite Auden, how-ever, enumerates 'lark, ruddock, willow-wren, nightingale, snipe, part-ridge, turtle-dove', and even 'the melodious mavis' whoever she may be.

Of the Pamina-Papageno duet:

> Auden is at his worst here. Again, too many syllables. He has deliberately turned the German iambic into an anapestic rhythm, so as to provide one syllable per note and destroy completely the beautiful legato line which Mozart achieved with tied notes. He has turned it into a Gilbert-and-Sullivan patter song.

And so on. No wonder I was nervous, the following summer, when I was invited again to Kirchstetten. But Wystan and Chester were their usual welcoming, relaxed, domestic selves, and the day passed as happily as ever. No mention was made of my savage comments of their *Zauberflöte* transla-tion, and I thought, 'Thank Christ, they haven't seen it.' Being driven to the station by Wystan was, comfortingly, the usual terrifying experience. It was only as I got into the Vienna-bound train, and turned to wave goodbye to Wystan, that he said gently 'If only you hadn't been so nasty to us, we'd have been able to have a copy of your book in the house.' The train moved off, and he stood on the platform looking rather pleased with himself.

At the beginning of 1966, I left *The London Magazine*, having been invited to join the staff of the Arts Council of Great Britain. ('You'll go mad, having to deal with boring cultural bureaucrats.' 'Worse than that, my dear Wystan, I shall become one.') The following year, I was involved in setting up the first *Poetry International*. Wystan came and read his poems, and amused the audience by being visibly impatient with the American poet Anne Sexton, whose reading of her confessional verse went on and on. And on. Before the evening was over, he had reduced her to tears. When I visited Kirchstetten the following summer, Ken Thomson, who was press officer for *Poetry International*, was with me. 'Don't have boring American women poets who whine on for four times as long as they're asked to,' said Wystan. 'You've got to entertain the audience, you know.' Ken suggested having Ogden Nash, who would certainly be entertaining. I decided to invite Nash. 'A good idea,' said Wystan, and at our press conference in London the follow-ing year he coolly announced that it was at his suggestion that Nash had been invited to appear.

After Wystan had been appearing regularly at *Poetry International* for two or three years, I felt that perhaps I was taking too great an advantage of his generosity. He used to earn four-figure sums with his poetry readings in the States, whereas I could offer him only twenty pounds! I wrote to thank him for having helped us so much, and explained that I would not be inviting him next year. But he had got into the habit of coming. 'Dear Charles,' he replied, 'thanks for your letter about the poetry festival. I'd be delighted to take part again next year . . .' I never again tried not to invite him.

Usually, when Auden appeared, we played to full houses. But, one year, on our first evening the weather was far too glorious for people to come indoors and listen to poetry. I led Wystan and other poets onto the stage of the Queen Elizabeth Hall to find that not many more than half the seats were occupied. 'You didn't tell me it was a private party, dear,' my star poet murmured as we bowed to the assembled few. They were, I remember, not only few but noisy: the coughing bounced off the walls throughout the performance. Still, I don't *think* there was any hidden message in Wystan's reading that evening, of his 'Song of the Devil', which ends with the line: 'I'm so bored with the whole fucking crowd of you I could *scream!*' It was a poem he enjoyed performing.

In 1970, at the behest of the *Sunday Times*, I kept a diary during the *Poetry International* week. It captured something of the atmosphere of the festival, and Wystan is well to the fore:

Tuesday: The poets begin to arrive. I sit in my office like some bemused Shakespearian monarch while messengers rush in to exclaim 'Thom Gunn has just arrived from San Francisco', and 'Soyinka has flown in from Stockholm, but we've lost him' (Stockholm? I was expecting him from Ibadan) and 'I met the plane from Rome but Pasolini wasn't on it.'

It was Pasolini and Tennessee Williams about whose arrival I have felt most sceptical. But Tennessee has actually made it, a few days ahead of schedule. Seeing him again after ten years, I found him as pleasant as before, but hesitant, easily bruised, his personality somehow fragmented. Shortly after he arrived, we talked and drank in his hotel room, until a journalist arrived with photographer, to interview him. Tennessee described how, in his opinion, he had been badly treated by his brother during his recent breakdown. 'Has your brother ever featured in any of your plays, Mr Williams?' asked the interviewer. 'He will,' promised Mr Williams.

I got up to go. 'Tennessee, I'm going to leave you with these press gentlemen.'

'How very brutal of you.'

Wednesday: At noon today we had a successful reception for the poets at the Martini Terrace. I didn't succeed in luring Tennessee to it, and W. H. Auden has not yet arrived (nor, of course, has Pasolini, of whom I begin to despair), but most of the others were there: the gentle Hungarian Sandor Weöres, clasping two dauntingly huge volumes said to contain his collected poems; Thom Gunn flashing his tattoos at the press; the delightful Carolyn Kizer; Stephen Spender wearing his endearing air of practised shyness; the quiet, friendly Octavio Paz and his beautiful wife. But we had promised the press all this and Tennessee too, so I spent much of the reception on the phone to his hotel. Couldn't he come along just for a few minutes? No, he thinks he's catching flu, and maybe he's had a heart flutter too. Impressed, I hang up and give up. But an American theatrical colleague of Tennessee's says, 'Forget it. We've been hearing about those flutters for twenty years. He's still the strongest swimmer I know.'

Thursday: They're all here now, except Pasolini. Whom can I find to replace him at such short notice? Try Robert Lowell again? Not much point: when I last spoke to him a few days ago, he said, 'The kind of poetry reading affair I don't like is when you have to share the programme with a number of other poets, and you're only allowed about twenty minutes, and they won't let you discuss anything with the audience . . .'

Thursday, later: A small, gaunt man in a light suit and dark glasses, unshaven and carrying a suitcase, has just been shown into my office. Pasolini, Eureka! Auden too, has flown in from Vienna. 'I believe we're *ausverkauft*' were his first words to me.

Friday morning: The first of our performances went very well last night. Tennessee's act was the most hilarious, Allen Tate's reading the least audible, Peter Porter's the fastest, Pasolini's the most impenetrable. In the interval, Pasolini asked me if he could meet his translator, Gavin Ewart. I found Gavin at the bar. He looked scared and distinctly unenthusiastic about the meeting. I introduced them to each other, and ran away.

Saturday: Auden, whom we look on now as our Poetry International mascot, made his first appearance last night to great applause. He doesn't read, he knows the poems, seeming to pluck the words from an invisible tele-prompter high in the back of the hall. 'Wystan,' I ask, 'do you know *all* of your poems by heart?' 'Heavens, no, I learn the ones I'm going to

322

perform. If I decide to do them again in a few months' time, I'll have to learn them all over again.'

Sunday: Tennessee, waving his claret-filled tea-cup and saucer at the audience, last night read his new poem, 'What's next on the agenda, Mr Williams?' Well, *he* says it's a poem. I thought it a magnificent dramatic monologue, whether prose or poetry.

This afternoon, I fly up to Edinburgh with five of the poets (Dennis Brutus replacing Wole Soyinka who has returned to Stockholm as suddenly and inexplicably as he had arrived) for a final performance in the Assembly Rooms this evening. 'I hope,' said Wystan, 'you'll be a stern chairman and not let any of us go on too long.' I promise. The other poets look harrowed.

Monday afternoon: The Edinburgh performance last night was a success. Full house, as in London. Afterwards, the Scottish Arts Council invited a few people to meet us at our hotel, the George. Carolyn Kizer, Wystan Auden and I walked from the Assembly Rooms to the George singing a lyric from *Pal Joey*, which Wystan has included in his commonplace book, *A Certain World*, recently published in the States. I compliment him on his firm baritone. 'Bass,' he corrects me.

This morning, after breakfast, Carolyn and I walk around Edinburgh in the sun . . . Back to the hotel to collect the others and be driven to the airport. Wystan says he must buy a haggis to take back to Austria, so we stop when we see a butcher's. Wystan leaps out on the wrong side, oblivious to murderous traffic, and ambles across the road, while Dennis Brutus, Thom Gunn, Carolyn and I bite our nails in suspense. He returns triumphantly with his haggis, peering at it as though it were a crystal ball.

At Edinburgh airport, we order dry martinis (American style). The drinks that arrive are a very curious colour, and the American poets reject them. Not wishing to upset the nice barmaid, I pour all three mystery drinks into a tumbler, and bravely drink while explaining to her how a martini is really made. Behind me, I hear Wystan's voice improbably asserting that the only place where you can get a decent martini in Britain is Ashby-de-la-Zouche. The most horrid drink he has ever been offered, he says, was a Taj Mahal Cola in Calcutta. 'I was terribly thirsty, but I simply couldn't swallow it.' He breaks off as the names of Auden and Gunn are called over the speaker system. They are requested to report to the check-in desk. I go with them. The clerk wishes to know where Mr and Mrs Sandor Weöres are. (They have decided to have an extra day in Edinburgh.) 'Do they think we've murdered them?' asks Wystan gaily. Then our flight is called, and Wystan leaps into action. In his ripest Baron

Ochs *Wienerisch*, 'Leupold,' he calls to me, 'wir gehen.' And he leads us across the tarmac and up the gangway. It's all over until next year.

Some months after this, I was asked to be Guest Editor for one issue of the magazine *Workshop*, and to select poems from the many submitted by unknown young poets eager to see themselves in print. I thought it would be encouraging to print these new young poets side by side with four or five established and well-known poets, and so I wrote to those among my friends and acquaintances whom I thought most likely to agree to be published for little or no payment: W. H. Auden, D. J. Enright, Thom Gunn, Ted Hughes and Peter Porter. I asked each to let me have a recent, unpublished poem, and I got five splendid poems almost by return of post. Auden's was 'Lines to Dr. Walter Birk on His Retiring From General Practice', which he had written in Kirchstetten in September to his local doctor. Dr Birk had looked after Wystan for several years: after his retirement Wystan often grumbled that he could simply not get used to being treated by doctors who did not know him personally.

When Wystan arrived for the 1971 *Poetry International*, he seemed older, crankier, short of breath and, occasionally, of temper. He repeated his stories within the hour now, instead of within the week. One evening he sat with me in the backstage bar at the Queen Elizabeth Hall. Dennis Enright joined us, and I introduced him to Auden who appeared not to remember him, although they had certainly met before. The three of us had a drink together, and chatted for a few moments. Then, while Dennis was still sitting with us, Wystan turned to me and asked 'How old *is* old Enright?'

He always claimed not to read reviews of the *Poetry International* performances, but seemed always to know what was said about him; and when the *Financial Times* wrote, of Ernst Jandl at the 1971 Festival, that 'the wittiest thing about his appearance was Charles Osborne's translations, which were dazzling exercises in essaying the impossible', Wystan introduced me to someone as 'the witty dazzler' and later advised me that it would have been wittier of me to have left Herr Jandl and his sound poetry in whatever beer hall I'd found them in!

A few days before the 1972 Festival, I received a phone call from Wystan in Austria. The young Russian-Jewish poet, Joseph Brodsky, who had been forced to live an underground life in his own country for years, and had spent some time in a prison camp, had now been expelled from the Soviet Union and given a visa to Israel. But he did not want to go to Israel, so he managed somehow to get to Vienna and telephone Wystan who swung into action on his behalf immediately. Could I help to get Brodsky into England? Well, I could try. Brodsky's eventual destination was America, and the British immigration authorities wanted to be sure the Americans were going to let him in before they issued him with a British visa. in other words, we were apparently only prepared to accept him in transit. Arrangements were complicated, and difficult to conclude within two or three days, but somehow it happened. I formally invited Brodsky to take part in *Poetry International*, he flew with Wystan from Vienna, and when they arrived at Heathrow poor Brodsky was mobbed by television cameramen, photographers and journalists. It must have been a very bewildering experience for him. All his life he had been persecuted for no better reason that that he was a poet, and now suddenly he was being treated as a hero apparently for the same reason, He had never been outside Russia before, and unlike other Soviet poets whom we had encountered he was no ebullient extravert. Wystan fussed about him like a mother hen, an unusually kindly and understanding mother hen.

I did not find the slightest difficulty in acceding to Wystan's request that, the following year, Chester be invited to take part in *Poetry International*. Chester was, after all, a poet with a voice of his own and a real lyric gift. If there was a place on our platform for Charles Olson, Robert Creeley, Robert Bly, Denise Levertov and Gregory Corso,[1] to mention only other American poets, then there was certainly a place for Chester Kallman and his humane, civilized, tightly knit lyric verse. So, in 1973, Chester accompanied Wystan to London. In any case, I had a favour or two to ask of Wystan. I knew that, as from the autumn of 1972, he would be based in Oxford for six months of each year, and I wanted to try to involve him more closely with literary life in Great Britain again. I was very conscious of the fact that he still thought of himself as an American or, rather, a New Yorker, and that it was to New York friends that he turned first when discussing new projects, or when wanting an opinion on something he had written. But he was essentially English, and if he was now going to live half of each year in England I thought I ought to rope him into the English literary scene in some way. The Chairman of the Arts Council's Literature Panel was at that time the distinguished philosopher, Stuart Hampshire. (Previous Chairmen with whom I'd worked had been Cecil Day Lewis, Angus Wilson and Frank Kermode.) I knew that Stuart's period of appointment was soon to end; acting on the assumption that the Arts Council would leap at the opportunity of including W. H. Auden among its members as Chairman of its Literature Panel, I tentatively broached the subject with Wystan. I was not disconcerted by his initial reaction which, out of deference to the Arts Council, I shall not describe, for I was confident that, in due course, I could win him over. Only then would I turn my powers of persuasion upon the Chairman and Secretary-General of the Arts Council. What I immediately said to Wystan was: 'Well, if you'd rather not get involved with the Arts Council, would you

[1] Though Corso never turned up: he was too stoned to get himself on to a plane.

consider joining the Board of Management of the Poetry Book Society? It's a book club, like those you've been associated with in the States, and it presents the annual poetry festival which you have graced with your presence since 1967.'

'But I'd have to come to *meetings*!' He made them sound like public hangings.

'Only once a quarter.'

He grunted. 'Oh, all right.'

As Secretary of the Poetry Book Society, I conveyed his gracious provisional acceptance to my Chairman and Board, and we elected him at our next meeting. I saw this as the first move in the game to get Wystan Auden onto the Arts Council of Great Britain. He would, I suppose, have needed to be a British citizen for this to be possible, but I hoped that, after he had been living in England again for a time, he would be willing to revert to his original nationality. As it was, he died while I was still contemplating my next move.

In the last year of his life, 1973, I saw Wystan both in Austria and in England. In May, when I paid my usual visit to him at Kirchstetten during the *Wiener Festwochen*, I thought that what Henry Moore called 'the monumental ruggedness of his face, its deep furrows like plough marks crossing a field' had become even more accentuated since the previous winter. The shuffling gait had acquired hesitancies, and there were occasions when he stood still, ready for action but momentarily undecided in which direction to move. For some time, his voice had shown a tendency to trail away into a curiously disturbing silence: now his limbs began to slow down into stillness, to similar effect. And then, suddenly, he would be all right again. But in those odd moments of hesitancy and indecision, he would look so lost that it was heartrending. The moments passed, and I almost persuaded myself that they hadn't occurred.

During the fortnight that I was in Vienna that spring, Wystan came into the city one day to visit his chiropodist, and he and Ken Thomson and I lunched together at a snack bar that Wystan liked, not far from the Opera House. He was at his most cheerful that day, and we discussed all sorts of plans for the future. He and I had talked often about Goethe, and we decided to collaborate in editing a Goethe Reader which would include the kind of extracts from Goethe which English-language readers would be most likely to enjoy. I agreed to produce a list of possible contents which we could discuss when Wystan returned to Oxford in the autumn. We would share the task of translating any pieces of which good English translations did not already exist, and Wystan would write a Foreword. I also agreed to sound out Charles Monteith of Faber & Faber when I returned to London, for there would be no point, said Wystan, in our going ahead unless they were willing to publish. I spoke to Charles, who made encouraging noises which I passed on to Wystan when he came to London for *Poetry International*. We planned to start work on Goethe later in the year.

On Sunday, at the end of the *Poetry International* week, Wystan and Chester came to lunch at my flat. Wystan and I were to take part in a television programme later in the day, and this was my way of ensuring not only that he would get to the right place at the right time but also that he would be reasonably sober. I planned to offer him no more than two cocktails before lunch, and to pretend that the two bottles of wine standing on the dining table were all I had in the flat. It didn't work, of course, and we were well oiled by the time we arrived at the Young Vic where we were to perform, and where the television people gave us more to drink. It didn't affect him, except perhaps to make his reminiscences a little more indiscreet than they normally were.

That Sunday in July was the last time I saw him. Less than three months later he was dead, and I was standing in the churchyard at Kirchstetten scattering earth onto his coffin. As I walked away from the grave, I overheard a snippet of conversation between two Austrians, one of whom must have been a Kirchstetten acquaintance of Wystan's. 'Wir waren erstaunt,' I heard him say, 'aber nicht *so* erstaunt . . . er war so müde.'[1] Immediately there came into my mind a famous poem by Goethe which Wystan and I had agreed summed up the problem of translating him, for it was so very beautiful in German, and yet impossible to put into an English which was not either banal or sentimental. 'You'll have to do that one,' he had said. 'I already have, years ago,' I replied, and I quoted my translation to him. He gave his familiar grunt. 'It'll do.'

Über allen Gipfeln	Over all the mountains
ist Ruh,	is peace,
in allen Wipfeln	in all the tree-tops
spürest du	you feel
kaum einen Hauch.	hardly a breath.
Die Vöglein schweigen im Walde.	The little birds are silent in the woods.
Warte nur: balde	Wait awhile: soon
ruhest du auch.	you too will rest.

[1] 'We were astonished, but not *so* astonished . . . he was so weary.'

Chapter Thirteen

Obiter dicta

With what conviction the young man spoke
When he thought his nonsense rather a joke;
Now, when he doesn't doubt any more,
No one believes the booming old bore.[1]

I love Italian, it's the most beautiful language to write in, but terribly hard for writers because you can't tell when you've written nonsense. In English you know right away.

Novels, even good ones, can be read simply to pass the time; music, even the greatest, can be used as background noise; but nobody has yet learned to consume a poem: either one cannot read it at all, or one must listen to it as its author intended it to be listened to.

There could be no opera if we did not, in addition to simply having emotions, insist upon having them at whatever inconvenience to ourselves and others.

Writers are usually in the unfortunate predicament of having to speak the truth without having the authority to speak it.

When I hear, as I heard the other day, a college girl ask for a bestseller because she said she wanted to be able to talk about it, I feel a sympathy with the fascist slogan *Kinder, Kuche, Kirche*. When I discover the literary taste of some great textual scholars, I also wonder.

The greatest educational problem of today is how to teach people to ignore the irrelevant, how to refuse to know things, before they are suffocated. For too many facts are as bad as none at all.

I always have two things in my head – I always have a theme and the form. The form looks for the theme, the theme looks for the form, and when they come together you're able to write.

The Germans tend to regard one of their classic authors as Jesus Kleist.

[1] From 'Shorts'.

I think we should do very well without politicians. Our leaders should be elected by lot. The people could vote their conscience, and the computers could take care of the rest.

Writers seldom make good leaders. They're self-employed, for one thing, and they have very little contact with their customers. It's very easy for a writer to be unrealistic.

I can't understand – strictly from a hedonistic point of view – how one can enjoy writing with no form at all. If one plays a game, one needs rules, otherwise there is no fun.

As great a poet as Dante might have been, I wouldn't have had the slightest wish to have known him personally. He was a terrible prima donna.

I live by my watch. I wouldn't know to be hungry if I didn't have my watch on!

Sorry, my dear, one mustn't be bohemian.

The problem with the behaviouralists is that they always manage to exclude themselves from their theories. If all our acts are conditioned behaviour, surely our theories are, too.

Sincerity always hits me something like sleep. I mean, if you try to get it too hard, you won't.

Italian and English are the language of Heaven, 'Frog' the language of Hell.

Jews are more complex than Gentiles.

No character in Dostoevsky would have made an amusing dinner companion, I think, whereas most of Dickens's characters, including many who were evil, would have been fascinating company at table.

Narcissus was a hydrocephalic idiot who thought 'On me it looks good'.

People who attend chamber music concerts are like Englishmen who go to church when abroad.

The older one gets, the more one values the age of friendship, as if it were a vintage.

When my time is up I'll want Siegfried's Funeral Music and not a dry eye in the house.

Ideally one should die upstairs, like Falstaff, while a party is in full swing below, and people are saying things like 'Now why doesn't the old boy get on with it?'

In spite of all that *einsam* rubbish, poets are no lonelier than anyone else. Poetry itself is lonely, of course, in the sense that few people read it.

Every time we make a nuclear bomb we are corrupting the morals of a host of innocent neutrons below the age of consent.

The trouble with dreams, of course, is that other people's are so boring.

I'm no advocate of the purely Uranian society myself. I mean, *I* certainly don't want to live *only* with queers.

The public thinks it can be unfaithful to a writer, but is shocked if the writer is unfaithful to it.

My face looks like a wedding-cake left out in the rain.

It's as if one said, 'It will rain tomorrow.' Perhaps, as it happens, it does, but one only said it because it rhymed with sorrow.

All this fuss over world government. It seems so simple to me. You just have to throw all passports in the sea, and tax incomes at the source.

If I had children, I would want them to be either physicians or ballet dancers. Then they'd always have a job.

I often spend time reading detective stories when I ought to be answering letters, but, if all detective stories were suppressed, I see no reason to believe that I should not find some other device for evading my duty.

The annual tonnage of publications is terrifying if I think about it, but I don't have to think about it. That is one of the wonderful things about the written word: it cannot speak until it is spoken to.

Thank God for books as an alternative to conversation.

If I lived under a dictatorship, I'd write children's stories. I'm sure one would get a lot in.

Poets are very vain, and wish they were the only one of them alive – and many persuade themselves they are.

I think a truly honest person would never wear a hat. Except in arctic weather a hat serves no purpose. The mitre, the Easter bonnet, the helmet, they function as insignia of power.

I have always found it remarkable that in poetry and romantic literature there is so much about sex and very little about food which is just as pleasurable and never lets you down.

To become preoccupied with beauty means a neurosis. There are people who stay always twenty inside. You look at them and think: 'My dear, if for one moment you'd allow your face to agree with your age!'

I don't go along with all this talk of a generation gap. We're all contemporaries, anyone walking this earth at this moment. There's a certain difference in memories, that's all.

My poetry doesn't change from place to place, it changes with the years. It's very important to be one's age. You get ideas you have to turn down – 'I'm sorry, no longer'; 'I'm sorry, not yet.'

I've noticed there are two classes of people who are very bad at reading poetry: those who are too shy like Marianne Moore, and those who are too conceited, like Robert Graves. I hope I'm neither.

It's very difficult for a woman poet to be sufficiently detached, whereas a man tends to become an aesthete, to become too detached, to say things not because he believes them but because they sound effective.

Both in conversation and in books people today are only too ready to take their clothes off in front of total strangers.

If the father is a novelist, the relationship is bound to be embarrassing, because he cannot help seeing the son as a character out of his novels.

The camera always lies. It just ain't art.

I love subways. I love being underground. Don't know what a psychiatrist would make of that.

What no critic seems to see in my work are its comic undertones. Only through comedy can one be serious.

In the end, art is small beer. The really serious things in life are earning one's living so as not to be a parasite, and loving one's neighbour.

Oxford was a place for England's elite. Which was all right. People can't be equal, it's absurd.

I admire the young when they're anti-money, but what they mustn't do is take money from papa and then criticize his way of life.

I didn't really learn to work until I got to the States. One of the besetting vices in all classes in England is idleness. I wonder why? Perhaps they worked too hard in the nineteenth century and got basically tired.

The duties of a writer as a writer and a citizen are not the same. The only duty a writer has as a citizen is to defend language. And this is a *political* duty. Because, if language is corrupted, thought is corrupted.

I think that at least one requirement for a lecturer is that he should have something to say.

Kiss Me, Kate is more fun than *The Taming of the Shrew*.

I'm against this idea in a culture that everybody has to have this kind of experience of 'falling in love'. It can be very bad when people imagine they've had it and it's something else.

Brecht was an admirable man, in the sense that one surely must admire someone who lived in a Communist country, but took out Austrian citizenship, kept his money in a Swiss bank, and hedged his bets when he was dying by sending for the priest, just in case.

A professor is one who talks in someone else's sleep.

Index

Figures in *italics* refer to illustrations

336